CW01082028

The London Bird Atlas

The London Bird Atlas

Ian Woodward   Richard Arnold   Neil Smith

Principal sponsor

Published jointly by the
London Natural History Society and **John Beaufoy Publishing**

2017

First published in the United Kingdom in 2017 by the London Natural History Society and John Beaufoy Publishing Ltd
11 Blenheim Court, 316 Woodstock Road, Oxford OX2 7NS, England
www.johnbeaufoy.com

10 9 8 7 6 5 4 3 2 1

Copyright © 2017 the London Natural History Society and John Beaufoy Publishing Limited
Copyright in text © 2017 Richard Arnold and Ian Woodward
Copyright in photographs © 2017 as listed below
Copyright in maps © 2017 Neil Smith

The authors assert their moral rights to be identified as the authors of this work.

Photograph captions
Front cover: Goldfinch. **Back cover:** Stonechat. **Half title page:** Juvenile Green Woodpecker. **Opposite title page:** Cuckoo. **Title page:** Kingfisher.

Photograph credits
Peter Alfrey 52, 124, 330; **John Archer** 184; **Joe Beale** 191; **Martin Bennett** cover front flap, 41, 122, 128, 129, 130, 166, 242, 257, 260, 272, 277, 282, 298, 302, 304, 318, 324, 338; **Julian Bhalerao Salthouse** 174; **Richard Bonser** 185; **Graham Brownlow** 70, 155, 157, 161, 165; **Michael Darling** 120, 126, 135, 146, 154, 201, 212, 226, 259, 316, 369; **Gehan de Silva Wijeyeratne** 3, 22, 28, 29, 34, 42, 48, 49, 57, 58, 60, 69, 73, 75, 95, 101, 109, 110, 138, 140, 148, 172, 186, 188, 192, 195, 227, 228, 233, 236, 245, 246, 274, 286, 290, 297, 303, 310, 312, 327, 328, 334, 366, 370, 371; **Lee Dingain** 177, 270; **Edmund Fellowes** front cover, 1, 2, 78, 144, 156, 235, 252, 264, 278, 321, 362; **John Hawkins** 89, 113, 159, 169, 209, 218, 224, 238, 251, 284, 288, 400; **Jonathan Lethbridge** 62, 182, 281 **Dominic Mitchell** 289; **Andrew Moon** cover back flap, 6, 24, 37, 38, 39, 44, 46, 50, 64, 66, 76, 77, 81, 82, 83, 84, 96, 97, 98, 102, 103, 104, 106, 114, 117, 118, 132, 136, 142, 150, 152, 158, 160, 162, 167, 199, 210, 214, 217, 219, 221, 222, 230, 231, 241, 249, 254, 266, 269, 279, 293, 300, 306, 322, 325, 332, 336, 337, 340, 342, 344, 348, 356, 361; **Garth Peacock** 36, 79, 80, 147, 164, 197, 207, 295, 346; **Nirosh Perera** back cover 23, 26, 27; **Roger Riddington** 180; **Peter Warne** 32, 54, 90, 92, 170, 179, 202, 204, 262, 308, 345, 350, 353, 364, 396; **Roy Woodward** 86, 119, 314, 355, 358.

All rights reserved. No part of this publication may be reproduced, stored in a retrieval system or transmitted in any form or by any means, electronic, mechanical, photocopying, recording or otherwise, without the prior written permission of the publishers.

Great care has been taken to maintain the accuracy of the information contained in this work. However, neither the publishers nor the authors can be held responsible for any consequences arising from the use of the information contained therein.

ISBN 978-1-909612-99-0

Designed by Gulmohur
Project management by Rosemary Wilkinson
Cartography by the London Natural History Society

Printed and bound in Malaysia by Times Offset (M) Sdn. Bhd.

London Natural History Society
Founded 1858

Honorary Vice-Presidents
A. J. Barratt, D. Bevan, FLS, R. M. Burton, MA, FLS,
J. A. Edgington, PhD, FLS, J. F. Hewlett, PhD, K. H. Hyatt, FLS

Officers for 2017
President: *Vacant.*

Vice-Presidents: Helen Baker, MBOU, Colin Bowlt, PhD, FLS, Mark Burgess, David J. Montier; Colin W. Plant, BSc, FRES, Pat J. Sellar, BSc (Eng), FRGS, MBOU; R. John Swindells, Edward Tuddenham, MD, H. Michael Wilsdon, MBOU

Secretary: David Howdon

Treasurer: Michael West

Assistant Treasurer: Robin Blades

London Bird Club
The London Bird Club is the section of the London Natural History Society for those with a particular interest in birds.

http://www.lnhs.org.uk > About Us> LNHS Sections> London Bird Club

twitter.com/londonbirdclub

Chair: Gehan de Silva Wijeyeratne, FLS
Secretary: Angela Linnell

Dunnock

Photographers

Andrew Moon
Dominic Mitchell
Edmund Fellowes
Garth Peacock
Gehan de Silva Wijeyeratne
Graham Brownlow
Joe Beale
John Archer
John Hawkins
Jonathan Lethbridge
Julian Bhalerao
Lee Dingain
Martin Bennett
Michael Darling
Nirosh Perera
Peter Alfrey
Peter Warne
Richard Bonser
Roger Riddington
Roy Woodward

London Natural History Society Committees 2017

President

Vacant.

Honorary Vice-Presidents

A. J. Barrett, D. Bevan FLS, R. M. Burton MA, FLS,
J. A. Edgington PhD, FLS, J. F. Hewlett PhD, K. H. Hyatt FLS

Council: *The affairs of the Society are managed by Council, whose members are the President, Secretary and Treasurer, one representative from each section and ten elected members.*

Officers for 2017

President: Vacant.

Vice-Presidents: Helen Baker MBOU, Colin Bowlt PhD FLS, Mark Burgess, David J. Montier, Colin W. Plant BSc FRES, Pat J. Sellar BSc (Eng) FRGS MBOU, R. John Swindells, Edward Tuddenham MD, Michael Wilsdon MBOU

Secretary: David Howdon

Treasurer: Michael West

Assistant Treasurer (Membership): Robin Blades

Independent Examiner: Meyer Williams

Representative Members of Council: David Bevan (Botany), Sarah Barnes (Ecol. & Ent.), Gehan de Silva Wijeyeratne (London Bird Club), Stuart Cole (Bookham Common Survey), to be appointed: (Hampstead Heath Survey)

Elected Members of Council: Robin Blades, Keiron Brown, Kat Duke, Jan Hewlett, Catherine Schmitt, Ian Woodward

Administration and Finance Committee: Deals with day to-day running matters and advises Council to whom it is responsible.

Members of Administration and Finance Committee:

Chairman: Michael Wilsdon, Secretary: Vacant, David Howdon (LNHS Secretary), Mike West (LNHS Treasurer), Robin Blades, Mark Burgess, Jo Hatton, Jan Hewlett, (one vacancy).

Library Committee: Chairman: John Swindells (Botany), David Allen (Librarian and Committee Secretary), David Howdon (LNHS Secretary), Mike West (LNHS Treasurer), Bill Dykes (E&E) & Iain Orr (LBC)

London Bird Report: Chairman of Editorial Board: Pete Lambert. Members: John Archer, Jonathan Lethbridge, Roger Payne, Mike Trier, Bob Watts, Gus Wilson

Editor, London Naturalist: Nick Rutter

Editor, Newsletter: Mark Burgess

Editor, Programme: Yu-Hsuan (Doris) Lin

Conservation Officer: David Bevan FLS

Librarian: David Allen

Minuting Secretary (General Meetings): Angela Linnell

Publications Sales: Catherine Schmitt

Website Manager: Malcolm Kendall

Bookham Common Survey

Chairman: *Vacant.*

Secretary: Steve Mellor

Committee: Dr. Alan Prowse, Ian Swinney, Stuart Cole.

Botany

Chairman: David Bevan FLS

Secretary: Sarah Graham-Brown

Indoor Meetings Secretary: Vacant.

Field Meetings Secretary: George Hounsome

Committee: Paul Bartlett PhD, Robin Blades, Annie Chipchase, Pippa A. Hyde, Ian Kitching, Maria L. Roberts, Mary Clare Sheahan, John Swindells.

Recorders

Flowering Plants and Vascular Cryptogams: Mark Spencer PhD FLS

Fungi: Andy Overall

Lichens: John Skinner

Bryophytes: Peter Howarth

Ecology and Entomology

Chairman: Mick Massie

Secretary: Nathalie Mahieu PhD

Treasurer: David Greeno

Indoor Meetings Secretary: Claudia Watts

Field Meetings Secretary: Tristan Bantock

Section Representative to Council: Sarah Barnes

Committee: Bill Dykes, Keiron Brown, Dawn Painter

Recorders

Arachnida (spiders and pseudoscorpions): J. Edward Milner BSc

Coleoptera (Carabidae & Coccinellidae/ground beetles & ladybirds): Paul Mabbott BSc

Coleoptera (all other beetles): Maxwell Barclay

Diptera (flies): Duncan Sivell

Hemiptera (true bugs): Tristan Bantock

Hymenoptera (ants): Mike Fox

Hymenoptera (bees, wasps): Vacant.

Lepidoptera (butterflies): Leslie Williams

Lepidoptera (moths) Syrphidae and invertebrates not otherwise listed: Colin W. Plant BSc FRES

Lumbricidae (earthworms): Keiron Brown

Mammals: Clive Herbert FLS MIoD

Orthoptera (grasshoppers & crickets): Sarah Barnes

Odonata (dragonflies & damselflies): Neil Anderson BSc

Plant galls: Tommy Root

Reptiles and Amphibians: Tom Langton BSc FRSB

Soil-dwelling Invertebrates (Symphyla, Diplura, Isopoda, Myriapoda): Andy Keay

London Bird Club

Chairman: Gehan de Silva Wijeyeratne

Secretary: Angela Linnell

Treasurer: George Kalli

Talks Organiser (Incoming): Georgina Gemmell

Talks Organiser (Outgoing): Kat Duke

Field Meetings Organiser: Shalmali Rao Paterson

Coach Trips Organiser: Vacant

Chair of London Bird Report Editorial Board: Pete Lambert

Chair of Rarities Committee: Bob Watts

Reading Circle Secretary: Angela Linnell

Library Representative: Iain Orr

Twitter Master: Lee Dingain

Committee: Ian Woodward, Nirosh Perera, Sally Middleton

Recorders

Chairman of Rarities Committee: Bob Watts

Bird Recorder for London: Andrew Self

Inner London: Richard Bonser

Bucks: Andrew Moon

Essex: Roy Woodward

Herts: Roger Payne

Kent: John Archer

Middlesex: Sean Huggins

Surrey: David Campbell

Ringing and BTO Reps

Ringing enquiries: Paul Roper

BTO North London Contact: *vacant*

BTO South London Contact: Richard Arnold

Figure 1: Map of the LNHS Atlas recording area

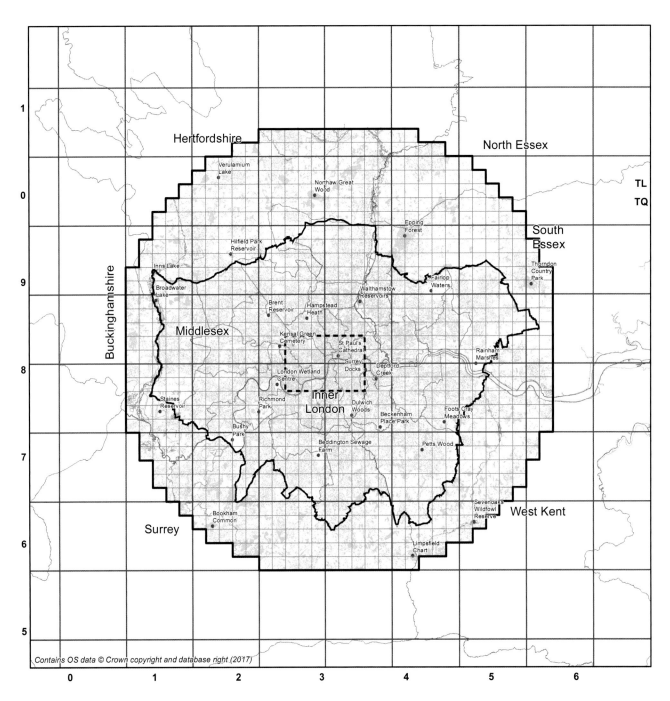

This map shows the recording area used for the three London Atlas projects. The atlas recording area is slightly larger than the official London area.

Contents

1. Introduction

The London area has a fantastic range of bird species, from the rare Black Redstart to the humble Feral Pigeon and the exotic Ring-necked Parakeet. It is also well studied, with publications on London's birds dating back to at least 1866 (Harting's *Birds of Middlesex*). The recorded changes in the bird life are fascinating, with species, numbers and distribution changing as a result of our activities both inside the city and far beyond it. Here, we chart the changes of the last 40 years and show the current distribution of the birds of the London area.

In this book, the London area is a region which covers the area within 20 miles (or approximately 32km) of St Paul's Cathedral (see p.10). This area includes all of the Greater London boroughs and a number of villages and towns outside the metropolis. It is just a little larger than the area now encircled by the M25 motorway. It contains vast areas of built-up land and private gardens, interspersed with squares, parks, commons, playing fields, allotments and various other forms of open land. The area is, of course, dissected by the Thames and its tributaries. It also includes areas of countryside surrounding London, including parts of the North Downs, the Colne Valley, the eastern fringe of the Chiltern Hills, the Lee Valley, Epping and Hainault Forests, the low-lying landscape of south Essex and the upper reaches of the Thames Estuary.

In 2007, the British Trust for Ornithology (the BTO), together with the Scottish Ornithologists' Club and BirdWatch Ireland, embarked on a project to map the distribution of the birds of the British Isles (Balmer *et al.*, 2013, referred to as the 'National Atlas' in this book). Alongside the national project, many local bird clubs took the opportunity to produce a detailed bird atlas at the local level. The London Natural History Society (LNHS) was one such organisation. This book is the report on the results of the survey in the London area.

This is the third time that an atlas survey of London's breeding birds has taken place, following the surveys in 1968–72 (Montier, 1977; hereafter referred to as 'Montier'), and in 1988–94 (Hewlett *et al.*, 2002; hereafter referred to as 'Hewlett *et al.*'). This, the third of the London atlases, also presents, for the first time, maps showing relative abundance of selected species and seasons, based on timed counts, and maps showing the distribution of birds in the London area during the winter.

The three atlas projects chart substantial changes in the birds of the London area since the late 1960s and provide a record of the decline of a number of once widespread species, as well as the appearance or re-appearance of other species. These changes are discussed in the species accounts and they are also summarised in the sections on 'Breeding Birds' and 'Wintering Birds' below, where some of the common themes are also discussed in more detail. Despite being the largest city in the UK and among the largest in the world, London continues to have a rich bird fauna within urban parks, green spaces, gardens and the more rural countryside surrounding Greater London that makes up the London area. In a time of increasing urbanisation and a rising human population, it is hoped that this book will highlight this rich fauna and will help to ensure that appropriate action and conservation efforts are taken to preserve the species in decline, so that future generations of Londoners can enjoy them. The species accounts include many negative stories but also highlight the positive ones.

2. The London Area

For recording purposes, the London area is divided into sectors: Middlesex, Essex, Hertfordshire, Buckinghamshire, Surrey and Kent. These sectors represent parts of or, in the case of Middlesex, the whole of, individual Watsonian vice-counties, which together comprise a nationwide series of recording areas (although for the purposes of recording birds the vice-counties of north and south Essex are combined). It is important to note that these vice-county boundaries differ in detail from present administrative boundaries.

In the city centre, a rectangular area of five miles (8km) from north to south and eight miles (12.8km) from east to west, centred on Charing Cross, is recognised as Inner London. Like the wider London area, the birds of this part of the city have been well studied (Cramp & Teagle, 1952b; Woodward & Arnold, 2012). Records attributed to Surrey, Hertfordshire, etc. in the text refer to the parts of the Watsonian vice-counties *outside* Inner London but *within* the wider London area.

Recording for this atlas project, as for the two previous London atlases, was based on tetrads. Tetrads are 2km x 2km squares and there are 25 tetrads within each 10km square in the national grid. The individual tetrads within each 10km square were identified by the national Ordnance Survey grid reference for the square followed by a suffix, A through to Z, with the letter O being omitted (see National Atlas, p.35). A consequence of the use of tetrads as recording units is that the London recording area for atlas-based surveys covers a slightly larger area than the official London recording area (see the map on p.10).

3. Methodology

The 2007–13 London Atlas was carried out initially in parallel with the BTO's National Atlas, with two additional years of survey work being carried out after fieldwork for the National Atlas ended in 2011. The aim was to document the breeding and wintering distribution of the birds in the London area and to identify changes in distribution since the previous two breeding atlases of the London area, in 1968–72 and 1988–94.

Timed tetrad counts

Surveyors were asked to make two timed visits to their allocated tetrads in summer (one in April or May and one in June or July) and two timed visits in winter (one in November or December and one in January or February). During each timed visit they walked a route of their choosing, which enabled them to visit all the main habitats within the tetrad and count all birds seen or heard for one hour, with the option of continuing for a second hour. The survey methodology for timed counts is described more fully in the National Atlas. For the National Atlas, timed counts were required in a minimum of eight out of the 25 tetrads in each 10km square in each season. However, for the London Atlas project, the aim was to carry out timed counts in both summer and winter in all 856 tetrads in the London area. Observers in the London area were encouraged to survey for the full two hours on all four visits.

The level of coverage achieved by the timed counts is summarised in Table 1.

Casual, or roving, recording

Timed counts of up to two hours enabled the surveyors to record and count most of the commoner species within a tetrad but may be insufficient to record the scarcer and/or more elusive species in the tetrad or to confirm breeding status. Therefore, observers were also encouraged to make additional visits to their tetrads to search for more elusive species and to record breeding evidence. These were called 'roving records' for the National Atlas project. In the London area, observers were asked to spread these additional visits out over the winter and the breeding season to try to ensure that all species were recorded. No minimum time was recommended. This contrasts with the second atlas, when a minimum survey time of twelve hours spread out across the breeding season was recommended. In practice, with such a large area to cover, survey effort was variable across the London area during 2007–13, as was the case for both previous atlases. Additional casual recording was undertaken by observers in most tetrads in the 2007 to 2013 period and coverage was generally excellent. However, a small number of tetrads received only timed counts (six in the breeding season and 17 in winter). The implications of this variable survey effort are discussed below ('Comparison with previous atlas maps').

Data from other sources

In addition to records input directly into the BTO's online Atlas website, data from other BTO datasets and other organisations were added to the atlas database by the BTO. These included records from the BirdTrack bird recording website (www.birdtrack.net), Garden BirdWatch (www.bto.org/gbw), Heronries Census (www.bto.org/heronries) and Nest Record Scheme (www.bto.org/nrs), as well as records from the BTO/JNCC/RSPB Breeding Bird Survey (www.bto.org/bbs) (see National Atlas,

Table 1: Timed count coverage achieved for the 856 tetrads in the London area. The main figure is the total number of tetrads in each category and the figure in brackets shows the percentage for that category:

Total timed count coverage	Breeding	Winter
4 hours (two counts both of 2 hours)	604 (70.6%)	643 (75.1%)
3 hours (one count of 2 hours and one of 1 hour)	75 (8.8%)	79 (9.2%)
2 hours (two counts of 1 hour)	117 (13.7%)	123 (14.4%)
2 hours (single count of 2 hours)	24 (2.8%)	9 (1.1%)
1 hour (single count of 1 hour)	15 (1.8%)	2 (0.2%)
No timed counts	21 (2.4%)	0

pp.42–45 for a list of other sources). Similarly, some records submitted to the London Bird Club (the ornithology section of the LNHS) were added to the atlas website, to fill gaps for both the National Atlas and the London Atlas.

The BTO linked any additional records to tetrads wherever possible, and we have reviewed many of the records submitted to the London Bird Club, in order to link them to the correct tetrad so that they can be used in the London Atlas. However, the location for some records refers to a site name rather than a grid reference. Many of these sites lie entirely within a single atlas tetrad and so the associated data could readily be used in the London Atlas project. Other sites extend across two (or more) tetrads and so the associated data could not easily be linked to a single tetrad. For these sites, the data were generally discarded or, in a small number of cases, added to the atlas dataset with the application of a little judgement on the appropriate tetrad. Therefore, some sightings that were submitted to the London Bird Club or elsewhere, and published in the *London Bird Report*, are omitted from the atlas maps.

In the instances when judgement was applied to data from large sites, the records were attributed to either (i) the tetrad within which the centre of the site is located, (ii) the tetrad in which most of a site is located or (iii) the tetrad which held most suitable habitat for the species. Alternatively, for some large well-watched sites, we sought the advice of local birdwatchers and allocated records to tetrads based on their local knowledge to ensure that the atlas data for the site is as accurate as possible. Despite there being some uncertainty about the precise tetrad, these approaches have been taken to ensure, as far as possible, that important records of scarcer species are not omitted from the map. Records have only been added in this way if suitable habitat is present in the tetrad *and* there are no other existing atlas records for that species in *any* of the other tetrads covered by the site.

Categories of breeding

During the breeding season, observers were asked to record evidence of breeding using the BTO's breeding evidence codes. These codes were allocated to one of four different breeding categories, as shown in Table 2.

The breeding categories have differed in the three London atlases. The second atlas used the simplest approach with just two categories, 'Present' (which is referred to in the species account tables as 'Seen Only') and 'Breeding or showing Evidence of Breeding' (which is referred to in the species account tables as 'Evidence of Breeding'). Therefore, to compare results from all three atlases in the species accounts, the categories from the first and current atlases have been aggregated to match, as closely as possible, the categories used in the second atlas (Table 2).

Although most of the categories can be matched closely across all three atlases, the way that some breeding evidence has been categorised may have been a little inconsistent, in particular for singing birds, pairs and territories. For example, in Montier, a 'singing male present on more than one date in the same place' was categorised as 'Probable Breeding' in that publication and transmuted to 'Breeding' in the second atlas and the comparison tables, whereas, in the current atlas, it would be categorised as 'Possible Breeding' (and therefore 'Seen Only' in the comparison tables) unless the observations were more than a week apart, in which case the evidence type would be upgraded to a territory and then categorised as 'Probable Breeding' (and therefore 'Breeding' in the comparison tables).

In practice, there may have been just as much variability in the treatment of singing birds, pairs and territories within each atlas. This is because, in spite of the definitions and advice provided, different observers may have differing perceptions of when to record a singing bird or pair as territorial. However, it is likely any variability in the treatment of singing birds, pairs and territories will have very little or no effect on the overall interpretation of changes in species distribution across the three atlases. Where appropriate, we have commented in the species accounts if we feel that it needs to be borne in mind when interpreting the maps.

In many cases, records of birds were submitted to the current atlas project without any evidence of breeding at all. Where these records could not subsequently be assigned a breeding evidence code (see section 'Survey Coverage'), they were assigned to the category of 'Present'.

Data submission and validation

Advances in technology since the last atlas meant that the majority of data for the current atlas was submitted online by the surveyors, using the BTO's online atlas data entry system (National

Atlas, pp.47–63). Validation of records (National Atlas pp.59–62) was carried out by BTO regional organisers and/or nominated validators in each BTO region.

A small proportion of the 950,000+ records that were submitted in the London area were removed or amended, either during validation or during the final checks of the distribution maps. Most amendments resulted from data entry errors, mapping errors or queries relating to breeding status, which were usually corrected by the surveyors themselves. Only a small minority of validation queries were about the identification. These related to national and local rarities, and, in a small number of instances, to records relating to scarcer or declining species in unexpected locations which were checked with the local recorders.

National rarities required acceptance by the Rare Breeding Bird Panel, and local rarities required acceptance by the London Bird Club's ID Panel. As parts of the London recording area also fall within the recording areas of the other county bird clubs,

Table 2: The BTO breeding evidence codes used during the 2008–13 fieldwork and how these relate to the breeding categories used in all three London atlases. For the first and current atlas, the equivalent term to that used in the second atlas is given in parentheses. For a full description of the breeding codes used in the current atlas, see National Atlas, p.42. Note that 'Breeding' in this table refers to the category titled 'Evidence of Breeding' in the second atlas.

BTO Breeding Evidence Code	First Atlas Breeding Category (1968–72)	Second Atlas Breeding Category (1988–94)	Current Atlas Breeding Category (2008–13)
F (Flying over)	None	None	None
M (suspected to still be on Migration)	None	None or Seen Only[1]	Migrant[2]
U (sUmmering non-breeder)	Unknown[3]	Seen Only	Present (=Seen Only)
H (present in suitable Habitat)	Possible (=Seen Only)	Seen Only	Possible (=Seen Only)
S (Singing male in suitable habitat)[4]	Possible or Probable (=Seen Only or Breeding)[4]	Seen Only or Breeding[4]	Possible (=Seen Only)
P (Pair observed in suitable habitat)[4]	Possible or Probable (=Seen Only or Breeding)[4]	Seen Only or Breeding[4]	
T (Territorial behaviour by one individual on two days a week apart, or by many individuals or one day)[4]			
D (courtship and Display near suitable habitat)	Probable (=Breeding)		Probable (=Breeding)
N (visiting probable Nest site)		Breeding	
A (Agitated behaviour suggesting young present nearby)			
I (brood patch on adult examined In hand)	Unknown[5]		
B (nest Building)	Probable/ Confirmed (=Breeding)[6]		
DD (Distraction Display observed)			
UN (Used Nest or eggshells found)			
FL (recently FLedged or downy young observed)			
ON (Occupied Nest)	Confirmed (=Breeding)	Breeding	Confirmed (=Breeding)
FF (Adult carrying Faecal sac or Food)			
NE (Nest containing Eggs)			
NY (Nest with Young seen or heard)			

1 In 1988–94, surveyors were asked to ignore migrant birds, but some birds suspected to be migrants were recorded as 'Present' (Hewlett *et al.*).

2 Known migrant birds are shown as a separate category on the 2008–13 atlas maps, but are excluded from the breeding categories in the tables in the species accounts, to permit direct comparison with the previous atlases.

3 No equivalent or similar breeding evidence code is listed by Montier. However, summering, non-breeding Grey Heron and gulls were omitted from the maps in the first atlas.

4 See main text for discussion about the recording of singing birds, pairs and territories. The distinction is based primarily on the number of occasions birds were heard singing at a location.

5 No equivalent or similar breeding evidence code is listed by Montier.

6 Nest building was regarded as confirmed breeding in Montier, except for birds of prey, waders, gulls, terns, owls, Carrion Crow, Rook, Jackdaw, Wren, *Acrocephalus and Sylvia* warblers.

it should be noted that there are a small number of local rarities which have been included in the National Atlas following acceptance by the relevant county validators, but have been excluded from the London Atlas maps as they were either not submitted or not accepted by the London ID Panel.

Records queried during validation have been omitted if the surveyor did not respond to the query raised, or if an identification was not accepted by the relevant recorder or ID panel. As is the case for the London Bird Report, exclusion of a record does not necessarily imply that the relevant ID panel believes an identification error has been made, but that the panel feels that insufficient evidence has been provided to prove the identification beyond doubt.

Presentation of data

Maps are shown for the majority of species, depending on whether the species is a summer visitor (one to three breeding season maps), a winter visitor (one or two winter maps), or present in the London area all year round (both breeding and winter maps).

(i) Maps showing current (2007–13) distribution

The breeding season maps show the highest breeding category that was recorded in each tetrad in any breeding season between 2008 and 2013 inclusive. Further details of the breeding categories are provided in the section 'Categories of breeding' above. The main breeding season surveys took place between 1st April and 31st July, but records of confirmed breeding occurring outside these months are also included. For migrant species, a small black dot is shown for tetrads where the only records submitted to the atlas were of birds considered to still be on migration. These tetrads are not included in the tables comparing the current and previous atlas results, as migrants were excluded from both previous London atlases.

The dots on the winter maps record presence in a tetrad between 1st November and 28th (or 29th) February, during any of the winters between 2007/08 and 2012/13 inclusive. A single record is sufficient for a dot to be shown on the map.

In both seasons, records of birds that *are known* to have flown straight over the tetrad, or given breeding evidence code 'F' (flying over) are excluded from the maps. The reason for doing so is to avoid showing birds as present in a tetrad of which they were making no use. This presents problems for

raptors because these species may spend time soaring over their breeding territory or hunting while in flight. The observer may therefore have recorded the birds as flying over when in fact the birds were making use of the tetrad. Conversely, many records of raptors were given no breeding evidence code at all and therefore shown as 'Present' on the maps. Some of these records could relate to flying birds, whether making use of the tetrad or not. Although the general pattern is believed to be accurate, the detail of the distribution maps for raptors should be interpreted with some caution.

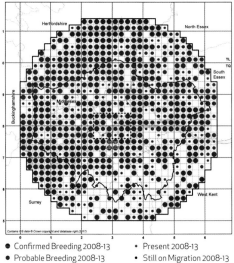

Figure 2: Breeding Distribution

● Confirmed Breeding 2008-13   · Present 2008-13
● Probable Breeding 2008-13   · Still on Migration 2008-13
· Possible Breeding 2008-13

(ii) Relative abundance maps

Relative abundance maps are shown for the more common and widespread species included in this volume.

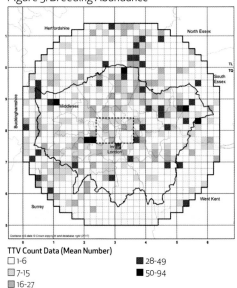

Figure 3: Breeding Abundance

TTV Count Data (Mean Number)
☐ 1-6   ■ 28-49
☐ 7-15   ■ 50-94
▨ 16-27

Further discussion about the methodology used to produce the abundance maps, and the interpretation of them, is provided in the section 'Relative abundance mapping' below. For both breeding and winter maps, darker colours represent higher *relative* abundance. The scales vary for each species and are shown next to the maps.

(iii) Comparison maps

Comparison maps are shown for the breeding season only and are not available for winter as there has been no previous tetrad-scale survey carried out during winter in the London area. The comparison maps show how the current distribution for a species differs from the distribution observed at the time of the first London Atlas (1968–72) and at the time of the second London Atlas (1988–94), by showing, *inter alia*, 'losses' (tetrads where a species has previously been recorded but was not recorded during the 2008–13 breeding season) and 'gains' (tetrads where a species had not been recorded previously but was recorded during 2008–13). Further discussion about interpreting differences between the three atlases is provided in the section 'Survey coverage' below.

Figure 4: Breeding Change

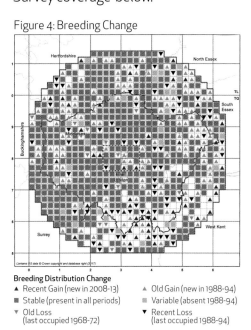

Contains OS data © Crown copyright and database right (2017)

Breeding Distribution Change

▲ Recent Gain (new in 2008-13)   ▲ Old Gain (new in 1988-94)
■ Stable (present in all periods)   ■ Variable (absent 1988-94)
▼ Old Loss   ▼ Recent Loss
(last occupied 1968-72)   (last occupied 1988-94)

(iv) Breeding Bird Survey graphs

The Breeding Bird Survey is an annual survey which started in 1994 and takes place across the UK. Its aims are to monitor changes in bird populations using repeated annual visits to sample 1km survey squares, carried out by volunteers. Results are produced for nine government regions in England,

including Greater London (BBS; Woodward, 2016), for all species that have occurred in an average of 30 or more squares in that region. BBS trend graphs for London are presented within the species accounts for the 26 species for which they are available. Note that the graphs show the trend in the Greater London government offices region, rather than the trend in the London area.

Relative abundance mapping

The breeding and winter abundance maps have been produced by calculating the mean of all available one hour timed counts for each tetrad for that season. Therefore, the abundance measure for each tetrad that received a timed count is based on data from a minimum of one and a maximum of four counts, from two timed visits of up to two hours each (see section 3.1, above, or National Atlas, pp.36–40, for further details about the timed counts). Over 70% of tetrads received the maximum of four hours of timed survey effort in the breeding season and over 75% of tetrads did so in winter.

The methodology for the timed counts was designed to produce relative abundance maps for the National Atlas at the 10km scale or higher and not at a tetrad scale. This used counts from eight or more tetrads in each 10km square to calculate relative abundance (National Atlas, pp.74–84). As the London atlas presents counts for each tetrad, it is particularly important to bear in mind that the relative abundance maps presented for the London area offer a much cruder measure of relative abundance. As well as real differences in relative abundance, there are likely to be substantial differences in tetrad-level counts because of other factors. Perhaps the most important of these for most species is that each tetrad will have been covered by a different observer, with observers having variable levels of field skills and knowledge varying considerably depending on their experience. Counts from more experienced surveyors are known to be higher than those who are less experienced (Eglington *et al.*, 2010). Other factors which may affect individual counts include the route followed (which was selected by the observer), the time and date of the survey, and the weather conditions. *Therefore, the relative abundance maps presented in this volume should be interpreted by looking at the general pattern they present for a species* because trying to compare relative abundance counts between individual tetrads may be misleading.

Figure 5: Comparison of numbers of species recorded in different tetrads with the numbers recorded in second atlas during the breeding season.

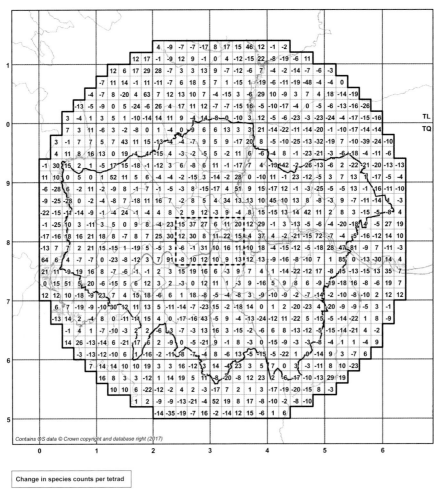

Change in species counts per tetrad

Mapping of scarce breeding species

Interim distribution maps were produced and distributed online during the fieldwork, to help promote the London Atlas and to give feedback about progress to observers. However, tetrad-level maps were not produced for a number of scarcer species, following the recommendations of the Rare Breeding Birds Panel.

For some of these species, we have included tetrad-level maps in this publication, following discussion with the London Bird Club. For most of these species, site based information has been published in the *London Bird Report* for many years (e.g. Pochard), so the production of distribution maps will not reveal any new information.

In a small number of cases, we have decided that publishing distribution maps to tetrad-level would be inappropriate. These are normally species for which site information is not published within the London Bird Report. The approach taken depended on the species. For some, the record of breeding was simply omitted from the map; for others, all records are shown but without an indication of breeding status and for others counts of tetrads in each of the recording sectors are given on the map.

Survey coverage and comparison with previous atlas maps

As a result of the advances in technology and the spread of social media since the second atlas, the number of observers and the number of records submitted to the current atlas far exceed the totals for the two previous London atlases. However, this does not necessarily mean that the effort made to record birds in a given tetrad was greater than for the previous atlases. In fact, the methodology used, and the ability to submit casual records online, means that survey effort was undoubtedly much more variable than in previous atlases. The result was that a large proportion of the records are from well-watched sites with multiple observers, while some, less-interesting tetrads, in both urban and rural areas, were surveyed by just a single observer.

Variation in survey effort is not unusual in atlas surveys. It was noted in both previous London atlases, with effort in the East London/Essex area thought to have been much more thorough during the second atlas than during the first atlas and the reverse believed to be true for parts of Surrey (Hewlett *et al.*).

During the current atlas, survey effort was believed to have been especially limited in the more rural parts of the Essex and Kent sectors when compared to the effort made to survey these areas in the second atlas. We do not have a record of the number of hours spent surveying in previous atlases so direct comparison of effort cannot be made. However, one observer is believed to have committed a substantial number of hours to survey work across the rural parts of the Essex sector during the second atlas (J. Hewlett, *pers. comm.*).

A comparison of the difference in the number of species recorded in each tetrad between the second and current atlases supports the belief that rural Essex and Kent were covered less well than other areas (Figure 5). However, it should be borne in mind that farmland birds are known to be in decline and that we would therefore expect a larger difference in the number of species recorded in these areas even if effort was the same for both atlases. In contrast, it should be noted that survey effort in Hertfordshire was particularly good during the current atlas. It is believed that a similar pattern of survey coverage occurred during winter.

A further complication is that many breeding season records submitted for the current atlas were simply of the presence of a species without information on breeding activity and so were of limited use for the atlas maps. Where this is the case for common species, breeding categories have been upgraded following a review of the data, where it is clear from the records submitted that a higher breeding category is appropriate. Resident, mainly sedentary, species (e.g. Robin, Blue Tit, House Sparrow) have been upgraded to have breeding evidence 'T' (territory, i.e. 'probable breeding' on the basis of high counts on a single day, whereas migrants and scarcer resident species (e.g. Coal Tit) were only upgraded to status 'T' if a series of records from the same site occurred during the same breeding season. In the case of records of migrant species with no breeding evidence, our assessment of breeding evidence considered whether any of the

records were outside the main passage period.

Another problem with migratory species was when observers did not input the appropriate 'M' code to indicate they were passage birds, and instead recorded the birds as singing 'S' or on territory 'T'. In some cases, we have marked such records as migrants where we know that no breeding habitat exists in the tetrad or that the birds are almost certainly migrants (for example all Whinchats and Wheatears were marked as migrants). However, we have usually left the breeding status unchanged and the status on the maps will therefore reflect what was input by the observer. In the case of Redstart and Wood Warbler, most if not all of the tetrads showing 'Present' or 'Possible breeding' will almost certainly relate to migrants, but it is conceivable that a small number relate to birds which considered the site suitable for breeding, albeit, in most cases, briefly. Species which are still widespread in our area but declining, like Willow Warbler, are also difficult to interpret and some records shown as present or with breeding evidence probably relate to passage birds.

Given the above, it is important to bear in mind when interpreting the species maps that survey effort may affect the comparison maps for some species, in particular scarcer and more elusive species, and also that the breeding evidence categories shown in some tetrads for all three atlases may be lower than would have been the case if additional survey effort was undertaken. However, it should also be noted that even in the broader areas with reduced survey effort during the current atlas, many of the tetrads were still surveyed very thoroughly. Therefore, for scarcer and more elusive species which have suffered substantial losses in tetrad occupation, it is likely that the maps offer a reasonably accurate assessment of their current distribution. More care is required for the species that show a more scattered distribution, as gaps on the map could reflect either a genuine absence or reduced effort. Further discussion is included within the species accounts where it is felt that consideration of survey effort is particularly important when interpreting the map for that species.

4. The Changing Environment
The changes to the London area (and to its birds) during the period from the time of the first atlas (1968–72) to the time of the second atlas (1988–94), were summarised in Hewlett *et al*. These changes included regeneration of many areas of derelict land including London's docklands, and development

around the urban fringe, including expansion of the motorway network, putting pressure on some of the outer parts of the London area. Hewlett *et al.* note that London's birds had also been affected by other factors that were having a wider effect in Britain, and elsewhere, and some of the main factors driving negative changes in our bird populations during this period must have been changes in agricultural practice outside the urban area and, potentially, land use changes within it.

Hewlett *et al.* also observed that some activities had positive effects on local bird populations during that period, for example, the creation of wetland habitat following sand and gravel extraction. In addition, the increasing interest in wildlife watching and nature conservation contributed to nature-focused management within some of London's parks and habitat improvement schemes, such as the creation of reed beds and the placement of purpose-built tern rafts on waterbodies, that enabled some species to colonise new areas.

Since the second atlas, further environmental changes, both positive and negative, have occurred. For example, between 1994 and 2004, an estimated 750 to 800 hectares of green space in London were lost to development (GLA, 2005b). The demands of an increasing human population mean that there is ongoing demand for housing and, in 2004, when Ken Livingstone was mayor, a strategic plan for Greater London was published (GLA, 2004). Some aspects of this 'London Plan' focused on key areas for development and regeneration which may have some negative effects on wildlife, such as in the Thames Gateway, although sustainability and green spaces also featured. Importantly, the Plan included policies to prevent development on greenfield sites, protect open spaces and re-focus development on brownfield, or previously developed, land at a high density. The Plan has been updated by future mayors (GLA, 2016), and it remains to be seen which aspects of the Plan have most influence over future policy, and hence on the environment and on our birds, in the longer term.

The threat of further large-scale development lingers over some sites, but with a few significant exceptions along the Thames Gateway (such as the Olympic site) and elsewhere, much of the development since the second atlas has been localised rather than large scale. Another feature of the last 20 years is the growth in development of high-rise buildings within central London, which has changed the city's skyline. Some of these, like 'The Gherkin' and 'The Shard' have become modern landmarks. As well as developments affecting the land upon which they are built, several studies have shown that high-rise buildings of glass and steel can result in bird mortality due to bird strike, particularly during migration (for example Loss *et al.*, 2014).

However, there is also increasing concern that small-scale decisions made by large numbers of homeowners may be having a cumulative effect over wide areas, which could in turn affect some species in London and other urban areas; for example the paving over of both front gardens (GLA, 2005) and back gardens (Smith *et al.*, 2011), and the blocking up of potential nesting cavities in walls and roofs during home improvements, such as at the Wyvil Estate, Stockwell, where numbers of Starling and House Sparrow nests dropped as a direct consequence of the nest holes being blocked during refurbishment (LBR 2013, 2014).

On a more positive note, the increase in conservation-minded management noted by Hewlett *et al.* has continued at many sites and conservation organisations have targeted London's population with the creation of relatively new but impressive wildlife reserves that rival others across the country. Many of the most popular UK nature reserves are often focused around wetlands as they enable a wide variety of species to be viewed easily. London is no exception and both the London Wetland Centre and Rainham Marshes RSPB reserve now attract visitors from the capital and beyond.

Wildlife-friendly management is not confined to large reserves. Habitat creation schemes have created or expanded habitat in many other locations, for example reed beds in the Royal Parks, and the creation of a network of newly planted recreational woodland in Havering, the Thames Chase Community Forest where 1.3 million trees have been planted since 1990 (www.thameschase. org.uk, 01/10/2016). Some rivers which were previously lined on either bank by concrete have been restored as naturalised rivers such as the River Brent at Tokyngton Park, Brent and the River Ravensbourne at Cornmill Gardens, Lewisham (The River Restoration Centre http://www.therrc.co.uk/ rrc, 29/03/2017). Many other smaller nature reserves and green spaces with visiting facilities and public information about wildlife now exist in the London area. Furthermore, in heavily built-up urban areas, new developments may now include features that are designed to promote biodiversity on a small scale, such as green roofs and Swift bricks. Often these occur as a result of planning conditions but in some cases developers may include such features themselves following consultation with ecologists and other experts. The focus, at least in policy, is now very much on sustainable development with significant harm to biodiversity either avoided, mitigated or compensated, see for example, the National Planning Policy Framework.

Although large-scale housing and infrastructure development, and major habitat creation projects, are often highly visible and therefore more noticeable in the London area, they are not the only potential drivers of bird population change and indeed they may not be the most important factors. As touched upon above, the cumulative effect of localised changes may be just as important as large-scale developments.

Furthermore, some changes to the environment are much less obvious or may even be invisible to Londoners as they go about their daily lives. However, for some species, one or more of these intangible or external factors may be much more important than development in driving population changes. The list below gives some other factors which may have driven negative and positive changes to some of London's bird species. This list is not necessarily comprehensive and is in no particular order:

• Change in agricultural practices (e.g. agricultural intensification, switch to autumn sown cereal crops) which is linked to population declines in farmland birds in rural and, potentially, suburban areas as well.
• Agri-environment schemes which may now be helping to slow or halt the declines in some farmland birds caused by agricultural intensification.
• Climate change which is linked to changes in the breeding and wintering ranges of birds, therefore causing local population changes, and changes in reproductive success rates.
• Problems for migratory species during migration or on their wintering or breeding grounds outside the London area; such problems may include hunting and habitat loss or degradation.
• Change in woodland management (e.g. cessation of coppicing) and deer abundance which may be resulting in a decline in some woodland species especially those which prefer a dense understorey.

• Planting of new woodlands which have benefited some generalist species and those which prefer coniferous woodland.
• Household improvements (e.g. re-roofing, plastic soffits, extensions, gardening, paving over) which may be reducing the availability of nesting opportunities and the availability of food.
• Wildlife-friendly gardening, including the provision of bird food and nest boxes in gardens which may offset some of the negative effects of home improvements.
• Disturbance of ground-nesting birds due to recreation activities, which has been shown to have negative effects on ground-nesting heathland birds, for example.
• *Trichomonosis* disease and possibly other diseases which have been demonstrated to negatively affect the populations of some bird species.
• Improving water quality of the Thames and its tributaries with subsequent improvements in the availability of food for fish-eating birds but potentially also negative effects on wading birds in the Thames Estuary as the nutrient levels, and therefore productivity, decline.
• Air pollution which may affect reproductive success in some bird species by, for example, causing shell thinning.

Research suggests that some of these factors can have a substantial effect on the populations of some bird species on a wide scale. Where this may be relevant to a particular species in the London area, this is referred to in the species accounts, for example the effect of *trichomonosis* on Greenfinch populations (Robinson *et al.*, 2010). However, for some of the factors, evidence that they have driven wider scale population changes is either anecdotal or harder to prove and requires further research (for example air pollution).

5. Breeding Birds

Hewlett et al. (pp.11–20) discussed the changes to bird life in the London area between the first and second atlases, contrasting the different trends in different habitats. Many of these trends have continued to the present day; wetland species have generally continued to do well, whereas farmland species have continued to decline. We briefly discuss below some of the general trends affecting the bird populations of some of these habitats since the second atlas.

Water and wetlands

In the second atlas, it was highlighted that increases in tetrad occupancy of more than 20% had occurred for 21 wetland species between the first two atlas periods, with a decrease of more than 20% occurring for just one species, the difficult to monitor Water Rail. There has been relatively little new wetland creation since the second atlas. However, Rainham Marshes has been opened to the public and work is now taking place in the north of our area to turn Walthamstow Reservoirs into another major urban nature reserve, 'Walthamstow Wetlands' opening in 2017 (www.walthamstow-wetlands.org.uk, 01/10/2016) and the same is happening in the south of our area at Beddington Farmlands Nature Reserve (http://bfnr.org.uk/, 30/03/2017). Despite this, the number of occupied tetrads has increased for several wetland species since the second atlas, most notably introduced species such as Greylag Goose, Egyptian Goose and Mandarin Duck. The current atlas also shows the colonisation of the London area by the Little Egret and a further increase in the number of tetrads occupied by Cetti's Warbler.

However, there is one subset of wetland birds that has fared less well since the second atlas, continuing the trend that was observed in that publication. These are the birds of wet grassland and meadows. Hewlett *et al.* stated that this was one of the most threatened habitats of the London area. Indeed, 64% of grazing marsh in the Greater Thames area was lost between the early 1930s and the mid-1980s and it is also a threatened habitat nationally (UKBAP, 1995). In the London area, further development has occurred along the outer Thames since the second atlas. It is perhaps not surprising therefore that the species using this habitat, such as Redshank, Lapwing, Snipe and Yellow Wagtail have all continued to decline, both in the London area and nationally, since the second atlas.

Farmland and rural areas

Five farmland species decreased in tetrad occupancy by more than 20% between the first and second atlases (Grey Partridge, Turtle Dove, Barn Owl, Rook and Tree Sparrow), with just one species increasing by more than 20% in the same period (the introduced Red-legged Partridge).

Since the second atlas, agricultural intensification has continued to affect farmland birds and they have continued to decline. The government's wild bird indicator showed a decline of 54% over the period 1970–2014 (Defra, 2015). However, there is some evidence that agri-environment schemes could be having a positive effect, or at least slowing the rate of decline, for some species of farmland birds (Bright *et al.*, 2015).

Unsurprisingly, given the bleak national picture, the current atlas shows that many farmland species continue to be in trouble in the London area. Of the five species that had been lost from more than 20% of previously occupied tetrads at the time of the second atlas, three are now close to extinction in the area (Grey Partridge, Turtle Dove and Tree Sparrow), and several other farmland species have also suffered further substantial declines since the second atlas period (for example Skylark, Bullfinch, Yellowhammer and Corn Bunting).

Woodland and woodland edge

The second atlas showed contrasting fortunes for woodland birds in the London area, with some species increasing and others decreasing in the number of occupied tetrads. The species with increased occupancy included four widespread generalists (Great Spotted Woodpecker, Blackcap, Nuthatch and Treecreeper) and two scarcer species (Lesser Spotted Woodpecker and Hawfinch),

Rose-ringed Parakeet

whereas the species with decreased occupancy nearly all have specialist habitat requirements (Nightingale, Redstart, Wood Warbler, Marsh Tit and Willow Tit).

The downward trends for many woodland specialists have continued. Redstart, Wood Warbler and Willow Tit no longer breed in our area, while the increases observed in the second atlas for Lesser Spotted Woodpecker and Hawfinch have been completely reversed and both are now also close to disappearing from the London area. Marsh Tit has also continued to decline. The current atlas also shows a decline in tetrad occupancy for a previously widespread woodland migrant, the Willow Warbler, which has declined sharply across south-east England over the last 20 years (National Atlas).

The changes in tetrad occupancy observed for woodland species in the London area generally reflect population trends elsewhere in southern England and in some cases across the rest of the UK. The contrast between the trends for woodland generalists and woodland specialists, has been highlighted by recent research (Hewson et al., 2007). This research also demonstrated that longer distance migrants (such as Nightingale, Redstart, Wood Warbler and Willow Warbler) were faring less well than short distance migrants (such as Blackcap and Chiffchaff).

The national declines in woodland birds probably result from multiple causes, potentially including climate change, a decrease in invertebrates, changes to woodland structure, resulting from both woodland management changes and the impact of increased deer numbers, and increased predation by Grey Squirrel *Sciurus carolinensis*, Great Spotted Woodpecker and members of the crow family (Fuller *et al.* 2005).

Urban green spaces, parks and gardens

London and other towns within our area have many green spaces, ranging from large parks, including the Royal Parks and Country Parks, which often include areas actively managed for nature, down to tiny squares sometimes containing no more than a lawn and some benches. For our birds, private domestic gardens are also important: these gardens make up around one-fifth of Greater London by area (GLA, 2005a).

By 2005, it was estimated that two-thirds of front gardens in Greater London were already covered by paving or other hard materials, the equivalent

Song Thrush

of 5,200 football pitches, often to create parking spaces (GLA, 2005a). Other green spaces have been lost too: between 1989 and 1999 an area equivalent to Richmond Park was lost to development; between 2001 and early 2005, the amount of greenfield land lost was lower but was still equivalent to three times the area of St James's Park each year (GLA, 2005b). It is likely that loss of greenfield land has occurred in other towns in our area. It is not known how much this affected our bird populations, as any effect is only likely if these spaces provided good habitat for birds before they were paved or built over. However, changes to the density of buildings and loss of suitable garden habitat in suburban areas in London are likely to have at least some localised effect on bird numbers (Dawson & Gittings, 1990).

For resident breeding species associated with this habitat, the key factor affecting bird populations in the London area seems to be the amount of deciduous trees and shrubs. Management measures which either promote or remove this type of vegetation across the area generally may be of more significance for bird populations than the loss of other types of open space (Chamberlain *et al.*, 2005).

Despite these changes, the trends for common birds in Greater London have generally been positive, with the BTO/JNCC/RSPB Breeding Bird Survey (BBS), covering the period 1995 to 2013, showing increases for 14 species in Greater London, many of which are associated with green spaces and gardens, and decreases for just six (BBS; Woodward, 2016). The new atlas distribution maps, also show that many species are holding or increasing their level of tetrad occupancy within urban areas, for example Green Woodpecker, Whitethroat and Jackdaw.

A fast-increasing species is the Ring-necked Parakeet, which has its most important UK population in our area. This species is controversial as it is a non-native species and there are concerns it may affect hole-nesting native species. It has spread from south-west London and can now be found in green spaces and gardens across the capital. There is, however, no evidence yet that the introduced Ring-necked Parakeet is affecting populations of woodland birds in the London area (Newson *et al.*, 2011).

Substantial losses from previously occupied tetrads have occurred for some species which make use of green spaces, including Spotted Flycatcher, Linnet and Bullfinch. There are also concerns about the six species that have recorded BBS declines in Greater London (Swift, Starling, Blackbird,

Song Thrush, Mistle Thrush and House Sparrow). Blackbird stands out in this list as BBS shows a decline in Greater London but an increasing trend elsewhere, including both the south-east England and east of England BBS regions. The different trend in Greater London remains unexplained, and the decline has not yet been reflected in any change in distribution in the London area. For common species, it may take many years for any decline to be reflected in the distribution map, as the species remains widespread even though numbers have declined. In the case of Blackbird, Sanderson (2013) reported a decline in numbers during the autumn bird counts in Kensington Gardens, from 191 in 1975 to 111 in 1995 and just 28 in 2010, and speculated that this might possibly be linked to a reduction in leaf litter due to changes in park management.

Buildings

Residential and commercial properties are an important component of the London area. Of the six species listed above that have declined significantly in Greater London since 1995, three (Swift, Starling and House Sparrow) are strongly associated with buildings and often nest in gaps under the eaves or in the brickwork. These gaps are now often blocked up during renovation work and lack of available nesting sites is one of the potential factors that may have contributed to declines of urban sparrows, although many other potential factors have also been suggested (BirdTrends; Crick *et al.*, 2002). Previous research has suggested that House Sparrows may have disappeared mainly from more affluent areas (Shaw *et al.*, 2008) perhaps reflecting the greater prevalence of renovation work in these areas. A mass participation survey in London supported this suggestion (RSPB/London Biodiversity Partnership, 2003). The abundance maps presented here for Starling and House Sparrow both appear to suggest that densities are higher in the less affluent areas of London.

Many modern developments and high-rise flats now have a sheer glass and steel construction and hence offer few niches for House Sparrows, Starlings and other birds. The London Swift group is attempting to reverse the decline of this species by encouraging housing developers and councils to provide nesting sites by including Swift bricks and/ or Swift boxes on new developments and existing buildings. Another aerial feeder which nests on buildings, the House Martin, is too scarce to be

Kestrel

monitored by BBS in Greater London but is also in steep decline across the south-east of England and large gaps in distribution have appeared in the London area.

In contrast, Herring and Lesser Black-backed Gulls have profited from nesting on rooftops, where they may benefit from the absence of their natural predators, the ready availability of waste food and, possibly, the extra warmth in urban areas (Ross-Smith *et al.* 2014). Both species have expanded substantially since the second atlas, and now nest in many parts of Greater London and in other towns such as Watford and Harlow. For the most part, they nest in industrial areas where they are undisturbed, although a few do nest on residential properties (for example in Camden).

Since the second atlas, the Peregrine has also colonised the London area, reaching a peak of 28 pairs present in 2011 (LBR). This is one of the few species that can take advantage of tall buildings in the city centre and elsewhere. Many of London's pairs are in urban areas including Inner London. They nest on buildings including industrial sites and tower blocks, sometimes benefiting from the provision of nesting platforms, and are well monitored by active Peregrine surveyors, who liaise with landowners and property managers to ensure that the birds continue to be protected. Another falcon, the Kestrel, also nests on buildings, but has suffered a reduction in the number of occupied tetrads since the second atlas, particularly in Greater London, and has perhaps been replaced by the Sparrowhawk (which nests in trees) as the most widespread raptor in the London area. The Kestrel has declined across most of its range in Britain and the causes are unclear (National Atlas). In London, this species has been known to prey on House Sparrows, and Kestrels nested close to some of the House Sparrow hotspots in central London in the 1990s. So, the sparrow decline could possibly have contributed to the loss of the Kestrel from some London tetrads (J. Hewlett, *pers. comm.*).

Wasteland or 'brownfield' sites

Hewlett *et al.* noted that the pressure for development since the 1980s had meant that wasteland and so-called 'brownfield' sites (i.e. sites which had previously been built on) had been developed more rapidly, leaving less opportunity for such sites to be occupied by birds (Hewlett *et al.*). At the time of the first atlas, the derelict

Surrey Docks in Inner London was used by several species including Lapwing and Little Ringed Plover, with both Skylark and Yellow Wagtail still breeding on the few remaining undeveloped plots by the time of the second atlas. Pressure on brownfield sites has continued to be high in London since the second atlas, particularly along the Thames corridor (Harrison & Davies, 2002; Raco & Henderson, 2006), and national and local initiatives and policies have focused on favouring development on brownfield land over 'greenfield' sites, especially since the publication of the London Plan in 2004 (GLA, 2004; GLA, 2005b).

Both Little Ringed Plover and Ringed Plover use brownfield sites, particularly along the Thames, and have both decreased since the second atlas, although they also use a variety of other sites and the losses could also be linked to other habitat changes, such as the growth of vegetation at some gravel pits.

A discussion of wasteland sites would not be complete without mention of the Black Redstart, an iconic London bird ever since it became associated with bombed-sites following the Second World War. The current atlas map suggests that the number of occupied tetrads has declined slightly since the second atlas, as might be expected with the loss of brownfield sites. However, it is still widespread in central London and reported numbers do fluctuate for this difficult-to-find species. Black Redstart was one of the species which was the focus of a Biodiversity Action Plan in London. The provision of green roofs may benefit this species and other wildlife (GLA, 2008).

Breeding bird trends, losses and gains

Hewlett *et al.* reported the loss of three breeding species to the London area since the first atlas. These were Wryneck, Red-backed Shrike and Cirl Bunting. A further six species had records with some evidence of breeding in 1988–94, but no such records during 2008–13 breeding seasons. These were Common Sandpiper, Willow Tit, Wood Warbler, Fieldfare, Whinchat and Wheatear. In addition, Redstart was restricted to just one 'probable breeding' record in the 2008–13 breeding seasons, which was of a singing male heard at a site on two dates only; it is no longer regarded as a breeding bird in our area. The 'loss' of Fieldfare is not surprising, as the 1991 breeding record was extremely unusual because this species is normally confined as a rare

Avocet

breeding species to the far north of Britain. Most of the other species listed above had very low breeding populations in the London area even in 1968–72 and so again, their loss as breeding species from the London area was not unexpected. However, Willow Tit was present in as many as 262 tetrads at that time (out of 856) and was still present in 181 tetrads during the second atlas, mainly in Hertfordshire and Essex. Its demise was already well under way by then and came about extremely rapidly, with the last confirmed breeding record occurring in 1995, just one year after the end of the second atlas period.

The current breeding status of several other species is also unclear. Although evidence of breeding was recorded for them in 2008–13, they were absent or on the brink of disappearing as breeding species in our area during the latter part of this period. Nightjar, Woodlark and Dartford Warbler have always had a tenuous position in our area as their habitat requirements are very specific. Nightjar may still cling on as a breeding species at the edge of our area, but the latter two were lost following the severe winters at the start of the atlas period, although their populations could recover and they may breed here again in future. These severe winters may have also caused the recent apparent loss of Woodcock from most of its remaining sites, and its capacity to return is more doubtful. Snipe, too, may no longer be breeding in the London area. Finally, evidence of breeding for Ruddy Duck occurred in 12 tetrads in total, but it was more or less extinct by 2013 following a national cull, which has divided opinion among birdwatchers.

Sadly, it looks likely that several other species

that were still widespread during the second atlas may go the same way as Willow Tit in the near future, with the current atlas showing substantial declines in the number of occupied tetrads for Grey Partridge, Turtle Dove, Lesser Spotted Woodpecker, Yellow Wagtail, Spotted Flycatcher, Marsh Tit, Tree Sparrow, Lesser Redpoll, Hawfinch and Corn Bunting. The majority of these species are farmland or woodland birds. Many of these declines are not surprising; these species are all of conservation concern (Eaton *et al.*, 2015) because they are among the fastest declining bird species in the UK in the long-term, as measured by combined Common Birds Census and Breeding Bird Survey trends covering 1967 to 2013. Indeed, four of them (Turtle Dove, Tree Sparrow, Willow Tit and Grey Partridge) have declined nationally by more than 90% over that period (BirdTrends).

In contrast, there have also been a number of gains to London's breeding birds since the end of the second atlas. Buzzard, Peregrine, Avocet and Black-headed Gull all nested soon after the second atlas period and were included in a special section about recent gains in that publication. Since then, additional gains have been Little Egret, Red Kite, Marsh Harrier, Great Black-backed Gull and Raven. Red-crested Pochard is also a nominal 'gain' in the current atlas. Although free-flying birds were already breeding at the time of the first atlas, this species was not included in the first two atlases because the population was not considered to be self-sustaining.

Four more species had records categorised as 'probable breeding' for the first time during the current atlas. These were Goldeneye, Bittern, Savi's Warbler and Great Reed Warbler. In the case of Goldeneye, a pair summered in 2010 and breeding was recorded after the end of the current atlas period (in 2014). However, the breeding female was ringed and was therefore presumed to be an escape. For the other three bird species, the records were of males present for more than one week, and therefore holding a 'territory', but it is very unlikely any of them bred on this occasion. The Great Reed Warbler at Amwell is a notable anomaly, as, despite having been recorded during the current London atlas, this species has still not officially been recorded in the London area at the time of writing (December 2016). This anomaly comes about because the London atlas recording area is slightly larger than the LNHS recording area (see the section 'London area' above).

6. Wintering Birds

Most of the birds which migrate to the British Isles for the winter are the wildfowl and waders which breed on the Arctic tundra and taiga, arriving here mainly from the north-west (from Iceland, Greenland and Canada) and from the north-east (Scandinavia, the Baltic and Russia). Many of these birds winter on our estuaries and coasts and hence the London area supports relatively low numbers of most wintering species. The Thames and the larger reservoirs and gravel pits are the best sites in the area to find them, and parts of the Thames Basin, Lee Valley and west London waterbodies are recognised as Special Protection Areas because of the numbers of winter wildfowl and other water birds. Elsewhere, the farmland surrounding the London area supports a small number of birds which migrate there for winter, and urban green spaces and gardens can also support others, particularly during periods of severe weather when the 'urban-heat island effect' may mean that Greater London stays free of snow and ice while the surrounding countryside does not.

Water and wetlands

The Thames estuary supports important numbers of Black-tailed Godwit, Avocet, Grey Plover, Dunlin, Knot and Redshank during winter (JNCC, 2016). Only comparatively small numbers reach as far upriver as the London area. The Thames Estuary beyond Crossness is the only part of the London area where these species can be said to overwinter annually, with the exception of Knot, which is currently a scarce visitor having overwintered in very small numbers in the past. Rainham Marshes is the site in our area from which most records of these species are received, though this may simply be because this site is so well watched. They are also regular at other sites including Crayford, Dartford, West Thurrock and Swanscombe Marshes.

In the London area, several other species spend the winter mostly along the Thames or on the adjacent marshes, also usually in very small numbers. These species include Pintail, Hen Harrier (occasional), Marsh Harrier, Merlin (occasional), Oystercatcher, Ringed Plover, Curlew, Ruff, Caspian Gull and Rock Pipit. Other species which are most likely to be encountered along the Thames, but which are too scarce to be considered regular winter visitors, include wintering swans and geese, sea ducks, other seabirds, Lapland Bunting and Snow Bunting.

Many of the species that are encountered along the Thames in winter also occur occasionally on or at the edges of the large reservoirs in the London

Black-tailed Godwit

area, particularly those in the south-west and in the Lee Valley, but also at other large wetland sites, such as the London Wetland Centre. In most cases, these species occur away from the Thames during autumn or spring passage and are short-stayers, so cannot be considered to be overwintering. However, cold weather movements do occasionally bring birds to the reservoirs during the middle of winter as well.

Furthermore, some species can be fully considered as winter visitors to the reservoirs and larger gravel pits. For example, Great Northern Diver is the most frequent diver species in the London area, and an average of four birds overwintered on the large reservoirs during the current atlas survey. Most of these birds are immatures, and the south-west waterbodies usually attract around three-quarters of the birds seen in our area. Another such species is Black-necked Grebe, with up to 30 wintering annually on William Girling Reservoir in the Lee Valley, and are incredibly faithful to this site, rarely visiting the adjacent King George V Reservoir. Over the last ten years, small numbers have also wintered on Staines Reservoir but records elsewhere are scarce.

Several other wetland species not mentioned above are widespread in winter both on the Thames and elsewhere, including Shoveler, Wigeon, Gadwall and Teal. The gravel pits and reservoirs of the Lee Valley and the Colne Valley are visited by some wildfowl species which are relatively scarce on the Thames Marshes, including Great Crested Grebe, Tufted Duck, Pochard, Goldeneye, Smew and Goosander. The Lee Valley and Wraysbury gravel pits are important for Smew, which winters in small numbers in Britain. Bittern also winters regularly at several sites and occasionally appears elsewhere, particularly during colder weather.

Farmland and rural areas

In the London area, the main areas of arable farmland are found in the Hertfordshire and Essex sectors. Only a small number of species can be said to be regular winter visitors to this habitat. Lapwing and Golden Plover still occur in farmland in small numbers but many of the highest winter counts of these species in our area now occur at wetland sites, in particular, Rainham Marshes and, for Lapwing, the London Wetland Centre, just outside Inner London. Woodcock and Snipe are also found occasionally on farmland, and are probably more widespread than the distribution maps suggest as they are often only observed if flushed. Meadow Pipit is also frequently encountered on farmland during winter.

Agricultural intensification and the planting of autumn cereals have caused a reduction in the availability of winter stubble fields. As a result, large areas of arable farmland can appear relatively bird-less for much of the winter, with Skylark, finches and Yellowhammer sometimes forming large flocks which move around to search for suitable feeding sites. Where there are stubble fields, they provide winter food for farmland birds (Gillings & Newson, 2005) and other agri-environment scheme options such as wild bird seed crops may fulfil a similar role (Baker et al., 2012).

Other species that are frequent winter visitors to farmland include Redwing, Fieldfare and the four commonest gull species, all of which can be found throughout the London area in winter. Large flocks of Woodpigeon can also sometimes be observed on farmland, and this species was the most abundantly recorded species in the London area during the timed counts (see section 7).

Woodland and woodland edge

Lapwing

Coot

Like farmland, London's woodlands can seem impoverished during winter when compared with the breeding season. Birdwatchers can sometimes walk for some time seeing (and hearing) very few birds, before experiencing a sudden flurry of activity when they come across a roving flock. Such flocks usually comprise mostly resident woodland species, such as tits, Nuthatch, Treecreeper and Goldcrest.

There are relatively few winter visitors to our woodlands. Wintering Chaffinches sometimes form large flocks, perhaps comprising a mixture of resident birds and migrants. These flocks may include a few Brambling too, with numbers varying depending on food availability further north and east. Two other finches, Siskin and Lesser Redpoll, can also be observed wintering in woodland, especially in wetter woods with good numbers of alder trees. In addition, groups of Redwing can often be found feeding on woodland leaf litter.

Although still scarce, another species which is more likely to be located during winter is the Woodcock. At this time of the year, this species is more widespread and may sometimes be flushed from even small patches of woodland.

Urban green spaces, parks and gardens
London and other towns in our area provide habitat in the form of buildings, gardens and parks. These are frequented by a wide variety of familiar common bird species, with use of gardens peaking in winter, when fewer resources are available in the wider countryside (Risely & Simm, 2016). During winter, they may be joined by woodland birds, including Lesser Redpoll, Siskin and Brambling. Blackcap is another garden visitor in winter, with most of our wintering Blackcaps thought to originate from breeding grounds in central Europe, a recent occurrence which began around the 1960s (Helbig *et al.*, 1994). This new migration route may have been supported partly by the provision of bird food in gardens (Plummer *et al.*, 2015).

In addition to the species found in gardens, urban parks and playing fields are used by gulls, particularly Black-headed Gull and Common Gull, and those containing ponds or lakes may support good numbers of wintering wildfowl, with such as Mallard, Gadwall, Shoveler, Teal, Tufted Duck, Pochard and Coot, with resident birds being supplemented by winter migrants.

The urban-heat island effect is a well-known phenomenon which keeps temperatures slightly higher in London than in the surrounding countryside, particularly at night (e.g. Wilby, 2003). Several winter roosts of 100 or more Pied Wagtail can be found in Greater London, usually in trees or shrubs. During extreme weather conditions, urban parks and streets can become a refuge for birds escaping harsher conditions in the wider countryside. Redwing and, especially, Fieldfare were more frequent and more widespread in Greater London during the more severe early winters of the atlas, when large numbers could sometimes be encountered along urban streets and in parks with trees bearing berries (e.g. Rowan *Sorbus aucuparia*). Such trees may also attract Waxwing during 'irruption' years, which occur when food resources are scarce in Scandinavia and north-east Europe, rather than being linked more directly to severe weather. Other species can also be encountered more frequently in urban green spaces during severe weather, including Meadow Pipit and Skylark, and some usually elusive species may become more visible as they are forced to use more open habitats, for example Woodcock, Snipe and Jack Snipe.

Buildings

Buildings are not a commonly used resource during the winter, although some nest sites will be used as winter roosts and some species, like the Peregrine, may continue to maintain their territories throughout the year.

This was not always the case. Starling roosts on buildings in central London numbered in the tens of thousands in the mid-twentieth century. These have now largely gone for reasons which are unclear but preventative measures which were installed on buildings from the mid-1980s could be a contributing factor (Self). Roosts still occur under some of the bridges in central London, although the roosts are a fraction of the size they used to be (Bowlt, 2008).

Wasteland or 'brownfield' sites

Brownfield sites have provided additional habitat for birds visiting the London area in winter, although as noted above, the availability of such sites is diminishing (GLA, 2005b). Relatively open brownfield sites can provide habitat for ground-feeding species such as Linnet and Meadow Pipit, whereas sites which have remained unmanaged for several years and become overgrown with bramble and other scrub, can provide habitat for wintering thrushes, Starlings, Blackcap and resident species including Dunnock, Robin and Wren.

Wintering bird trends, losses and gains

As this is the first winter atlas for the London area, we are unable to show maps comparing results from this atlas with previous London atlas surveys or make detailed comparison of tetrad occupancy. It will therefore be interesting to see whether distribution changes have occurred for these and other species, if and when another wintering atlas is carried out in London.

We do know that all the bird species which regularly winter in number in the London area now have been doing so for many years. Some wintering bird species have certainly increased in distribution, such as Bittern, Avocet and Black-tailed Godwit; we also know that others have a wider distribution, such as Wigeon, and that others probably have a reduced distribution, such as Lapwing. The Great Grey Shrike is perhaps the only contender for a regular wintering species (in addition to the lost resident species described under breeding birds) which has been lost as a wintering bird from the London area since the 1990s (LNHS, 1964; Self). For the future, one of the main factors affecting the birds which winter in the London area may be climate change, with birds moving their core wintering grounds either away from or towards our area in response to the changing climatic conditions.

7. Which Species are Most Common in the London Area?

There are two ways that we can assess which species are the most commonly *recorded* species in the London area. First, we can rank species according to the number of tetrads in which they were recorded: this is a measure of how widespread they are. As one would expect, the most widespread species are more generalist species which can be found in a wide variety of habitats, in particular those which are familiar in urban areas through their use of gardens and open green spaces. A total of four species was recorded in all 856 tetrads in the London area during the breeding season (Woodpigeon, Blue Tit, Blackbird, Robin) and six species were recorded in all tetrads during winter (Woodpigeon, Magpie, Carrion Crow, Great Tit, Blackbird, Robin).

The undertaking of timed counts during the current atlas project gives us the opportunity of using a second method of ranking species in the London area, which was not possible for either of the previous London atlases. All birds were counted during the time counts, and therefore species can be ranked according to the number of birds counted.

Table 3: The most abundantly recorded species in the London area during the atlas timed counts.

	Winter				Breeding season		
	Species	Total counted	Mean per hour		Species	Total counted	Mean per hour
1	Woodpigeon	124,442	40.47	1	Woodpigeon	51,711	17.59
2	Black-headed Gull	104,205	33.89	2	Starling	36,326	12.36
3	Starling	57,356	18.65	3	Feral Pigeon	34,025	11.57
4	Feral Pigeon	54,507	17.73	4	Carrion Crow	29,080	9.89
5	Carrion Crow	39,442	12.83	5	Blackbird	24,858	8.46
6	Blue Tit	34,034	11.07	6	Blue Tit	22,427	7.63
7	Blackbird	24,623	8.01	7	House Sparrow	21,169	7.20
8	Magpie	23,892	7.77	8	Robin	19.116	6.50
9	Jackdaw	22,501	7.32	9	Wren	18,672	6.35
10	Robin	21,952	7.14	10	Magpie	16,318	5.55
11	Great Tit	21,828	7.10	11	Mallard	15,954	5.43
12	Fieldfare	21,215	6.90	12	Chaffinch	14,769	5.02
13	Mallard	20,986	6.82	13	Great Tit	14,466	4.92
14	Redwing	20,949	6.81	14	Jackdaw	13,717	4.67
15	Coot	20,117	6.54	15	Coot	10,635	3.62
16	Chaffinch	18,914	6.15	16	Canada Goose	9,395	3.20
17	Common Gull	16,895	5.49	17	Swift	9,392	3.19
18	House Sparrow	15,876	5.16	18	Greenfinch	8,660	2.95
19	Canada Goose	13,511	4.39	19	Black-headed Gull	8,637	2.94
20	Tufted Duck	12,595	4.10	20	Collared Dove	6,907	2.35

This ranking takes account of some 2,940 hours of timed counts during the breeding season, and 3,075 hours of timed counts during winter, with counts covering all 856 tetrads in the London area.

These counts do not necessarily show which are the most common species in the London area. Instead, they show which species were *the most abundantly recorded*. This is a very important distinction as the detectability of different species will vary according to how secretive and vocal they are and may also vary at different times of the year. Some species are much more easily detected and a high proportion of the birds present are likely to be counted, whereas other species may be equally abundant, but are harder to detect apart from when they are singing. In the most recent population estimates (Musgrove *et al.*, 2013), Wren is listed as the most common breeding species in Great Britain (7.7 million pairs) but it was only 9th in the top 20 breeding season list for the London area and does not appear in the top 20 in winter, when it is less vocal (it ranked 28th). Dunnock is also a widespread and common garden species (2.3 million pairs) but fails to make either list (it ranked 22nd in the breeding

season), perhaps because of its generally secretive behaviour or perhaps because it is genuinely only found at relatively low densities in London.

Although a few species, such as Wren and Dunnock, were exceptions due to being more easily detected when singing, counts of the most abundantly recorded species were generally higher during the winter than during the breeding season. Resident bird populations are likely to be higher in autumn and the early part of the winter following the previous breeding season. The higher counts may also reflect an influx into the London area during winter for some of the species listed, or that some birds may be easier to observe during winter when the trees lose their foliage and birds may spend more time in the open in search of food. It is also notable that many of the top ranked wintering species form wintering flocks which may also make them easier to find. The presence of several water birds on both lists may be (at least partly) because they are often highly visible compared to some other very common species.

Species Accounts

The species accounts are generally ordered according to the eighth edition of the *British List* (BOU, 2013). However, some minor changes to the species order have been made for reasons of presentation.

Merlin

Mute Swan

Cygnus olor

Common breeding resident; amber list.

The Mute Swan is our only resident swan species. It is found throughout the British Isles, where suitable habitat occurs. It requires wetland that is of sufficient size and can make use of larger lakes and rivers or canals that are sufficiently wide and have feeding opportunities. The UK population is currently increasing although in south-east England the population has remained broadly stable since 1994 at least (BBS).

It is widely distributed in the London area but with some gaps, most notably in an area spanning the Kent sector and in parts of Surrey, which is broadly coincident with the North Downs, and Middlesex. Outside the Greater London boundary, the most important areas are the west London waterbodies, the Colne Valley, the Lee Valley and the Thames Marshes. The current distribution across the London area is similar to that recorded in both previous atlases. There have been widespread gains in the number of tetrads occupied since 1994, suggesting the species have benefited from the creation of wetlands and improvements in water quality in rivers.

The wintering population may comprise birds which breed in our area and birds which breed elsewhere. Regardless of origin, the wintering birds can exploit a wider range of waterbodies, which explains the more widespread occurrence of this species in the London area during this season.

Breeding Distribution

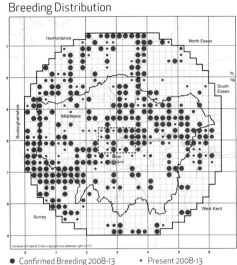

- ● Confirmed Breeding 2008-13
- ● Probable Breeding 2008-13
- ● Possible Breeding 2008-13
- · Present 2008-13
- · Still on Migration 2008-13

Period	Number of Tetrads		
	Evidence of Breeding	Seen Only	Total
Breeding 1968–72	178	59	237
Breeding 1988–94	186	98	284
Breeding 2008–13	264	94	358
Winter 2007/8–2012/13	-	-	407

However, on some waterbodies, particularly the smaller lakes, a breeding pair will remain in residence and maintain their territory throughout the winter by chasing off other swans (except their own young which may be allowed to remain until late winter or early spring). At other sites, the Mute Swan is not territorial and congregates in large groups. The highest site count during the atlas period was 237 at Harrow Lodge Park, Essex in January 2011 (LBR). Large numbers of non-breeding birds remain at this site throughout the year and three figure counts occur here regularly.

Breeding Change

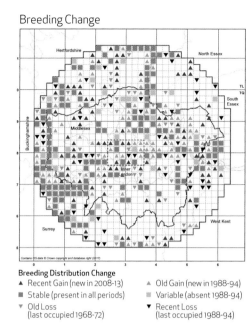

Breeding Distribution Change
- ▲ Recent Gain (new in 2008-13)
- ■ Stable (present in all periods)
- ▼ Old Loss
  (last occupied 1968-72)
- ▲ Old Gain (new in 1988-94)
- ■ Variable (absent 1988-94)
- ▼ Recent Loss
  (last occupied 1988-94)

Winter Distribution

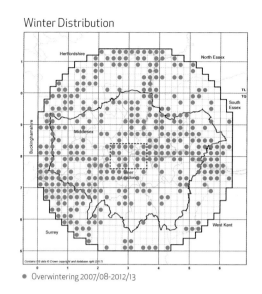

- ● Overwintering 2007/08-2012/13

Bewick's Swan

Cygnus columbianus

Scarce migrant, usually in autumn, and winter visitor; amber list.

Bewick's Swan is a winter visitor to the British Isles from European Russia, with the biggest numbers in Britain being found in the fenlands of eastern Britain, especially the Ouse and Nene Washes (National Atlas).

It is a scarce visitor to the London area, with only a small number of sightings in most years, usually consisting of just a few birds. It is most likely to be encountered at the major wetland sites in the area, such as the west London waterbodies, the Lee Valley and Rainham Marshes.

During the atlas period, the only significant arrivals occurred during the 2010/11 winter, when double figure counts were made at eight sites (LBR). It is likely that the same birds were involved in at least some of the counts. Five of these counts were made on 3rd December 2010, including 27 on the Thames between Rainham and Crayford Marshes. Up to 18 birds were then recorded in the Harmondsworth area from 29th December 2010 into January 2011. The only other double figure counts during the atlas survey period were made on 19th January 2013, when approximately 30 flew over Walthamstow Reservoirs and 21 were later seen at Bowyer's Water, both records presumably involving birds from the same flock (LBR).

All records of known flyovers are excluded from the map. However, some of the plotted points may still represent birds which were flying over our area.

Winter season tetrads: 18

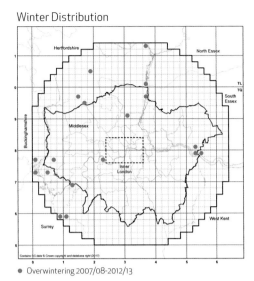

Winter Distribution

● Overwintering 2007/08-2012/13

Whooper Swan
Cygnus cygnus

Rare winter visitor; amber list.

The wintering population of Whooper Swan in the British Isles is believed to comprise the whole of the Icelandic breeding population (National Atlas) plus birds which breed in Russia and Fennoscandia (Migration Atlas). The majority winter in Scotland and Ireland (National Atlas) and this species is rarer than Bewick's Swan in the London area even though, in the British Isles as a whole, the Whooper Swan is a more widespread (National Atlas) and more numerous (Musgrove et al., 2013) winter visitor than Bewick's Swan.

During the current atlas period, a total of just 11 wild birds was seen in the London area. A flock of five birds was seen at Cheshunt Gravel Pits, Crossness and then Rainham Marshes on 23rd January 2010; three were at Rainham on 24th December 2010; and one in Hyde Park/Kensington Gardens on 7th November 2011.

Another bird at Walthamstow Reservoirs in October 2009 is not shown on the map as it departed on 31st, one day before the winter survey period began, and another seen flying down the Thames at Crayford on 11th Dec 2012 is also excluded from the map, as it was not seen to land.

One free-flying bird at Cheshunt Gravel Pits in December 2007 was considered an escape (LBR). Records of captive birds and non-flying escapes such as the bird at the London Wetland Centre are excluded from the map, as are three additional records, which were not submitted to the London Bird Club ID Panel.

Winter season tetrads: 5

Winter Distribution

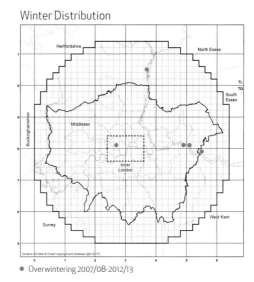

● Overwintering 2007/08-2012/13

Bean Goose

Anser fabalis

Rare winter visitor; amber list.

Bean Goose is a scarce, and primarily coastal, winter visitor in Britain, with annual numbers only in the low hundreds (Musgrove et al., 2013). Those that do spend the winter here are concentrated on the Slamannan Plateau in Stirlingshire, the Sefton coast and in East Anglia, with small numbers of, usually transient, birds recorded elsewhere, particularly along the east coast (National Atlas).

Given the scarcity and generally coastal distribution, and the fact that the other wintering grey geese with which the Bean Goose is often found are scarce in the London area, it is no surprise that the Bean Goose is a rare visitor to the London area, with most records coming from around the Thames.

Two separate forms of Bean Geese occur in the UK: Taiga Bean Goose *A. f. fabalis* and Tundra Bean Goose *A. f. rossicus*. During the atlas period, all those recorded in the London area that were identified to race, were the Tundra Bean Goose.

Away from the Rainham area, where several birds occurred, including the maximum count of 12 in December 2007, a first winter Bean Goose was at Tyttenhanger Gravel Pits from 26th November to 1st December 2011, and a single bird was seen at three sites in west London in February and March 2012. Flyover birds (excluded from the map) were also seen at Beddington Farmlands, Crossness and West Thurrock.

Winter season tetrads: 9

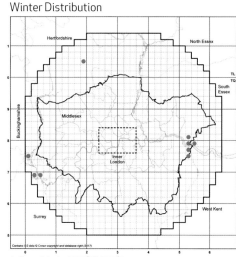

Winter Distribution

● Overwintering 2007/08-2012/13

Pink-footed Goose
Anser brachyrhynchus

Scarce winter visitor; amber list.

The Pink-footed Goose breeds in Iceland and Greenland and winters in north-west Europe (BirdLife). The species winters in large numbers in Norfolk and this is the normal southernmost limit of its wintering range in Britain (National Atlas). It is therefore a rare bird in the London area.

Like other wild geese and swans, larger flocks are occasionally recorded flying over the area, but do not usually stop. During the current atlas period, these included a flock of 71 over Rainham Marshes on 21st January 2010. The only records of longer staying birds during the current atlas period were of two birds in the Rainham area in February 2010, between two and six in the same area in November 2010, and up to two in the Lee Valley in 2010/11 (with one of these, or a different bird, also seen at the Roding Valley Nature Reserve). All other records were of birds which were present in our area only briefly in the winter of 2010/11, and came from Holmethorpe Sand Pits, Tyttenhanger Gravel Pits, Sevenoaks Wetland Reserve and fields near Cobham.

Small numbers of feral birds are also known to be present in Britain, for example at Abberton Reservoir in Essex (Wood, 2007). The record of this species from Cobham mentioned above is thought to be of an escaped or feral bird (LBR) and it is possible that some of the other records were also feral birds rather than truly wild birds.

Winter season tetrads: 15

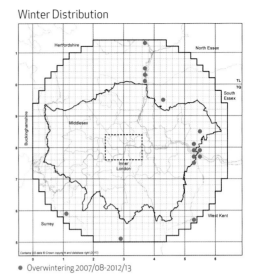

Winter Distribution

● Overwintering 2007/08-2012/13

White-fronted Goose

Anser albifrons

Scarce winter visitor and passage migrant; red list.

Two subspecies of White-fronted Goose winter in the British Isles. The Greenland race *flavirostris* winters largely in south-west Scotland and Ireland, whereas a small proportion of the Eurasian race *albifrons* winters in southern England (Migration Atlas). This distinction is not always made when records of this species are submitted; however, all the London Atlas records which were attributed to a subspecies were, unsurprisingly, *albifrons*. Numbers of the *albifrons* race have declined in Britain since the 1950s and increased in the Netherlands, possibly as a result of a shift in winter distribution due to milder continental winters (Migration Atlas).

The White-fronted Goose is scarce in the London area, with the nearest regular wintering flocks occurring on the Swale in North Kent and the Essex coast, where numbers increase in harsher continental winters (Wood, 2007).

Most records in our area are of small groups of birds that are present only briefly, though larger flocks can sometimes be encountered. For example, during 20th to 22nd December 2010, birds were seen flying over at least 13 different sites, with more than 100 birds seen at three locations: Stoke Newington Reservoir, Wanstead Flats and Barking Bay. This occurred during the coldest December for 100 years and followed snow in November and December originating from the continent, including heavy snowfall on 20th December (Met Office, 2016).

Small numbers of apparently wild birds sometimes linger, usually in the lower Thames area. These include a small group of three to four birds, first seen in February 2009, that apparently returned to the Ingrebourne Valley for at least three winters in succession and were present for a couple of months each year. Single birds may also sometimes be encountered amongst flocks of Greylags. These are often relegated to the 'escapes' section of the London Bird Report, although it is possible that such records may occasionally involve genuinely wild birds that have become isolated from their own species and associated themselves with feral geese.

The map shows all records of free-flying birds which were found to be using a tetrad, including those thought likely to be feral birds. Excluded from the map are records of over-flying birds and records from sites where captive birds are present, unless it is known for certain that the records did not relate to birds in the collection.

Winter season tetrads: 22

Winter Distribution

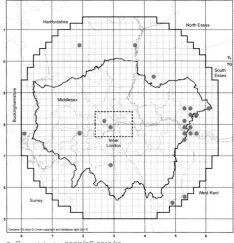

● Overwintering 2007/08-2012/13

Greylag Goose

Anser anser

Common, introduced breeding resident; amber-listed but this refers to the largely migratory, wintering population that does not occur in the London area.

In Britain, the wintering population includes both birds from the Icelandic breeding population and resident birds, including an expanding resident feral population that is now present across most of Britain (National Atlas). The breeding population of principally feral birds in the UK increased by 215% (26% to 564%) over the period 1995 to 2013 (BBS).

The Greylag Goose population in London is, of course, part of the feral resident population, and may have originated from restocking programmes by wildfowling organisations in the late 1950s and early 1970s, and/or from free-flying young raised by captive birds in St James's Park (Hewlett *et al.*).

The Greylag Goose can now be found in many urban parks, especially in Greater London, as well as in more open wetland areas such as the Outer Thames Estuary and the Lee and Colne Valleys. At many sites, the numbers of Greylag Goose remain small in comparison with Canada Goose, with just one or two pairs typically present.

However, at some sites, a much larger population has become established. Flocks of several hundred birds are now regularly recorded within the London area, with the biggest counts during the atlas period coming from Hyde Park/Kensington Gardens, with a count of 450 in December 2010; Rainham Marshes, with 376 in December 2012; and Sevenoaks Wildlife Reserve, with 345 in November 2010. Although it was not in the atlas survey seasons, an even higher count of 523 was made in September 2010 at the latter site.

Not surprisingly, the number of tetrads occupied by Greylag Goose has increased substantially within the London Area since the 1988–94 atlas.

Period	Number of Tetrads		
	Evidence of Breeding	Seen Only	Total
Breeding 1968–72	4	2	6
Breeding 1988–94	47	57	104
Breeding 2008–13	112	121	233
Winter 2007/8–2012/13	-	-	217

The winter distribution is similar to the breeding season distribution, with most birds remaining in the same area throughout the year.

Breeding Distribution

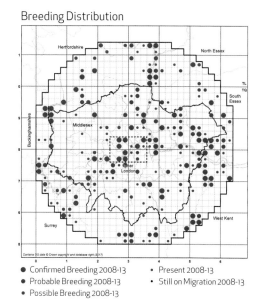

- ● Confirmed Breeding 2008-13
- ● Probable Breeding 2008-13
- ● Possible Breeding 2008-13
- • Present 2008-13
- • Still on Migration 2008-13

Breeding Change

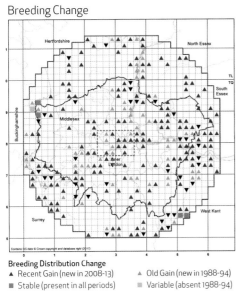

Winter Distribution

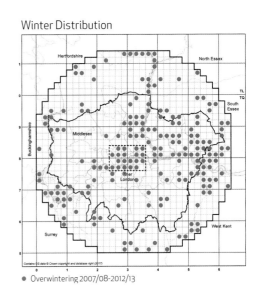

● Overwintering 2007/08-2012/13

Breeding Distribution Change
▲ Recent Gain (new in 2008-13)   ▲ Old Gain (new in 1988-94)
■ Stable (present in all periods)   ■ Variable (absent 1988-94)
▼ Old Loss
(last occupied 1968-72)   ▼ Recent Loss
(last occupied 1988-94)

Greater Canada Goose

Branta canadensis

Very common, introduced breeding resident; not listed as it is a non-native species.

The Canada Goose is the most abundant non-native waterbird species in Britain (WeBS), and the UK population grew by 66% (37% to 106%) over the period 1995 to 2013 (BBS).

Free-flying populations of the Canada Goose have been breeding in the London area since the 1950s, when wildfowling organisations brought birds to sites around the outskirts of London (Hewlett *et al.*). The species expanded its range rapidly during the 1960s, 70s and 80s, and is now fully established, being found wherever there are suitable areas of water including lakes, ponds and canals.

During the current atlas period, the Canada Goose was recorded across most of urban London, with the main gaps in distribution occurring in more rural areas. However, it is still present in rural areas where there are waterbodies, including small ponds. The distribution is not strictly limited to tetrads containing water features, as feeding birds sometimes move away from water to feed on nearby agricultural fields and grassland, including sports pitches in urban areas (for example tetrad TQ48X).

Canada Goose has further increased the number of tetrads occupied since the second breeding atlas though the rate of expansion has slowed, possibly reflecting the fact that most potential breeding sites are already in use.

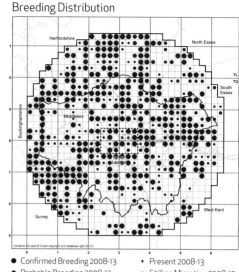

Breeding Distribution

- Confirmed Breeding 2008-13
- Probable Breeding 2008-13
- Possible Breeding 2008-13
- Present 2008-13
- Still on Migration 2008-13

Period	Number of Tetrads		
	Evidence of Breeding	Seen Only	Total
Breeding 1968–72	56	21	77
Breeding 1988–94	287	115	402
Breeding 2008–13	342	158	500
Winter 2007/8–2012/13	-	-	486

The winter distribution is similar to that observed in the breeding season. During the winter the highest counts for this species during atlas fieldwork (timed counts) came from the Lee Valley and Fairlop Waters/ Gravel Works.

Breeding Change

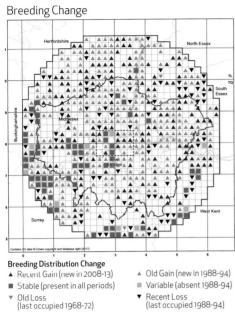

Winter Distribution

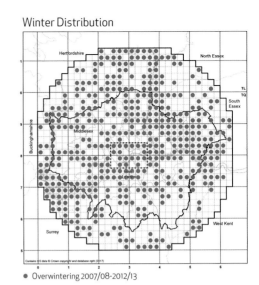

Breeding Distribution Change
- ▲ Recent Gain (new in 2008-13)
- ■ Stable (present in all periods)
- ▼ Old Loss (last occupied 1968-72)
- ▲ Old Gain (new in 1988-94)
- ■ Variable (absent 1988-94)
- ▼ Recent Loss (last occupied 1988-94)

- ● Overwintering 2007/08-2012/13

Barnacle Goose

Branta leucopsis

Introduced resident, breeding rarely, and scarce winter visitor; amber listed but this refers to the migratory wintering population.

The Barnacle Goose breeds mainly in the Arctic and winters further south. Those which winter in Britain are found mainly in Scotland and Ireland (Black *et al.* 2014). In addition to migratory birds, there is a growing naturalised population in Britain (National Atlas).

The species has bred in the London area, with the first record from the Lee Valley in 1986 (Hewlett *et al.*). However, there are no populations in the London area that are considered to constitute a self-sustaining population.

Records of feral Barnacle Goose are often single birds amongst Canada Goose flocks and are relegated to the 'escapes' section of the London Bird Report. The largest flock of resident birds during the atlas period was a group of approximately ten birds at Walton Reservoir during the early years of the survey, with numbers dropping to approximately six in 2012, then two in the winter of 2012/13 and one or two in 2013 (LBR). This was the only site where successful breeding by Barnacle Goose was confirmed during the atlas period, apart from a bird which produced a single hybrid young with a Greylag Goose at Sevenoaks Wildlife Reserve in 2009.

Although Barnacle Goose was recorded more widely during the current atlas period than previously, its status in the London area is still uncertain.

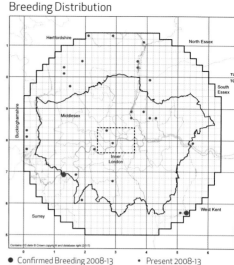

Breeding Distribution

● Confirmed Breeding 2008-13
● Probable Breeding 2008-13
● Possible Breeding 2008-13
• Present 2008-13
• Still on Migration 2008-13

Period	Number of Tetrads		
	Evidence of Breeding	Seen Only	Total
Breeding 1968–72	0	0	0
Breeding 1988–94	2	5	7
Breeding 2008–13	2	26	28
Winter 2007/8–2012/13	-	-	38

The winter distribution in the London area is usually similar to the breeding season, with the resident feral birds being largely sedentary. However, apparently wild birds do occur occasionally, with the Netherlands probably the most likely source of origin of these birds. During the atlas period, the largest flock recorded was at Rainham Marshes, where 82 were counted on 21st December 2007, increasing to 88 birds from 24th to 29th December, with 37 remaining until 16th January 2008. Some observers noted iron-staining around the faces of some birds. This suggests a strong likelihood of wild origin (LBR, 2007) as such staining in geese indicates they have been feeding in wetlands with deposits of iron oxides (Alisauskas *et al.*, 1998), which are not found locally. Other notable flocks included 50 on the west London waterbodies in January and February 2010 and 52 at Apps Court Farm in December 2012.

Breeding Change

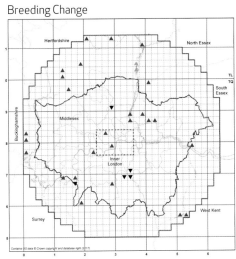

Winter Distribution

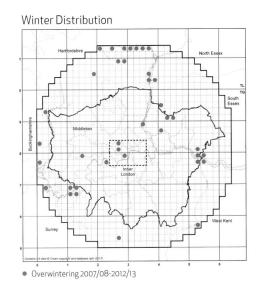

Breeding Distribution Change
▲ Recent Gain (new in 2008-13)
■ Stable (present in all periods)
▼ Old Loss
  (last occupied 1968-72)

▲ Old Gain (new in 1988-94)
■ Variable (absent 1988-94)
▼ Recent Loss
  (last occupied 1988-94)

● Overwintering 2007/08-2012/13

Brent Goose

Branta bernicla

Occasional passage migrant and winter visitor; amber list.

Two populations of Brent Goose winter in the British Isles. The pale-bellied form (*B. b. hrota*) breeds in Svalbard and Greenland and winters in western Britain and Ireland. The dark-bellied form (*B. b. bernicla*) breeds in Russia and winters in north-west Europe, including eastern Britain (Migration Atlas). This latter form winters in Essex and records in London normally relate to this subspecies. However, a Pale-bellied Brent Goose *B. b. hrota* was recorded during the current atlas period at Rainham Marshes on 22nd December 2010, the third ever record for the London area (LBR).

The Brent Goose is a coastal species, usually found on salt marsh and estuaries. Significant numbers occur within the Thames estuary, particularly in autumn when 40% to 50% of the total wintering population of Britain may be present there (Wood, 2007). As might be expected, the vast majority of records in the London area, including those submitted during the current atlas period, are from the lower Thames. Even here, it usually only occurs in small numbers and does not often linger. Records elsewhere within the London area are generally flyovers but single birds or small groups occasionally alight on the larger reservoirs.

Excluding known flyovers, the highest winter count during the current atlas period was 22 birds at Rainham Marshes on 21st January 2010, with 20 landing on King George VI Reservoir on 8th November 2011, and 15 at Hilfield Park Reservoir on 19th February 2008 (LBR). However, like other species, Brent Goose can sometimes turn up in unexpected locations, such as the bird seen grazing on Hampstead Heath on 17th November 2011 (LBR). Birds which were known to have only been seen flying over are excluded from the map.

Winter season tetrads: 27

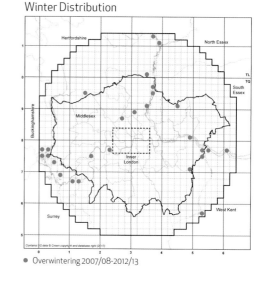

Winter Distribution

● Overwintering 2007/08-2012/13

Egyptian Goose
Alopochen aegyptiaca

Increasing introduced breeding resident; not listed as it is a non-native species.

As the name suggests, the natural range of the Egyptian Goose is in Africa. In Britain, the species first became established in East Anglia. Its range across Britain has expanded recently and the number of Wetland Bird Survey sites where the species was recorded almost doubled between 2007/08 and 2012/13 (WeBS).

The first recorded breeding of the Egyptian Goose in the London area occurred in the Lee Valley in 1979, with further nesting recorded there in 1981 and 1986 (Hewlett *et al.*).

Following the expansion of the Canada Goose and Greylag Goose, the Egyptian Goose is the third non-native goose species to become established in the London area (the Barnacle Goose is not considered to have become established). Like the two more numerous established species, the Egyptian Goose can now be found breeding in urban parks as well as other wetland habitats.

During the second atlas period, the Lee Valley was still the best place to find the Egyptian Goose in the London area. However, in the late 1990s and early 2000s, a population became established in the south-west of the London area, with breeding occurring at Old Oxted, Bushy Park, Denham Court Lake and Kew Gardens (Hewlett *et al.*). It seems likely that it is this population that was the source of later expansion of this species into Inner London and then into the north and east of Greater London during the 2000s.

During the second atlas period, it was recorded in just seven tetrads. However, its rapid spread across the London area has coincided with the expansion in Britain seen in the WeBS survey results and the number of occupied tetrads in the London area has increased by more than twentyfold since 1988–94.

Period	Number of Tetrads		
	Evidence of Breeding	Seen Only	Total
Breeding 1968–72	0	0	0
Breeding 1988–94	4	3	7
Breeding 2008–13	109	62	171
Winter 2007/8–2012/13	-	-	174

Much of the increase appears to have occurred very recently. In 2006, there were records of just six pairs/broods at four sites, with records coming from 59 sites altogether, mostly in Surrey and Middlesex (LBR). By 2010, there were 34 confirmed breeding pairs/broods at 25 sites with records from 116 sites in total and then by 2013, there were 55 confirmed breeding pairs/broods at 34 sites with records from nearly 200 sites in total (LBR).

The wintering distribution is similar to the distribution in the breeding season.

Breeding Distribution

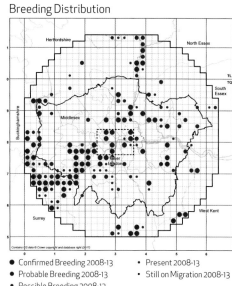

- ● Confirmed Breeding 2008-13
- ● Probable Breeding 2008-13
- ● Possible Breeding 2008-13
- • Present 2008-13
- • Still on Migration 2008-13

Breeding Change

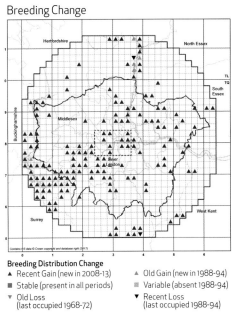

Breeding Distribution Change
▲ Recent Gain (new in 2008-13)   ▲ Old Gain (new in 1988-94)
■ Stable (present in all periods)   ■ Variable (absent 1988-94)
▼ Old Loss   ▼ Recent Loss
(last occupied 1968-72)   (last occupied 1988-94)

Winter Distribution

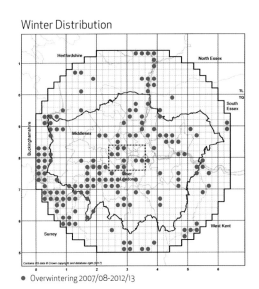

● Overwintering 2007/08-2012/13

Shelduck

Tadorna tadorna

Breeding resident on Lower Thames and major inland waters; amber list.

The Shelduck is predominantly a coastal species, wintering on estuaries around the British Isles but, since the 1960s, it has expanded its range in Britain and now breeds inland in many areas (National Atlas). Its status in the London area matches the national picture, with substantial increases in occupied tetrads noted between the first and second atlas periods.

During the current atlas period, broods were noted in 27 tetrads, with probable breeding occurring at a further 28 tetrads, for example, where a pair was observed during summer but breeding not confirmed. As might be expected, the Thames estuary is a stronghold, with broods seen more or less annually at Rainham Marshes and Crossness. A post-breeding flock of 190 was recorded in Barking Bay on 6th July 2011. Away from the Thames, breeding also occurs on larger gravel pits and reservoirs, and broods were observed in three or more atlas years at Walthamstow Reservoir, Queen Mother Reservoir, Queen Mary Reservoir and Holmethorpe Sand Pits.

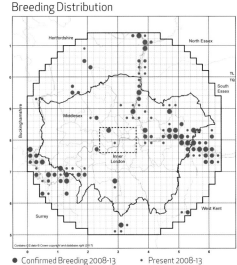

Breeding Distribution

- ● Confirmed Breeding 2008-13
- ● Probable Breeding 2008-13
- ● Possible Breeding 2008-13
- • Present 2008-13
- • Still on Migration 2008-13

Period	Number of Tetrads		
	Evidence of Breeding	Seen Only	Total
Breeding 1968–72	4	0	4
Breeding 1988–94	60	33	93
Breeding 2008–13	55	62	117
Winter 2007/8–2012/13	-	-	92

The Shelduck population in the London area appears to have peaked at approximately 55 pairs around the year 2000 (Self) but has since fallen to around 20 pairs, not all of which successfully produce young (LBR). Despite the fall in numbers, and some losses from tetrads in the Lee Valley, the number of occupied tetrads during the current atlas period is similar to the second atlas.

Shelduck is also found in the Royal Parks in Inner London and breeding is occasionally reported from there, including one instance in Regent's Park during the current atlas period which involved free-flying birds. However, the origin of the breeding birds, whether truly wild or originating from the wildfowl collections, is not always clear.

The majority which breed in Britain are thought to migrate to the Wadden Sea (Netherlands/Germany) in late summer to moult (Migration Atlas), and recent counts suggest that a greater number are now wintering in the Netherlands rather than in Britain, perhaps in response to warmer winter conditions on the continent (Holt *et al.*, 2012).

However, the wintering distribution in the London area is similar to the breeding season, with most Shelduck found along the Thames in Essex and Kent, where counts of over 100 may occur, for example, 169 at Barking Creekmouth in January 2009. As well as along the Thames, smaller numbers can also be found on the larger waterbodies in our area, in particular the reservoirs and gravel pits of the Lee Valley and the south-west.

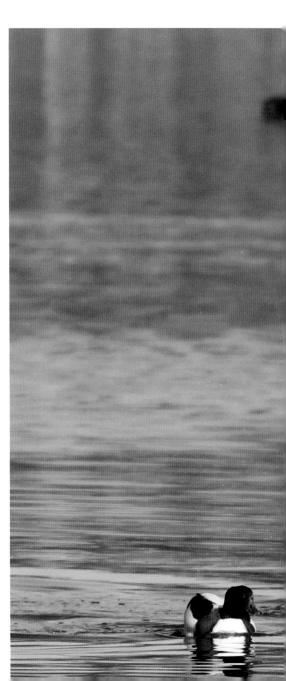

Breeding Change

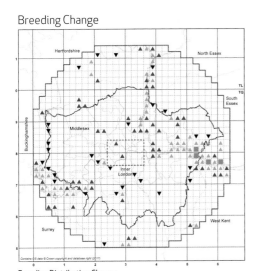

Winter Distribution

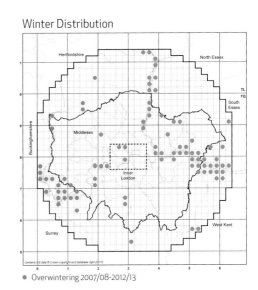

Breeding Distribution Change

▲ Recent Gain (new in 2008-13)   ▲ Old Gain (new in 1988-94)

■ Stable (present in all periods)   ■ Variable (absent 1988-94)

▼ Old Loss
(last occupied 1968-72)   ▼ Recent Loss
(last occupied 1988-94)

● Overwintering 2007/08-2012/13

Mandarin Duck
Aix galericulata

Introduced breeding resident, locally common; not listed as it is a non-native species.

The Mandarin Duck originates from East Asia, but became established in Britain in the early twentieth century. Its preferred habitat is woodland with ponds. It has greatly expanded its range in Britain over the last 40 years and is now found across much of south-east England, with other populations centred on the Severn Vale and the Peak District (National Atlas).

The earliest populations in the London area were in the south-west, probably the result of expansion from its original strongholds around Virginia Water and Windsor Great Park, which lie in Surrey just outside the London area. The Mandarin was already established in these areas at the time of the first confirmed breeding in the London area, near Thorpe in 1946 (Self). By the second atlas period, it was widespread in the south-west and breeding in several locations elsewhere, particularly in north London and the Hertfordshire sector, as well as Epping Forest. It was also recorded as present in Inner London at Regent's Park.

The current atlas shows losses from a small number of tetrads in Surrey but increased occupancy in most other areas, confirming that Mandarin Duck is fully established in the London area. In Inner London, breeding appears to have occurred amongst birds of captive origin in St James's Park in the late 1990s (Self), followed by a pair at Hyde Park/Kensington Gardens in 2007 and subsequently other Royal Parks (Self).

Breeding Distribution

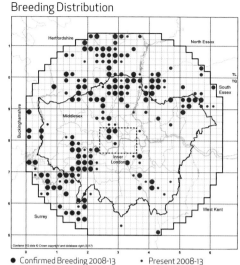

● Confirmed Breeding 2008-13
● Probable Breeding 2008-13
● Possible Breeding 2008-13
• Present 2008-13
• Still on Migration 2008-13

Period	Number of Tetrads		
	Evidence of Breeding	Seen Only	Total
Breeding 1968–72	24	9	33
Breeding 1988–94	54	38	92
Breeding 2008–13	126	66	192
Winter 2007/8–2012/13	-	-	151

During winter, the distribution of the Mandarin Duck is similar to the breeding season, both nationally and within London. Compared to the breeding season, it was found in fewer tetrads within the London area. However, birds are more often seen in larger flocks and may be more visible, particularly if they are forced into more open water by cold weather. The biggest count during the atlas period came from Grovelands Park, north London, with 158 in November 2009. A three figure count also occurred at Regent's Park, where 103 were recorded in December 2010 (LBR), possibly relating to birds moving into London as a result of cold weather.

Breeding Change

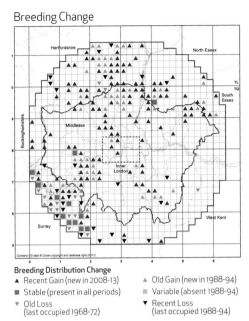

Winter Distribution

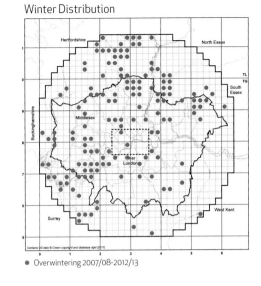

Breeding Distribution Change

▲ Recent Gain (new in 2008-13)   ▲ Old Gain (new in 1988-94)

■ Stable (present in all periods)   ■ Variable (absent 1988-94)

▼ Old Loss
(last occupied 1968-72)   ▼ Recent Loss
(last occupied 1988-94)

● Overwintering 2007/08-2012/13

Wigeon
Anas penelope

Common winter visitor, occasionally summers; amber list.

The Wigeon is predominantly a winter visitor to Britain, and differs in behaviour from most other wintering duck species in being a grazer. As a result, it needs habitat containing large, open areas of grassland (or other vegetation), where it can feed without being disturbed, and waterbodies, that provide a safe place to roost. Consequently, it is less likely to be found wintering in urban parks than the other common dabbling duck species that prefer aquatic food resources (such as Mallard, Gadwall, Teal and Shoveler).

As shown by the atlas map, the most important areas for Wigeon in the London area are around the lower Thames, the west London waterbodies, the Lee Valley and the Colne Valley. By far the most significant site is Rainham Marshes, in the lower Thames area, where counts of approximately 700 occurred each winter during the start of the current atlas period rising to 1,500 in January 2011 and 2012. Other counts of more than 400 came from Bowyers Water (580 in November 2007), Holyfield Lake (405 in February 2012), Queen Mary Reservoir (646 in December 2010) and Staines Reservoir (442 in January 2010; 425 in December 2010; 504 in February 2012) (LBR).

The London Wetland Centre is the only site located in the urban area providing good habitat for Wigeon and up to 100 birds spend the winter there. However, with large numbers of Wigeon wintering in the London area, occasional birds do turn up briefly at other urban sites, usually staying for a day or less. In Inner London, there were records from Regent's Park, Hyde Park/Kensington Gardens and the River Thames at Rotherhithe.

Although the species is mainly a winter visitor to south-east England, there are occasional breeding records (National Atlas). A small number of birds also summered in our area during the current atlas period (LBR), but there were no confirmed or probable breeding records and most of the breeding season records relate to late staying winter birds still present in April.

Breeding season tetrads: 35

Winter season tetrads: 155

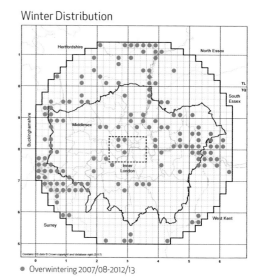

Winter Distribution

● Overwintering 2007/08-2012/13

Gadwall

Anas strepera

Local breeding resident and common winter visitor; amber list.

The number of Gadwall wintering in the UK has risen steadily over the last thirty years (WeBS). Some of these breed in continental Europe or Iceland (National Atlas), but the UK breeding population is also expanding and is estimated to be between 690 and 1,730 breeding pairs (Musgrove *et al.*, 2013) and, as a result, breeding records are no longer collected by the Rare Breeding Birds Panel.

In the London area, as elsewhere, Gadwall is associated with wetland habitats including some urban sites. The earliest breeding birds in London may have originated from the St James's Park collection. Free-flying young, believed to be from the park, were recorded at Barn Elms regularly from 1936 until the 1950s (Hewlett *et al.*). Since then, the breeding range within London (and Britain) has expanded which may have been aided by the increasing number of sand and gravel pits (Hewlett *et al.*). However, the breeding distribution remains relatively restricted compared to other expanding wildfowl species and the number of breeding pairs in the London area is probably fewer than 50 (LBR). Breeding has continued in the Lee Valley, where it first occurred during the first atlas period, and the west London waterbodies and the outer Thames area, where it occurred during the second atlas period. It has expanded in the Colne Valley since the second atlas period. Breeding is also shown for Inner London and at Brent Reservoir for the first time during the current atlas period. However, some of the apparent 'gains' in Inner London may simply reflect differing assumptions on whether birds breeding in the Royal Parks were captive or not between now and previous atlas periods.

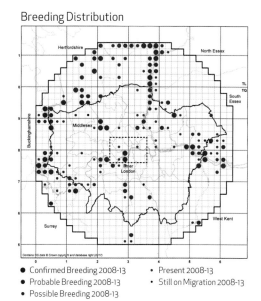

Breeding Distribution

- Confirmed Breeding 2008-13
- Probable Breeding 2008-13
- Possible Breeding 2008-13
- Present 2008-13
- Still on Migration 2008-13

Period	Number of Tetrads		
	Evidence of Breeding	Seen Only	Total
Breeding 1968–72	9	0	9
Breeding 1988–94	23	30	53
Breeding 2008–13	81	83	164
Winter 2007/8–2012/13	-	-	247

In Britain, most birds are thought to make only local movements (Migration Atlas) and some of the Gadwall in the London area probably continue to frequent the same waterbodies within which this species also breeds, with the Lee Valley, Colne Valley, west London waterbodies and the Thames Marshes being especially favoured. However, at least the majority of the birds are winter visitors, and the Gadwall is more widespread in our area at this time of year. The highest counts during the atlas period occurred during the cold winter of 2010/11, and included counts exceeding 800 in three successive months at Wraysbury/Horton GP, with a peak of 1,004 in January 2011 (LBR). Other counts of more than 300 during the current atlas period came from: Brent Reservoir, Rainham Marshes, Bowyers Water, Crossness, Rye Meads, Aldenham Country Park and Barking Creekmouth (LBR).

Breeding Change

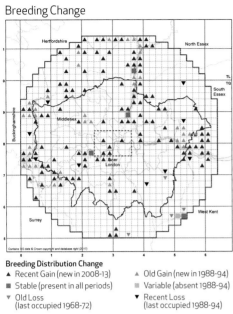

Winter Distribution

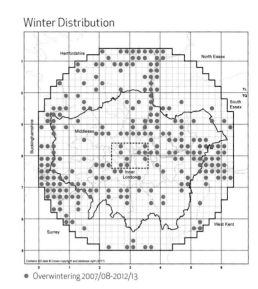

Breeding Distribution Change
- ▲ Recent Gain (new in 2008-13)
- ▲ Old Gain (new in 1988-94)
- ■ Stable (present in all periods)
- ■ Variable (absent 1988-94)
- ▼ Old Loss (last occupied 1968-72)
- ▼ Recent Loss (last occupied 1988-94)

● Overwintering 2007/08-2012/13

Teal

Anas crecca

Common winter visitor and rare breeder; amber list.

The Teal is a widespread and familiar wintering bird in Britain and the London area, with birds arriving in Britain from their breeding grounds in Iceland, Scandinavia and north-west Siberia (Migration Atlas). Small numbers of Teal also remain in south-east England to breed, although many records in spring probably relate to late-departing migrants (National Atlas).

The presence of wintering birds lingering into the breeding season makes interpretation of the breeding season map difficult. Records of pairs and individual birds in suitable habitat in only April have been given the status 'present' on the atlas map. The apparent increase in the total number of occupied tetrads between the second and current atlas periods almost certainly relates to differences in the way these birds were recorded rather than a genuine increase in tetrad occupancy.

The only confirmed breeding during the current atlas period in the London area was recorded at the London Wetland Centre in 2012. This was the first confirmed breeding record in the London area since 2002. This is fewer than during the second atlas period, when ten confirmed nesting pairs were found, six of which were at Rainham Marshes (Hewlett *et al.*). However, during the current atlas period there were also birds present in June at several other sites.

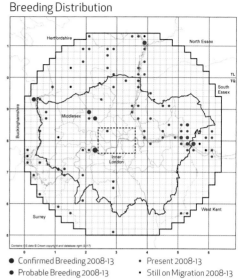

Breeding Distribution

● Confirmed Breeding 2008-13 • Present 2008-13
● Probable Breeding 2008-13 • Still on Migration 2008-13
● Possible Breeding 2008-13

Period	Number of Tetrads		
	Evidence of Breeding	Seen Only	Total
Breeding 1968–72	5	13	18
Breeding 1988–94	11	48	59
Breeding 2008–13	6	78	84
Winter 2007/8–2012/13	-	-	264

In the London area, the favoured wintering area for this species is along the lower Thames, including Rainham Marshes (where there was a peak count of 2,500 during the current atlas period in January 2011), Crossness (1,068 in February 2010), Barking Creekmouth (700 in January 2009 and December 2010) and East India Dock Basin (430, December 2010). Elsewhere, 570 were counted at the London Wetland Centre in February 2012 and 515 at Beddington Farmlands in November 2010 (LBR).

Smaller numbers winter annually at other sites across the London area, predominantly at the main wetland sites (Lee Valley, Colne Valley, west London waterbodies). Like Wigeon, Teal does not winter regularly in urban parks, although small numbers do appear from time to time. Unlike Wigeon, they sometimes linger in Greater London parks for an extended period; for example there were between one and four birds at Regent's Park from January to March 2008 and up to five in Hyde Park/Kensington Gardens in the same period of the following year (LBR).

Breeding Change

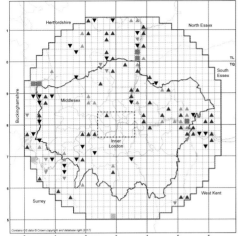

Winter Distribution

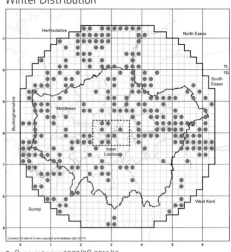

Breeding Distribution Change
- ▲ Recent Gain (new in 2008-13)
- ■ Stable (present in all periods)
- ▼ Old Loss (last occupied 1968-72)
- ▲ Old Gain (new in 1988-94)
- ■ Variable (absent 1988-94)
- ▼ Recent Loss (last occupied 1988-94)

- ● Overwintering 2007/08-2012/13

Mallard

Anas platyrhynchos

Very common and widespread breeding resident; amber list.

The breeding population of the Mallard in the UK increased by between 3% and 27% between 1995 and 2013 (BBS). The south-east England region also appears to have experienced an increase in the Mallard population during the same period. Conversely, the Mallard population in London appears to have been declining since 2005 (BBS, see graph).

The Mallard is the most familiar duck in the London area and can be found on the smallest of ponds and streams. It is resident in many town parks where it readily takes bread handed out by visitors. It was found across most of the London area during all three atlas periods. The population was widespread at the time of the second atlas, when the most significant gap was in the south of the area; in Kent, Surrey and south-east London, including the area which broadly corresponds to the North Downs, where suitable habitat is scarce. The apparent decline in the Mallard population in the London area is not visible on the atlas map, with the number of occupied tetrads in the current atlas similar to the second atlas. There are still a number of small gaps, principally in rural Essex and in north-west London, in addition to that corresponding with the North Downs and that in south-east London.

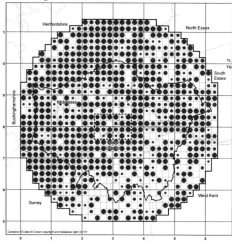

Breeding Distribution

- ● Confirmed Breeding 2008-13
- ● Probable Breeding 2008-13
- ● Possible Breeding 2008-13
- · Present 2008-13
- · Still on Migration 2008-13

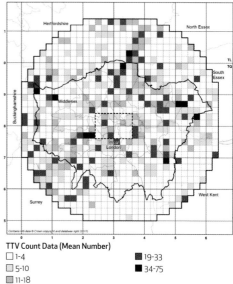

Breeding Abundance

TTV Count Data (Mean Number)
- □ 1-4
- ▨ 5-10
- ▨ 11-18
- ▨ 19-33
- ■ 34-75

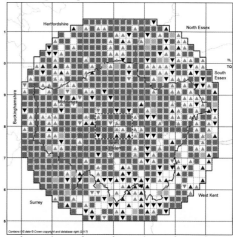

Breeding Change

Breeding Distribution Change
- ▲ Recent Gain (new in 2008-13)
- ■ Stable (present in all periods)
- ▼ Old Loss (last occupied 1968-72)
- ▲ Old Gain (new in 1988-94)
- ▨ Variable (absent 1988-94)
- ▼ Recent Loss (last occupied 1988-94)

Period	Number of Tetrads		
	Evidence of Breeding	Seen Only	Total
Breeding 1968–72	470	100	570
Breeding 1988–94	553	153	706
Breeding 2008–13	550	169	719
Winter 2007/8–2012/13	-	-	668

At many sites, the 'pure' Mallard are accompanied by domestic varieties, ranging from pure white Aylesbury-type ducks to birds with plumage that is very similar to 'pure' Mallard, but which stand out due to their noticeably larger size. During the current atlas period the domestic varieties of Mallard were recorded in as many as 14% of tetrads in the London area (119 tetrads). It may well be that domestic varieties are even more widespread than this, as some surveyors probably included such birds within the total Mallard count, rather than recording them separately.

The winter distribution of the Mallard, both nationally and in London, is similar to the breeding distribution. Birds which breed in Britain are joined in the winter by a substantial number of birds which breed on the continent, with up to three-quarters of wintering birds being migrants (Migration Atlas). However, the numbers wintering in Britain have declined from about the year 1990 onwards (WeBS). The decline is thought to be because birds may have stayed in mainland Europe rather than travelling on to spend the winter in Britain. This could be a result of warmer winters due to climate change (Sauter *et al.*, 2010).

Despite these recent declines, large numbers of Mallard still winter in our area. The highest winter counts during the current atlas period came from the River Thames, between Putney and Barnes which regularly supports in excess of 400 birds and the River Wandle at Carshalton (468 in December 2009) (LBR). Most of the higher totals during the timed counts came from the large and well-known sites where significant numbers of wildfowl gather during the winter.

Winter Distribution

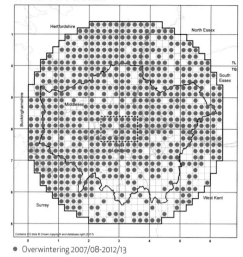

● Overwintering 2007/08-2012/13

Winter Abundance

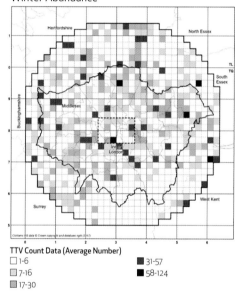

TTV Count Data (Average Number)
□ 1-6
□ 7-16
□ 17-30
■ 31-57
■ 58-124

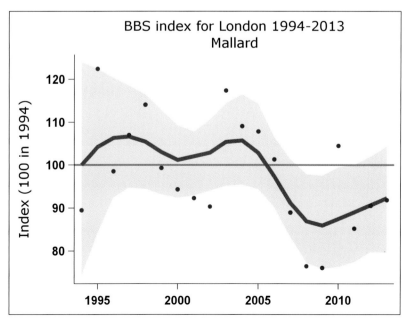

BTO/JNCC/RSPB Breeding Bird Survey (BBS)

Pintail

Anas acuta

Passage migrant/winter visitor in small numbers; amber list.

The elegant Pintail is a rare and localised breeding species in Britain and there were a few breeding records from the Ouse Washes during the current atlas period (National Atlas). However, this species is mainly a winter visitor to the UK with around 29,000 birds present during this season (Musgrove *et al.*, 2013).

Pintail was recorded in 18 tetrads in the London area during the breeding seasons of the current atlas period. These few and scattered records are likely to relate to escapes, feral birds or late staying winter visitors. However, apparently wild birds have occasionally summered in the London area in the past (Self). The possibility of feral birds referred to above relates to a small population that became established in the Barnes area in 1999, with a pair from this population breeding at the London Wetland Centre in 2001 (Self).

In the London area, the Pintail is an uncommon winter visitor and is the least widespread of the wintering dabbling ducks. It tends to stay away from smaller waterbodies in urban areas, preferring more natural sites with marsh or similar habitat. The main wintering sites for the species are Rainham Marshes and Crayford Marshes, which are the only locations where more than ten birds regularly occur. Normally a peak of around 20 to 30 birds occurs at Rainham each winter, but the highest contemporary count during the atlas period was 120 on 24th December 2007 (LBR). Smaller numbers of apparently wild birds also occur at the London Wetland Centre annually in winter, including 32 birds in December 2011 (LBR).

This species can occasionally be seen elsewhere during the winter, with records during the current atlas period coming from several tetrads in the Lee Valley, the west London waterbodies and Brent Reservoir. It is not regular in these areas but small numbers do sometimes linger. For example, there was a pair in the Seventy Acres Lake/Hall Marsh area in January 2008, two to three birds at Amwell in January and February 2009 and a female in the King George VI Reservoir area from October to December 2009. Other records from closer to Inner London may be of feral birds, possibly including some of those from the London Wetland Centre.

Breeding season tetrads: 18

Winter season tetrads: 61

Breeding Distribution

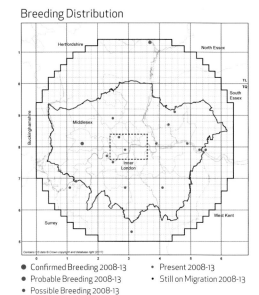

- ● Confirmed Breeding 2008-13
- ● Probable Breeding 2008-13
- ● Possible Breeding 2008-13
- • Present 2008-13
- • Still on Migration 2008-13

65

Winter Distribution

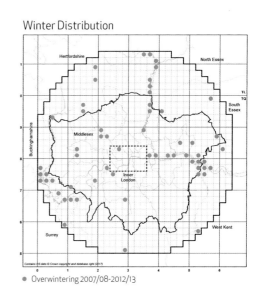

● Overwintering 2007/08-2012/13

Garganey
Anas querquedula

Scarce passage migrant, occasionally breeds, rare in winter; amber list.

The Garganey is found across Eurasia and, unlike all other wildfowl species, it is a summer visitor to Britain, wintering in the central part of Africa. Britain marks the western edge of its range and the species has a scattered distribution in Britain with perhaps 100 pairs present annually (Musgrove *et al.* 2013), mainly in England but a few birds are present across the Scottish central belt (National Atlas). It is not of conservation concern internationally but it is on the amber list in the UK due to recent population declines.

In the breeding season, it requires wetland habitat with abundant edge vegetation such as marshes and wet meadows. Consequently, it is especially uncommon in the London area and breeding can be difficult to confirm. During the first London atlas period, a male held territory at Stanwell Moor and it was recorded in four other tetrads. In the second atlas period, broods were seen at Kings Mead/Amwell in 1989 and a pair was observed mating at Beddington Sewage Farm in 1993. Birds were recorded as present in a further 27 tetrads, including a party of nine juveniles at Rye Meads in 1993, that may have been raised elsewhere, and a pair displaying at Rainham Marshes in 1991 (Hewlett *et al.*).

The current distribution is similar to that of the second atlas period, with five sites (six tetrads) having records of probable breeding, relating to pairs present in June or birds which stayed long enough to be recorded as being on 'territory'. At Kempton Nature Reserve, a nesting attempt in 2009 was thought to have failed due to the activities of foxes (LBR). At Rainham Marshes, a pair summered in 2013, and birds were observed in spring until late May 2010 and until 3rd June 2011, but breeding was not confirmed. Excluding records marked as migrants by the observers, birds were present in 26 additional tetrads. As is the case for the second atlas, many of these records are likely to be of passage birds, but, given the secretive nature of this species, a small number may well relate to breeding attempts.

Breeding Distribution

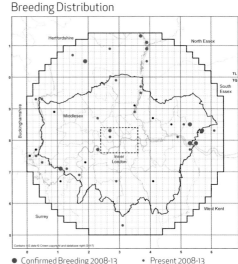

- ● Confirmed Breeding 2008-13
- ● Probable Breeding 2008-13
- ● Possible Breeding 2008-13
- • Present 2008-13
- • Still on Migration 2008-13

Period	Number of Tetrads		
	Evidence of Breeding	Seen Only	Total
Breeding 1968–72	1	4	5
Breeding 1988–94	2	27	29
Breeding 2008–13	6	26	32
Winter 2007/8–2012/13	-	-	5

Although Garganey is a summer visitor, birds occur in winter very occasionally and it occurred in five tetrads in the London area during the winter in the current atlas period. Some records probably involved late autumn migrants or early spring migrants, but others in mid-winter were suggestive of wintering, including a bird recorded intermittently at the London Wetland Centre each month between November 2007 and February 2008, and one at Holmethorpe Sand Pits from 7th December 2011 to 6th January 2012 (LBR).

Breeding Change

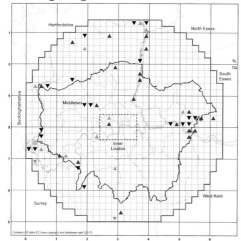

Winter Distribution

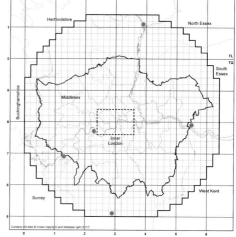

Breeding Distribution Change

▲ Recent Gain (new in 2008-13)   ▲ Old Gain (new in 1988-94)

■ Stable (present in all periods)   ■ Variable (absent 1988-94)

▼ Old Loss
(last occupied 1968-72)   ▼ Recent Loss
(last occupied 1988-94)

● Overwintering 2007/08-2012/13

Shoveler

Anas clypeata

Common passage migrant and winter visitor, scarce breeder; amber list.

The Shoveler is a relatively scarce but widely distributed breeder in the British Isles that is more widespread as a winter visitor (National Atlas).

The status in London is similar to that in the rest of the UK, with a few pairs breeding each year and greater numbers during the winter. Evidence of breeding occurred at six sites in the London area during the first atlas period, with considerable expansion of its breeding distribution recorded in the Lee Valley and the Rainham area by the time of the second atlas, during which breeding evidence was recorded at 20 sites.

The number of tetrads with evidence of breeding during the current atlas was similar to the second atlas, though there were fewer probable or confirmed breeding records from the Lee Valley. Most records came from larger wetland sites; for example, there was confirmed breeding at Rainham Marshes, the London Wetland Centre, Kempton Nature Reserve, Brent Reservoir, Maple Lodge, Stocker's Lake and three sites in the Lee Valley. Although the Shoveler is shown on the atlas map as more widely present in the breeding season now than during the last atlas, this may not be a true reflection of its breeding distribution, as many records of 'presence' were in April and so probably relate to late wintering birds rather than summering birds. Some of the 'probable' breeding records could also relate to late wintering pairs.

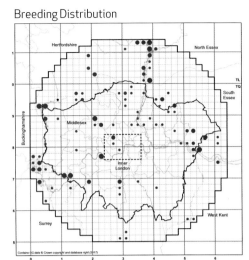

Breeding Distribution

● Confirmed Breeding 2008-13 · Present 2008-13
● Probable Breeding 2008-13 · Still on Migration 2008-13
● Possible Breeding 2008-13

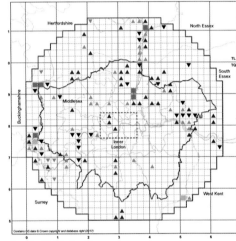

Breeding Change

Breeding Distribution Change
▲ Recent Gain (new in 2008-13) ▲ Old Gain (new in 1988-94)
■ Stable (present in all periods) ■ Variable (absent 1988-94)
▼ Old Loss ▼ Recent Loss
(last occupied 1968-72) (last occupied 1988-94)

Period	Number of Tetrads		
	Evidence of Breeding	Seen Only	Total
Breeding 1968–72	6	8	14
Breeding 1988–94	20	47	67
Breeding 2008–13	28	66	94
Winter 2007/8–2012/13	-	-	237

As noted above, the Shoveler is much more numerous and widespread during the winter in the London area. Passage and wintering birds in Britain originate from northern Europe, the Baltic and Russia (Migration Atlas). This species is most numerous in the London area at the major wetland sites, such as the Thames Marshes, the Lee Valley, the Colne Valley, the London Wetland Centre and the west London waterbodies, but it can also be found, often in small numbers, in many urban parks. The largest count during the current atlas period was 409 at Creekmouth (Barking) in December 2010 (LBR).

Winter Distribution

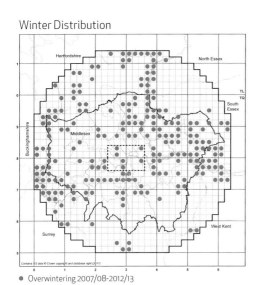

● Overwintering 2007/08-2012/13

Winter Abundance

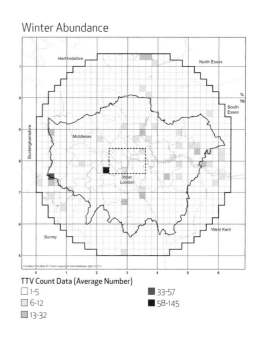

TTV Count Data (Average Number)

☐ 1-5
☐ 6-12
☐ 13-32
■ 33-57
■ 58-145

Red-crested Pochard

Netta rufina

Introduced breeding resident, probably also rare visitor from the continent; not listed.

The Red-crested Pochard is a naturalised breeding resident in England, with the main population in the Cotswolds (National Atlas). There are reportedly only around 10 to 21 breeding pairs in total (Musgrove *et al.*, 2013); however much larger numbers are recorded in winter possibly indicating a larger breeding population as well as perhaps some migrants.

In the London area, birds in the Royal Parks have been allowed to breed and raise free-flying young since at least the early 1950s (Self). Free-flying birds were present in the London area during the time of the second atlas. However, this species was not included in the second atlas because all records were believed to be derived from the wildfowl collections of the Royal Parks. Therefore, data from only the current atlas period is presented in the table below. Since the year 2000, birds have been seen more regularly across the London area. The population has now become established and is considered to be self-sustaining (LBR, 2010).

The breeding season map shows that the population is concentrated around the Royal Parks in central and south-west London, with breeding also confirmed in Esher and at Stocker's Lake. Scattered records from elsewhere during the breeding season suggest that the number of tetrads where breeding occurs may increase in the future.

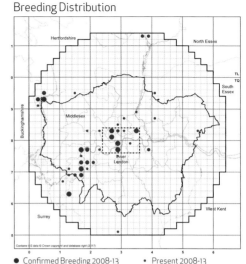

Breeding Distribution

● Confirmed Breeding 2008-13   • Present 2008-13
● Probable Breeding 2008-13   • Still on Migration 2008-13
● Possible Breeding 2008-13

Period	Number of Tetrads		
	Evidence of Breeding	Seen Only	Total
Breeding 2008–13	15	26	41
Winter 2007/8–2012/13	-	-	70

In winter, between 200 and 400 are reported in England (WeBS) and, in the London area, this species is more widespread during winter. This is particularly the case in the south-west of the London area, with records also from sites within the Lee Valley, the Colne Valley, the Ingrebourne Valley and a number of other scattered sites. There is a possibility that a small number of these are wintering birds which breed on the continent. However, most are likely to be resident birds which are making winter movements.

Winter Distribution

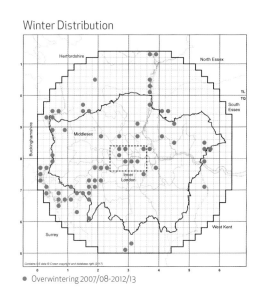

● Overwintering 2007/08-2012/13

Pochard

Aythya ferina

Common winter visitor and migrant, scarce breeder; red list.

The Pochard breeds in lowland areas of Britain, including London and the surrounding area, which is an important population centre for this species (National Atlas).

The breeding population in London probably descends mainly from captive birds in St James's Park, perhaps supplemented by wild birds periodically. Apart from one earlier record, the growth of the breeding population commenced in the first half of the twentieth century and has risen to a total breeding population of about 50 to 60 pairs (Self), which is about 10% of the total in Britain (Musgrove *et al.*, 2013). The two previous atlases show the increasing breeding distribution of the Pochard within our area, with the number of tetrads occupied in the breeding season doubling to over a 100 by the time of the second atlas; many of these occupied tetrads are within Greater London. The breeding distribution has not changed much since then; urban parks and other sites within Greater London still account for the majority of breeding sites. Elsewhere, breeding still occurs within the other major wetland sites in the London area, including the Lee Valley, the west London waterbodies and the Colne Valley.

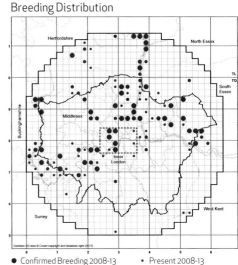

Breeding Distribution

- ● Confirmed Breeding 2008-13
- ● Probable Breeding 2008-13
- ● Possible Breeding 2008-13
- • Present 2008-13
- • Still on Migration 2008-13

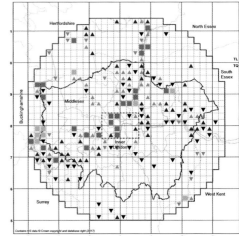

Breeding Change

Breeding Distribution Change
- ▲ Recent Gain (new in 2008-13)
- ■ Stable (present in all periods)
- ▼ Old Loss (last occupied 1968-72)
- ▲ Old Gain (new in 1988-94)
- ■ Variable (absent 1988-94)
- ▼ Recent Loss (last occupied 1988-94)

Period	Number of Tetrads		
	Evidence of Breeding	Seen Only	Total
Breeding 1968–72	23	32	55
Breeding 1988–94	48	69	117
Breeding 2008–13	55	67	122
Winter 2007/8–2012/13	-	-	225

Of course, the Pochard is primarily a winter visitor to Britain. It is therefore much more numerous and widespread both nationally and in the London area during the winter when the resident population is supplemented by birds mostly from the Baltic and from Russia (Migration Atlas). Although wintering numbers have declined since the mid-1990s following increases in the 1970s and 1980s (WeBS), the total population in Britain in winter is around 38,000 birds (Musgrove *et al.*, 2013).

As would be expected, the winter distribution of the Pochard in the London area encompasses the main wetland areas, including the Lee Valley; Ingrebourne Valley/Thames Marshes; the west London waterbodies and the Colne Valley. Small numbers of Pochard also frequent smaller waterbodies during the winter, especially across north and north-east London and South Essex. The highest count recorded during the current atlas period was 629 at Staines Reservoir in January 2010 (LBR) and contemporary records indicate a wintering population in the London area of fewer than 1,500 (LBR).

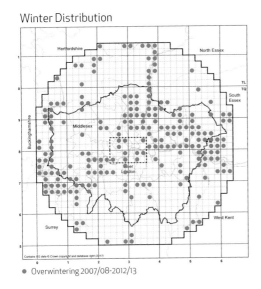

Winter Distribution

● Overwintering 2007/08-2012/13

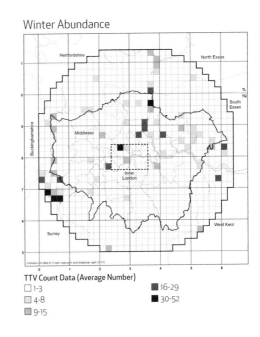

Winter Abundance

TTV Count Data (Average Number)
- ☐ 1-3
- ☐ 4-8
- ☐ 9-15
- ■ 16-29
- ■ 30-52

Tufted Duck

Aythya fuligula

Resident breeder and common winter visitor; amber list.

The Tufted Duck is a common breeding bird in Britain, with 17,000 breeding pairs (Musgrove *et al.*, 2013), and is even more numerous during winter when there are estimated to be 110,000 individuals present in Britain. Its status in London reflects the national picture.

In line with the national trend, the number of pairs breeding in London increased during the twentieth century, until the mid-1980s and, following a survey in 1984, it was estimated that there were between 800 and 1,000 pairs in the London area in late May and early June, mostly on reservoirs, gravel pits and park lakes (Oliver, 1985). This was accompanied by an expansion in its breeding distribution, with the number of occupied tetrads in London during the breeding season nearly doubling between the first and second atlas periods. The current atlas shows that the distribution of this species has remained relatively unchanged since the second atlas. The Tufted Duck continues to frequent a wide variety of wetland habitats, including relatively small waterbodies in urban parks, and it is distributed widely across the London area where suitable waterbodies exist.

This species is a late breeder in comparison with many other bird species, with broods sometimes not appearing until August, after the end of the atlas breeding survey period. It is possible, therefore, that breeding evidence may have been missed in some tetrads. In July and August, large post-breeding congregations also occur at some of the major reservoirs.

Period	Number of Tetrads		
	Evidence of Breeding	Seen Only	Total
Breeding 1968–72	108	76	184
Breeding 1988–94	193	145	338
Breeding 2008–13	253	114	367
Winter 2007/8–2012/13	-	-	364

As noted above, large numbers of birds arrive into the British Isles from continental Europe in winter. Despite this, the broad distribution of the Tufted Duck in the winter remains much the same as during the breeding season in Britain (National Atlas) and in the London area.

Also during the winter, significant aggregations of Tufted Duck are encountered at some sites in the London area, including nationally important numbers at three sites in 2010/11; the Lee Valley gravel pits, Staines Reservoir and Walthamstow Reservoir (Self). The largest winter count during the current atlas period was 1,430 at Queen Mother Reservoir in January 2010 (LBR).

Although Tufted Duck remains widespread in Britain, range contractions have occurred in Ireland (National Atlas), and recent research suggests that the wintering range is shifting to the north-east with more birds now wintering in Scandinavia, possibly in response to climate change (Lehikoinen *et al.*, 2013). If this trend continues, it is possible that wintering numbers in London could decline in the long-term.

Breeding Distribution

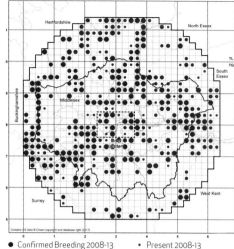

● Confirmed Breeding 2008-13   • Present 2008-13
● Probable Breeding 2008-13   • Still on Migration 2008-13
● Possible Breeding 2008-13

Breeding Change

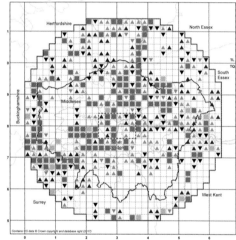

Breeding Distribution Change

▲ Recent Gain (new in 2008-13)   ▲ Old Gain (new in 1988-94)
■ Stable (present in all periods) ■ Variable (absent 1988-94)
▼ Old Loss   ▼ Recent Loss
(last occupied 1968-72)   (last occupied 1988-94)

Winter Distribution

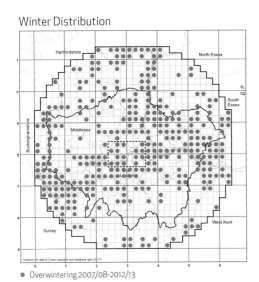

● Overwintering 2007/08-2012/13

Winter Abundance

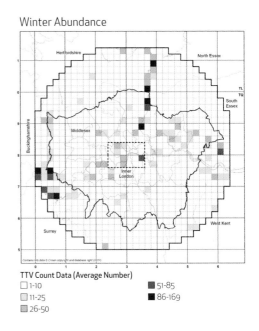

TTV Count Data (Average Number)

☐ 1-10   ☐ 51-85
☐ 11-25   ■ 86-169
☐ 26-50

Scaup
Aythya marila

Uncommon winter visitor and passage migrant; red list.

Scaup is predominantly a winter visitor to the British Isles, with small numbers occasionally lingering into spring or summer (National Atlas). It is mainly found in coastal areas and does not normally move inland; this is reflected in its status in the London area as an uncommon winter visitor.

Most records in the London area during the current atlas period were along or near the outer Thames, in the Lee Valley and on the west London waterbodies. Records of genuine overwintering birds are unusual in the London area and most observations were of birds that were present for a single day or just a few days. However, there are records of birds which stay for longer periods in most winters, occasionally involving small groups. During the current atlas period, these included: up to seven birds moving between several of the west London waterbodies in 2008/09; four in the Millwall Docks/Greenland Docks area in 2010/11; up to five at Staines Reservoir in 2011/12 and two to four at the same site in 2012/13 (LBR). The highest count made during atlas fieldwork was seven, at both Queen Mother Reservoir in January 2009 (LBR) and on the River Thames at Gallions Reach in January 2011.

Breeding season tetrads: 9

Winter season tetrads: 48

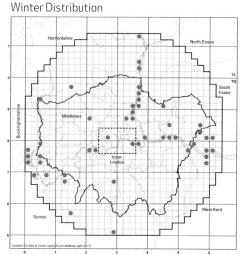

Winter Distribution

● Overwintering 2007/08-2012/13

Eider

Somateria mollissima

Scarce visitor, usually in winter; amber list.

The Eider is a coastal species which is resident in Britain. It breeds mainly in the north but it is found around most of the coast of Britain during the winter (National Atlas) when the total population is around 60,000 birds (Musgrove *et al.*, 2013). It rarely moves inland and it is therefore a scarce winter visitor to the London area.

During the current atlas period, all records of this species in the London area were during the winter of 2010/11, including 12 on the River Thames at Grays on 15th December 2010 and eight on the William Girling Reservoir from 19th December 2010, with three remaining at this site until 27th December 2010. A long-staying bird at Walthamstow Reservoir from 22nd January to March 2011 may have been one of those recorded earlier at the William Girling Reservoir. A bird was also seen in Surrey at Queen Elizabeth II Reservoir and Buckland Sand Pits in January 2011 (LBR). An Eider seen flying over Stoke Newington Reservoir during the same winter did not settle and is not shown on the map. Clearly, a very small proportion of the total population of Eider ever visits the London area; the largest flock ever recorded comprised 35 birds (Self).

Winter season tetrads: 10

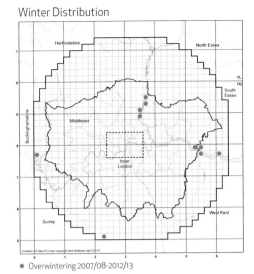

Winter Distribution

● Overwintering 2007/08-2012/13

Long-tailed Duck

Clangula hyemalis

Scarce winter visitor; red list.

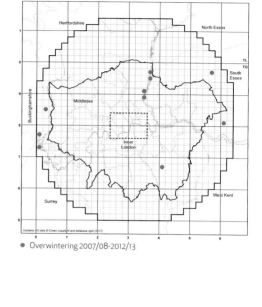

Winter Distribution

● Overwintering 2007/08-2012/13

The Long-tailed Duck is a winter visitor to the British Isles. It is a coastal species with the largest numbers found around the coast of Scotland (National Atlas). Like other sea ducks, it is a scarce visitor to the London area.

Perhaps surprisingly for a sea duck, when this species is present in the London area, it is usually at large, inland waterbodies rather than the tidal River Thames (Self). Indeed, all records from the current atlas period were away from the River Thames. There was a maximum of six individuals, which were recorded in ten different tetrads during the winter period, all during the final two winters of the atlas period, 2011/12 and 2012/13. There were up to two birds which moved between Walthamstow, William Girling and King George V Reservoirs in the Lee Valley in winter 2012/13 (November to February). There were also single birds at Wraysbury Reservoir/Queen Mother Reservoir during the same period and at Grange Waters the same winter (December 2012). Smaller waterbodies were also visited by this species. A female or immature bird frequented Hayes Farm Trout Lake in November and December 2011, and one was seen at the Mores, near Brentwood, on 26th December 2012 (LBR). A drake that appeared in Hyde Park/Kensington Gardens on 12th October 2012 is not shown on the map as it occurred before the winter period.

Both long-staying individuals wintering in 2012/13 stayed until April 2013 and so were also recorded during the breeding season surveys. Unusually, a female summered in 2013 on various waterbodies in south-east London (Self), including Canada Water and Surrey Water in Inner London. These birds accounted for records from nine tetrads in total during the breeding season.

Breeding season tetrads: 9

Winter season tetrads: 10

Common Scoter

Melanitta nigra

Passage migrant and occasional winter visitor, never numerous; red list.

While there is a small breeding population of about 52 pairs in the flow country in Scotland (Musgrove *et al.*, 2013), and another small breeding population in Ireland, the Common Scoter is predominantly a winter visitor that is found around the coast of the British Isles (National Atlas), with about 100,000 present annually in UK waters (Musgrove *et al.*, 2013).

As a marine species, the Common Scoter is unusual in the London area, though small numbers are occasionally seen here, particularly in spring and autumn when birds are moving between their wintering and breeding sites.

Although the Common Scoter does not breed in our area, it does occur during the breeding season while on migration. Passage birds can sometimes be observed in late spring or even early summer, with returning birds observed from as early as July. Records during the breeding season included counts of 24 at Rainham Marshes on 11th April 2009, and 28 on the River Thames in the Rainham/Crossness area on 26th July 2010 (LBR).

The majority of winter atlas records were in November (57) or the first seven days of December (13), so were probably associated with late autumn movements. Just nine records occurred during the remainder of the atlas winter period (8th December to the end of February), with all the records in January and February being of birds on the Thames. Away from the Thames, most records came from the west London waterbodies, with additional records from William Girling Reservoir, Amwell Nature Reserve, Hilfield Park Reservoir and Brent Reservoir. The only double figure count during winter was made at Gallions Reach, with 12 birds on 7th February 2012 (LBR).

Breeding season tetrads: 12

Winter season tetrads: 17

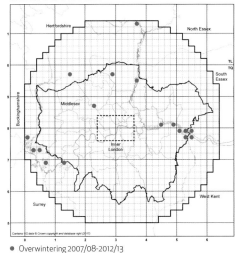

Winter Distribution

● Overwintering 2007/08-2012/13

Velvet Scoter

Melanitta fusca

Rare passage migrant and winter visitor; red list.

The Velvet Scoter is only a winter visitor to British coastal waters and is much less regular inland, and much less numerous overall, than the Common Scoter (National Atlas).

During the current London atlas period, all records of this species came from the west London waterbodies. Most records were from the winter, when there were single birds on the Queen Mother Reservoir on 15th and 16th January 2008 and 8th December 2008; up to four birds frequenting various reservoirs in the 2010/11 winter; and two on Island Barn Reservoir from 28th November to 9th December 2012 (LBR). A bird seen on William Girling and King George V Reservoir in March 2010 is not shown on the map as it was outside the atlas survey seasons. One of the 2010 wintering birds remained until April at King George VI and Staines Reservoirs. The only other record during the breeding season came from the same tetrad, comprising five birds on Staines Reservoir on 13th April 2009. These birds were presumably stopping off while on migration to their breeding grounds in Northern Europe.

Winter season tetrads: 5

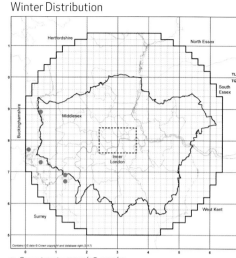

Winter Distribution

● Overwintering 2007/08-2012/13

Smew

Mergellus albellus

Winter visitor in variable numbers; amber list

For many bird watchers, the sight of a male Smew is a highlight of the winter. Small numbers of Smew, between 100 and 200, winter in Britain (Musgrove *et al.*, 2013). Recent declines in this population are attributed to a change in wintering distribution possibly caused by climate change. However, two cold spells during the atlas period led to small influxes of birds to Britain (National Atlas).

The Smew frequents gravel pits and London's bird watchers are fortunate that some of the pre-eminent British sites for this species are in the London area. These sites include Wraysbury Gravel Pit, where average counts are among the highest in Britain, the Lee Valley (particularly Amwell and Cheshunt Gravel Pits) and Thorpe Water Park.

Away from the main wintering sites in the London area, individuals or small groups of Smew occur sporadically or sometimes spend the winter. This is particularly so on small to medium sized waterbodies for example in the Colne Valley and in south-west Essex. They also occur, usually briefly and during harsher weather, on the Thames and the larger reservoirs. From time to time, wild Smew also appear in the Inner London parks, and birds were seen in both Hyde Park and Regent's Park during the current atlas period. These included a first-winter male at Regent's Park in 2012 which stayed from 6th February to 19th March, and was sometimes seen in the wildfowl enclosure alongside the captive wing-clipped Smew (LBR). The atlas map clearly shows the association of this species with the Lee and Colne Valleys, with another cluster of records in north-east London and south Essex.

Winter season tetrads: 60

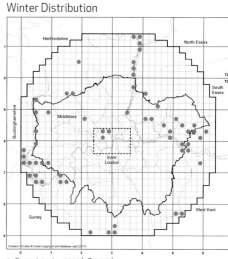

Winter Distribution

● Overwintering 2007/08-2012/13

Red-breasted Merganser

Mergus serrator

Scarce winter visitor and passage migrant; green list

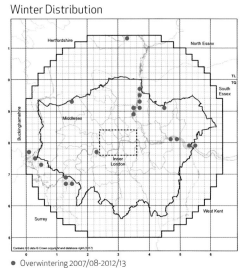

Winter Distribution

● Overwintering 2007/08-2012/13

In Britain, the Red-breasted Merganser breeds in Scotland, north-west England and north Wales and winters around the coast (National Atlas). Like other species that are predominantly coastal during the winter, it is a scarce winter visitor to the London area.

In the London area, it occurs as a scarce passage migrant in March and April and records of birds during the summer are unusual. During the current atlas period such records included a female that was recorded on the Thames at Rainham/Crayford from 15th to 27th June 2010 and again on 6th July 2010.

During the winter, most records of this species relate to short-staying birds on the Thames or the major reservoirs. However, at least two birds overwintered in the area during the atlas period, perhaps accounting for around half of the occupied tetrads shown on the map. The first of these was a juvenile which was seen intermittently on Walton Reservoir, Island Barn Reservoir and the Queen Elizabeth II Reservoir in the winter of 2008/09 before moulting into male plumage by March 2009. The second was a female, which has apparently wintered every year in the Lee Valley since 2005/06. It was observed intermittently at Walthamstow, Banbury, William Girling and King George V Reservoirs each winter until 2011/12, but then failed to appear for the final winter of the current atlas period.

Winter season tetrads: 20

Goosander

Mergus merganser

Regular winter visitor; green list.

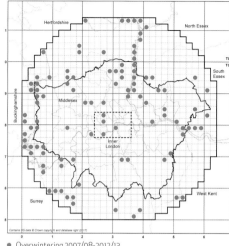

Winter Distribution

● Overwintering 2007/08-2012/13

The Goosander is a resident species in Britain, breeding in Scotland, northern England, Wales and Devon (National Atlas). Most of these birds are thought to winter within around 150km of their breeding sites. Therefore, most of the birds wintering in lowland Britain, including the London area, probably breed on the continent (Migration Atlas). In winter, this species frequents freshwater sites, including gravel pits and reservoirs.

Records of Goosander in the London area during the breeding season relate to late departing wintering birds. During the current atlas period, the latest observation was made on 23rd May 2012 at Thorney Gravel Pit (LBR).

The main wintering populations in our area are in the Lee Valley and on the west London waterbodies. Even at these locations, this species is not numerous with typically fewer than 100 birds reported each winter in the London area during the current atlas period (LBR). Away from these main sites, the Goosander occurs regularly, but in low numbers and for short periods, at suitable waterbodies within the London area. Examples during the current atlas period include the Colne Valley and sites in Inner London.

As the atlas map indicates, the distribution of the Goosander is relatively sparse across the London area because this species is usually found on medium to large waterbodies and rivers. This species differs from most other wintering wildfowl, as it makes regular use of medium width rivers and canals as well as more open waterbodies. For example, birds in the Lee Valley can often be found on the River Lee and the Lee Navigation canal; the New River in Enfield is also used.

Numbers in the London area seem to be declining (Self). This could potentially be because, like Tufted Duck and Goldeneye, recent research suggests that the wintering range of Goosander is shifting north-eastwards, possibly as a result of climate change (Lehikoinen *et al.*, 2013).

Breeding season tetrads: 12

Winter season tetrads: 105

Goldeneye
Bucephala clangula

Common winter visitor, occasionally summers; amber list.

The Goldeneye breeds in small numbers in Scotland (about 200 females), but it is much more common in winter when about 20,000 birds migrate to Britain from Fennoscandia and Russia (Musgrove *et al.*, 2013; National Atlas). There has been a recent decline in the numbers of Goldeneye wintering in the UK (WeBS), which may be related to a north-eastern shift in the core wintering range as a result of milder continental weather (Lehikoinen *et al.*, 2013).

It is primarily a winter visitor to the London area, however the Goldeneye was recorded in the breeding season during the current atlas period. Such records usually relate to late-staying migrants. However, a pair is believed to have summered at Troy Mill Lake (Hertfordshire) in 2010 and there were records in June from nearby sites in 2011 and 2012 (LBR).

The main wintering areas are the Lee Valley and the west London waterbodies, with several sites in each of these areas regularly supporting more than ten birds. During the current atlas period, the highest count was 76 at Staines Reservoir on 1st March 2013, although this was outside the atlas survey periods, during which the highest count was 63 at King George V Reservoir in January 2008 (LBR).

Away from the Lee Valley and the west London waterbodies, more than 10 birds regularly occur at Stocker's Lake and at Broadwater Lake in the Colne Valley. Single birds or small groups occur elsewhere, for example in east London and south Essex and in the Colne Valley. At many of the sites, the birds are only present briefly. This species is also occasionally recorded in the Inner London parks, with all records during the current atlas period relating to single birds which stayed for short periods.

Winter season tetrads: 76

Winter Distribution

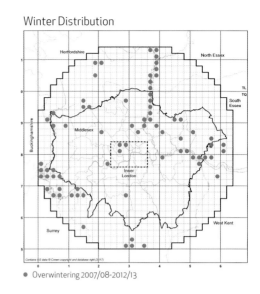

● Overwintering 2007/08-2012/13

Ruddy Duck

Oxyura jamaicensis

Rare (if not now extinct) introduced resident, declining through control; not listed as it is a non-native species.

The Ruddy Duck is a North American species which was introduced into collections in England, from which birds escaped in the 1950s and established a feral population in Gloucestershire (Hewlett *et al.*).

The population expanded and the Ruddy Duck was first reported in the London area in 1965 (Hewlett *et al.*). It became an established breeding species in our area by the 1990s. A decision was made to eradicate the species in the UK to prevent inter-breeding with the closely related White-headed Duck *O. leucocephala* in Spain. The cull began in 2005 (National Atlas; Henderson, 2009).

The Ruddy Duck was not recorded in the London area during the first atlas period but was present in more than 50 tetrads at the time of the second atlas, with evidence of breeding observed in 32 tetrads. Subsequent records (LBR) suggest that further colonisation occurred in London up until the cull.

A number of birdwatchers were opposed to the cull and stopped reporting the Ruddy Duck as a result, so it is likely that the maps and the figures in the table under-represent the true status of the species at least during the early years of the current atlas period. Despite this, it is known that this species was still relatively widespread in the London area at the start of the current atlas period, with breeding confirmed from 12 tetrads. However, there were no breeding records received at this time from the south-west of the London area, which was its stronghold previously.

By 2009, numbers of Ruddy Duck in the UK had already been reduced by almost 90% (Henderson, 2009) and by 2013 around 50 birds survived in the wild in the UK (Henderson, 2013). In the London area, the last successful breeding by this species is thought to have occurred in 2012 at both Brent Reservoir and Hilfield Park Reservoir, with breeding again attempted at Brent Reservoir in 2013, when groups of up to ten birds were still being reported (LBR).

Period	Number of Tetrads		
	Evidence of Breeding	Seen Only	Total
Breeding 1968–72	0	0	0
Breeding 1988–94	32	21	53
Breeding 2008–13	18	22	40
Winter 2007/8–2012/13	-	-	53

The winter distribution, both nationally and in London, is similar to the breeding distribution, with scattered populations at key wetland sites. Large counts were still being made in the early years of the current atlas period, including 113 at Staines Reservoir in both 2007/08 and 2008/09. However, the highest count during the final winter of the atlas period was just 11 birds at Brent Reservoir in December 2012 (LBR). As in summer, non-reporting has probably occurred, masking its presence in some tetrads.

Without the effects of the cull, it seems certain that both maps would have shown considerable gains like several other naturalised waterfowl species in the London area. As it is, both maps indicate a wider distribution than must now be the case because the population declined so sharply during the atlas period.

Breeding Distribution

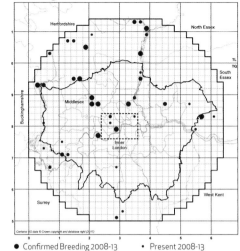

- ● Confirmed Breeding 2008-13
- ● Probable Breeding 2008-13
- ● Possible Breeding 2008-13
- · Present 2008-13
- · Still on Migration 2008-13

Breeding Change

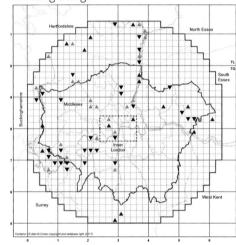

Breeding Distribution Change
- ▲ Recent Gain (new in 2008-13)
- ■ Stable (present in all periods)
- ▼ Old Loss (last occupied 1968-72)
- ▲ Old Gain (new in 1988-94)
- ■ Variable (absent 1988-94)
- ▼ Recent Loss (last occupied 1988-94)

Winter Distribution

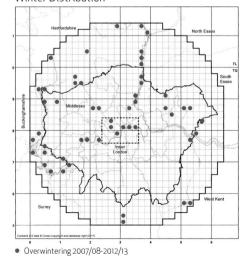

- ● Overwintering 2007/08-2012/13

Quail

Coturnix coturnix

Rare summer visitor; amber list.

During the breeding season, the Quail can be found throughout lowland England and in eastern Scotland. The numbers in Britain fluctuate from year to year. During the current atlas period, a good 'Quail year', when this species was relatively numerous and widespread, occurred in 2011 (National Atlas). The breeding population in Britain is estimated to be just 540 pairs (Musgrove *et al.*, 2013).

In the London area, this species has been scarce since at least the end of the 19th century (Self). Records are mainly from the outer part of the area where cereal crops occur, particularly in the south-east and east of our area. The occurrence of Quail is sporadic and usually unpredictable; one exception seems to be the Orsett area where Quail was recorded during the second atlas period and in five out of six summers during the current atlas period (LBR). Unfortunately none of the recent records were of territorial birds.

Breeding by Quail at a particular locality is extremely difficult to prove at least partly because apparently territorial males may move on if they fail to attract a mate. The six birds recorded as breeding during the first atlas relate to birds heard calling on more than one date (Hewlett *et al.*) which may have over-represented the breeding distribution at that time. No territorial birds were recorded at all during the second atlas. With one, or possibly two, exceptions, all the records shown on the current atlas map also involved birds apparently present for a few days at most, with most being seen (or more often heard) for a single day only.

The first exception was a male present at Crayford Marshes for two weeks in June 2012. The second was even more unusual as it involved one or two birds close to central London at Wormwood Scrubs. A male was heard singing on 17th May 2011 and it, or a different bird, was heard again on 31st May and 1st June (LBR). The Crayford bird is shown as 'Probable breeding' on the atlas map, however there is some doubt that this was the case.

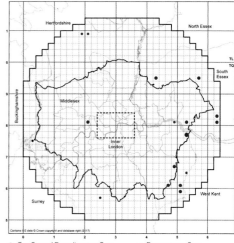

Breeding Distribution

- ● Confirmed Breeding 2008-13
- ● Probable Breeding 2008-13
- ● Possible Breeding 2008-13
- • Present 2008-13
- • Still on Migration 2008-13

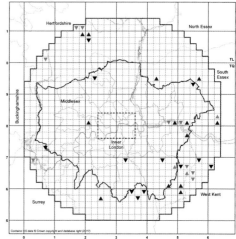

Breeding Change

Breeding Distribution Change
- ▲ Recent Gain (new in 2008-13)
- ■ Stable (present in all periods)
- ▼ Old Loss (last occupied 1968-72)
- ▲ Old Gain (new in 1988-94)
- ■ Variable (absent 1988-94)
- ▼ Recent Loss (last occupied 1988-94)

Period	Number of Tetrads		
	Evidence of Breeding	Seen Only	Total
Breeding 1968–72	6	3	9
Breeding 1988–94	0	15	15
Breeding 2008–13	1	15	16

Red-legged Partridge
Alectoris rufa

Introduced breeding resident; not listed.

The Red-legged Partridge became established in Britain as a result of introductions, which began in the 18th century, for shooting (Hewlett *et al.*). Releases of birds for that purpose still occur (National Atlas). Indeed, the number of Red-legged Partridge released for shooting in the UK is increasing and is now nearly 200 times higher than in 1961 (Aebischer, 2013). In Britain, the Red-legged Partridge now outnumbers the native Grey Partridge by approximately two to one (Musgrove *et al.*, 2013). This has been brought about as much by the decline in Grey Partridge as increases in Red-legged Partridge. However, the proportion of Red-legged to Grey Partridges is substantially higher than 2:1 in the London area.

In the London area, the Red-legged Partridge is restricted to the rural outskirts, predominantly in the Hertfordshire and Essex sectors, which have been the stronghold for this species since at least the time of the first atlas. The number of occupied tetrads has increased in parts of Surrey and in Hertfordshire and Middlesex, where gains have occurred close to and within the Greater London boundary. Losses have occurred in some parts of Essex, including tetrads along the Thames within Greater London such as at Barking Bay.

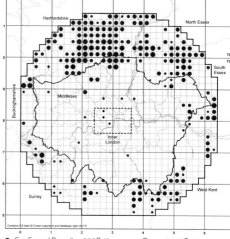

Breeding Distribution

- ● Confirmed Breeding 2008-13
- ● Probable Breeding 2008-13
- ● Possible Breeding 2008-13
- • Present 2008-13
- • Still on Migration 2008-13

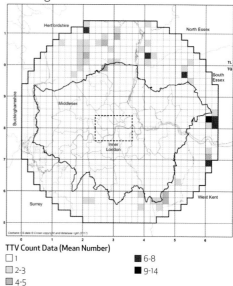

Breeding Abundance

TTV Count Data (Mean Number)
- ☐ 1
- ☐ 2-3
- ☐ 4-5
- ■ 6-8
- ■ 9-14

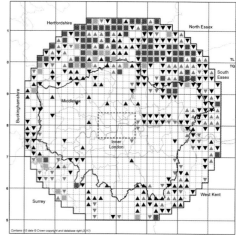

Breeding Change

Breeding Distribution Change
- ▲ Recent Gain (new in 2008-13)
- ■ Stable (present in all periods)
- ▼ Old Loss (last occupied 1968-72)
- ▲ Old Gain (new in 1988-94)
- ■ Variable (absent 1988-94)
- ▼ Recent Loss (last occupied 1988-94)

Period	Number of Tetrads		
	Evidence of Breeding	Seen Only	Total
Breeding 1968–72	105	86	191
Breeding 1988–94	179	94	273
Breeding 2008–13	147	77	224
Winter 2007/8–2012/13	-	-	176

To what extent the maps show 'natural' changes in distribution is difficult to ascertain due to historic and potentially ongoing releases at some locations within the London area.

Occasionally, wandering individuals turn up at sites in the middle of urban areas, particularly during spring. During the fieldwork for the current atlas, these included a bird which stayed at Brent Reservoir from 28th March to 27th April 2010 (although it almost certainly was not breeding it is shown as a 'probable breeding' record as it was on 'territory' for more than a week) and birds at Stoke Newington Reservoir (13th April 2009) and Hampstead Heath (1st to 2nd April 2012) (LBR). A bird which visited several tetrads in Inner London in April 2013 (LBR) is regarded as a migrant because most of the sites it visited, including Westminster and the canal towpath at Little Venice, were clearly unsuitable for breeding.

As may be expected for a relatively sedentary species, the winter distribution of the Red-legged Partridge is similar to the breeding distribution, and includes unusual, and typically brief, appearances within Greater London.

As well as releases for shooting, the picture may also be clouded by deliberate releases by falconers. In September 2014, falconers were observed releasing two Red-legged Partridges at Staines Moor and this practice could possibly account for some of the records from urban areas (LBR, 2013).

Winter Distribution

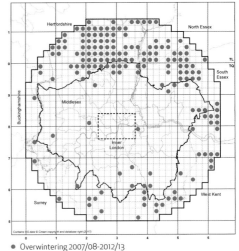

● Overwintering 2007/08-2012/13

Winter Abundance

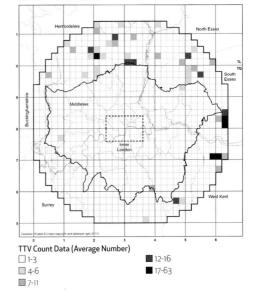

TTV Count Data (Average Number)
☐ 1-3 ■ 12-16
☐ 4-6 ■ 17-63
☐ 7-11

Grey Partridge

Perdix perdix

Breeding resident, declining; red list.

The native Grey Partridge is red-listed following a significant decline in the UK. It decreased by 59% (51% to 66%) over the period 1995 to 2013 (BBS). However, the decline began before 1995 and, over the period 1967 to 2013, this species is thought to have declined by around 91%, making it one of the fastest declining breeding species in Britain (BirdTrends).

At the time of the first London Atlas, the Grey Partridge was found in much of the outer part of the London area and was present in nearly twice as many tetrads as the Red-legged Partridge. The Grey Partridge has now all but vanished from our area and was found in just 32 tetrads during the breeding season of the current atlas period, with breeding confirmed in just three tetrads. This equates to a decrease in tetrad occupation of more than 80% since the second atlas period.

It is unclear how many of the recent records in the London area relate to recently released partridges rather than surviving populations of truly wild birds. However, it is likely that a small number of wild birds persisted in the London area during the current atlas period. The majority of records are from Hertfordshire. However, the highest count made during fieldwork for the current atlas in any one tetrad was 14 near Malden Rushett, Surrey in August 2010.

A record from Queen Mother Reservoir in April 2013 was particularly unusual. However, as noted previously, falconers were observed releasing two Red-legged Partridges at nearby Staines Moor in September 2014 (LBR), so this Grey Partridge may have originated from the same source.

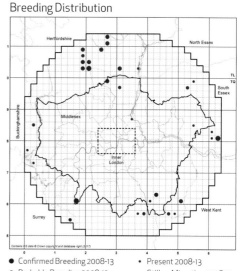

Breeding Distribution

● Confirmed Breeding 2008-13 · Present 2008-13
● Probable Breeding 2008-13 · Still on Migration 2008-13
● Possible Breeding 2008-13

Period	Number of Tetrads		
	Evidence of Breeding	Seen Only	Total
Breeding 1968–72	223	126	349
Breeding 1988–94	115	83	198
Breeding 2008–13	14	18	32
Winter 2007/8–2012/13	-	-	18

The distribution of the Grey Partridge during the winter is much the same as during the breeding season. In Hertfordshire, and in the London area as a whole, the largest counts during the winter season of the current atlas period were at Redwell Wood Farm, with at least 18 present on 24th January 2009 and then at least 24 on 7th February 2009. In Essex, up to 21 were seen at Grey Goose Farm (North Stifford) from November 2007 to January 2008 and then ten at the same locality on 1st February 2009. Elsewhere, a scattering of records included 15 at Cheverells, Surrey in February 2012 (LBR). The Inner London record relates to a bird found in a gutter in Salisbury Street in January 2010 (LBR), which seems most likely to be an escaped or released bird.

Breeding Change

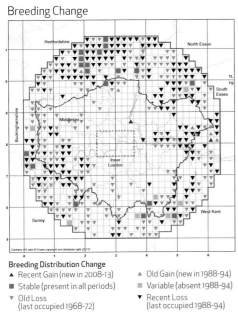

Contains OS data © Crown copyright and database right (2017)

Winter Distribution

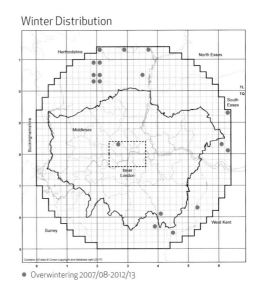

Contains OS data © Crown copyright and database right (2017)

● Overwintering 2007/08-2012/13

Breeding Distribution Change
▲ Recent Gain (new in 2008-13) ▲ Old Gain (new in 1988-94)
■ Stable (present in all periods) ■ Variable (absent 1988-94)
▼ Old Loss
 (last occupied 1968-72) ▼ Recent Loss
 (last occupied 1988-94)

Pheasant

Phasianus colchicus

Common breeding resident, introduced; not listed.

Although the Pheasant is not native to this country, it is thought to have been resident in Britain for many hundreds of years. The exact origins are unclear but it is probable that it was introduced to England in the 11th century (Brown & Grice, 2005). It is found across most of Britain (National Atlas), and the naturalised population continues to be supplemented on an annual basis by birds reared in cages for game shooting, though only a small proportion of these are thought to join the wild population (Hewlett *et al*).

Pheasant has shown a similar breeding distribution during all three London atlases. As a farmland bird species, it breeds across most of the non-urban parts of the London area and can also be found breeding closer to central London in places where suitable habitat exists, such as at Tottenham Marshes. Since the second atlas there have been losses from tetrads in south-west London and along the Thames, but gains have occurred elsewhere within the Greater London boundary.

Pheasant also occasionally strays into more urban areas in March and April, presumably as a result of local 'passage' movement. For example, one appeared in Hyde Park/Kensington Gardens from 16th to 20th March 2009 and a male was present on the north bank of Brent Reservoir from 21st March to 16th April 2009 (LBR). Occasionally, this species is found in urban areas at other times of the year, such as the injured male at Hyde Park/Kensington Gardens in the summer of 2010.

Period	Number of Tetrads		
	Evidence of Breeding	Seen Only	Total
Breeding 1968–72	295	138	433
Breeding 1988–94	343	140	483
Breeding 2008–13	255	259	514
Winter 2007/8–2012/13	-	-	472

In winter, the distribution of Pheasant, both nationally and in the London area, is similar to during the breeding season. During periods of colder weather, birds occasionally turn up unexpectedly in very urbanised and/or sub-optimal sites.

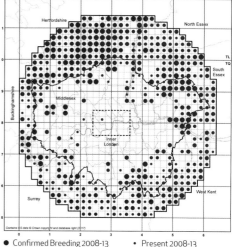

Breeding Distribution

● Confirmed Breeding 2008-13   • Present 2008-13
● Probable Breeding 2008-13   • Still on Migration 2008-13
● Possible Breeding 2008-13

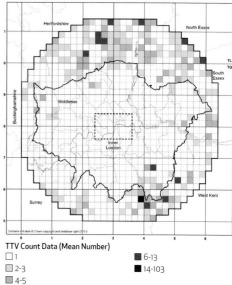

Breeding Abundance

TTV Count Data (Mean Number)
□ 1   ■ 6-13
□ 2-3   ■ 14-103
▨ 4-5

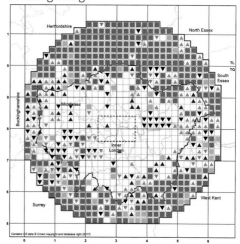

Breeding Change

Breeding Distribution Change
▲ Recent Gain (new in 2008-13)   ▲ Old Gain (new in 1988-94)
■ Stable (present in all periods)   ▨ Variable (absent 1988-94)
▼ Old Loss (last occupied 1968-72)   ▼ Recent Loss (last occupied 1988-94)

Winter Distribution

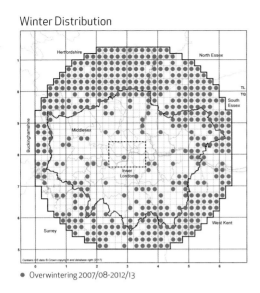

● Overwintering 2007/08-2012/13

Winter Abundance

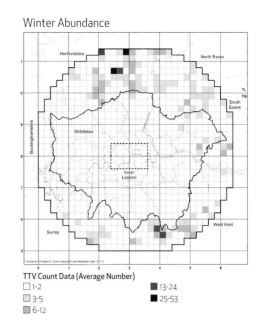

TTV Count Data (Average Number)

☐ 1-2 ▨ 13-24
☐ 3-5 ■ 25-53
▨ 6-12

Red-throated Diver

Gavia stellata

Rare winter visitor and occasional migrant; green list.

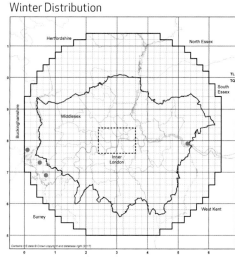

Winter Distribution

● Overwintering 2007/08-2012/13

In Britain, the Red-throated Diver breeds mainly in Scotland, with the highest wintering concentrations occurring along the North Sea coast (National Atlas), when birds that breed in Britain are joined by others which breed in Scandinavia and Greenland (Migration Atlas). In total, approximately 17,000 birds spend the winter around the coast of Britain (Musgrove *et al.*, 2013). Offshore aerial surveys suggest that large numbers winter off the coast of south-east England, especially in the Greater Thames area (National Atlas).

Although good numbers winter close to London, this species is infrequent in the London area because it is so strongly associated with the sea during winter.

With two spring passage records excluded, there were just four winter records during the current atlas period; two from Rainham Marshes and two from the west London waterbodies. Both records from Rainham were of birds that were present for a single day only (in February 2008 and November 2008). The birds on the west London waterbodies both stayed for longer periods, the first visiting King George VI Reservoir, Queen Mary Reservoir and Queen Mother Reservoir in December 2010 and the second visiting King George VI Reservoir and Staines Reservoir from January 2013, remaining in the area until the exceptionally late date of 10th June. Another bird reported at William Girling Reservoir in November 2011 (Essex Bird Report) and included in the National Atlas, is excluded from the map as no description was submitted to the London Bird Club.

Breeding season tetrads: 2

Winter season tetrads: 4

Black-throated Diver
Gavia arctica

Rare winter visitor and occasional migrant; amber list.

Within the British Isles, the Black-throated Diver breeds in Scotland and the Outer Hebrides and winters around the coast of Britain (National Atlas). Approximately 560 birds spend the winter around the coast of Britain making this the least numerous winter visitor of the three divers commonly observed in Britain (Musgrove *et al.*, 2013).

The Black-throated Diver is an irregular visitor to the larger waterbodies of the London area, with some individuals staying for an extended period. Although much less numerous during the winter in Britain, the Black-throated Diver is observed about as often as the Red-throated Diver in our area (LBR).

There were just three birds recorded in the winter during the current atlas period, which between them visited a total of six tetrads. The first bird spent a month on the William Girling Reservoir from 17th January to 17th February 2010 and was also seen on the adjacent King George V Reservoir. The following winter, a juvenile was recorded on Queen Mary Reservoir on four dates in December 2010. Another juvenile was recorded from 12th January 2013 on the Queen Mother Reservoir, before moving to the King George VI Reservoir in late January, staying there until March and also visiting Staines Reservoir towards the end of this period.

Two additional spring passage birds were observed outside the defined winter survey season and are therefore omitted from the atlas map.

Winter season tetrads: 6

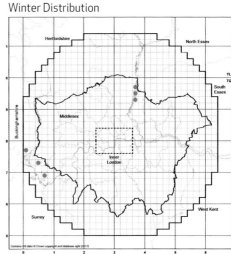

Winter Distribution

● Overwintering 2007/08-2012/13

Great Northern Diver

Gavia immer

Scarce winter visitor and occasional migrant; amber list.

The Great Northern Diver breeds mainly in the Arctic, occurring in winter around most of the coast of the British Isles, with the largest concentrations off the coasts of Scotland and Ireland (National Atlas). Approximately 2,500 birds spend the winter around the coast of Britain (Musgrove *et al.*, 2013).

This species is by far the most common diver species found in the London area and the only one that can be considered a regular winter visitor, averaging four a year during the current atlas period, with 10 or 11 birds seen in the winter of 2009/10. Most birds that frequent the London area are juveniles and they regularly remain in the area until April or May, with the latest summer record during the current atlas period coming from Wraysbury Reservoir on 21st May 2011.

The majority are found on the west London waterbodies, with roughly three-quarters of the birds recorded during the Atlas being seen here. These birds often move regularly between these reservoirs over the course of the winter and sometimes also visit other large waterbodies in the area. During the current atlas period, birds were present here annually, including up to seven that were seen mainly on King George VI Reservoir in January and February 2010.

The other favoured area is the Lee Valley, where one or two birds were present in the winters of 2008/09, 2009/10 and 2011/12. The King George V and William Girling Reservoirs are usually preferred by longer staying birds but this species was also recorded at Amwell, Nazeing Gravel Pits and Walthamstow Reservoirs and one of the birds observed in the Lee Valley also visited the nearby Stoke Newington Reservoirs in February 2009.

Away from the west London waterbodies and the Lee Valley, there were just three records: one at Hilfield Park Reservoir on 16th December 2012 and two that were seen along the Thames that are omitted from the atlas map as both were only seen in flight.

Winter season tetrads: 18

Winter Distribution

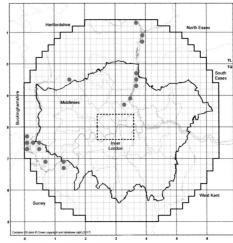

● Overwintering 2007/08-2012/13

Cormorant

Phalacrocorax carbo

Increasing breeding resident and common winter visitor; green list.

At one time Cormorant was restricted to coastal areas in Britain during the breeding season, but many inland colonies have now formed, the majority in the last 20 years. Birds from the continental race *P. c. sinensis* were thought to be responsible for the initial colonisation of inland sites but an increasing proportion of birds from the nominate race, *P. c. carbo*, now breed at inland colonies, making up just under 40% of inland breeders in the UK in 2012 (Newson *et al.*, 2013). The Cormorant can now be found across much of Britain throughout the year (National Atlas).

The first breeding behaviour in the London area occurred at Stocker's Lake in 1984 when a single bird built a nest. This was followed by successful breeding at Broadwater Lake in 1987 and Walthamstow Reservoir from 1991 (Self). These were the only two sites where breeding occurred during the second atlas period. Since then, the Cormorant has made substantial gains across the London area and is now widespread, being found wherever there are suitable waterbodies. Breeding activity remains restricted to a small number of sites. Walthamstow Reservoir is the largest breeding colony, with numbers peaking here in 2004 at 360 pairs and declining slightly since. The Walthamstow Reservoir breeding population is now around 3% of the breeding population in Britain, making this site of national importance for this species. A small number of new colonies have been formed elsewhere with confirmed breeding occurring at ten sites during the current atlas period.

Period	Number of Tetrads		
	Evidence of Breeding	Seen Only	Total
Breeding 1968–72	0	0	0
Breeding 1988–94	2	72	74
Breeding 2008–13	10	333	343
Winter 2007/8–2012/13	-	-	438

The Cormorant is even more widespread in winter, with individuals able to travel long distances to feeding sites and often being seen flying over central London and other built-up areas. The feeding sites do not need to be large and small numbers appear on lakes in town parks, along canals, and on fishing lakes in both urban and rural areas. However, as may be expected, the larger aggregations in winter are found on the larger reservoirs, particularly those in the south-west of the London area, but also at Walthamstow Reservoir. In recent years, a significant winter roost became established in Inner London at Battersea Park, with 220 birds being counted here on 14th February 2013. There is also a heronry at the park, and both roost sites and heronries are favoured sites for the establishment of new Cormorant breeding colonies (Newson *et al.*, 2007), so perhaps this species could soon be breeding in Inner London.

Breeding Distribution

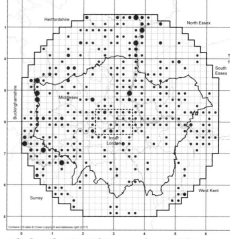

- ● Confirmed Breeding 2008-13
- ● Probable Breeding 2008-13
- ● Possible Breeding 2008-13
- · Present 2008-13
- · Still on Migration 2008-13

Breeding Change

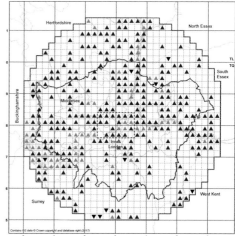

Breeding Distribution Change
- ▲ Recent Gain (new in 2008-13)
- ▲ Old Gain (new in 1988-94)
- ■ Stable (present in all periods)
- ■ Variable (absent 1988-94)
- ▼ Old Loss (last occupied 1968-72)
- ▼ Recent Loss (last occupied 1988-94)

Winter Distribution

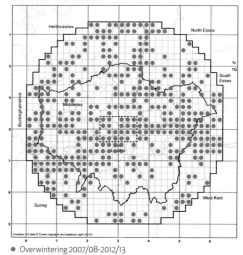

- ● Overwintering 2007/08-2012/13

Birds known to be flying over are excluded from both distribution maps, but it is likely that some dots showing birds as 'present' relate to flyover birds which were not recorded as such.

Winter Abundance

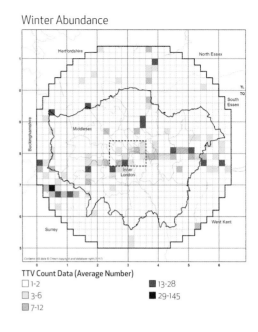

TTV Count Data (Average Number)

- ☐ 1-2
- ☐ 3-6
- ☐ 7-12
- ☐ 13-28
- ☐ 29-145

Shag
Phalacrocorax aristotelis

Irregular visitor, usually in winter; red list.

Unlike the Cormorant, the closely related Shag has remained a predominantly coastal species. Although the Shag is sometimes seen everywhere around the British Isles, it is much more numerous on the northern and western coasts and is a scarce visitor to the south-east coast. Consequently, it is also scarce in the London area.

During the current atlas period, there was an average of approximately five records per year in our area, with birds occurring in autumn, winter and spring. Most of the winter records shown on the map were of short-staying birds but two did overwinter, both on the west London waterbodies. The first bird was on the Queen Mother Reservoir from 11th December 2007 to 11th February 2008, and the second was mostly on Staines Reservoir, from 19th September 2011 to 14th May 2012, but also visited some other nearby sites during this period.

Breeding season tetrads: 4

Winter season tetrads: 7

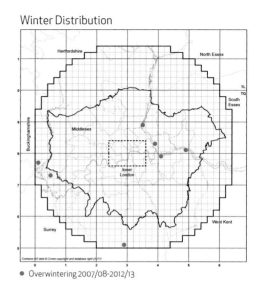

Winter Distribution

● Overwintering 2007/08-2012/13

Bittern

Botaurus stellaris

Scarce winter visitor; amber list.

As a result of habitat restoration and creation, the number of booming Bitterns in Britain increased from 11 in 1997 to 104 in 2011 (National Atlas), though its requirement for extensive reedbeds means that it is restricted to a small number of suitable sites (National Atlas).

There are no confirmed records of breeding in the London area (Self) but it is hoped that this species will eventually breed here as a result of habitat creation in the Lee Valley. Hopes were raised of such an event when booming males were heard at both Amwell and Cheshunt Gravel Pit in 2009 but breeding was not confirmed and there have been no subsequent records from these localities as yet.

Breeding Distribution

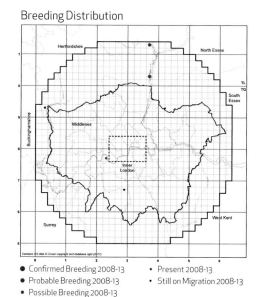

- ● Confirmed Breeding 2008-13   · Present 2008-13
- ● Probable Breeding 2008-13   · Still on Migration 2008-13
- ● Possible Breeding 2008-13

Period	Number of Tetrads		
	Evidence of Breeding	Seen Only	Total
Breeding 1968–72	0	0	0
Breeding 1988–94	0	0	0
Breeding 2008–13	0	4	4
Winter 2007/8–2012/13	-	-	57

The Bittern is much more widespread in Britain in winter (National Atlas), when the species makes use of much smaller reedbeds. It can also sometimes be seen at sites without reeds, particularly during periods of harsh weather.

The Bittern is a regular but scarce wintering visitor to the London area. The Lee Valley has been visited annually from as long ago as the early 1980s, leading to the creation of the popular Bittern Watchpoint at Cheshunt Gravel Pits. Although one female wintering in the Lee Valley was ringed as a nestling in Lincolnshire (Harris, 2006), it is unclear whether most of the other birds using the Lee Valley in winter nest elsewhere in Britain or on the continent, or a mixture of the two. Since the turn of the millennium, the Ingrebourne Valley and the London Wetland Centre have also become regular wintering sites and the Bittern is now encountered more frequently elsewhere across the London area. However, records from Rainham Marshes are surprisingly scarce given that the habitat appears to be suitable, and it may be that the precise habitat conditions on the reserve fail to meet the requirements for this species. The Bittern is, of course, a very secretive bird so it is possible that any wintering birds could escape detection for long periods, especially if they spend their time in the non-public part of this reserve.

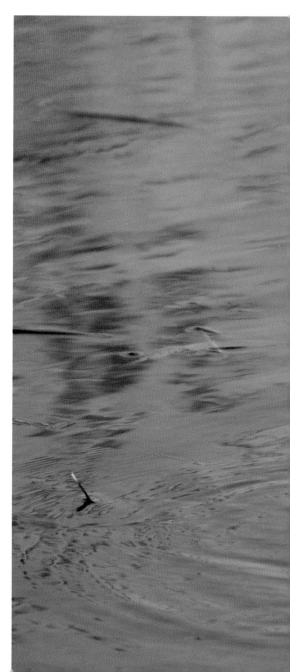

Winter Distribution

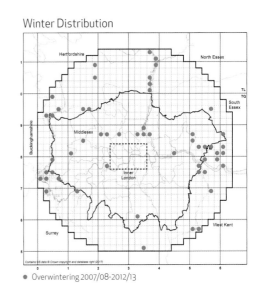

● Overwintering 2007/08-2012/13

Little Egret
Egretta garzetta

Rare breeder and increasingly frequent visitor; green list.

The rapid spread of Little Egret across the British Isles has been one of the major ornithological stories of the last 20 years. Breeding was confirmed in more than 160 10km squares in England, Wales and Ireland (National Atlas). It is hard to believe that it was still officially on the national rarity list at the start of the second atlas and was only removed from the list at the end of 1990.

The first record in the London area was in 1956 and the second in 1972, then the number of records started to pick up from the late 1980s onwards, increasing dramatically in the early 2000s (Self). The species was not included in either of the first two London atlases. The first recorded breeding in the London area was within the heronry at Walthamstow Reservoirs in 2006, and the resultant Little Egret colony is the largest in the London area. During the current atlas period, probable or confirmed breeding was reported from a further nine tetrads.

Like the Grey Heron, this species may fly long distances to feeding sites and its widespread presence during the breeding season may reflect this. However, at Walthamstow Reservoir, nests are usually difficult or impossible to see as they are hidden amongst vegetation and additional breeding sites may therefore have been overlooked elsewhere, particularly if they are at sites without a pre-existing heronry.

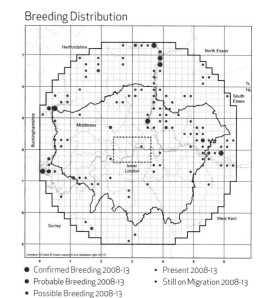

Breeding Distribution

- ● Confirmed Breeding 2008-13
- ● Probable Breeding 2008-13
- ● Possible Breeding 2008-13
- • Present 2008-13
- • Still on Migration 2008-13

Period	Number of Tetrads		
	Evidence of Breeding	Seen Only	Total
Breeding 1968–72	0	0	0
Breeding 1988–94	0	0	0
Breeding 2008–13	10	113	123
Winter 2007/8–2012/13	-	-	232

The spread of Little Egret across Britain was particularly evident in winter, with the species showing the greatest range expansion of any wintering species included in the national atlas. The Little Egret shows a widespread but scattered distribution across the London area at this time of the year. It can be encountered along rivers and canals, and at ponds and other wetland areas, both within and outside urban areas, including occasional records in the parks in Inner London.

The two harsher winters during the current atlas period do not seem to have affected its spread, so it seems likely that further range consolidation and expansion will occur both within the London area and the rest of Britain. It may also become a breeding bird in Inner London in future years.

Winter Distribution

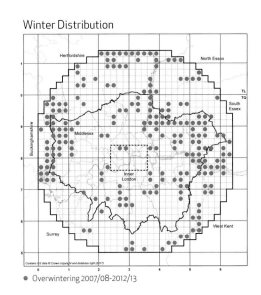

● Overwintering 2007/08-2012/13

Grey Heron
Ardea cinerea

Common breeding resident; green list.

The Grey Heron is widely distributed throughout the British Isles in both the breeding season and during winter (National Atlas) and it is well monitored during the breeding season by the BTO's Heronries Census. The census showed the Grey Heron to be more numerous in the early 2000s than at any time in the last 80 years. However, the population is known to be susceptible to harsh winters and there was a sharp drop in numbers following the severe winters that occurred during the current atlas period (BirdTrends).

A substantial increase in the number of heronries was noted between the first two London atlas periods and subsequent increases during the 1990s are observable in the current breeding distribution map, with breeding activity being observed in more tetrads now than during the second atlas period. However, the number of apparently occupied nests in the London area has fallen since 2010, partly as a result of reduced counts at the main site, Walthamstow Reservoirs.

The species often travels long distances from its breeding sites to its feeding sites and so is also found away from breeding colonies. Consequently, the Grey Heron can now be observed across much of the London area during the breeding season.

Period	Number of Tetrads		
	Evidence of Breeding	Seen Only	Total
Breeding 1968–72	9	91	100
Breeding 1988–94	36	394	430
Breeding 2008–13	63	460	523
Winter 2007/8–2012/13	-	-	605

The winter distribution is similar to the breeding distribution in both Britain and in the London area. Generally, the main gaps in distribution in the London area occur in the areas lacking major wetland habitats or water. However, birds may also be observed in apparently less promising habitat, including urban areas where garden ponds may provide a food source, and even in the middle of crop fields. In winter, the biggest numbers occur around the breeding sites. This is likely to be explained both by better quality habitat in these areas, and by the fact that many individuals have already returned to their colonies in or before February, to begin nesting activity (which of course is within the winter survey season for the atlas).

Breeding Distribution

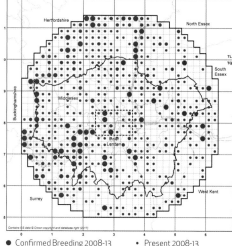

- ● Confirmed Breeding 2008-13
- ● Probable Breeding 2008-13
- ● Possible Breeding 2008-13
- · Present 2008-13
- · Still on Migration 2008-13

Breeding Change

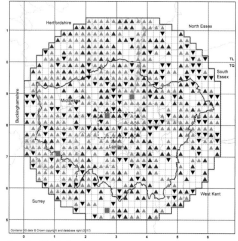

Breeding Distribution Change
- ▲ Recent Gain (new in 2008-13)
- ■ Stable (present in all periods)
- ▼ Old Loss (last occupied 1968-72)
- ▲ Old Gain (new in 1988-94)
- ■ Variable (absent 1988-94)
- ▼ Recent Loss (last occupied 1988-94)

Winter Distribution

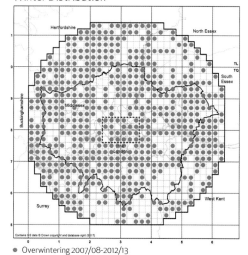

- ● Overwintering 2007/08-2012/13

Winter Abundance

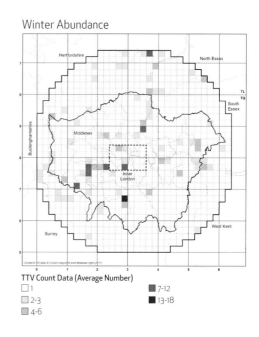

TTV Count Data (Average Number)

- ☐ 1
- ☐ 2-3
- ☐ 4-6
- ☐ 7-12
- ■ 13-18

Little Grebe

Tachybaptus ruficollis

Widespread breeding resident and winter visitor; green list.

The Little Grebe is a widespread breeding resident, present across most of the low-lying areas of Britain (National Atlas). The longer term trend suggests that, following an increase in the late 1970s, a large decrease occurred in the 1980s (BirdTrends). This decrease occurred primarily before the last atlas period, since when numbers have been stable (BBS).

Indeed cold winters may have caused declines ahead of both previous atlas periods (Hewlett *et al.*), though the Little Grebe was still widespread in the London area in both instances. Breeding also occurred widely, including within two tetrads in Inner London during the second atlas period.

The Little Grebe can still be found at all the major wetland sites in the London area, including the Lee Valley, the west London waterbodies the Colne Valley and the Thames Marshes, with the highest numbers found at sites such as Rye Meads, Walthamstow Reservoirs, Rainham Marshes and the London Wetland Centre.

The species is also able to find and make use of smaller sites away from the major wetland areas. Since the second atlas period, the most noticeable change has been an increase in the number of breeding sites within Greater London, where the species uses ponds in urban parks and sometimes urban canals and rivers, such as the River Wandle in south London. Water quality improvements may have helped facilitate this expansion, as well as active habitat management at some sites, such as the planting of reeds and other vegetation. Elsewhere, the distribution within the London area is relatively unchanged apart from some losses from tetrads in rural Essex.

Breeding Distribution

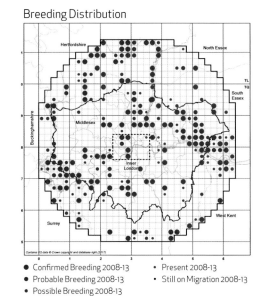

- ● Confirmed Breeding 2008-13
- ● Probable Breeding 2008-13
- ● Possible Breeding 2008-13
- · Present 2008-13
- · Still on Migration 2008-13

Period	Number of Tetrads		
	Evidence of Breeding	Seen Only	Total
Breeding 1968–72	107	32	139
Breeding 1988–94	165	42	207
Breeding 2008–13	154	83	237
Winter 2007/8–2012/13	-	-	282

The winter distribution, both in Britain and in the London area, is similar to the breeding distribution. However, the species is locally more widespread during winter, when it can frequent additional sites where no suitable nesting habitat exists. This is especially apparent in north-east London, and in Surrey and south-west London. It is possible that occupancy of these waterbodies may increase in colder weather when sites within Greater London may be among the last to freeze over as a result of the 'urban heat-island effect'.

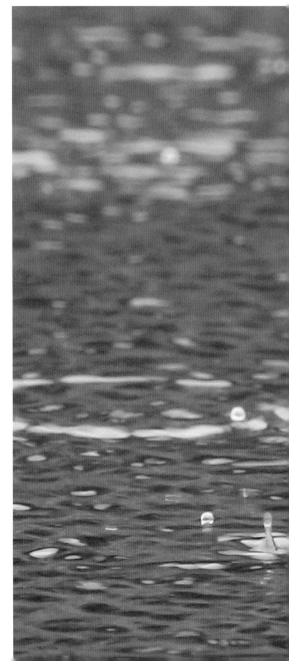

Breeding Change

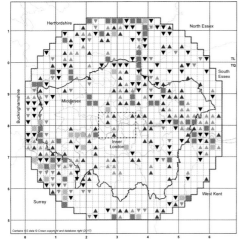

Winter Distribution

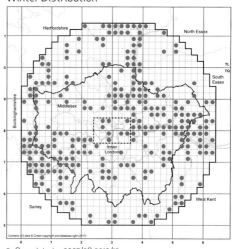

Breeding Distribution Change

▲ Recent Gain (new in 2008-13) ▲ Old Gain (new in 1988-94)
■ Stable (present in all periods) ■ Variable (absent 1988-94)
▼ Old Loss
(last occupied 1968-72) ▼ Recent Loss
(last occupied 1988-94)

 Overwintering 2007/08-2012/13

Great Crested Grebe
Podiceps cristatus

Common breeding resident and winter visitor; green list.

The Great Crested Grebe was one once hunted for its feathers which adorned the hats of the wealthy. As a result, it was one of the earliest species subject to conservation concern and one of the drivers behind the formation of the Royal Society for the Protection of Birds in the early twentieth century. The Great Crested Grebe increased in numbers during the twentieth century, benefiting from protection and from the creation of gravel pits. Numbers in Britain have remained stable since the 1990s (BBS).

In the London area, it has colonised many of the suitable sites in both urban and rural areas, and more than doubled its population between the first and second atlases, with tetrad occupancy showing a similar increase (Hewlett *et al.*). Following these gains, the breeding distribution in the current atlas period remained similar to that of the last.

During the breeding season, the Great Crested Grebe has a similar distribution to Little Grebe, and can be found at the major wetland sites and at suitable waterbodies in urban areas. Most of the differences in the distributions of these two species could be explained by slightly different habitat requirements.

Period	Number of Tetrads		
	Evidence of Breeding	Seen Only	Total
Breeding 1968–72	98	18	116
Breeding 1988–94	184	39	223
Breeding 2008–13	189	42	231
Winter 2007/8–2012/13	-	-	216

In winter, locally resident Great Crested Grebes may be joined by others that breed elsewhere in Britain or abroad (Migration Atlas). The birds tend to congregate on some of the larger waterbodies in the London area, particularly in areas where a network of waterbodies is present, such as the west London waterbodies and the Lee Valley. The largest flocks are usually found on the west London waterbodies, especially Queen Mary Reservoir. This is especially so in cold weather, when movement to large waterbodies may lead to especially large counts, for example the 676 birds recorded on Queen Mary Reservoir on 19th December 2010 (LBR). It is also during severe winter weather that birds are most likely to be seen on the Thames in Inner London, for example one or two birds were present there during the period 10th–14th January 2010.

However, this species is not restricted to larger waterbodies in winter and small numbers (often ones and twos) can also be found on many smaller lakes and gravel pits in the London area, provided the weather remains temperate and these waterbodies do not freeze over. The birds at the sites may be breeding birds retaining their territory through the winter. Indeed, the Great Crested Grebe is one of a small number of species that has been known to occasionally attempt to breed during the winter in the London area; for example a pair nest building in Regent's Park on 22nd January 2014.

Breeding Distribution

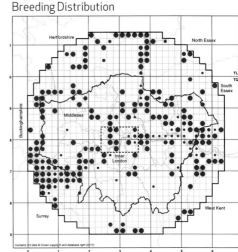

- ● Confirmed Breeding 2008-13
- ● Probable Breeding 2008-13
- ● Possible Breeding 2008-13
- · Present 2008-13
- · Still on Migration 2008-13

Breeding Change

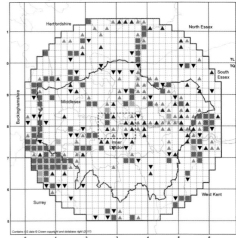

Breeding Distribution Change
- ▲ Recent Gain (new in 2008-13)
- ■ Stable (present in all periods)
- ▼ Old Loss (last occupied 1968-72)
- ▲ Old Gain (new in 1988-94)
- ■ Variable (absent 1988-94)
- ▼ Recent Loss (last occupied 1988-94)

Winter Distribution

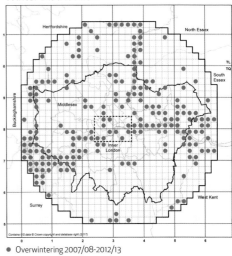

- ● Overwintering 2007/08-2012/13

Red-necked Grebe

Podiceps grisegena

Scarce winter visitor and passage migrant; red list.

The Red-necked Grebe is a regular but scarce winter visitor to Britain, with some birds occasionally lingering into spring and early summer. It is mainly found along the North Sea coast (National Atlas).

It is the rarest regularly occurring grebe species in the London area, averaging just three birds per year during the current atlas period. Some of these records relate to spring or autumn passage birds and are therefore not shown on the atlas distribution map.

The only long staying birds during the current atlas period were all on the west London waterbodies, including an individual which overwintered in 2010/11. This individual was mainly at the King George VI Reservoir but also visited several other reservoirs in the area. There were also birds at Queen Mother Reservoir from 8th to 25th November 2009 and from 19th November to 15th December 2012. Elsewhere, records are scattered, with most birds present for a maximum of two days, with the exception of one at Sevenoaks Wildlife Reserve from 8th to 15th December 2010. The locations include William Girling Reservoir in three different winters.

Breeding season tetrads: 2

Winter season tetrads: 10

Winter Distribution

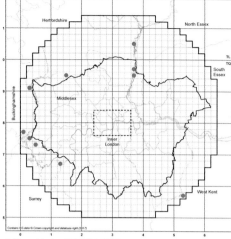

● Overwintering 2007/08-2012/13

Black-necked Grebe

Podiceps nigricollis

Passage and winter migrant and rare breeder; amber list.

The Black-necked Grebe is a scarce breeding species in Britain, with a scattered breeding distribution at mainly inland sites in eastern and central England. It is slightly more widespread in winter when it prefers sheltered coastal waters and large reservoirs (National Atlas).

In the London area, it did not feature in the first breeding atlas but it has bred at Hilfield Park Reservoir since the 1990s. A pair was also observed displaying at Beddington Sewage Farm during the second atlas period but they did not breed. Then, in 2002, a pair successfully raised two young at Rainham Marshes but this has so far not been repeated (Self).

Hilfield Park Reservoir remains the pre-eminent site for this species in the London area, with as many as nine broods counted there in 2010 and 2011. There are only around 40 breeding pairs in Britain, making the Reservoir of national importance for this species.

There have been signs of possible expansion within the London area away from this site, with unsuccessful breeding at a second site in the Hertfordshire sector in 2011 and possible breeding in the Essex sector in 2012. Since the end of the current atlas survey period, successful breeding has been confirmed in 2014 at Rye Meads (LBR). To protect breeding sites, full details are not shown on the map apart from at Hilfield Park Reservoir. Some sightings at other sites in spring which were presumed to involve passage birds are not shown.

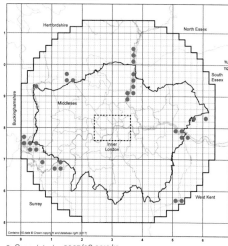

Breeding Distribution

- ● Confirmed Breeding 2008-13
- ● Probable Breeding 2008-13
- ● Possible Breeding 2008-13
- · Present 2008-13
- · Still on Migration 2008-13

Winter Distribution

- ● Overwintering 2007/08-2012/13

Period	Number of Tetrads		
	Evidence of Breeding	Seen Only	Total
Breeding 1968–72	0	0	0
Breeding 1988–94	1	1	2
Breeding 2008–13	5	15	20
Winter 2007/8–2012/13	-	-	31

The main wintering site for this species in London is William Girling Reservoir in the Lee Valley, where counts of 20+ regularly occur each year, with the birds normally present from August until late March or early April. The total wintering population in Britain is estimated to be around 130 individuals (Musgrove *et al.*, 2013) and so this reservoir is of national importance for this species during the winter.

The reservoir must perfectly meet the wintering requirements for this species, as the birds are remarkably faithful to the site. They are only occasional visitors to other reservoirs in the Lee Valley. Even the King George V Reservoir, which is superficially the same as the William Girling and is approximately 100m to the north, is only occasionally visited.

Away from the Lee Valley, the only other regular wintering site is Staines Reservoir. Numbers at this site are usually low during the first part of the winter (two or three birds), but peak in February and March at approximately 10 birds. Occasional wintering birds also occur elsewhere in the London area, including the other west London waterbodies, the

Colne Valley and waterbodies around the outer Thames.

Although the numbers in summer and winter are similar, it is not currently known whether the same birds make short distance movements and are therefore present in London throughout the year, or whether two different populations are involved.

Slavonian Grebe

Podiceps auritus

Scarce winter visitor and passage migrant; red list.

The Slavonian Grebe is a scarce breeding bird in Britain, being mostly restricted to Scotland during this season. It is more widespread in winter when it is mainly found at coastal sites around the British Isles (National Atlas). However, it is uncommon around most of the south-east coast of England and is a scarce visitor to the London area, averaging approximately eight birds per year over the current atlas period. The majority of these have appeared in winter, probably as a result of cold weather movements, and they often stay for only short periods. However, wintering birds can stay for longer periods and sometimes linger into April, when passage birds may also occur. May records are rare but a bird at Staines Reservoir in May 2011 was last observed on 20th.

The most usual locations of the London area for this species are the well-watched west London waterbodies, where single individuals overwintered in both 2008/09 and 2010/11. The 2010/11 bird also visited the nearby Broadwater Lake, and the 2008/09 bird on King George VI Reservoir was joined by a second individual in February 2009. One was also present at Thorpe Water Park in November 2012. Away from the south-west of the London area, the Slavonian Grebe can also be found occasionally in the Lee Valley and on or near the outer Thames, including one at Rainham from 24th January 2010, which was sadly found dead on 8th February, and a well-watched and showy bird which frequented a tiny pool at Littlebrook in Kent from 19th January to 16th February 2013. Away from these areas, the only winter record during the current atlas period was a bird on Fairlop Waters on 20th December 2009.

Breeding season tetrads: 5

Winter season tetrads: 19

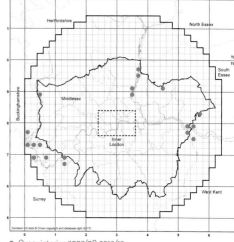

Winter Distribution

● Overwintering 2007/08-2012/13

Red Kite

Milvus milvus

Increasing visitor and breeder, following re-introduction to the Chilterns; green list.

The reintroduction of the Red Kite at several sites in England and Scotland is one of the conservation success stories of the late twentieth and early twenty-first centuries. Following these reintroductions, the population in Britain has increased by an estimated 874% (489% to 1,657%) over the period 1995 to 2013 (BBS), and it was recorded in seven times the number of 10km squares as it occupied at the time of the second atlas (National Atlas).

The Red Kite was famously abundant in London in 15th and 16th centuries but by the mid-19th century it had become a rare visitor (Self). The closest reintroduction site to the London area was in the Chilterns, where reintroductions began in 1989 (Evans *et al.*, 1999). The species quickly became a regular sight along the M40 motorway. The population has slowly spread out from the reintroduction site, including in the direction of London, with the number of records in the London area increasing steadily through the 2000s.

About 50% of all sightings of Red Kite in the London area occur between March and June and many of these are likely to be passage birds or juveniles, either dispersing across London or looking for new areas in which to breed. Resident birds are also displaying at that time of year and are therefore far more visible. Nevertheless, birds can be highly mobile throughout the year and the number of reports in other months has increased over the period of the atlas.

The core range of the Red Kite in the London area was initially in the Hertfordshire sector but by the end of the atlas period, birds could be seen daily in the Buckinghamshire sector and elsewhere in the west of our area. The spring peak has declined gradually between 2007 and 2013, reflecting an increase in the number of birds colonising the parts of our area closest to the Chilterns, where many birds will undoubtedly have originated from. A pair bred just beyond the London area boundary in 2005 (Self), with breeding within the boundary first confirmed in 2007 and occurring in a total of eight tetrads by 2013.

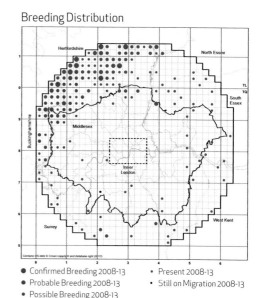

Breeding Distribution

● Confirmed Breeding 2008-13   • Present 2008-13
● Probable Breeding 2008-13   • Still on Migration 2008-13
● Possible Breeding 2008-13

Period	Number of Tetrads		
	Evidence of Breeding	Seen Only	Total
Breeding 1968–72	0	0	0
Breeding 1988–94	0	0	0
Breeding 2008–13	22	169	191
Winter 2007/8–2012/13	-	-	125

The distribution in the London area is more restricted in winter. The regular provision of food in some areas may lessen the need for birds to roam more widely at this time.

Birds which were recorded as only flying over have been excluded from the atlas maps. These include several birds recorded flying over central London. The Red Kite covers large distances whilst searching for food from the air and so the occupied tetrads shown on both maps away from core areas should be considered representative.

Winter Distribution

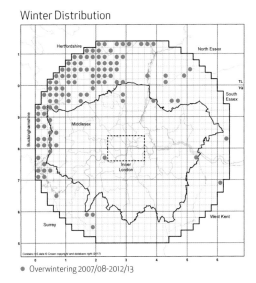

● Overwintering 2007/08-2012/13

Sparrowhawk
Accipiter nisus

Common breeding resident; green list.

Like several other raptor species, the population of the Sparrowhawk in Britain has increased significantly since suffering a large decline in the mid-twentieth century, when the use of organochlorine pesticides such as DDT was thought to be a major contributory factor (for example Newton & Wyllie, 1992). The long-term population trend shows that numbers have increased by 115% (46% to 290%) over the period 1975 to 2013, peaking in around 2005 and dropping slightly since (BirdTrends). As a result, the Sparrowhawk is once again a widespread and familiar breeding resident. The short term trend indicates that the population has declined slightly (-15%) during the period 1995 to 2013 (BBS).

In the London area, the Sparrowhawk was historically common in some rural areas but had become scarce by the 1860s (Self). It was still extremely scarce at the time of the first breeding atlas. However, the number of occupied tetrads increased by more than tenfold by the time of the second atlas, when it was recorded in 579 tetrads (68% of the total number of tetrads). At that time, most of the occupied tetrads were found in the countryside around Greater London, but some birds had successfully colonised the urban area, including Inner London, particularly at sites where larger wooded areas exist.

The expansion of its range in London continued up to the time of the current atlas and the Sparrowhawk can now be found across most of the London area during the breeding season. As a result of its increase in distribution, and the decline of the Kestrel within central London, the Sparrowhawk is perhaps now the raptor that is most frequently encountered in Greater London, though in central urban areas the Peregrine would be another contender for this title.

Across the London area as a whole, the number of occupied tetrads is almost unchanged since the second atlas, but the species may be more widespread than shown on the breeding map. Many of the gaps in distribution during the current atlas period are in tetrads where survey effort was less thorough, such as parts of rural Essex and Kent.

Breeding Distribution

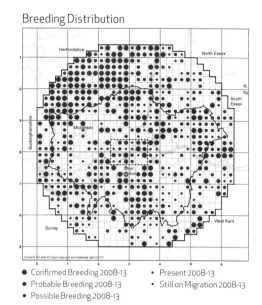

- Confirmed Breeding 2008-13
- Probable Breeding 2008-13
- Possible Breeding 2008-13
- Present 2008-13
- Still on Migration 2008-13

Period	Number of Tetrads		
	Evidence of Breeding	Seen Only	Total
Breeding 1968–72	19	31	50
Breeding 1988–94	327	252	579
Breeding 2008–13	264	314	578
Winter 2007/8–2012/13	-	-	667

The winter distribution of the Sparrowhawk, both in London and in Britain, is similar to the breeding distribution. However, the species was recorded more widely in the London area during winter and it may be that the winter map is more representative of its status in our area.

123

Breeding Change

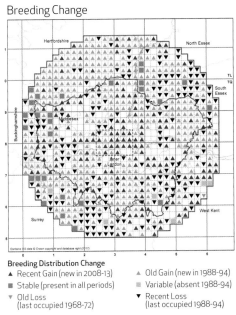

Winter Distribution

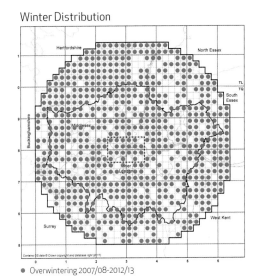

Breeding Distribution Change
▲ Recent Gain (new in 2008-13)
■ Stable (present in all periods)
▼ Old Loss
(last occupied 1968-72)

▲ Old Gain (new in 1988-94)
■ Variable (absent 1988-94)
▼ Recent Loss
(last occupied 1988-94)

● Overwintering 2007/08-2012/13

Buzzard

Buteo buteo

Increasing breeding resident and regular migrant/visitor; green list.

Like several other raptors, the Buzzard was one of the good ornithological news stories of the late twentieth century. By the 1950s, it had become restricted to western parts of Britain, but its spread eastwards since then has been so marked that it has re-colonised the whole of Britain, becoming the sixth most widespread wintering species in Britain (National Atlas). As a result, the population in Britain has continued to grow, with the long-term trend in England suggesting there may be eight times as many Buzzards as there were in 1967 and that the increase has mainly occurred since around 1990 (BirdTrends).

The Buzzard population had reached to just west of the London area by the early 1990s and was recorded as present in eight tetrads during the second London atlas. The first confirmed breeding in the London area in recent times occurred in 1998 in the Copped Hall area in Essex (Self). It has since rapidly colonised the remainder of the non-urban parts of our area, as the breeding distribution map shows. Most breeding records are from the Hertfordshire sector: This matches the findings of Oliver (2011) who reported that records from the Hertfordshire sector were considerably higher in most years but also that they were variable and this pattern may be influenced by observer effort.

The Buzzard can also be encountered flying over central London during suitable weather conditions. The peak time for such encounters is during spring and autumn when continental birds may be migrating through the London area. However, some movement also occurs at other times of year and may involve more local birds. It will be interesting to see whether any of the larger open spaces in Greater London, such as Richmond Park, will be able to support a breeding pair in the future.

Period	Number of Tetrads		
	Evidence of Breeding	Seen Only	Total
Breeding 1968–72	0	0	0
Breeding 1988–94	0	8	8
Breeding 2008–13	179	214	393
Winter 2007/8–2012/13	-	-	411

In winter, the distribution is similar to the breeding season.

Breeding Distribution

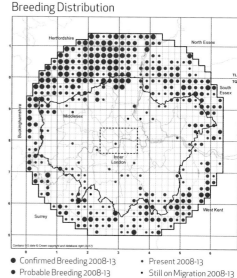

● Confirmed Breeding 2008-13   • Present 2008-13
● Probable Breeding 2008-13   • Still on Migration 2008-13
● Possible Breeding 2008-13

Breeding Change

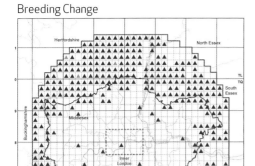

Contains OS data © Crown copyright and database right (2017)

Breeding Distribution Change
▲ Recent Gain (new in 2008-13)   ▲ Old Gain (new in 1988-94)
■ Stable (present in all periods)   ■ Variable (absent 1988-94)
▼ Old Loss
(last occupied 1968-72)   ▼ Recent Loss
(last occupied 1988-94)

Winter Distribution

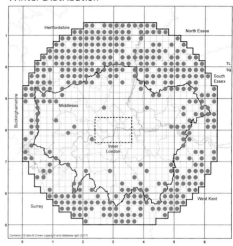

Contains OS data © Crown copyright and database right (2017)

● Overwintering 2007/08-2012/13

Marsh Harrier

Circus aeruginosus

Scarce, but increasing passage migrant; has bred; amber list.

The population of Marsh Harrier in Britain has increased in recent years following a low in the 1970s (National Atlas). The Marsh Harrier may have benefited from conservation work to increase the size and number of reedbeds to aid the recovery of the Bittern population.

For the 200 years prior, the Marsh Harrier has only been known as a passage migrant in the London area, moving through in small numbers in spring and autumn. The species was not recorded in the first London atlas and was only observed in one tetrad during the second atlas period. As the population in Britain has increased, it has been seen far more regularly in the London area and there have been more sightings during the spring and summer, and the species is now present at the lower Thames Marshes throughout the year (LBR); nevertheless, spring remains the peak period (Self).

As a result of these changes, Marsh Harrier was observed more widely in our area during the current atlas period. The majority of records in the London area come from the area around Rainham Marshes, with birds occasionally summering there. Elsewhere, a bird also summered at Rye Meads in 2013.

In 2010, a pair successfully raised two young in the Essex sector, the first breeding record in the London area for 200 years (Self). Although most breeding Marsh Harriers nest in reedbeds, a UK survey in 1995 demonstrated that nests can be in very small patches of reeds or ditches and that small numbers also nest in oil-seed rape or winter cereal fields (Underhill-Day 1998). It is therefore conceivable that additional pairs of Marsh Harrier have nested in the less well-watched arable parts of the London area, but most, if not all, of the spring records in the London area probably relate to passage birds.

So that the breeding site cannot be identified, the details are not shown on the map and some 'dots' have been shifted slightly.

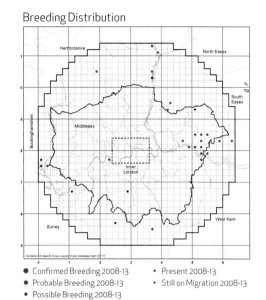

Breeding Distribution

● Confirmed Breeding 2008-13   · Present 2008-13
● Probable Breeding 2008-13   · Still on Migration 2008-13
● Possible Breeding 2008-13

Period	Number of Tetrads		
	Evidence of Breeding	Seen Only	Total
Breeding 1968–72	0	0	0
Breeding 1988–94	0	1	1
Breeding 2008–13	1	20	21
Winter 2007/8–2012/13	-	-	30

The Thames marshes is also the area where the Marsh Harrier is most likely to be encountered during winter, and in 2012 and 2013 birds were seen at Rainham Marshes in every month of the year. Away from this area, most records are of birds seen on one day only. It is likely that these birds moved straight through our area, though in some cases it is possible that they were actively hunting or were present in the area for more than one day. Like breeding birds, wintering Marsh Harriers are not necessarily restricted to marshland and sometimes hunt over farmland.

Winter Distribution

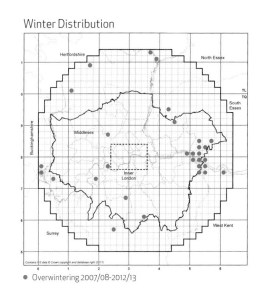

● Overwintering 2007/08-2012/13

Hen Harrier

Circus cyaneus

Scarce passage migrant and rare winter visitor; red list.

The Hen Harrier is a winter visitor to the south of England. In the 1980s, the species regularly wintered on the Lower Thames Marshes (Self) but it is now much scarcer in the London area, with just a handful of records each year. The prime area for Hen Harrier is still the lower Thames including Rainham Marshes.

During the atlas period, records from Rainham Marshes occurred in all winters apart from 2008/09. A juvenile or female (known as a ringtail) was seen there regularly but intermittently between January and April 2011, but it is unclear whether any birds wintered in other years as there were long gaps between sightings. Other records in this area came from Crayford/Dartford Marshes, the Ingrebourne Valley and Crossness, with a male lingering briefly at the latter site in January 2010 and being seen on three days between the 19th and the 23rd.

There is a scattering of records away from the lower Thames. Most, if not all, of these records seem likely to relate to individuals that were moving through the London area rather than genuine wintering birds. The only individual away from the Thames Marshes that was recorded on more than one day was a bird at Canon's Farm (Surrey) which was seen on two successive dates on 8th and 9th November 2010.

Breeding season tetrads: 2

Winter season tetrads: 17

Winter Distribution

● Overwintering 2007/08-2012/13

Merlin

Falco columbarius

Uncommon winter visitor; red list.

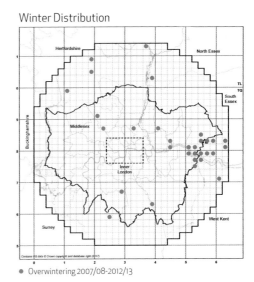

Winter Distribution

● Overwintering 2007/08-2012/13

The Merlin breeds mainly on moorland in the British Isles, especially in the north of Britain (National Atlas). During winter, when numbers are supplemented by birds which breed in Iceland (Migration Atlas), it can be found across the remainder of Britain, though it is sparse or absent from some areas (National Atlas).

The Merlin is relatively uncommon in the London area (National Atlas) compared to some other parts of lowland Britain. The only regular wintering area is the Thames Marshes, where it is a scarce winter visitor to such localities as Rainham Marshes, Crayford/Dartford Marshes and the Ingrebourne Valley. Because Merlin is a species that requires a description in the London area, away from the lower Thames Marshes, the picture elsewhere is complicated by the fact that many reported sightings are lost each year from the published record, because no descriptions are submitted to the London Bird Club. This includes a number of reported atlas records which have been omitted.

It is likely that the scattering of records shown on the map away from the Thames Marshes mostly relate to late autumn passage records rather than wintering birds. Over half of the records away from the Thames sites occurred in November, and all of them were of birds seen on a single date only. However, even at Rainham Marshes, sightings are often irregular, so some of these birds may have stayed for longer periods, particularly those seen in agricultural areas that are not regularly watched.

Winter season tetrads: 31

Kestrel

Falco tinnunculus

Common breeding resident; amber list.

In contrast to most other raptor species, the Kestrel is now declining in the UK and, as a result, it has been placed on the amber list of birds of conservation concern. It has suffered a range contraction of 6% in the UK since the 1968–72 atlas, but can still be found throughout England, although in lower abundance in most parts of its range than in 1988–91 (National Atlas). The short-term trend shows a drop of approximately 40% in the breeding population between 1995 and 2013 (BBS).

All raptor species were thought to have become extinct as breeding birds in London by the late nineteenth century by Hudson, who wrote in 1898 that "It is exceedingly improbable that any of the raptorial species which formerly inhabited London – Peregrine Falcon, Kestrel and Kite – will ever return" (Hudson, 1898). However, as soon afterwards as 1909, Kestrel was reported as being not uncommon in London, having bred in Cheapside, with further confirmed breeding occurring in the 1920s (Fitter, 1949). The Kestrel became widespread and by the second atlas period, it was found in 94% of the tetrads in the London area. It remains a familiar species throughout the area but it now has a much sparser distribution, both within urban areas and in the surrounding countryside. Its abundance has certainly declined across much of the London area since the second atlas period (National Atlas).

Despite losses from some tetrads, it continues to breed successfully in Inner London where good habitat and breeding locations exist, for example in Regent's Park where boxes are provided and some areas of grass are left uncut for the benefit of wildlife, including small mammals. Outside Greater London, tetrad occupancy levels appear to have remained high in some areas, for example within the Hertfordshire sector, but appear to have reduced elsewhere.

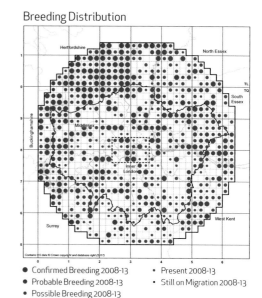

Breeding Distribution

● Confirmed Breeding 2008-13   · Present 2008-13
● Probable Breeding 2008-13   · Still on Migration 2008-13
● Possible Breeding 2008-13

Period	Number of Tetrads		
	Evidence of Breeding	Seen Only	Total
Breeding 1968–72	377	295	672
Breeding 1988–94	523	285	808
Breeding 2008–13	291	341	632
Winter 2007/8–2012/13	-	-	639

In winter, Kestrel is slightly more widespread than during the breeding season, both within Greater London and in the surrounding countryside. However, there are still gaps in a number of areas, particularly within the Greater London boundary.

Breeding Change

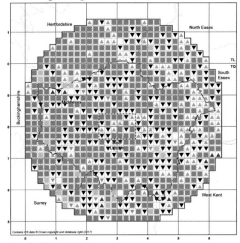

Contains OS data © Crown copyright and database right (2017)

Breeding Distribution Change
- ▲ Recent Gain (new in 2008-13)
- ■ Stable (present in all periods)
- ▼ Old Loss
  (last occupied 1968-72)
- ▲ Old Gain (new in 1988-94)
- ■ Variable (absent 1988-94)
- ▼ Recent Loss
  (last occupied 1988-94)

Winter Distribution

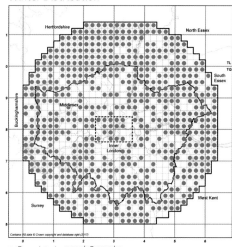

Contains OS data © Crown copyright and database right (2017)

- ● Overwintering 2007/08-2012/13

Hobby

Falco subbuteo

Breeding summer visitor and passage migrant; green list.

Hobby is a summer visitor to the southern half of Britain, and experienced a fourfold increase in the occupation of 10km squares within its range since 1968–72 (National Atlas).

It was scarce in the London area during the first atlas period, being recorded in just 19 tetrads, mostly in Surrey. However, a substantial increase occurred over the next 20 years with it being recorded in almost fifteen times more tetrads during the second atlas period.

The distribution map for the second atlas period shows a scattering of records throughout the London area, with probable or confirmed breeding occurring widely, in both urban and rural areas. The current distribution is broadly similar to that of the second atlas, with fewer tetrads occupied in Kent and south-east London compared to other areas.

Recent gains in tetrad occupation close to central London confirm that Hobby is able to make use of green spaces within more densely urban areas, and a pair bred successfully in Inner London in 2011. The Hobby can be secretive during the breeding season and it is a relatively late breeder, so it is perhaps less likely to be confirmed as a breeding species than others. However, Hobby can roam widely during the breeding season (National Atlas) which may also explain the relatively high number of tetrads occupied relative to the likely size of the breeding population.

In the second London Atlas, it was suggested that further range expansion could be anticipated, possibly as a result of climate change. However, the current atlas does not show substantial gains in the number of occupied tetrads. The number of breeding pairs reported annually in the London Bird Report has been very variable during the current atlas period, ranging from a low of 16 pairs in 2008 to a high of 40 pairs in 2009, and the population appears to be either stable or increasing. The variation may reflect the amount of time and effort required to locate breeding pairs, and the true annual total is probably closer to the higher figure.

So that the breeding sites cannot be identified, the detail has been removed from the breeding season map and some 'dots' have been shifted slightly.

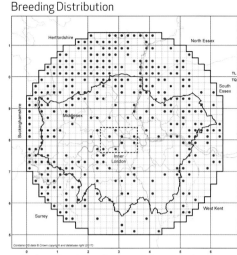

Breeding Distribution

● Confirmed Breeding 2008-13
● Probable Breeding 2008-13
● Possible Breeding 2008-13
· Present 2008-13
· Still on Migration 2008-13

Period	Number of Tetrads		
	Evidence of Breeding	Seen Only	Total
Breeding 1968–72	5	14	19
Breeding 1988–94	84	191	275
Breeding 2008–13	97	230	327

Breeding Change

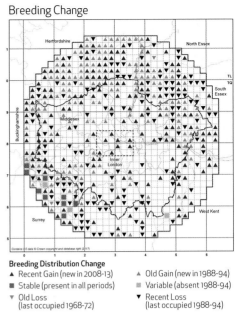

Breeding Distribution Change
- ▲ Recent Gain (new in 2008-13)
- ■ Stable (present in all periods)
- ▼ Old Loss (last occupied 1968-72)
- ▲ Old Gain (new in 1988-94)
- ▣ Variable (absent 1988-94)
- ▼ Recent Loss (last occupied 1988-94)

Peregrine

Falco peregrinus

Increasing breeding resident and winter visitor; green list.

The Peregrine is another raptor species that has recovered its distribution in Britain over recent decades and it can now be found across much of Britain throughout the year, though it remains more common in the north and west (National Atlas). It has also moved into urban areas, with many documented examples in Britain and elsewhere (Drewitt, 2014). Cities, such as London, provide plenty of taller buildings with suitable perches and also ledges on which to nest, with boxes also sometimes specially provided by helpful birdwatchers or conservationists. Electricity pylons are also commonly used by this species, particularly in more open areas that lack suitable tall buildings.

It did not feature in the main accounts for either of the previous London atlases but was included in the second atlas in a section describing species breeding just after the end of the atlas, following successful breeding at Silvertown in 1998 (Hewlett *et al.*). Since then, the Peregrine population has increased substantially and by the end of the atlas period there were more than 20 pairs nesting in the London area (LBR). There are several publicised sites where this species can be seen, including the pair that takes its fledglings to the chimney of the Tate Modern, where they are the subject of an RSPB watchpoint. Conservationists liaise with landowners to help provide and protect nest sites and maintain a watch on many of London's birds. Prey items can be surprisingly varied; as well as pigeon, London's Peregrines (as well as those in other UK cities) have been found to eat migrant bird species, including some that normally migrate at night (Drewitt, 2014).

Most breeding sites are kept secret to protect the birds and therefore the detail has been removed from the breeding season map and some 'dots' have been shifted slightly.

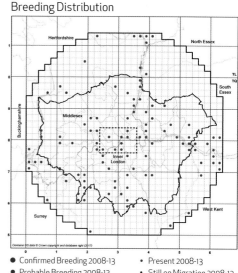

Breeding Distribution

- ● Confirmed Breeding 2008-13
- ● Probable Breeding 2008-13
- ● Possible Breeding 2008-13
- • Present 2008-13
- • Still on Migration 2008-13

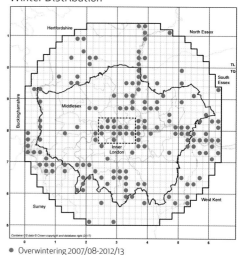

Winter Distribution

- ● Overwintering 2007/08-2012/13

Period	Number of Tetrads		
	Evidence of Breeding	Seen Only	Total
Breeding 1968–72	0	0	0
Breeding 1988–94	0	0	0
Breeding 2008–13	31	79	110
Winter 2007/8–2012/13	-	-	169

The Peregrine is more widespread in winter than it is in the breeding season, both in Britain and in London. In our area, it was recorded in one and a half times as many tetrads during the winter months as during the breeding season. Pairs breeding in cities usually remain on their territories throughout the year (Drewitt, 2014), so this increased distribution is probably the result of the dispersal of juveniles and seasonal movement by adults from elsewhere.

Water Rail

Rallus aquaticus

Common, but elusive, winter visitor; scarce breeder; green list.

Breeding Distribution

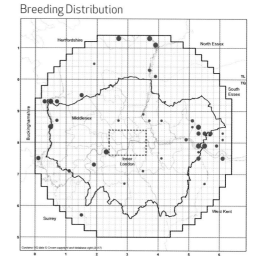

● Confirmed Breeding 2008-13   • Present 2008-13
● Probable Breeding 2008-13   • Still on Migration 2008-13
● Possible Breeding 2008-13

Though uncommon, the national distribution and abundance of the Water Rail appear stable and this species is not currently of conservation concern. Numbers increase during winter.

In the London area, as nationally, the breeding distribution of the Water Rail, is patchy and associated with suitable wetland habitat, with only some of the habitat available apparently occupied. Where this species breeds in the London area, it does so in small numbers with usually one or two (maximum seven) breeding pairs recorded per tetrad.

In the three atlas periods, the average number of tetrads occupied by this species where there was evidence of breeding was 18.7, with the highest at 21 during the first atlas period.

In the last atlas, there was speculation that this species could become established as part of the breeding fauna of the 'Barnes Wetlands'; this has now happened, making this the closest breeding occurrence of this species to Inner London during any of the atlas periods.

Period	Number of Tetrads		
	Evidence of Breeding	Seen Only	Total
Breeding 1968–72	21	15	36
Breeding 1988–94	16	10	26
Breeding 2008–13	19	21	40
Winter 2007/8–2012/13	-	-	156

Again, reflecting the national picture, this species is recorded more widely during the winter period indicating that larger numbers may be present. As would be expected, there is a clear association with the major river valleys; Lee, Colne, Darent, Mole and the Thames outside Inner London. There are also scattered records from other wetlands, including The London Wetland Centre; in Inner London at Regent's Park, where it was recorded in all six winters; in Hyde Park/Kensington Gardens, where it was recorded in four of the six winters. At Regent's Park, two to three individuals overwintered in most years during the atlas period.

Recent studies using playback to monitor Water Rails elsewhere in the UK during the breeding season have found that numbers have been far higher than previous estimates (Holling & RBBP, 2013). A December 2009 count using this method at the London Wetland Centre found 41 birds, 3.5 times higher than the previously recorded winter high of 12 (LBR, 2009). It is interesting to speculate whether a similar study in the London area during the breeding season would find Water Rail present at sites where it is currently only known to occur in winter.

Breeding Change

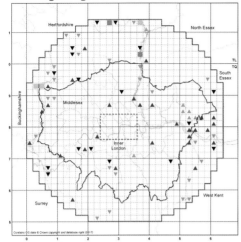

Winter Distribution

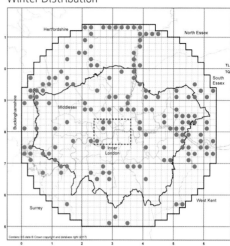

Breeding Distribution Change
- ▲ Recent Gain (new in 2008-13)
- ■ Stable (present in all periods)
- ▼ Old Loss
  (last occupied 1968-72)
- ▲ Old Gain (new in 1988-94)
- ■ Variable (absent 1988-94)
- ▼ Recent Loss
  (last occupied 1988-94)

● Overwintering 2007/08-2012/13

Moorhen

Gallinula chloropus

Very common breeding resident; green list.

The Moorhen is an abundant and widespread species occurring wherever there is water with fringing vegetation in lowland Britain (National Atlas).

In the London area, this species is similarly found breeding wherever there is a suitable body. This is the case in most tetrads except for those within the broad swathe of the North Downs where this species is much more thinly distributed. This pattern was also evident in both previous London Atlases.

Earlier publications suggest that the breeding distribution of the Moorhen in the London area has remained more or less stable for at least 100 years and may be expanding, having been found in 100 more tetrads in this current atlas period than in the first.

Moorhen can be found even on very small ponds and along streams, unlike the Coot, which tends to prefer slightly larger waterbodies and wider canals or rivers. This is reflected in the fact that Moorhen was found in nearly 80% of the tetrads in our area, 21% more than Coot.

Period	Number of Tetrads		
	Evidence of Breeding	Seen Only	Total
Breeding 1968–72	497	85	582
Breeding 1988–94	570	70	640
Breeding 2008–13	570	112	682
Winter 2007/8–2012/13	-	-	689

During the winter, the distribution of Moorhen in the London area is much the same as during the breeding season.

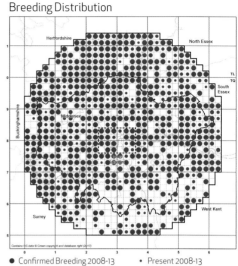

Breeding Distribution

- Confirmed Breeding 2008-13
- Probable Breeding 2008-13
- Possible Breeding 2008-13
- Present 2008-13
- Still on Migration 2008-13

Breeding Change

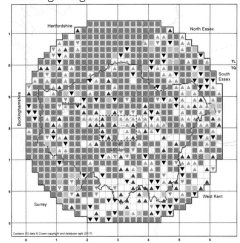

Winter Distribution

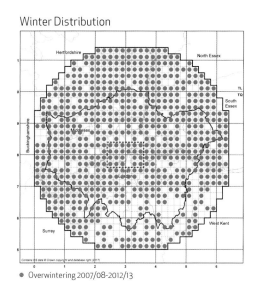

Breeding Distribution Change
- ▲ Recent Gain (new in 2008-13)
- ■ Stable (present in all periods)
- ▼ Old Loss (last occupied 1968-72)
- ▲ Old Gain (new in 1988-94)
- ▣ Variable (absent 1988-94)
- ▼ Recent Loss (last occupied 1988-94)

● Overwintering 2007/08-2012/13

Coot

Fulica atra

Very common breeding resident and winter visitor; green list.

The Coot is an abundant, widespread and familiar species of open water. It is not currently of conservation concern and its population in Britain has shown a long term increase.

Like the Moorhen, the Coot shows a distinct absence from much of the North Downs. Elsewhere, it is clearly associated with areas which have larger areas of open water, such as along river valleys, reservoirs, lakes and gravel pits. A comparison of the maps from the three atlases indicates that this species has expanded its distribution around the main river valleys, perhaps an indication of population growth during this period.

Breeding Distribution

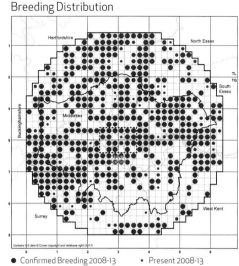

- ● Confirmed Breeding 2008-13
- ● Probable Breeding 2008-13
- ● Possible Breeding 2008-13
- · Present 2008-13
- · Still on Migration 2008-13

Period	Number of Tetrads		
	Evidence of Breeding	Seen Only	Total
Breeding 1968–72	250	45	295
Breeding 1988–94	399	45	444
Breeding 2008–13	448	59	507
Winter 2007/8–2012/13	-	-	478

During the winter, the distribution of Coot in the London area is much the same as during the summer. However, numbers during the winter season are, in places, much higher than in the breeding season, reflecting the influx of birds from Scandinavia, the Baltic States and other parts of northern Europe (Migration Atlas). The highest counts of wintering Coot in the London area made during the atlas timed visits were from the Lee Valley and Brent Reservoir, but high counts can also occur during winter at other large waterbodies, including four-figure counts from two sites in Buckinghamshire: Horton Gravel Pit, with 1,020 on 26th December 2010 and 1,115 on 2nd January 2011, and Wraysbury Gravel Pit, with 1,030 on 15th January 2010.

Breeding Change

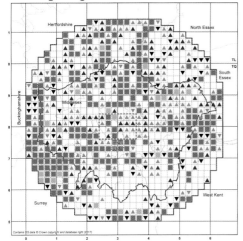

Contains OS data © Crown copyright and database right (2017)

Breeding Distribution Change
- ▲ Recent Gain (new in 2008-13)
- ■ Stable (present in all periods)
- ▼ Old Loss (last occupied 1968-72)
- ▲ Old Gain (new in 1988-94)
- ■ Variable (absent 1988-94)
- ▼ Recent Loss (last occupied 1988-94)

Winter Distribution

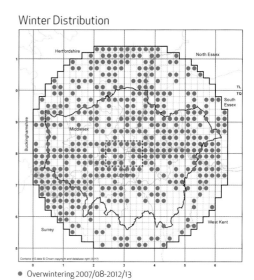

Contains OS data © Crown copyright and database right (2017)

- ● Overwintering 2007/08-2012/13

Avocet

Recurvirostra avosetta

Occasional breeder and scarce visitor; amber list.

The Avocet was a rare species in Britain at the start of the twentieth century but returned to breed during the Second World War (Cadbury & Olney 1978), and has since successfully increased in both population and range.

It normally breeds in shallow coastal lagoons and did not feature in the species accounts for either of the first two London atlases. However, it does appear in the second atlas in a section providing short accounts of species which nested after the end of the atlas survey period: a pair bred in 1996 at Kempton Park Reservoir, successfully raising one young. This was the only breeding in the London area until 2005, when three pairs nested at Rainham Marshes, with four pairs nesting the following year. One pair was successful in both years.

During the current atlas period, two confirmed nesting attempts were made, both at different sites: London Wetland Centre (2008) and the Lower Thames Marshes (2013). In the first instance the nests were deserted after eggs had definitely been laid. Nest desertion was also suspected in the second case but an adult was seen with a juvenile in August so this attempt may have been successful (LBR). A pair was also at Rainham Marshes during the breeding season in 2008. Other birds were recorded as present at several other sites where they were likely to be passage migrants.

In order to withhold the identity of the site, the Lower Thames breeding record is not mapped.

Period	Number of Tetrads		
	Evidence of Breeding	Seen Only	Total
Breeding 2008–13	3	5	8
Winter 2007/8–2012/13	-	-	10

During winter, the Avocet is found on estuaries where it sometimes forms large flocks. In the London area, it has occasionally been found along the Thames in small numbers. In recent years, West Thurrock Marshes has been a regular wintering site and the Avocet flock here has increased substantially in size in recent years. A count of 71 during an atlas timed count on Christmas day in 2010 was a record count for London at the time. This was subsequently beaten just two months later by a count of 80 at the Queen Elizabeth II Bridge, and then by 82 at West Thurrock in February 2012 (LBR).

Breeding Distribution

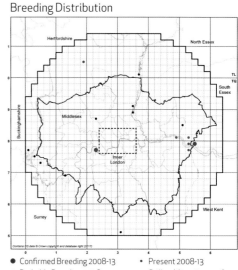

- ● Confirmed Breeding 2008-13
- ● Probable Breeding 2008-13
- ● Possible Breeding 2008-13
- • Present 2008-13
- • Still on Migration 2008-13

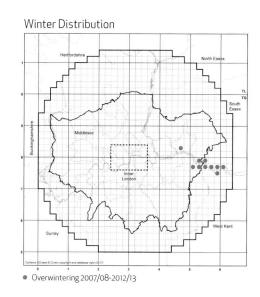

Winter Distribution

Overwintering 2007/08-2012/13

Oystercatcher

Haematopus ostralegus

Localised breeding resident, passage migrant and winter visitor; amber list.

Formerly almost restricted to coasts, the Oystercatcher colonised inland wetland sites during the 1970s and 1980s; a period of population growth (Gibbons *et al.*, 1993). In England, the breeding range and population continues to grow (National Atlas). The Oystercatcher is amber listed because the UK population represents more than a fifth of the total European population (Eaton *et al.*, 2015).

In line with the national trend, the Oystercatcher was first recorded breeding in the London area, at Rainham, in 1971 (Self). This coincided with the first atlas period. By the time of the second atlas, this species had expanded its breeding distribution along the Thames Estuary as far upstream as Thamesmead and breeding was also attempted at two gravel pits; however numbers were low, up to five pairs per year. The expansion has continued, with breeding behaviour observed in the Lee and Colne Valleys, and several other wetland sites during the current atlas period. Despite the expanded distribution, the number of pairs successfully breeding has remained low.

Period	Number of Tetrads		
	Evidence of Breeding	Seen Only	Total
Breeding 1968–72	2	1	3
Breeding 1988–94	9	5	14
Breeding 2008–13	21	35	56
Winter 2007/8–2012/13	-	-	35

The distribution in the London area in winter is much the same as during the breeding season, although not so extensive along the Lee and Colne Valleys and more concentrated on the Thames Estuary. This is in line with the national picture: most inland breeding Oystercatchers leave their breeding sites and move to the coast in winter, although in recent years some have started returning to breeding sites as early as February (National Atlas).

Breeding Distribution

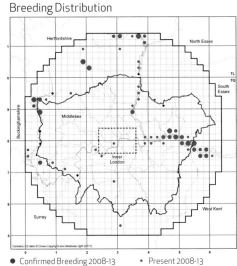

- ● Confirmed Breeding 2008-13
- ● Probable Breeding 2008-13
- ● Possible Breeding 2008-13
- • Present 2008-13
- • Still on Migration 2008-13

Breeding Change

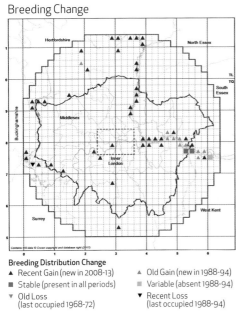

Winter Distribution

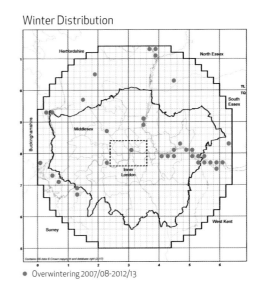

- ● Overwintering 2007/08-2012/13

Breeding Distribution Change
- ▲ Recent Gain (new in 2008-13)
- ■ Stable (present in all periods)
- ▼ Old Loss
  (last occupied 1968-72)
- ▲ Old Gain (new in 1988-94)
- ■ Variable (absent 1988-94)
- ▼ Recent Loss
  (last occupied 1988-94)

Golden Plover

Pluvialis apricaria

Regular winter visitor; amber list.

The Golden Plover is a breeding bird of the uplands which winters in the lowlands and on the coast. The majority of the population which winters in Britain breeds overseas (Migration Atlas). It is on the amber list because of the international importance of the population which winters in Britain.

London and the area to the south have some of the lowest densities of wintering Golden Plover in Britain (National Atlas). However, it is present in the London area as a winter visitor, associated mainly with farmland in Hertfordshire, the Thames Estuary and the Lee and Colne Valleys. The flocks encountered during the atlas timed counts were mostly of less than 100 birds but three larger counts were made in Hertfordshire, including one of 1,100 (at TL21A). Contemporary records include flocks of 2,500 birds in this county although most flocks are much smaller than this (LBR).

Small numbers of non-breeding birds were also recorded during the breeding season in this atlas period. These records certainly relate to passage migrants on their way to breeding grounds in the uplands and beyond. These birds were most strongly associated with the Thames Estuary.

Breeding season tetrads: 10

Winter season tetrads: 58

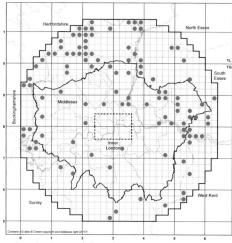

Winter Distribution

● Overwintering 2007/08-2012/13

Grey Plover

Pluvialis squatarola

Passage migrant and scarce winter visitor; amber list.

The Grey Plover is a migratory species with a circum-global distribution, breeding in high northern latitudes and wintering further south (BirdLife). The birds which winter in Britain breed in the tundra in Russia (Migration Atlas). Birds which winter further south also pass through Britain on their way to and from breeding grounds during the spring and autumn. Winter habitat is very much coastal but, when on migration, inland wetland sites are also used. Grey Plover is on the amber list because of the international importance of the population that winters in Britain.

The Thames Estuary as a whole supports internationally important numbers of Grey Plover during the winter and this is reflected in our area; most of the occupied tetrads were along the Thames Estuary as far upstream as Woolwich. Whilst this species can form large flocks, it is more often seen alone or in small groups. Some individual birds may return to use and defend the same winter feeding areas from year to year (Townshend 1985).

Grey Plover is regular in the Thames Estuary, including at Rainham Marshes, where peak winter counts are normally around 20, with small numbers also wintering elsewhere in our area along the Thames. The other two tetrads where this species was recorded contain a large gravel pit or reservoir. During fieldwork for the breeding season, migrating birds were recorded in similar locations to those in winter. The London Wetland Centre provided the closest occupied tetrad to Inner London, albeit briefly.

Breeding season tetrads: 13

Winter season tetrads: 18

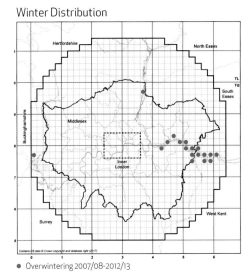

Winter Distribution

● Overwintering 2007/08-2012/13

Lapwing
Vanellus vanellus

Widespread breeding species, common winter visitor;
red list.

Nationally, the Lapwing population is undergoing a steep decline,
associated with changing farming practice, and a range contraction to the
east. As a consequence of the decline, this species is on the red list.

The Lapwing is a farmland and wetland bird which strongly influences its
distribution in the London area, being principally found in low-lying areas
and river valleys in the green belt. Interestingly, this species also bred in
Bushy, Richmond and Hampton Court Parks, as well as other urban green
spaces, when parts were ploughed for food production in the 1940s (Self).

A decline in numbers was reported in the first atlas and again in the
second. Despite the decline, evidence of breeding was recorded in a
similar number of tetrads in both atlases. The distribution is remarkably
similar in the current atlas, although some gaps seem to be enlarging,
notably on the North Downs and in parts of Essex.

The London area and the south-east now have one of the lowest
population densities for this species in Britain (National Atlas). During the
breeding season, fewer than 10 birds were counted in most of the tetrads
where this species was encountered. Larger numbers still breed at some
sites, including Rainham Marshes, Beddington Farmlands and the London
Wetland Centre, but some of the other larger counts may relate to flocks
of non-breeding or post-breeding individuals.

Period	Number of Tetrads		
	Evidence of Breeding	Seen Only	Total
Breeding 1968–72	179	123	302
Breeding 1988–94	193	134	327
Breeding 2008–13	153	73	226
Winter 2007/8–2012/13	-	-	338

The winter distribution of Lapwing in the London area is much the same
as the breeding distribution, though the arrival of continental birds in late
summer and autumn (Migration Atlas) means that more birds are present
in our area at this time of year.

Winter flocks recorded during the atlas period during timed counts were
mostly fewer than 150 with the only timed counts over 400 coming from
the Thames Estuary around Rainham. Lapwing was much more numerous
and widespread in the area during the winter in the last century. Referring
to the 1950s, the LNHS (1964) reported that "For nine months of the year
[the Lapwing] occurs in flocks of 1,000 or more, commonly frequenting
agricultural land...". Other counts undertaken during the current atlas
period show that it is still possible to see flocks of Lapwing comprising
1,000 or more birds but these now occur almost exclusively in the Lower
Thames area.

Breeding Distribution

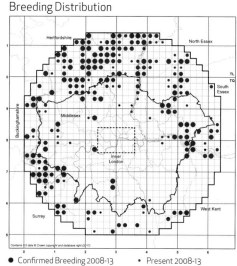

● Confirmed Breeding 2008-13   • Present 2008-13
● Probable Breeding 2008-13   • Still on Migration 2008-13
● Possible Breeding 2008-13

Breeding Change

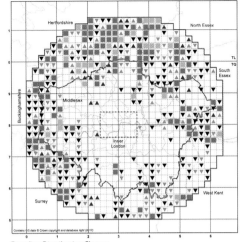

Breeding Distribution Change

▲ Recent Gain (new in 2008-13)　　▲ Old Gain (new in 1988-94)

■ Stable (present in all periods)　　■ Variable (absent 1988-94)

▼ Old Loss
(last occupied 1968-72)　　▼ Recent Loss
(last occupied 1988-94)

Winter Distribution

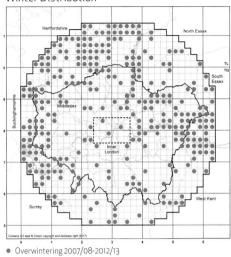

● Overwintering 2007/08-2012/13

Little Ringed Plover

Charadrius dubius

Breeding summer visitor and passage migrant; green list.

The Little Ringed Plover is a relatively recent colonist, with the first breeding in Britain occurring in 1938. It is a specialist breeder on bare sand and gravel which has been able to take advantage of gravel pits and similar sites, with a consequent effect on its distribution and population.

The first breeding in the London area occurred in 1944 (Self). By the time of the first atlas, this species had colonised most areas offering suitable habitat, notably along the Lee and Colne Valleys and the Thames Estuary. By the second atlas period, there had been further expansion to new gravel pits, notably in Hertfordshire, but with some losses at older gravel pits. Broadly, this pattern persists although the number of breeding pairs during the current atlas period may be around half of what they were in the early 1990s. The London area now holds about 2% to 4% of the British population.

So that the breeding sites cannot be identified, a sector level summary is shown for the breeding season instead of a tetrad map.

Breeding Distribution

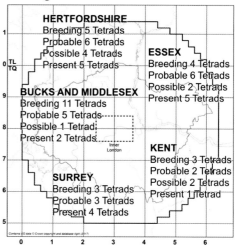

Period	Number of Tetrads		
	Evidence of Breeding	Seen Only	Total
Breeding 1968–72	61	8	69
Breeding 1988–94	80	34	114
Breeding 2008–13	48	26	74

Little Ringed Plover is a migratory species which does not winter in our area.

Ringed Plover
Charadrius hiaticula

Localised breeder and winter visitor, common passage migrant; amber list.

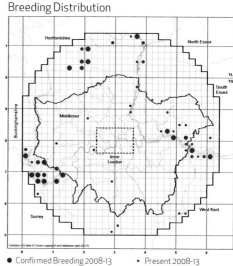

Breeding Distribution

- ● Confirmed Breeding 2008-13
- ● Probable Breeding 2008-13
- ● Possible Breeding 2008-13
- • Present 2008-13
- • Still on Migration 2008-13

The Ringed Plover is more strongly associated with the coast than the Little Ringed Plover but the Ringed Plover also breeds inland at the same type of man-made site; gravel pits, reservoirs, etc. The Ringed Plover is amber listed because of recent declines in its population.

The Ringed Plover is a recent re-colonist of the London area, with the first modern record of breeding in 1957 (Self). It has breed in most years since then. At the time of the first atlas, this species was associated with three distinct areas; the Thames Estuary, the Lee Valley and Wraysbury. An expansion was evident in the second atlas. This was centred on the original localities but also included new sites, particularly around the Colne and Lee Valleys. By the current atlas period, there appears to have been a marked contraction in occupied tetrads in the Lee Valley but not around Wraysbury and the Thames Estuary. The number of breeding pairs per year mirrors the expansion and contraction in occupied tetrads. In the first and this atlas periods the total number of pairs was probably fewer than 10, with a peak of at least 34 pairs during the second atlas in 1994 (Hewlett *et al.*).

Period	Number of Tetrads		
	Evidence of Breeding	Seen Only	Total
Breeding 1968–72	12	0	12
Breeding 1988–94	45	26	71
Breeding 2008–13	22	29	51
Winter 2007/8–2012/13	-	-	19

Ringed Plover has a more coastal distribution during the winter nationally and this is reflected in the London area, with winter records concentrated on the Thames Estuary, plus scattered occurrences at or near to those locations where this species was observed during the breeding season.

Breeding Change

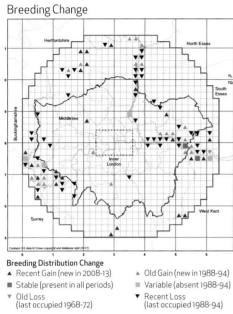

Breeding Distribution Change
- ▲ Recent Gain (new in 2008-13)
- ■ Stable (present in all periods)
- ▼ Old Loss
  (last occupied 1968-72)
- ▲ Old Gain (new in 1988-94)
- ■ Variable (absent 1988-94)
- ▼ Recent Loss
  (last occupied 1988-94)

Winter Distribution

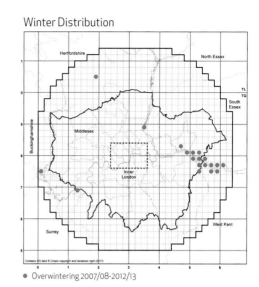

● Overwintering 2007/08-2012/13

Curlew

Numenius arquata

Winter visitor and passage migrant; red list.

The Curlew breeds in Britain mainly in moorland, marsh and other open habitats in northern England, eastern Scotland and central Wales (National Atlas). Much of this population migrates south or west for the winter, while birds which breed in similar habitats in Scandinavia and northern Europe make their way to Britain, and elsewhere (Migration Atlas). During the winter, this species is very much a bird of estuaries and mudflats, as well as adjacent wet grassland and arable fields.

The Curlew is a passage migrant and winter visitor to our area. The majority of the birds wintering in south-east England, and hence in our area, are birds which breed on the continent (Migration Atlas). During the 1980s, the Curlew stopped wintering in our area for a brief period, but started doing so again in the 1990s (Self). The Thames Estuary as a whole is of national importance for this species, supporting around 4,000 birds and, as would be expected, most of the records for this species during the current atlas period were from the Thames, as far upstream as the confluence with the River Lea. Rainham typically has the highest numbers reported annually (usually up to 30), though the highest count during atlas fieldwork was 33 at West Thurrock on 4th January 2008. There are scattered records elsewhere, often associated with the main wetland sites, such as the London Wetland Centre and the Lee Valley. The records away from the Thames usually involve birds which are present for a short time only, often just one day or less.

Breeding season tetrads: 20

Winter season tetrads: 52

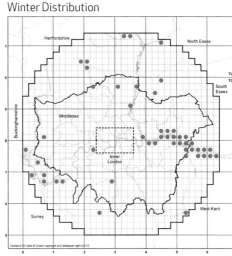

Winter Distribution

● Overwintering 2007/08-2012/13

Black-tailed Godwit

Limosa limosa

Passage migrant and winter visitor; red list.

The Black-tailed Godwit is a rare breeding species in Britain. Birds which breed in Britain and Europe, of the race *limosa*, winter in southern Europe and Africa, while most of the birds observed in Britain in winter have come from Iceland, of the race *islandica* (Migration Atlas). It is a wetland bird, breeding in open marshy areas and wintering mainly in estuaries and on the coast. It is on the red list due to historical population declines suffered by the *limosa* race, although the *islandica* race is increasing.

The Black-tailed Godwit has a very straightforward distribution in the London area during the winter, being found almost exclusively on the Thames downstream of Woolwich. The Thames Estuary as a whole is internationally important for this species, supporting over 5,000 birds in winter (WeBS). Most of these, though, are outside our area. Rainham is the main site for this species in our area, with the highest count during atlas fieldwork being 568 on 19th January 2012, made from the opposite side of the river at Crayford Marshes. Adjoining areas of the estuary can also support good numbers, especially Crossness and Dagenham Riverside. This species does occasionally occur away from the coast, especially during migration periods, as illustrated on the map. These tend to be small groups or single birds which do not remain long.

Breeding season tetrads: 19

Winter season tetrads: 26

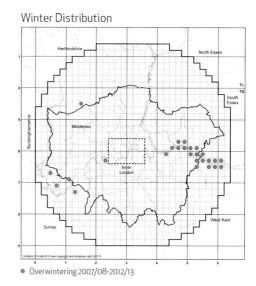

Winter Distribution

● Overwintering 2007/08-2012/13

Bar-tailed Godwit

Limosa lapponica

Passage migrant. Scarce in winter; amber list.

The Bar-tailed Godwit population which breeds in Fennoscandia and Russia winters around the coast of Britain, with only occasional birds occurring inland (National Atlas).

The Thames Estuary is an internationally important wintering area for this species (WeBS) and the second most important area for this species in Britain, after the Wash. However, this species does not normally move upriver as far as the London area, and mainly occurs here on spring and autumn passage. Most winter records are of birds which stay for a short period, often single birds, but there is a suggestion that winter records may be becoming more regular (LBR), and the species does occasionally linger for longer periods along the part of the Thames in our area. For example, there were one or two birds present there in December 2010 and up to three from January to March 2013. The highest winter count in the London area during the current atlas period was 16 at West Thurrock on 5th February 2012.

Breeding season tetrads: 11

Winter season tetrads: 12

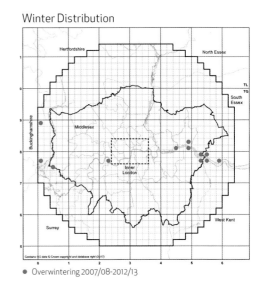

Winter Distribution

● Overwintering 2007/08-2012/13

Knot

Calidris canutus

Passage migrant and rare winter visitor; amber list.

The Knot has a circum-global distribution, breeding in the high Arctic, with most of the birds wintering in Britain being from the *islandica* race from Greenland and eastern Canada (Migration Atlas). The species forms large flocks in winter on coastal mudflats.

The Thames Estuary is an internationally important wintering site for this species (WeBS). Small numbers did winter on the Lower Thames Marshes in our area from the 1970s to the 1980s (Self), but nowadays the wintering flocks do not normally move far enough upriver to be within the London area, with just a few birds recorded here each year during the winter, usually present for a brief time only. These include a flock of 29 at Rainham Marshes on 27th January 2010. There were no records of birds over-wintering within the London area during the current atlas period. The species is more widespread during spring and autumn passage, when birds stop over for short periods at wetland sites. Passage largely falls outside the winter survey period; however one or two late autumn or early spring passage birds account for the occupied tetrads shown on the map away from the Thames.

Winter season tetrads: 11

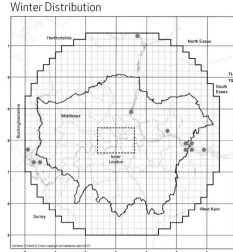

Winter Distribution

● Overwintering 2007/08-2012/13

Dunlin

Calidris alpina

Common passage migrant and winter visitor; amber list.

The Dunlin is a migratory species with a circum-global distribution, breeding in high northern latitudes and wintering further south. Most of the birds which winter in Britain breed in the taiga and tundra of northern Finland and Norway and western Siberia, while birds which breed in Greenland and Iceland, as well birds which breed in northern Britain, pass through when migrating further south for the winter and again on their return in spring (Migration Atlas). In winter, Dunlin typically form large flocks which feed on estuarine mudflats. Dunlin is amber-listed due to declines in the wintering population.

The Thames Estuary is internationally important for wintering Dunlin and this is reflected in the atlas map with this species being recorded as far upstream as the confluence with the River Lea. The larger flocks, though, are typically found further downstream at Crossness, Rainham, West Thurrock and Stone where counts of over 1,000 regularly occur. The largest counts made during the atlas period were 3,000 at West Thurrock on 3rd January 2009 and 3,400 at the same site on 3rd February 2012 (LBR).

The Dunlin is also found away from the Thames in our area; typically birds which stay for short periods, during the spring and autumn migration periods and in smaller flocks or singly. The atlas map clearly show that these records are associated with larger expanses of water such as gravel pits and reservoirs. The Lee and Colne Valleys produced most records but this species was also found at wetlands elsewhere, including the London Wetland Centre.

Breeding season tetrads: 23

Winter season tetrads: 46

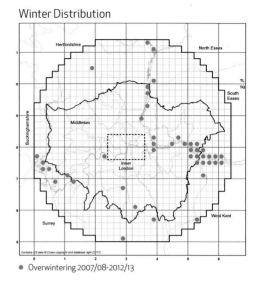

Winter Distribution

● Overwintering 2007/08-2012/13

Ruff

Philomachus pugnax

Passage migrant and scarce winter visitor; red list.

Ruff is a scarce breeding bird in Britain, but is common in Fennoscandia and Russia (Migration Atlas). Most of the population winters in Africa (Migration Atlas), but around 800 birds winter in the UK (Musgrove *et al.*, 2011).

The Rainham Marshes area is the only regular wintering site for this species in the London area, albeit in very small numbers with just two to four birds present most winters and up to six from January to March 2010. It can also be found at other nearby Thames sites. The Ruff is occasionally recorded elsewhere during spring and autumn passage.

Breeding season tetrads: 5

Winter season tetrads: 19

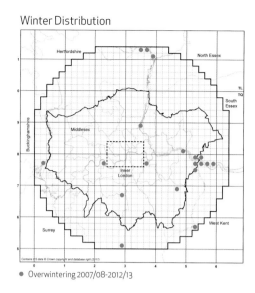

Winter Distribution

● Overwintering 2007/08-2012/13

Common Sandpiper

Actitis hypoleucos

Common passage migrant and localised winter visitor; amber list.

The Common Sandpiper is a migratory species which breeds right across Europe, including Northern Britain, and Asia, except the far north. It winters mainly to the south of the Tropic of Cancer, however, some winter in southern Britain, parts of Western Europe and North Africa (BirdLife). During the breeding season it is primarily a bird of fast-moving rivers and streams with exposed shingle banks. In Britain, this means that it is primarily a breeding species of the north and west.

During the last century, a pair bred in our area in 1910, with small numbers breeding, or attempting to breed, in the 1950s, 1960s and 1980s (Self). However, there have been no recent breeding records. The records of this bird during the breeding season in the current atlas period are therefore all considered to be passage migrants moving through the area on spring migration, which occurs during April and May. During these months, this species can turn up anywhere that there is water, with records from many of the usual wetland sites. This species also passes through our area during autumn passage, when numbers can be considerably higher; however, this falls outside both of the atlas survey periods.

Winter Distribution

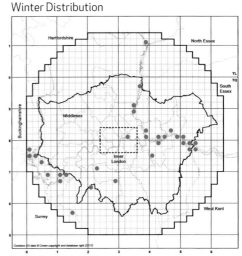

● Overwintering 2007/08-2012/13

Period	Number of Tetrads		
	Evidence of Breeding	Seen Only	Total
Breeding 1968–72	4	10	14
Breeding 1988–94	1	28	29
Breeding 2008–13	0	0	0
Winter 2007/8–2012/13	-	-	31

The winter distribution map shows an association with large wetland sites, with most records coming from the Thames Estuary and the major reservoirs (in west London and the Lee Valley), plus a few records from elsewhere. Only a small number of birds remain in our area at this time, with records usually coming from between 10 and 20 sites each winter. The maximum number recorded during atlas fieldwork from within one tetrad was five at Barking Bay in November 2012.

Green Sandpiper
Tringa ochropus

Widespread winter visitor and passage migrant; amber list.

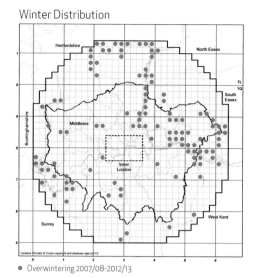

Winter Distribution

● Overwintering 2007/08-2012/13

The main breeding range for the Green Sandpiper is a broad swathe across Scandinavia, northern Europe and Asia, where it lays its eggs in the abandoned nests of other birds in trees (BirdLife). Although very small numbers breed in Scotland, it is primarily a winter migrant to the British Isles, with a preference for the lowlands in the south and east (National Atlas). At this time, it is generally associated with small bodies of fresh water.

In our area, there is a peak in numbers during the autumn migration (June to October) with a few birds over-wintering until March, followed by spring migration (March and April). This pattern accounts for the presence of this species in both the breeding and winter seasons. The principal localities for this species are the main river valleys, associated gravel pits and reservoirs, and the marshland around the Thames Estuary. However, it can also be found on smaller waterways and ponds where other waders apart from Snipe are usually absent, for example, the Mardyke in Essex and Gores Brook in Dagenham. The maximum number recorded in one tetrad during atlas fieldwork was 11, at both Beddington Farmlands (January 2009) and Crayford Marshes (February 2010), which reflects the habit of this species to occur singly or in small flocks.

Breeding season tetrads: 47

Winter season tetrads: 116

Redshank

Tringa totanus

Common winter visitor and passage migrant, declining and localised breeder; amber list.

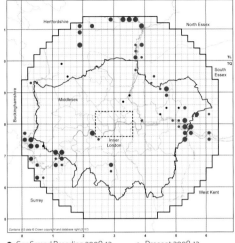

- ● Confirmed Breeding 2008-13
- ● Probable Breeding 2008-13
- ● Possible Breeding 2008-13
- ● Present 2008-13
- ● Still on Migration 2008-13

The Redshank breeds at inland freshwater marshes and coastal saltmarshes while its winter habitat is more coastal (National Atlas). The breeding population is in decline (BBS) and there has been a corresponding range contraction (National Atlas). The Essex and north Kent coasts have relatively high breeding densities of this species for mainland Britain, as do Lancashire and the Pennines. High breeding densities also occur on the Scottish Islands (National Atlas).

In the first London atlas period, Redshank was recorded breeding principally in the Thames marshes east of Woolwich, with other populations in the Darent, Mole, Colne and Lee Valleys. By the time of the second atlas, the populations in the Darent and Mole Valleys had gone but this was offset by new breeding locations at other inland sites, especially in the Colne Valley, and at Beddington, Hogsmill and Perry Oaks Sewage Treatment Works (the last of which was subsequently demolished for the construction of Terminal 5 of Heathrow). The picture in the current atlas period is of a similar, but reduced, distribution. This is a reflection of the long-term decline in the breeding population of this species in our area (and elsewhere). The current number, perhaps 20 to 30 known breeding pairs (LBR), mostly on the Lower Thames Marshes, is around half of what it was in the1990s, when it reached at least 61 pairs (Self). Breeding has recently been established at the London Wetland Centre, however.

Period	Number of Tetrads		
	Evidence of Breeding	Seen Only	Total
Breeding 1968–72	38	12	50
Breeding 1988–94	55	38	93
Breeding 2008–13	31	24	55
Winter 2007/8–2012/13	-	-	58

During the winter, migrants arrive primarily from Iceland, with some passing through and some of the birds that breed in Britain also migrating further south (Migration Atlas). The net effect is that the population of Redshank in Britain more than doubles in winter and there is a corresponding increase in the number of Redshank in our area during this season. However, the Redshank distribution in our area barely changes during the winter and by far the majority occur in the Thames Estuary, which is of international importance for this species. Crossness, Rainham and West Thurrock marshes regularly support a few hundred (LBR). This is about 10% of the whole Thames Estuary population. The highest count in this area during atlas fieldwork was 510 at Crayford Marshes in November 2011, followed by 500 at West Thurrock in December 2008.

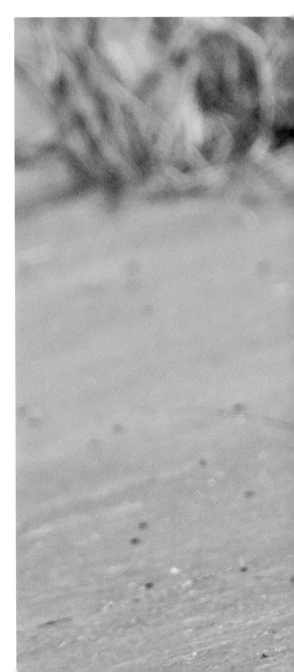

Breeding Change

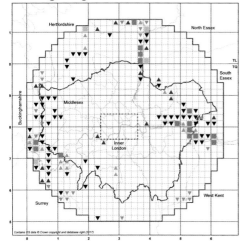

Winter Distribution

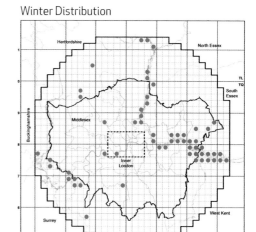

Breeding Distribution Change
- ▲ Recent Gain (new in 2008-13)
- ■ Stable (present in all periods)
- ▼ Old Loss
  (last occupied 1968-72)
- ▲ Old Gain (new in 1988-94)
- ■ Variable (absent 1988-94)
- ▼ Recent Loss
  (last occupied 1988-94)

● Overwintering 2007/08-2012/13

Greenshank

Tringa nebularia

Regular passage migrant, rare in winter; amber list.

Greenshank breeds mainly in Fennoscandia and northern Russia (BirdLife), with a small proportion of the population also breeding in the north of Scotland and on the Western Isles (National Atlas). In winter, some birds which breed in Scotland are believed to move to the west of Britain and to Ireland (Migration Atlas), while most of the birds that breed elsewhere winter to the south of the Tropic of Cancer (BirdLife). So, the species is more abundant in winter in the west of the British Isles and much scarcer on the east coast of Britain (National Atlas).

Consequently, it is mainly observed as a spring and autumn passage migrant in the London area, with the birds we see most likely to be those which breed in Scandinavia (Migration Atlas). In spring, most birds pass through our area in April and May, and this species was therefore observed during the atlas breeding season survey visits with most records coming from the lower Thames Marshes and west London waterbodies, and additional records from other well-watched wetland sites such as the London Wetland Centre and Beddington Farmlands.

However, the Greenshank does occasionally spend the winter in the London area, with overwintering birds previously recorded at Tyttenhanger Gravel Pits, from 2000/01 to 2003/04, and Rainham Marshes in 2002/03 and 2003/04 (Self).

During this atlas period, there were no instances where Greenshank was confirmed to overwinter although one individual spent two weeks at Walton Reservoir in February 2009, and another was at Island Barn Reservoir from 24th December 2011 to 2nd January 2012. Other sightings came from a further five sites (from four new tetrads), two in November and three in December. All of these additional records were observed on a single day only and presumably related to late migrant birds. Then, in the winter 2013/14, after the end of the current atlas period, a bird overwintered at Crossness (LBR).

Breeding season tetrads: 23

Winter season tetrads: 6

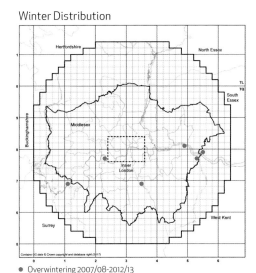

Winter Distribution

● Overwintering 2007/08-2012/13

Spotted Redshank

Tringa erythropus

Scarce passage migrant; amber list.

Spotted Redshank is predominantly a passage migrant in Britain, visiting *en route* from Scandinavia and northern Russia to its wintering grounds in Africa (Migration Atlas). Small numbers winter in western Europe, including around 100 birds wintering in Great Britain (Musgrove *et al.*, 2013), with a slow increase in wintering numbers being observed since the 1980s (National Atlas).

It is scarce in the London area, usually only observed on passage, with an average of fewer than ten a year since 2000 (Self). Such birds account for the occupied tetrads in the west of our area that are shown on the distribution map. However, during the atlas period, a single bird wintered in the Crayford Marshes and Rainham Marshes area in both 2011/12 and 2012/13. It seems likely that this was the same returning individual, and a record of a single bird flying over Dartford Marshes on 2nd December 2010 (LBR) suggests a possibility that it may have also been present in our area during the preceding winter.

Winter season tetrads: 5

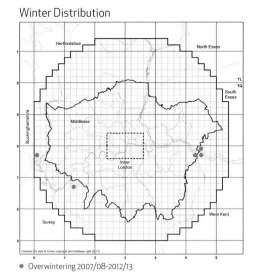

Winter Distribution

● Overwintering 2007/08-2012/13

Turnstone

Arenaria interpres

Passage migrant and localised winter visitor; amber list.

The Turnstone is a winter visitor to Britain, being found around the whole of the British coast (National Atlas), with most birds originating from Canada and Greenland (Migration Atlas). The species is highly site faithful in winter with birds staying in stable flocks and often moving only short distances, particularly if food supplies remain stable (Migration Atlas).

In the London area, Turnstone is a scarce passage migrant and winter visitor, with very small numbers wintering along the lower Thames, where numbers since the year 2000 have varied from two to 23 individuals (Self). Wintering records during the atlas period were all from here, with the furthest upriver from Creekmouth (Barking). Spring passage occurs from late April to early June and autumn passage occurs from mid-July through to September. During these periods, small numbers stop briefly at large inland waterbodies, such as Staines Reservoir, as well as the Thames Estuary.

Breeding season tetrads: 15

Winter season tetrads: 8

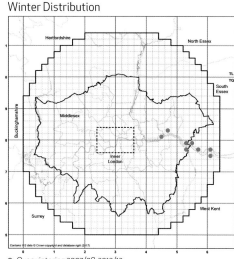

Winter Distribution

● Overwintering 2007/08-2012/13

Jack Snipe

Lymnocryptes minimus

Widespread but elusive winter visitor and passage migrant; green list.

The Jack Snipe is a migratory species which breeds in the taiga of northern Europe, Scandinavia and Siberia and winters further south, including in Britain (BirdLife). Like the Snipe, this species is associated with wetlands, including freshwater swamps and marshes. It is nearly always solitary. In Britain, it shows a distinct preference for the lowlands including those in south-east England (National Atlas).

The winter distribution of Jack Snipe in the London area broadly mirrors that of Common Snipe, except it was recorded in fewer tetrads and in smaller numbers. A few individuals, either wintering birds which have stayed later than usual or passage migrants, were also observed in similar locations during the breeding season. Being highly secretive, Jack Snipe can be very difficult to observe during fieldwork unless flushed, though birds can sometimes become more visible during cold weather. The difficulty in surveying this species is perhaps reflected in the fact that most of the records are from very well-watched areas, and it is likely to be more widespread than the map suggests.

Breeding season tetrads: 10

Winter season tetrads: 86

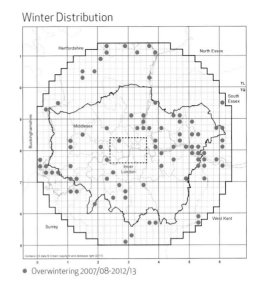

Winter Distribution

● Overwintering 2007/08-2012/13

Woodcock

Scolopax rusticola

Declining breeding species, widespread passage migrant and winter visitor; red list.

The Woodcock breeds in damp woodland and heath, and winters in much the same habitat. The national picture is a decline and retreat into areas with extensive woodland, which it favours (Heward *et al.*, 2015).

The London area is one of the areas from which the Woodcock is retreating and this is clearly shown by comparison of the three London atlases. Taken together, the first and second atlases show breeding clusters in seven broad areas; (i) around Malden Rushett, (ii) Kent/Surrey border, (iii) around Brentwood, (iv) Epping Forest (second atlas only), (v) the Hertfordshire woodlands, (vi) around Uxbridge/Ruislip, and (vii) Richmond Park (first atlas only). Data collected for the current atlas, and contemporary reports, suggest that only four of these populations remain and, even at these, the number of occupied tetrads has diminished.

There may have been as few as ten to 20 pairs breeding annually in our area at the start of the current atlas period (LBR), although this may be an under-estimate as the species is difficult to monitor. The decline has apparently continued over the course of the atlas period. For example, three roding males were recorded in Epping Forest in 2008 and 2–4 in 2009 (LBR) but there were no records of this species in Epping Forest in 2012 and 2013, even though surveys took place (*per* ELBF). Indeed, potential breeding records came from only two other sites in both 2012

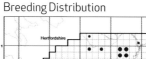

Breeding Distribution

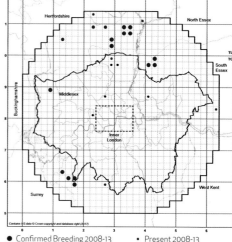

- ● Confirmed Breeding 2008-13
- ● Probable Breeding 2008-13
- ● Possible Breeding 2008-13
- • Present 2008-13
- • Still on Migration 2008-13

Breeding Change

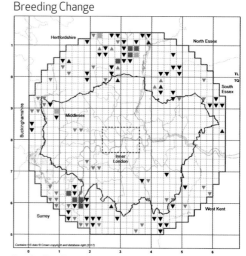

Breeding Distribution Change
- ▲ Recent Gain (new in 2008-13)
- ■ Stable (present in all periods)
- ▼ Old Loss (last occupied 1968-72)
- ▲ Old Gain (new in 1988-94)
- ■ Variable (absent 1988-94)
- ▼ Recent Loss (last occupied 1988-94)

Period	Number of Tetrads		
	Evidence of Breeding	Seen Only	Total
Breeding 1968–72	49	31	80
Breeding 1988–94	48	22	70
Breeding 2008–13	14	8	22
Winter 2007/8–2012/13	-	-	250

and 2013 (LBR).

In the winter, the resident Woodcock population is joined by migrants that breed in Scandinavia and northern Europe. This is reflected in the much wider occurrence of this species in our area (and elsewhere) during the winter. When on migration, this bird can turn up almost anywhere. The same is true during periods of severe weather, when the birds search for better feeding conditions. Indeed, there are a few records each year of exhausted birds in highly urban environments.

Winter Distribution

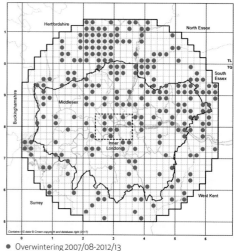

- ● Overwintering 2007/08-2012/13

Snipe
Gallinago gallinago

Common winter visitor and passage migrant, former scarce breeder; amber list.

The Snipe is associated with freshwater wetland habitats. Nationally, the breeding distribution of Snipe appears to be retreating to the north and west, with London and the south-east having some of the lowest densities of Snipe in the whole of Britain (National Atlas).

All three London atlases show a similar pattern in the breeding season with this species concentrated in six distinct locations, with five of these outside the built-up area. These are the Lee Valley, the Colne Valley, Thames Estuary marshes, around Tyttenhanger Gravel Pits, Sevenoaks and Beddington Sewage Farm. During the first atlas period, Snipe was recorded definitely breeding in seven tetrads, with breeding thought probable in a further 11 tetrads. In the second atlas, breeding was confirmed for one location, Rye Meads, and evidence of breeding was reported from another 19 tetrads. In total, there were estimated to be around four breeding pairs in the whole of the London area each year during the early 1990s (Self). There were just two tetrads where breeding was recorded as probable during the current atlas period. These were Kempton Nature Reserve, where a 'drumming' male was recorded in April 2009, and Longford Moor, where an apparently territorial bird was present in late May 2010. Despite this limited evidence of breeding activity, breeding has not been confirmed for this species in the London area so far in the 21st century (Self), and it is unlikely that this species currently breeds in the London area.

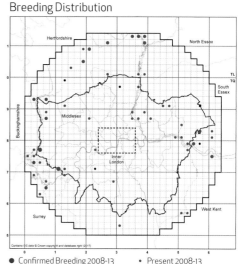

Breeding Distribution

- ● Confirmed Breeding 2008-13
- ● Probable Breeding 2008-13
- ● Possible Breeding 2008-13
- · Present 2008-13
- · Still on Migration 2008-13

Period	Number of Tetrads		
	Evidence of Breeding	Seen Only	Total
Breeding 1968–72	18	32	50
Breeding 1988–94	20	49	69
Breeding 2008–13	2	52	54
Winter 2007/8–2012/13	-	-	235

Some of the population that breeds in Britain remains in winter, to be joined by birds which breed in Iceland, northern Europe and Scandinavia, while others migrate south (Migration Atlas). The net result is that the winter population in Britain is more than ten times the size of the breeding population (Musgrove *et al.*, 2013). This is reflected in the atlas maps. In winter, this species still shows an association with the six areas mentioned above, and clearly avoids the higher and drier ground in the North Downs and Essex, but is otherwise of much wider occurrence than during the breeding season. An interesting element of the distribution is the extent to which this species enters the built-up area during winter. The strong association with wetland habitat is maintained though; these records are typically from parks with wetland features, such as Regent's Park and Hyde Park. Most observations were of fewer than six birds, with a few higher counts, including a count of 75 at Sevenoaks Wildlife Reserve. There are even counts of over 100 at very few sites, for example Rainham and Rye Meads (LBR).

Breeding Change

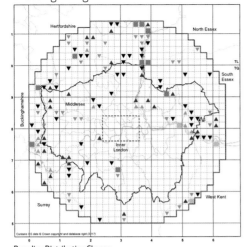

Winter Distribution

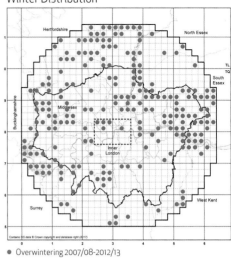

Breeding Distribution Change
- ▲ Recent Gain (new in 2008-13)
- ■ Stable (present in all periods)
- ▼ Old Loss (last occupied 1968-72)
- ▲ Old Gain (new in 1988-94)
- ■ Variable (absent 1988-94)
- ▼ Recent Loss (last occupied 1988-94)

 Overwintering 2007/08-2012/13

Common Tern

Sterna hirundo

Common summer visitor and passage migrant; amber list.

The Common Tern is well known as a long distance migrant with a circum-global distribution, breeding in the northern hemisphere and wintering mainly to the south of the Tropic of Cancer (BirdLife). Those which breed in Britain typically winter along the west coast of Africa and South Africa (Migration Atlas).

The three London atlases chart the rise of the Common Tern as a breeding species in our area. Following the first breeding attempt in 1958, and successful nesting in 1963 (Self), the first atlas shows two main clusters of breeding activity, the first of these in the Lee Valley and the second in the Colne Valley around Staines. There were also isolated records from South Ockendon, Swanscombe Marsh and Sevenoaks Wildlife Reserve. From these localities, the breeding distribution expanded along the Lee and Colne Valleys and, by the time of the second atlas, also encompassed sites along the Thames and reservoirs away from these rivers, including Brent Reservoir. Breeding also occurred in two Inner London tetrads at Shadwell Basin and at Surrey and Canada Water. A critical factor in enabling this range expansion was the provision of nesting rafts at key wetland sites, perhaps coupled with improvements in water quality and consequential supply of fish. In the current atlas period, the breeding distribution had expanded a little further with other wetland sites being used for breeding, including for example, at Richmond Park. However, there has been a decline in the number of breeding pairs reported since the peak in 2001 (Self). The recent arrival of Black-headed Gull as a breeding bird at some sites provides competition for the rafts and may be a factor behind this decline, as the gulls are on territory before the terns have completed their migration back to the British Isles. Gulls took over the rafts at Staines (Self) and have also taken over some rafts in the Lee Valley; the Lee Valley Park conservation team has recently started leaving some rafts covered until just before the terns return in order to ensure they are not already occupied (C. Patrick, *pers. comm.*).

Breeding Distribution

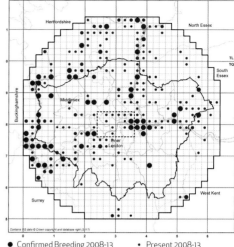

- ● Confirmed Breeding 2008-13
- ● Probable Breeding 2008-13
- ● Possible Breeding 2008-13
- • Present 2008-13
- • Still on Migration 2008-13

Period	Number of Tetrads		
	Evidence of Breeding	Seen Only	Total
Breeding 1968–72	12	3	15
Breeding 1988–94	51	78	129
Breeding 2008–13	58	169	227

Breeding Change

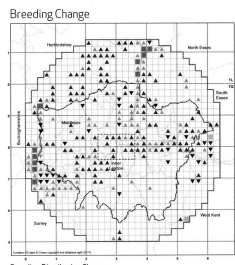

Breeding Distribution Change
▲ Recent Gain (new in 2008-13)   ▲ Old Gain (new in 1988-94)
■ Stable (present in all periods)   ▣ Variable (absent 1988-94)
▼ Old Loss
(last occupied 1968-72)   ▼ Recent Loss
(last occupied 1988-94)

Black-headed Gull

Chroicocephalus ridibundus

Very common winter visitor. Increasing breeder; amber list.

The Black-headed Gull nests at coastal and inland wetland sites, often in large colonies.

There were no breeding colonies of Black-headed Gull in our area during either the first or second atlas periods but this does not tell the full story. During the 1940s, there was a gullery at Perry Oaks Sewage Treatment Works, which peaked at around 300 nests, then declined to nothing by 1965. Another small colony was briefly established in the early 1960s at Maple Cross. These were followed by occasional attempts at breeding in the 1980s and 1990s, culminating in the establishment of a colony at Staines Reservoir in 1997 (Self).

During the current atlas period, the Staines Reservoir colony remained the most substantial breeding colony of this species in our area; with up to 186 pairs recorded (in 2013), nesting on tern rafts. Much smaller numbers, sometimes just one pair, also breed or attempt to breed at a small number of other wetland sites in the London area. However, at some of these sites, numbers have increased very quickly after the initial establishment of the colony; for example Bedfont Lakes Country Park (established 2006; 59 pairs in 2013), Rye Meads (2008; 89), Stocker's Lake (2010; 31) and Amwell Nature Reserve (2011; 40) (LBR).

Breeding Distribution

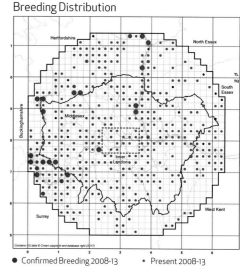

- ● Confirmed Breeding 2008-13
- ● Probable Breeding 2008-13
- ● Possible Breeding 2008-13
- • Present 2008-13
- • Still on Migration 2008-13

Period	Number of Tetrads		
	Evidence of Breeding	Seen Only	Total
Breeding 2008–13	22	369	391
Winter 2007/8–2012/13	-	-	818

During the winter, the Black-headed Gull population in Britain swells considerably due to birds arriving from Iceland, Scandinavia and Northern Europe, with some of the birds that breed in Britain travelling southwards to winter along the European, and, to a lesser extent, West African Atlantic coast (Migration Atlas). The numbers in the London area also increase considerably during this time, with playing fields being a favourite haunt, as well as wetland and coastal areas. As can be seen from the map, this species occurs in pretty much every tetrad during the winter and is generally evenly distributed. However, there are a few sites (up to around 15) where over 2,000 birds can be counted during the winter, with the largest counts typically coming from sites where this species gathers to roost. During the atlas fieldwork, the highest counts were 16,300 at Thames Ditton and 15,000 at Hilfield Park Reservoir. The ubiquity and abundance of this species in the urban area during the winter is a relatively recent phenomenon, beginning with small numbers of birds in the late nineteenth century (Self).

Breeding Change

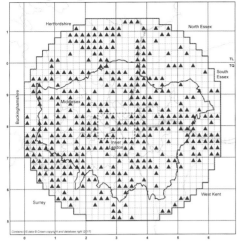

Winter Distribution

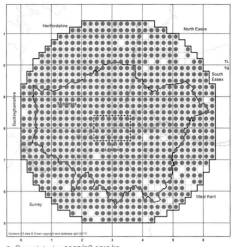

Breeding Distribution Change
- ▲ Recent Gain (new in 2008-13)
- ■ Stable (present in all periods)
- ▼ Old Loss
  (last occupied 1968-72)
- ▲ Old Gain (new in 1988-94)
- ■ Variable (absent 1988-94)
- ▼ Recent Loss
  (last occupied 1988-94)

● Overwintering 2007/08-2012/13

Mediterranean Gull

Larus melanocephalus

Regular winter visitor and passage migrant; amber list.

As a breeding bird, the Mediterranean Gull is a recent colonist to Britain. Having first bred here in 1968, the number of pairs is now estimated to be 600 (Musgrove *et al.*, 2013).

The Mediterranean Gull is a species primarily of the south and east of Britain, with concentrations during the breeding season around the Solent and Thames Estuary. Despite this, and that the first record of this species in England is from Greater London in 1866 (Brown & Grice, 2005), it is not yet a breeding bird of the London area. The nearest breeding occurs to the east of our area in Kent (National Atlas).

However, this species is now a regular winter visitor to our area and it is also present as non-breeding birds during the breeding season and as a passage migrant. The general pattern is for numbers to be higher during the winter (November to February) than during other months of the year. It is usually observed in small numbers, often just single birds, though a flock of 43 was seen flying east at Northfleet on 26th June 2013.

The Mediterranean Gull is widely regarded as a species with a coastal distribution during the winter. Despite this, there are records from most of the main inland wetland sites, and a few more besides, within our area during the winter. For example, this species was reported annually from Inner London during the current atlas period.

Single Mediterranean Gulls are sometimes found amongst flocks of Black-headed Gulls at the same site year after year. It seems likely that such records usually involve the same returning individual as gulls can be faithful to particular sites in winter (Lack, 1986). Indeed, there are at least two examples of birds with coloured rings on their legs returning to our area. A bird ringed in Germany was at Kensington Gardens in 2008/09 and 2009/10 and a bird given the name 'Valentino' has wintered at Valentine's Park in Ilford from 2000/01 to at least 2013/14, returning to Belgium to breed each summer (LBR).

Breeding season tetrads: 31

Winter season tetrads: 81

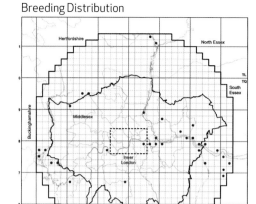

Breeding Distribution

● Confirmed Breeding 2008-13   • Present 2008-13
● Probable Breeding 2008-13   • Still on Migration 2008-13
● Possible Breeding 2008-13

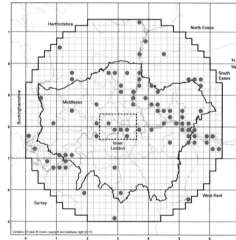

Winter Distribution

● Overwintering 2007/08-2012/13

Common Gull

Larus canus

Common winter visitor and passage migrant; amber list.

The Common Gull is a migratory bird with a circum-global breeding distribution which extends across northern Europe, northern Asia and North America, inland as well as coastal. During the winter, this species aggregates into three broad regions, one of which is centred on the North Sea (BirdLife).

As a breeding species in the British Isles, its distribution is very much northern and western, primarily Scotland and the west of Ireland (National Atlas). There are a small number of breeding records for the coasts of southern England (National Atlas) but none in the London area. It was, however, recorded widely in our area during the fieldwork for the breeding season, most of these being late departing birds in April, or returning or migrating birds in late July, but with some also being recorded in the intervening months.

During the winter, migrants arrive from northern Europe and Scandinavia resulting in a sevenfold increase in numbers (Mitchell *et al.*, 2004; Banks *et al.*, 2007). This species is then widespread in lowland Britain and most abundant in the east (National Atlas). It is clearly not averse to urban areas and was recorded in the majority of tetrads in our area during the winter. Its favoured habitats are wetlands and grasslands, especially playing fields, which explains the near ubiquitous distribution in Greater London. The highest count during the atlas period was 1,000 at both Wanstead Flats and Hilfield Park Reservoir, while contemporary records show that counts of 100 to 500 birds are not infrequent, and include a count of 3,200 at William Girling Reservoir (LBR).

Breeding season tetrads: 130

Winter season tetrads: 732

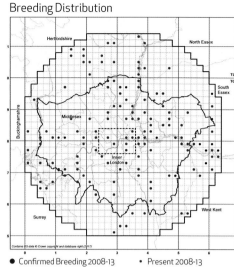

Breeding Distribution

● Confirmed Breeding 2008-13
● Probable Breeding 2008-13
● Possible Breeding 2008-13
• Present 2008-13
• Still on Migration 2008-13

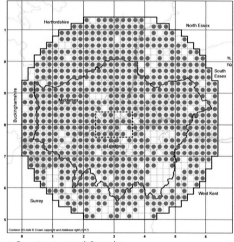

Winter Distribution

● Overwintering 2007/08-2012/13

Lesser Black-backed Gull

Larus fuscus

Common in autumn and winter, increasing breeder; amber list.

The Lesser Black-backed Gull typically breeds in northern latitudes and winters further south, with a huge wintering range that extends from the Gulf of Bothnia to the coast of South Africa (BirdLife). In Britain, it is primarily a breeding bird of the coast and, more recently, urban areas, becoming more widespread during the winter (National Atlas).

The three atlases document the rise and rise of the Lesser Black-backed Gull as an urban breeding bird in our area. Territorial pairs were recorded from two inner London tetrads (Regent's Park and Hyde Park) during the first atlas period and breeding was attempted at Regent's Park in 1969 (Self). By the time of the second atlas period, breeding was recorded in five tetrads, three of these in Inner London. These comprised small colonies of up to 11 pairs nesting on rooftops. The number of tetrads in which this species is found, both breeding and non-breeding, has increased dramatically since then. As a breeding bird, this species remains associated with the rooftops of Inner London and the surrounding urban area. Breeding evidence was also recorded from the Lee Valley and urban areas outside and to the north of Greater London, in Harlow and Watford, for example. Not all birds use rooftops, however, and nesting also occurs on barges, jetties and other structures along the Thames, and on an island at Walthamstow Reservoirs, for example. Where they do nest on rooftops, potential breeding sites can be extremely difficult to view and therefore it is likely that a small number of breeding sites will have been missed during the current survey.

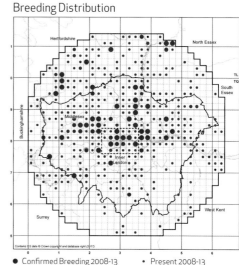

Breeding Distribution

● Confirmed Breeding 2008-13 · Present 2008-13
● Probable Breeding 2008-13 · Still on Migration 2008-13
● Possible Breeding 2008-13

Period	Number of Tetrads		
	Evidence of Breeding	Seen Only	Total
Breeding 1968–72	2	0	5
Breeding 1988–94	5	54	59
Breeding 2008–13	57	331	388
Winter 2007/8–2012/13	-	-	549

Until the 1980s, the Lesser Black-backed Gull was primarily a summer visitor in Britain but now some remain during the winter and these are supplemented by migratory birds from further north (Migration Atlas; Ross-Smith *et al.*, 2014), the net effect being that the wintering population is about half the size of the breeding population (Musgrove *et al.*, 2013). During the winter, this species is very much a bird of the lowlands and, as noted above, is certainly not restricted to the coast. This is reflected in our area, with records generally throughout but a notable gap in distribution around the North Downs and in rural Essex. The Lesser Black-backed Gull is often to be found with our other species of gull in winter, at wetland sites, playing fields and rubbish tips. It is one of the less numerous species but counts of several hundred are not infrequent at the larger wetland sites. The highest number recorded during atlas fieldwork was 700 at Grange Waters area, Essex (TQ68B) in December 2009. There were also 600 at Rainham Marshes in January 2011 (LBR).

Breeding Change

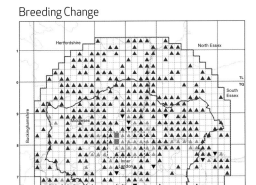

Winter Distribution

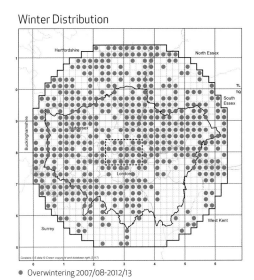

Breeding Distribution Change

▲ Recent Gain (new in 2008-13)
■ Stable (present in all periods)
▼ Old Loss
(last occupied 1968-72)

▲ Old Gain (new in 1988-94)
■ Variable (absent 1988-94)
▼ Recent Loss
(last occupied 1988-94)

● Overwintering 2007/08-2012/13

Herring Gull

Larus argentatus

Most common in winter, increasing breeder; red list.

The (European) Herring Gull breeds around the coasts of northern Europe, Scandinavia and Iceland, as well as inland in, for example, Finland and adjoining parts of Russia (BirdLife). In Britain, it is primarily a breeding bird of the coast but, like the Lesser Black-backed Gull, it has become a breeding bird of urban areas as well.

Famously, the Herring Gull first nested in our area near the sea lions at London Zoo in the early 1960s (Montier). As a breeding bird of the London area, it was a slightly earlier colonist than the Lesser Black-backed Gull and its spread is also demonstrated by the three atlases. In the first atlas, breeding activity was recorded in five tetrads, four of these in the urban centre and one in Sevenoaks. By the time of the second atlas, the breeding distribution had spread slightly, having adopted rooftops and sites along the River Thames. Non-breeding birds were also recorded fairly widely along the Thames and at scattered wetland sites elsewhere in our area during the breeding season. The current atlas illustrates a dramatic spread in the occurrence of this species during the breeding season. Inner London remains the core breeding area but evidence of breeding was also found in a number of tetrads along the River Lea and elsewhere, including perimeter towns such as Watford and Harlow. Herring Gull can often be found breeding in mixed colonies with the Lesser Black-backed Gull. However, the recent spread of the Herring Gull has not been as extensive and at most breeding sites the Herring Gull is outnumbered by its close relative. As for Lesser Black-backed Gull, some Herring Gull breeding sites may have been missed where potential sites on rooftops are impossible to view.

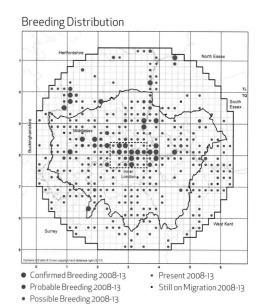

Breeding Distribution

- ● Confirmed Breeding 2008-13
- ● Probable Breeding 2008-13
- ● Possible Breeding 2008-13
- • Present 2008-13
- • Still on Migration 2008-13

Period	Number of Tetrads		
	Evidence of Breeding	Seen Only	Total
Breeding 1968–72	5	1	6
Breeding 1988–94	10	38	48
Breeding 2008–13	32	313	345
Winter 2007/8–2012/13	-	-	574

The population of Herring Gull in Britain almost trebles in winter (Mitchell *et al.*, 2004; Banks *et al.*, 2007) due mainly to arrivals from further north. It is most abundant around the coasts and in the lowlands (National Atlas). In our area, this species is widespread, although the map indicates that the North Downs and rural Essex are somewhat avoided. Elsewhere, it is associated with larger bodies of water (the Thames, gravel pits, reservoirs, etc.) and playing fields, hence the wide distribution. It is the second most numerous of our wintering gull species (after Black-headed), with counts of several thousand at some key sites (LBR). The highest count during atlas fieldwork was 10,000 at Beddington Sewage Farm (November 2007).

Breeding Change

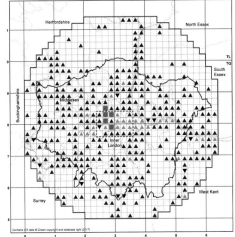

Winter Distribution

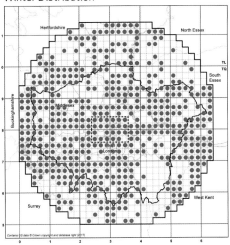

Breeding Distribution Change
- ▲ Recent Gain (new in 2008-13)
- ■ Stable (present in all periods)
- ▼ Old Loss (last occupied 1968-72)
- ▲ Old Gain (new in 1988-94)
- ■ Variable (absent 1988-94)
- ▼ Recent Loss (last occupied 1988-94)

● Overwintering 2007/08-2012/13

Yellow-legged Gull
Larus michahellis

Regular late summer and autumn visitor, some occurring at other times of year; amber list.

The Yellow-legged Gull is less well known than most other British gull species, having only been formally recognised as a full species in 2005 (Sangster *et al.*, 2005). It breeds on the continent, although a few pairs do breed on the south coast of Britain each year (National Atlas). This species is widespread across lowland England late in the breeding season, when juvenile and post-breeding birds arrive from Europe, and in winter (National Atlas).

In the London area, most records of this species during the breeding season came from the Thames and the west London waterbodies and a few other well-watched sites where large numbers of gulls occur, such as Beddington.

In winter, the Yellow-legged Gull shows a more widespread distribution in our area. In addition to the above sites, it can be found in the Lee Valley and at scattered locations elsewhere, particularly in north London. The Thames stands out as a hotspot for this species in winter and it was observed along almost the entire length of the river from central London to the eastern edge of our area. The highest counts usually come from Rainham or Crayford/Dartford Marshes.

Breeding season tetrads: 31

Winter season tetrads: 85

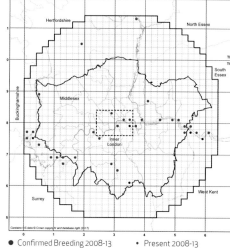

Breeding Distribution

- Confirmed Breeding 2008-13
- Probable Breeding 2008-13
- Possible Breeding 2008-13
- Present 2008-13
- Still on Migration 2008-13

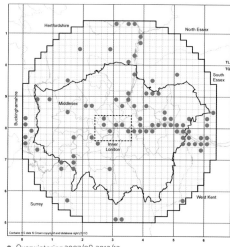

Winter Distribution

- Overwintering 2007/08-2012/13

Caspian Gull
Larus cachinnans

Scarce visitor mainly in winter; amber list.

Like the Yellow-legged Gull, the Caspian Gull is another newly recognised species that many birdwatchers have become aware of only relatively recently. It breeds in Eastern Europe eastwards into Asia, and has recently spread into Poland and eastern Germany (BirdLife). Migratory birds begin to arrive in Britain in late summer and reach their peak in winter (National Atlas).

The distribution maps confirm that the situation in London mirrors the national picture, with Caspian Gull being present in only a few tetrads in late summer and becoming more widespread in winter. Unsurprisingly, almost all the records came from the Thames and from other well-watched sites, where large numbers of gulls gather as well as experienced 'gullophiles' who are skilled at picking out this species. Indeed, the London area is one of the best places to locate this species in Britain, with 45, 75 and 56 individuals estimated to be present over the respective years 2011 to 2013 (LBR).

It seems unlikely that Caspian Gull will become as widespread in Britain as the other wintering gull species in the near future. However, recording of this species may become more frequent as birdwatchers become more familiar with its identification features and are able to distinguish it more readily from other species of gull.

Breeding season tetrads: 8

Winter season tetrads: 27

Breeding Distribution

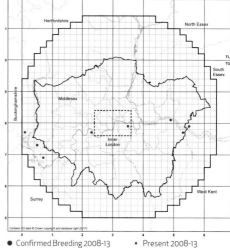

● Confirmed Breeding 2008-13   • Present 2008-13
● Probable Breeding 2008-13   • Still on Migration 2008-13
● Possible Breeding 2008-13

Winter Distribution

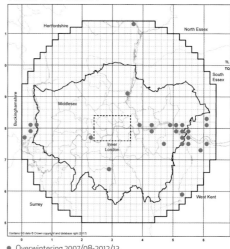

● Overwintering 2007/08-2012/13

Great Black-backed Gull
Larus marinus

Fairly common winter visitor in small numbers, recent breeder; amber list.

The Great Black-backed Gull is typically resident around the coasts of the North Atlantic, including Ireland, Scotland, Wales and the west coast of England (BirdLife). Some populations are migratory, particularly those that breed in northern latitudes. Perhaps as a consequence, this species is also widespread around the coast and in the lowlands in the east of Britain during the winter (National Atlas).

The Great Black-backed Gull is the latest gull species to colonise the London area as a breeding species. In the context of its national distribution, this is remarkable. Very few pairs breed in the east of England (themselves recent colonists) and few, if any, in Britain breed as far from the coast as those in London. The first record of confirmed breeding was on a barge on the Thames near Wandsworth Park in 2008 and the second confirmed breeding was at the Isle of Dogs in 2010, where breeding was again confirmed in 2013 (LBR). In addition, there were three records of recently fledged young in 2009, which are shown here as confirmed breeding although it is not known precisely where the birds nested. These records comprised a pair with recently fledged young on the Strand and adults with begging young at both Barking Bay and Queen Elizabeth II Reservoir. A territorial pair had been seen at Barking Bay earlier in the same year so it seems likely that at least this pair did nest in the tetrad where the young were seen. This species was observed in other places in our area during the breeding season, including elsewhere along the Thames, the Lee, Thames and Colne Valleys and at Brent Reservoir, and other pairs have been noted but breeding was not confirmed.

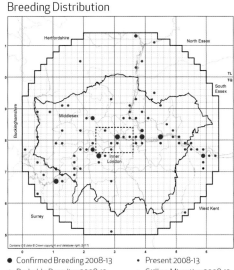

Breeding Distribution

- ● Confirmed Breeding 2008-13
- ● Probable Breeding 2008-13
- ● Possible Breeding 2008-13
- • Present 2008-13
- • Still on Migration 2008-13

Period	Number of Tetrads		
	Evidence of Breeding	Seen Only	Total
Breeding 1968–72	0	0	0
Breeding 1988–94	0	0	0
Breeding 2008–13	8	72	80
Winter 2007/8–2012/13	-	-	187

The population in Britain during winter is about double that of the breeding season (Musgrove *et al.*, 2013) and significantly higher in our area during the winter due to the arrival of birds that bred elsewhere. During the winter, it is more strongly associated with large wetland sites, especially the Thames Estuary, than the other common species of gull but the Great Black-backed Gull can also join these on playing fields. Counts of more than 50 are not unusual at key wetland sites (LBR). The highest number recorded during atlas fieldwork was 170 at Rainham Marshes in November 2008 but there was a contemporary count of c.500 at Queen Mother Reservoir in December 2007 (LBR).

Winter Distribution

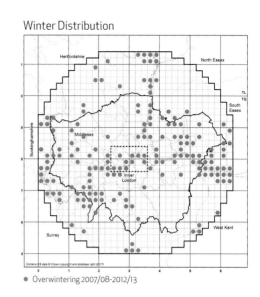

● Overwintering 2007/08-2012/13

Feral Pigeon

Columba livia

Abundant feral resident; green list.

The Feral Pigeon was under-recorded in the first atlas so a comparison with this period is difficult. The second and current atlases show a similar pattern; near ubiquity in Greater London with more patchy distribution in the surrounding counties, particularly on the higher ground of the North Downs and rural Essex. The abundance maps show a clear picture of higher abundance in Inner London. The highest breeding season count made during atlas fieldwork was 500 in Regent's Park in May 2012 and counts of over 200 birds are not unusual (LBR).

There is an apparent decline in this species, with Breeding Bird Survey data for the London region showing a 23% decline between 1995 and 2013. It is plausible that the return of the Peregrine Falcon, and other birds of prey, may be having an effect on Feral Pigeon numbers. Certainly, the available research indicates that Feral Pigeon may account for just under half the urban Peregrine diet (Drewitt & Dixon, 2008). However, a more likely cause of decline is a shift in the attitudes of people towards urban pigeons and the consequential introduction of control measures. Certainly, the large flocks of Trafalgar Square are a thing of the past since licenced pigeon-food sellers ceased trading in the square in 2001. Nevertheless, the Feral Pigeon was the third most abundantly recorded

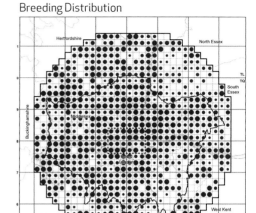

Breeding Distribution

● Confirmed Breeding 2008-13   • Present 2008-13
● Probable Breeding 2008-13   • Still on Migration 2008-13
● Possible Breeding 2008-13

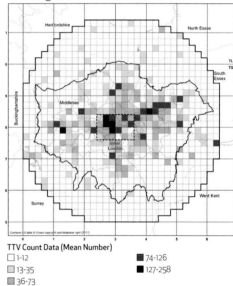

Breeding Abundance

TTV Count Data (Mean Number)
☐ 1-12   ■ 74-126
☐ 13-35   ■ 127-258
☐ 36-73

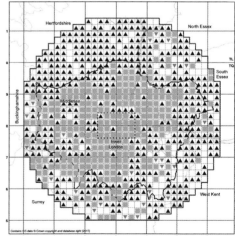

Breeding Change

Breeding Distribution Change
▲ Recent Gain (new in 2008-13)   ▲ Old Gain (new in 1988-94)
■ Stable (present in all periods)   ■ Variable (absent 1988-94)
▼ Old Loss
(last occupied 1968-72)   ▼ Recent Loss
(last occupied 1988-94)

Period	Number of Tetrads		
	Evidence of Breeding	Seen Only	Total
Breeding 1968–72	201	101	302
Breeding 1988–94	503	243	746
Breeding 2008–13	473	250	723
Winter 2007/8–2012/13	-	-	759

species during the timed counts in the breeding season surveys and the fourth commonest during winter.

As you would expect for a mostly sedentary species, the winter distribution is similar to the breeding distribution. However, the slightly more widespread presence of this species in rural areas during the winter may reflect the presence of small groups which can be found feeding in arable fields at this time of year. The highest count recorded during winter atlas fieldwork was 1,200 at Tyttenhanger Gravel Pits in November 2008.

Winter Distribution

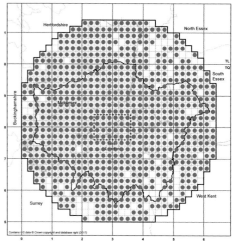

● Overwintering 2007/08-2012/13

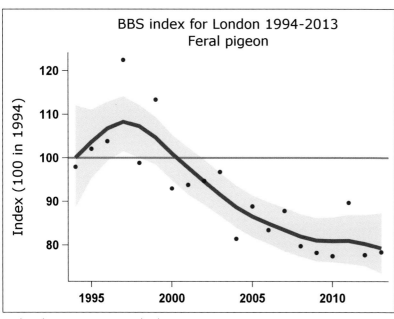

BTO/JNCC/RSPB Breeding Bird Survey (BBS)

Winter Abundance

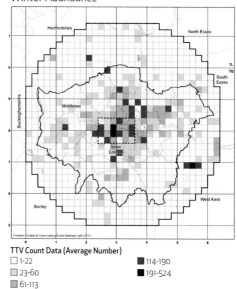

TTV Count Data (Average Number)
☐ 1-22 ■ 114-190
☐ 23-60 ■ 191-524
■ 61-113

Stock Dove

Columba oenas

Breeding resident and passage migrant; amber list.

In the first part of the last century, the Stock Dove was considered, in the London area, to be a common resident with a localised distribution (LNHS, 1964). The Thames Marshes was a notable stronghold and birds were nesting in Inner London parks during this time (Montier). This was followed by a marked decline in the national and local population in the 1950s and 1960s, linked to the use of organochlorine seed dressings (O'Connor & Mead, 1984). Since the restriction of use of these chemicals, which began in 1961, the Stock Dove population has recovered (BirdTrends). It is on the amber list because of the high proportion of the European population that is present in the UK.

By the time of the first atlas, this species had returned as a breeding species in the Inner London parks and was found in 328 tetrads altogether, of which the majority were in the more rural areas around London. There was, however, a notable lack of records from its previous stronghold, the Thames Marshes. The second atlas indicates that this species consolidated its distribution in the rural area, becoming, once again, a breeding species of the Thames Marshes, as well as many parks and open spaces within Greater London. The current atlas shows further consolidation of its distribution and, in particular, further advances into the urban area, with all but those areas most devoid of open spaces inhabited.

Despite this, the Stock Dove is nowhere particularly numerous as a breeding species in our area, with timed counts during the breeding season typically yielding no more than five birds per tetrad. Indeed, the National Atlas shows a marked reduction in density for this species in London. Nevertheless, records include a count of 1,251 from a farm near Maple Cross in April 2009 which is the highest count ever made in the London area and a similarly high count (912) from nearby in April 2010 (LBR). Self considers these to be 'part of a substantial breeding population within flying distance of these sites'. This seems likely because, in Britain, the Stock Dove is typically sedentary (half of all ringing recoveries were within 6km of where they were ringed) and passage birds are only observed in relatively small, and declining, numbers (Migration Atlas).

Period	Number of Tetrads		
	Evidence of Breeding	Seen Only	Total
Breeding 1968–72	185	143	328
Breeding 1988–94	352	221	573
Breeding 2008–13	415	238	653
Winter 2007/8–2012/13	-	-	554

The distribution of this species in the London area changes little between the breeding season and the winter; however, some higher counts were made, especially in the Thames Marshes where flocks of over 100 were recorded, with the highest count being 300 at Orsett Fen in January 2011.

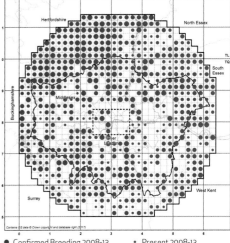

Breeding Distribution

● Confirmed Breeding 2008-13   • Present 2008-13
● Probable Breeding 2008-13   • Still on Migration 2008-13
● Possible Breeding 2008-13

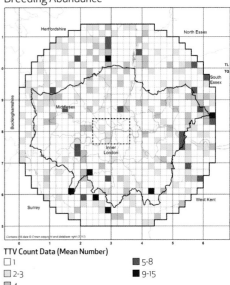

Breeding Abundance

TTV Count Data (Mean Number)
☐ 1   ■ 5-8
☐ 2-3   ■ 9-15
▨ 4

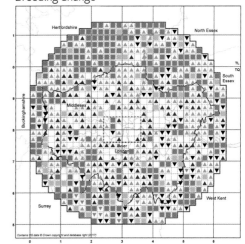

Breeding Change

Breeding Distribution Change
▲ Recent Gain (new in 2008-13)   ▲ Old Gain (new in 1988-94)
■ Stable (present in all periods)   ▨ Variable (absent 1988-94)
▼ Old Loss (last occupied 1968-72)   ▼ Recent Loss (last occupied 1988-94)

Winter Distribution

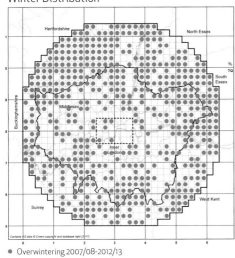

● Overwintering 2007/08-2012/13

Winter Abundance

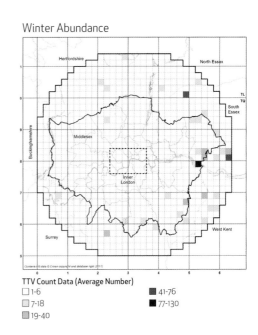

TTV Count Data (Average Number)
☐ 1-6   ◼ 41-76
☐ 7-18   ■ 77-130
◼ 19-40

Woodpigeon

Columba palumbus

Abundant breeding resident, passage migrant and winter visitor; green list.

The Woodpigeon may be the most common bird species in the UK (BBS). It is found in almost every region except the highlands of Scotland but is at its most abundant in the lowlands of England (National Atlas). It is not currently of conservation concern.

The Woodpigeon colonised urban London rapidly in the latter part of the nineteenth century, beginning in the central parks and spreading outwards from there (LNHS, 1964). By the time of the first atlas, it had achieved ubiquity across the whole of our area; the few tetrads where it was not recorded being attributed to survey coverage rather than actual absence. In the second and current atlases, the Woodpigeon was recorded in every single tetrad, with evidence of breeding in the vast majority. The atlas survey work indicates that this species is relatively more abundant in the north and east of our area and it was the most common species recorded in the London area during both the breeding and winter timed counts.

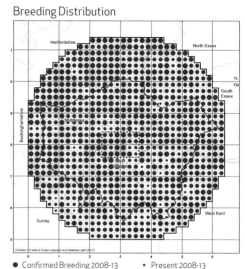

Breeding Distribution

● Confirmed Breeding 2008-13   • Present 2008-13
● Probable Breeding 2008-13   • Still on Migration 2008-13
● Possible Breeding 2008-13

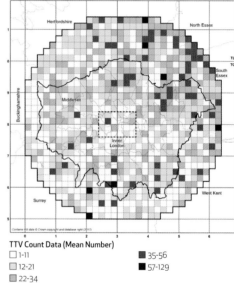

Breeding Abundance

TTV Count Data (Mean Number)
□ 1-11   ■ 35-56
□ 12-21   ■ 57-129
■ 22-34

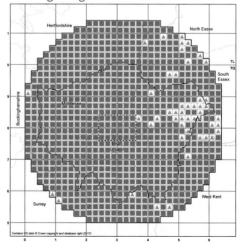

Breeding Change

Breeding Distribution Change
▲ Recent Gain (new in 2008-13)   ▲ Old Gain (new in 1988-94)
■ Stable (present in all periods)   ■ Variable (absent 1988-94)
▼ Old Loss   ▼ Recent Loss
  (last occupied 1968-72)   (last occupied 1988-94)

Period	Number of Tetrads		
	Evidence of Breeding	Seen Only	Total
Breeding 1968–72	734	75	809
Breeding 1988–94	809	47	856
Breeding 2008–13	789	67	856
Winter 2007/8–2012/13	-	-	856

During the winter, the distribution of this species in our area is unchanged, it being recorded in every single tetrad. However, the abundance mapping confirms that this species is much more numerous during the winter season, with an average of 40.47 birds per hour recorded during the winter timed counts compared to 17.59 per hour in the breeding season. This is due partly to a post-breeding peak in population size and partly to immigration from the north. Wintering flocks can comprise more than 1,000 birds. Excluding counts of flocks flying over, the highest number recorded in any one tetrad during the atlas fieldwork was 2,275 around Epping Green in Essex (in tetrad TL40H).

The atlas data does not show the large flocks of this species which pass through (and over) our area every year during autumn passage, with contemporary accounts giving estimates of tens of thousands travelling south or south-west. The origin and destination of these birds are probably elsewhere in Britain, as the British population is resident and continental migrants from northern Europe are thought to mainly bypass Britain on their southwards migration to France and the Iberian Peninsula (Migration Atlas). Despite this, rather small numbers of birds ringed in Britain are occasionally recovered from Europe and vice versa (Migration Atlas).

Winter Distribution

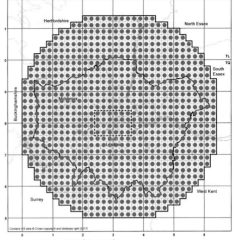

● Overwintering 2007/08-2012/13

Winter Abundance

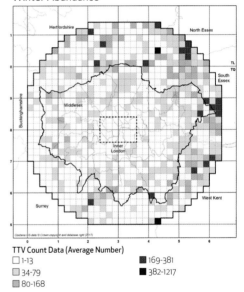

TTV Count Data (Average Number)
☐ 1-13   ■ 169-381
☐ 34-79   ■ 382-1217
☐ 80-168

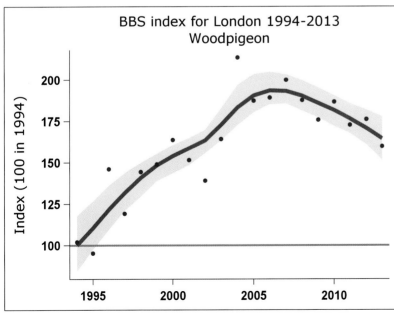

BTO/JNCC/RSPB Breeding Bird Survey (BBS)

Collared Dove
Streptopelia decaocto

Common breeding resident; green list.

The Collared Dove was first recorded breeding in Britain in 1955 (Hudson, 1965). There followed rapid expansion and rapid population growth between then and 2005, such that the population now numbers 980,000 pairs (Musgrove *et al.*, 2013) with a range that encompasses all areas of lowland Britain and Ireland (National Atlas).

It was first recorded in the London area in 1957 (Montier). By the time of the first atlas, evidence of breeding was recorded in 285 tetrads and it was present in 392 altogether. At that time, it was very much a bird of the outer suburbs and the towns surrounding Greater London, with very rural and very urban areas largely unoccupied. By the time of the second atlas, this species had consolidated its distribution in the rural and sub-urban parts of our area but was generally absent from all of the Inner London boroughs. The notable exception was occasional nesting in the Inner London parks, though just one pair nested within Inner London during the second atlas survey period itself (in St James's Park, unsuccessfully).

The current atlas indicates some slight further advancement towards the centre and with probable breeding status in one Inner London tetrad, in Regent's Park where 1-2 birds were seen throughout 2012 (LBR). However, it is also possible that some gaps have opened up in the distribution of this species, notably in Greenwich. The national atlas very distinctly shows a lower density for this species in London compared to the surrounding counties, within which lowland areas are clearly favoured. Reflecting this, the density of this species in our area is higher in north-east London and south Essex and surrounding lowlands.

Period	Number of Tetrads		
	Evidence of Breeding	Seen Only	Total
Breeding 1968–72	285	107	392
Breeding 1988–94	619	143	762
Breeding 2008–13	591	184	775
Winter 2007/8–2012/13	-	-	742

The distribution of this species in winter is very similar to that during the breeding season. This species can form flocks outside the breeding season, which in our area can comprise up to 100 birds, or occasionally more. The largest number recorded in any one tetrad during the winter period was a remarkable 250, in November 2009, during one hour of a timed count in the Darenth area (TQ57Q).

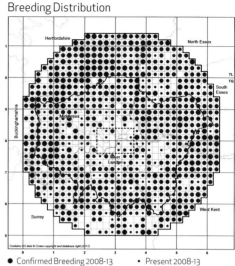

Breeding Distribution

● Confirmed Breeding 2008-13
● Probable Breeding 2008-13
● Possible Breeding 2008-13
· Present 2008-13
· Still on Migration 2008-13

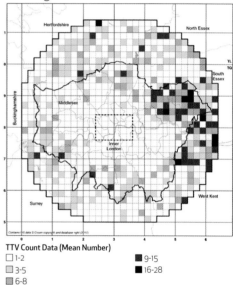

Breeding Abundance

TTV Count Data (Mean Number)
□ 1-2
□ 3-5
■ 6-8
■ 9-15
■ 16-28

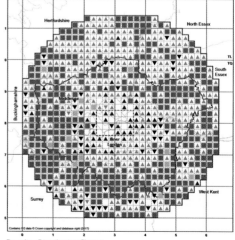

Breeding Change

Breeding Distribution Change
▲ Recent Gain (new in 2008-13)
■ Stable (present in all periods)
▼ Old Loss (last occupied 1968-72)
▲ Old Gain (new in 1988-94)
■ Variable (absent 1988-94)
▼ Recent Loss (last occupied 1988-94)

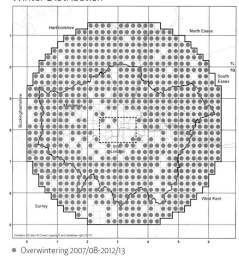

Winter Distribution

● Overwintering 2007/08-2012/13

BBS index for London 1994-2013
Collared Dove

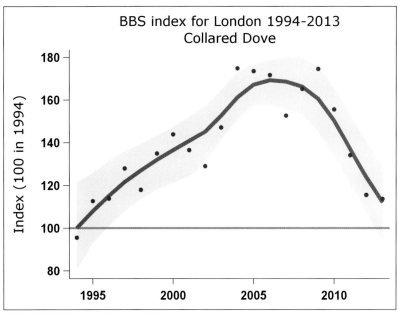

BTO/JNCC/RSPB Breeding Bird Survey (BBS)

Winter Abundance

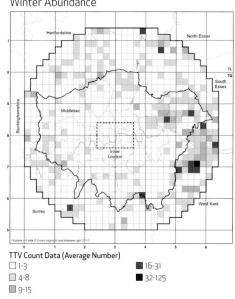

TTV Count Data (Average Number)
- 1-3
- 4-8
- 9-15
- 16-31
- 32-125

Turtle Dove

Streptopelia turtur

Localised and now scarce breeding summer visitor and passage migrant; red list.

The Turtle Dove is a migrant, wintering in the Sahel region of Africa and breeding further north in Africa, Europe, Asia and the Middle East (BirdLife). In Britain, this species has undergone a range contraction. Having retreated from former breeding areas in Wales and south-west and northern England, it is now mainly restricted to eastern England (National Atlas). At the same time, it has suffered a population decline of an estimated 91% between 1995 and 2013 (BBS).

The Turtle Dove is a bird of rural areas and this was strongly reflected in the earlier London atlases. At the time of the first atlas, this species was present in a consistent ring around the built-up area with the majority of the rural tetrads occupied, if not supporting breeding pairs. The second atlas shows a significant reduction in the number of occupied tetrads, with losses from tetrads to the south, west and north-west of our area but continuing presence in the rural tetrads in the north, east and south-east.

The current atlas shows a massive further reduction in distribution, with very few tetrads now occupied and these being mainly in the east, especially rural Essex. Excluding known migrants, this species was recorded from under 7% of the tetrads in our area, with some of these records probably passage birds. This compares to 53% at the time of the first atlas. Indeed, the current atlas map probably overstates the breeding distribution at the end of this atlas period, for example at Greensted (TL50G), three territorial birds were present in 2009, one singing bird was observed in 2010 and none were found in 2011. In 2013, the only known territorial bird was at Swanley Park in Kent, and there were none reported in rural Essex (LBR), though this part of our area is not well-watched so one or two pairs may still persist there. The actual number of breeding pairs in our area each year may now be fewer than ten and, sadly, it seems inevitable that the Turtle Dove will soon become extinct as a breeding bird in the London area.

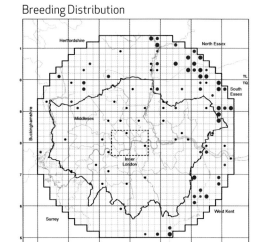

Breeding Distribution

● Confirmed Breeding 2008-13   • Present 2008-13
● Probable Breeding 2008-13   • Still on Migration 2008-13
● Possible Breeding 2008-13

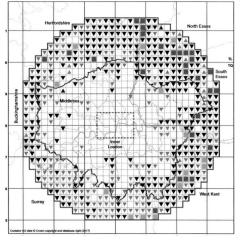

Breeding Change

Breeding Distribution Change
▲ Recent Gain (new in 2008-13)   ▲ Old Gain (new in 1988-94)
■ Stable (present in all periods)   ■ Variable (absent 1988-94)
▼ Old Loss (last occupied 1968-72)   ▼ Recent Loss (last occupied 1988-94)

Period	Number of Tetrads		
	Evidence of Breeding	Seen Only	Total
Breeding 1968–72	360	95	455
Breeding 1988–94	202	127	329
Breeding 2008–13	19	39	58

Ring-necked Parakeet

Psittacula krameri

Naturalised breeding resident, increasing

The natural distribution of the Ring-necked Parakeet is sub-Saharan Africa and India. Free flying Ring-necked Parakeets have been present in Britain occasionally since the 1850s; however, earlier populations did not persist and breeding by the present population of Ring-necked Parakeets was not confirmed until 1969 (Brown & Grice, 2005). The origins of the Ring-necked Parakeet in the London area are the subject of folklore.

The three London atlases show the progressive, although not especially rapid, colonisation of our area by this species. This is despite a many fold population increase over the period 1995 to 2013 (BBS). This species was present in the London area during the majority of the first atlas period, with breeding first confirmed in the London area in 1971 (Hewlett *et al.*). Despite this, there is no mention of Ring-necked Parakeets in the first atlas publication.

In the second atlas, evidence of breeding was reported from 29 tetrads and birds were seen in an additional 74 tetrads. The distribution was concentrated into two main population centres, one in south-west London and the adjoining areas of Surrey and Berkshire and the second in south-east London, with scattered records of breeding elsewhere, including Croydon and the Woodford/Epping Forest area. It is clear that, from the main centres identified in 1988–1994, this species has consolidated its range within the London area such that it now includes the majority of Greater London, with records from every London borough. The parts of the Counties of Surrey, Kent, Berkshire and Buckinghamshire, Hertfordshire and Essex which fall within the London area now also have records.

The abundance mapping shows reasonably clearly that the highest densities of this species are to be found close to the main population centres that were present at the time of the second atlas, although the London Borough of Richmond and especially Richmond Park now have the highest densities of parakeets found anywhere in London.

Period	Number of Tetrads		
	Evidence of Breeding	Seen Only	Total
Breeding 1988–94	29	74	103
Breeding 2008–13	324	228	552
Winter 2007/8–2012/13	-	-	572

In our area, the winter distribution of the Ring-necked Parakeet is almost identical to that of the breeding season. The Ring-necked Parakeet roosts communally with such roosts being at their maximum size between August and October, then decreasing to their minimum size in April (Pithon & Dytham, 2002): Therefore, peak aggregations typically fall outside the two seasons covered by atlas fieldwork. During the current atlas period, the larger night-time roosts were found to support more than 2,000 birds, including an astonishing count of 15,353 birds at Hersham Gravel Pits in July 2010 (LBR).

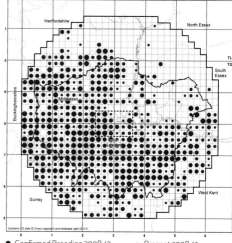

Breeding Distribution

- ● Confirmed Breeding 2008-13
- ● Probable Breeding 2008-13
- ● Possible Breeding 2008-13
- · Present 2008-13
- · Still on Migration 2008-13

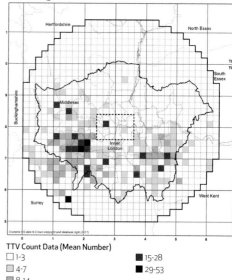

Breeding Abundance

TTV Count Data (Mean Number)
- ☐ 1-3
- ☐ 4-7
- ☐ 8-14
- ■ 15-28
- ■ 29-53

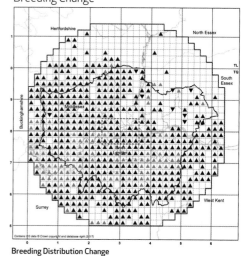

Breeding Change

Breeding Distribution Change
- ▲ Recent Gain (new in 2008-13)
- ■ Stable (present in all periods)
- ▼ Old Loss (last occupied 1968-72)
- ▲ Old Gain (new in 1988-94)
- ■ Variable (absent 1988-94)
- ▼ Recent Loss (last occupied 1988-94)

Winter Distribution

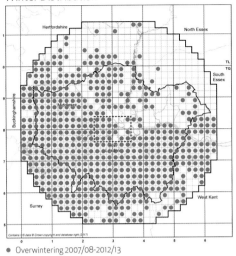

● Overwintering 2007/08-2012/13

Winter Abundance

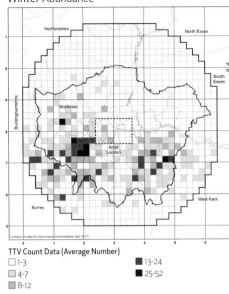

TTV Count Data (Average Number)
□ 1-3
□ 4-7
■ 8-12
■ 13-24
■ 25-52

Cuckoo

Cuculus canorus

Breeding summer visitor and passage migrant; red list.

The Cuckoo is a long distance migrant; the breeding range extending right across Eurasia, as well as parts of North Africa, and wintering in Africa, Madagascar and Thailand (BirdLife). Recent work by the BTO indicates that the population breeding in Britain overwinters in and around the Congo rainforest (Hewson *et al.*, 2016).

The breeding population in England and Wales (but not Scotland) has undergone a rapid decline, beginning in the 1980s (BBS). As a consequence, this species is on the red list. Despite the population decline, the distribution of this species across Britain has changed little during the same period (National Atlas).

The three London atlas maps also show little change in the distribution of the Cuckoo in our area. This species shows a clear preference for rural areas; however, it was also found occasionally in a few large areas of open, semi-natural habitats within Greater London, such as Richmond Park and Wimbledon Common.

The most recent national atlas clearly shows lower population density in and around London, again reflecting the preference for rural areas. No more than three were recorded in an hour in any one tetrad during the atlas timed counts.

Period	Number of Tetrads		
	Evidence of Breeding	Seen Only	Total
Breeding 1968–72	329	128	457
Breeding 1988–94	295	191	486
Breeding 2008–13	99	227	326

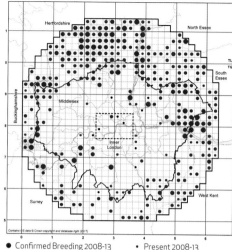

Breeding Distribution

● Confirmed Breeding 2008-13   • Present 2008-13
● Probable Breeding 2008-13   • Still on Migration 2008-13
● Possible Breeding 2008-13

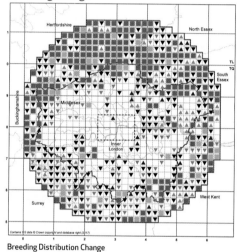

Breeding Change

Breeding Distribution Change
▲ Recent Gain (new in 2008-13)   ▲ Old Gain (new in 1988-94)
■ Stable (present in all periods)   ■ Variable (absent 1988-94)
▼ Old Loss (last occupied 1968-72)   ▼ Recent Loss (last occupied 1988-94)

Barn Owl

Tyto alba

Rare breeding resident and scarce winter visitor; green list.

Following a range contraction and decline in the Barn Owl population, which perhaps reached its lowest point in the 1980s and 1990s (BirdTrends), this species has recovered much of its former range across England and Wales and may have even expanded northwards in Scotland. The highest numbers are now in eastern England. However, following a peak in 2009, the population now seems to be declining again.

The Barn Owl is a rural bird. Nevertheless, it is thinly present in our area, especially outside Greater London in the Hertfordshire and Essex sectors.

The three London atlases reflect the national picture. The first atlas shows scattered breeding evidence in mostly rural locations but also Richmond Park and a few other suburban locations. The second atlas, which coincided with the low point described above, shows a range contraction with evidence of breeding coming only from the east of a line drawn between Woolwich and St. Albans. Since then, there may have been something of a recovery, with the distribution now more closely resembling that of the first atlas than the second, with a return to breeding in Surrey, for example. That said, there are a number of tetrads in east London/Essex area which seem to have lost their Barn Owls between then and now. Like all owls, this species can be difficult to find without crepuscular or night-time visits and so it may be more widespread than the number of occupied tetrads suggests.

To what extent the recovery of the population described above is attributable to releases of captive bred birds in the latter half of the twentieth century is matter for debate (Meek *et al.*, 2003); other potential contributing factors include the cessation of organochlorine pesticide use (Newton *et al.*, 1991), the provision of nest boxes (BirdTrends) and the creation of rough grassland along field margins as a result of agri-environment schemes (Bond *et al.*, 2005).

So that the breeding sites cannot be identified, a sector level summary is shown for the breeding season instead of a tetrad map.

Breeding Distribution

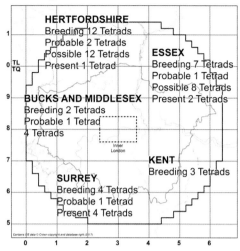

Period	Number of Tetrads		
	Evidence of Breeding	Seen Only	Total
Breeding 1968–72	48	61	109
Breeding 1988–94	22	44	66
Breeding 2008–13	33	31	64
Winter 2007/8–2012/13	-	-	71

The distribution of Barn Owl in our area during the winter is, as elsewhere in Britain, similar to that in the breeding season. Changes in occupied tetrads do occur from season to season and may relate to local movements made by birds in autumn and winter, including young birds seeking territories.

Winter Distribution

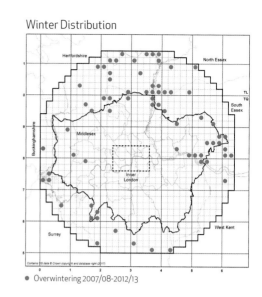

● Overwintering 2007/08-2012/13

Little Owl

Athene noctua

Introduced, localised breeding resident.

The Little Owl was introduced in the latter part of the nineteenth century and has since colonised much of lowland England and parts of Wales and, to a very limited extent, Scotland. However, the population, particularly in western England, is currently in decline (National Atlas).

In our area, the distribution of this species has remained much the same between the first and current atlases. This species is primarily a bird of low-lying, open but lightly wooded country and that is reflected in the atlas maps. Most of the records come from outside Greater London and particularly the Hertfordshire and Essex sectors. There are however breeding populations in some of the larger open spaces within the built-up area, including Richmond Park, where 18 pairs were recorded in 2008 (LBR). This species has also penetrated Inner London. It is reported in the second atlas that a bird was often seen in Regent's Park in 1989 and at least one pair bred successfully here several times during the current atlas period. A pair also bred in Hyde Park/Kensington Gardens during the current atlas period.

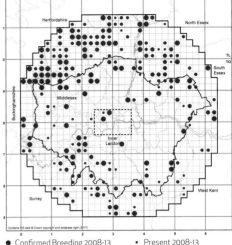

Breeding Distribution

- Confirmed Breeding 2008-13
- Probable Breeding 2008-13
- Possible Breeding 2008-13
- Present 2008-13
- Still on Migration 2008-13

Period	Number of Tetrads		
	Evidence of Breeding	Seen Only	Total
Breeding 1968–72	161	114	275
Breeding 1988–94	171	98	269
Breeding 2008–13	131	99	230
Winter 2007/8–2012/13	-	-	213

Although it has a large home range, the Little Owl is a sedentary species. As a consequence, the distribution of this species in our area during the winter is much the same as during the breeding season.

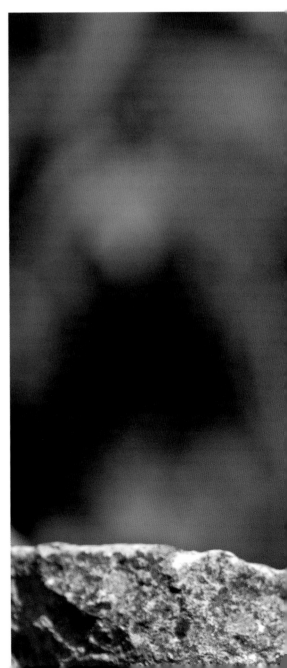

Breeding Change

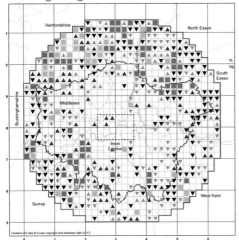

Contains OS data © Crown copyright and database right (2017)

Breeding Distribution Change
▲ Recent Gain (new in 2008-13)
▲ Old Gain (new in 1988-94)
■ Stable (present in all periods)
■ Variable (absent 1988-94)
▼ Old Loss
(last occupied 1968-72)
▼ Recent Loss
(last occupied 1988-94)

Winter Distribution

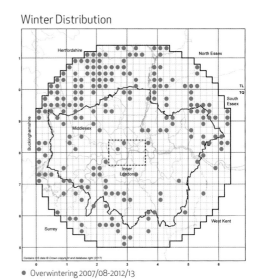

Contains OS data © Crown copyright and database right (2017)

● Overwintering 2007/08-2012/13

Tawny Owl

Strix aluco

Common breeding resident in the outer parts of the London area, scarcer towards the centre; amber list.

The Tawny Owl is found throughout Britain apart from the highlands (National Atlas). Due to the long-term decline in the Tawny Owl population, it is now on the amber list.

Despite the decline, the Tawny Owl remains the most common breeding owl species in the London area and, since the 1930s, has even been well established in built-up areas, provided there are sufficient trees. Its distribution has therefore included Inner London and, in particular the central London parks such as Regent's Park, since at least the 1950s (Cramp and Teagle, 1952a).

The first and second London atlases give a similar impression; the distribution shown in both is much the same, however, the number of tetrads in which this species was recorded was lower in the second atlas. These observations suggest a general thinning out of the population between these two periods.

In the current atlas, that trend appears to have continued with a further thinning out of the population. The area which is both to the east of the Lee Valley and the north of the Thames seems to have fared worst. Perhaps this is a reflection of the potential population decline occurring nationally. However, as for other owl species, it is also possible that it reflects reduced survey effort at night time compared to the second atlas.

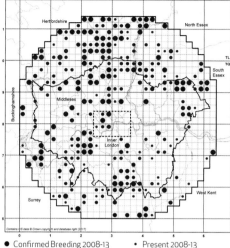

Breeding Distribution

- ● Confirmed Breeding 2008-13
- ● Probable Breeding 2008-13
- ● Possible Breeding 2008-13
- • Present 2008-13
- • Still on Migration 2008-13

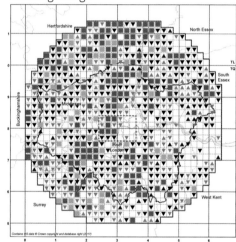

Breeding Change

Breeding Distribution Change
- ▲ Recent Gain (new in 2008-13)
- ■ Stable (present in all periods)
- ▼ Old Loss (last occupied 1968-72)
- ▲ Old Gain (new in 1988-94)
- ■ Variable (absent 1988-94)
- ▼ Recent Loss (last occupied 1988-94)

Period	Number of Tetrads		
	Evidence of Breeding	Seen Only	Total
Breeding 1968–72	374	162	536
Breeding 1988–94	310	156	466
Breeding 2008–13	141	135	276
Winter 2007/8–2012/13	-	-	262

Although it was perhaps a little less widely recorded during atlas fieldwork, the distribution of the Tawny Owl is much the same during the winter as it is in the breeding season.

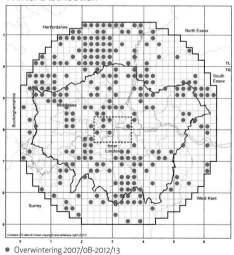

Winter Distribution

- ● Overwintering 2007/08-2012/13

Long-eared Owl
Asio otus

Scarce winter visitor and passage migrant, rare breeder; green list.

The Long-eared Owl is a breeding bird of woodland, especially coniferous woodland. It is an uncommon breeding species in Britain, with the majority of 10km squares within which breeding was recorded lying to the north and east of a line between the Thames and the Mersey Estuaries (National Atlas).

Consequently, it is a rare breeding bird in our area with probably only up to three pairs breeding in any one year in the twenty-first century (Self). This seems to have been the case during all three atlas periods, although the breeding population did increase in the late 1990s and four to seven pairs bred in 1999 (Self). The distribution of records has shifted though; in the first atlas the breeding records were all in the north, especially in Hertfordshire. In the second atlas, the records were mainly in Essex sector with most, but not all, of the Hertfordshire sector tetrads apparently vacated. During the current atlas period, there were no breeding records in the Hertfordshire sector but this species retained its presence in Essex. In addition, this species also attempted to breed in our area to the south of the Thames, where it also nested in the early decades of the twentieth century (LNHS, 1964).

So that the breeding sites cannot be identified, a sector level summary is shown for the breeding season instead of a tetrad map.

Period	Number of Tetrads		
	Evidence of Breeding	Seen Only	Total
Breeding 1968–72	8	5	13
Breeding 1988–94	5	6	11
Breeding 2008–13	3	3	6
Winter 2007/8–2012/13	-	-	14

Although birds that breed in southern England are joined by those that breed in Fennoscandia (Migration Atlas), this species remains uncommon and widely scattered in our area during the winter. During this season, this species was recorded mainly from wetland sites, including several within the Greater London area such as the London Wetland Centre, Brent Reservoir and Beddington. Most records are of single birds but as many as five have been recorded roosting together in our area, at Beddington Farmlands, several times during the current atlas period (LBR). Such roosts used to be more regular in our area. For example, around the turn of the 21st century about 25 birds wintered at four sites (Self).

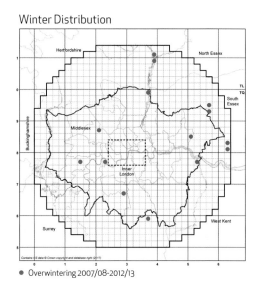

Breeding Distribution

HERTFORDSHIRE
Present 2 Tetrads

ESSEX
Breeding 2 Tetrads

SURREY
Probable 1 Tetrad
Present 1 Tetrad

Winter Distribution

● Overwintering 2007/08-2012/13

Short-eared Owl

Asio flammeus

Scarce winter visitor and passage migrant, rare breeder; amber list.

The Short-eared Owl has a circum-global distribution. It is migratory, with a breeding range which includes Northern Europe and Asia and a wintering range which includes Western and Southern Europe (BirdLife). In Britain, this species typically breeds in open, moorland areas and winters in the lowlands, including around the coast. Birds from Northern Europe also overwinter in Britain, meaning that numbers are higher.

The Short-eared Owl was solely an occasional winter visitor in our area up until the late 1980s, with successful breeding first confirmed in 1988 (Self). Breeding, probably by just one pair, also occurred in subsequent years, including once during the current atlas period, in 2008. The other, more widely scattered records relate to birds on passage as these can be encountered in April and May. Apparently non-breeding birds have also spent the summer in our area, including in 1990 and 1995 (Hewlett *et al.*). The breeding records in the second and current atlas periods are all from the Thames Marshes.

So that the breeding sites cannot be identified, a sector level summary is shown for the breeding season instead of a tetrad map.

Period	Number of Tetrads		
	Evidence of Breeding	Seen Only	Total
Breeding 1968–72	0	0	0
Breeding 1988–94	1	3	4
Breeding 2008–13	1	24	25
Winter 2007/8–2012/13	-	-	66

During the winter, this species is recorded more often in our area but still infrequently. The majority of the records are from open marsh and wetland sites. Many of these are single birds which move on quickly; Rainham Marshes was the site which most often had long staying individuals during the winter, with peak counts of between three and five birds, but the peak count occurred at King George VI Reservoir, where up to six birds were present in winter 2012/13.

Breeding Distribution

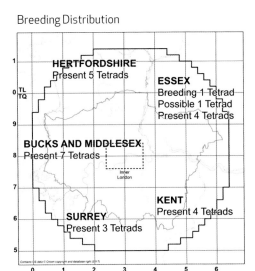

HERTFORDSHIRE
Present 5 Tetrads

ESSEX
Breeding 1 Tetrad
Possible 1 Tetrad
Present 4 Tetrads

BUCKS AND MIDDLESEX
Present 7 Tetrads

KENT
Present 4 Tetrads

SURREY
Present 3 Tetrads

Winter Distribution

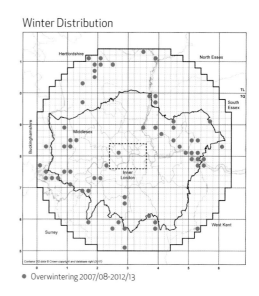

Contains OS data © Crown copyright and database right (2017)

● Overwintering 2007/08–2012/13

Nightjar
Caprimulgus europaeus

Rare passage migrant, occasionally breeding; red list.

The Nightjar is a long-distance migrant which breeds in Europe and Asia and winters in Africa (BirdLife). In Britain and Ireland, it is a breeding bird of heathland and new or recently felled forestry plantations (National Atlas). Following a range contraction and population decline in the middle of the latter half of the twentieth century, its range in England has recovered some of its previous ground (National Atlas; Langston *et al.*, 2007). Southern England is its stronghold.

In our area, this species was much more frequent at the beginning of the twentieth century than now. Its haunts at that time included many of the heathy commons and parks within Greater London, including Wimbledon Common, Richmond Park, Hampstead Heath and even Kew Gardens. It has been lost as a breeding species from all these sites, with the last regular breeding in Richmond Park in 1930 (another pair nested in 1950) (Self).

By the time of the first atlas, this species was breeding in a small number of tetrads in the outer parts of our area, including a cluster of tetrads near Broxbourne and another two clusters in the Surrey sector. The second atlas shows a reduction the Nightjar's distribution, with evidence of breeding reported from just three tetrads. Two of these were in the north of our area, again near Broxbourne. Breeding may also have taken place elsewhere at undisclosed locations during that period.

The current atlas indicates the loss of the Broxbourne population. However, evidence of breeding came from one tetrad in the south-west of our area, not far from where this species was also recorded breeding at the time of the first atlas.

It is likely that no more than two pairs bred in our area at the beginning of the current atlas period and that this may now have ceased (LBR). In 2009, there were only two records of birds 'churring', each on just one day. From 2010 onwards there were no records of birds exhibiting breeding behaviour at all in the LNHS area, although probable breeding occurred in 2013 in a tetrad within the atlas survey area but outside the official LNHS boundary. Another report of probable breeding in 2013 is excluded, as no description was submitted to the London Bird Club. This species is also encountered in our area as a passage bird, including one recorded in Regent's Park in May 2010.

So that the breeding sites cannot be identified, a sector level summary is shown for the breeding season instead of a tetrad map.

Period	Number of Tetrads		
	Evidence of Breeding	Seen Only	Total
Breeding 1968–72	23	7	30
Breeding 1988–94	3	6	9
Breeding 2008–13	1	3	4

Breeding Distribution

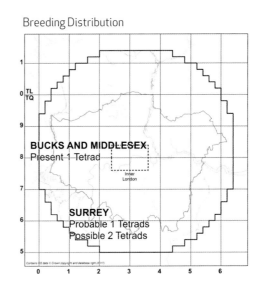

BUCKS AND MIDDLESEX
Present 1 Tetrad

Inner
London

SURREY
Probable 1 Tetrads
Possible 2 Tetrads

Contains OS data © Crown copyright and database right (2011)

Swift

Apus apus

Common, though probably declining, breeding summer visitor and passage migrant; amber list.

The Swift is found throughout the British Isles, though its occurrence is patchy across north-west Scotland and there has been a widespread decline in its abundance, with the breeding population in the UK falling between 34% and 51% between 1995 and 2013 (National Atlas; BBS). The Swift is difficult to monitor using traditional survey techniques as it can range a long way from its nesting sites.

Although the Swift remains widespread in the London area, declines are similar here to the rest of the UK, with the London trend being a steep drop since the end of the 1990s (BBS). This species was recorded in nearly 98% of tetrads during the second London atlas period but this has dropped to fewer than 90% of tetrads during the current London atlas period, with the number of confirmed or probable breeding records also falling.

Breeding Distribution

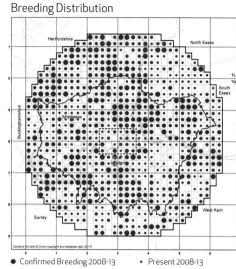

- Confirmed Breeding 2008-13
- Probable Breeding 2008-13
- Possible Breeding 2008-13
- Present 2008-13
- Still on Migration 2008-13

Period	Number of Tetrads		
	Evidence of Breeding	Seen Only	Total
Breeding 1968–72	424	265	689
Breeding 1988–94	408	430	838
Breeding 2008–13	259	496	755

The unoccupied tetrads are scattered across the whole London area suggesting general declines, though there are still a few areas with clusters of occupied tetrads with confirmed or probable breeding evidence. The maps are difficult to interpret (as was the case for both previous London atlases) as both passage and breeding birds can occur in large numbers away from breeding sites. However, there are gaps in south-east London and across the North Downs, while many other areas have no breeding evidence.

A reduction in the number of nest holes because of roof maintenance and new construction techniques is one possible reason behind the decline (Mayer, 2014). In some parts of London, local councils and developers have erected Swift boxes, or included Swift bricks in new buildings, to provide nest sites for Swifts. There have been a number of successes (Mayer, 2014).

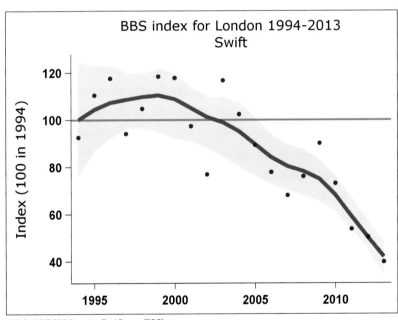

BTO/JNCC/RSPB Breeding Bird Survey (BBS)

Breeding Abundance

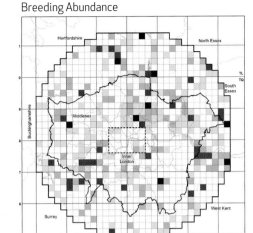

TTV Count Data (Mean Number)
- ☐ 1-4
- 5-10
- 11-18
- ■ 19-29
- ■ 30-65

Breeding Change

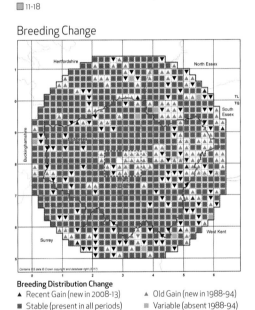

Breeding Distribution Change
- ▲ Recent Gain (new in 2008-13)
- ■ Stable (present in all periods)
- ▼ Old Loss (last occupied 1968-72)
- ▲ Old Gain (new in 1988-94)
- Variable (absent 1988-94)
- ▼ Recent Loss (last occupied 1988-94)

Kingfisher
Alcedo atthis

Locally common breeding resident with additional birds in winter; amber list.

The sight of a Kingfisher is unmistakable, though sadly often all too brief. The species is a widespread resident in Britain, and is found along lowland rivers, lakes and ponds throughout the year (National Atlas). In the UK, breeding numbers fell in the 1980s, then made a recovery and have since fallen slightly again but population levels remain much higher than the low experienced in the 1980s (BirdTrends; BBS). The population levels appear to be influenced by the severity of the preceding winter (BirdTrends).

During the breeding season, the distribution is restricted as a sandy bank, usually adjacent to water, is required to dig out a nest tunnel. Each pair defends a large territory which usually extends for 2–3km (Hamilton James. 1997). Breeding sites are sparsely scattered across the London area, with the main concentrations occurring in the area around the west London waterbodies, the Colne Valley and the Lee Valley. There appear to have been losses from some tetrads since the second atlas period in a number of areas, particularly in the east of our area. In spite of the recent losses, the Kingfisher remains more widespread in our area than at the time of the first atlas.

Period	Number of Tetrads		
	Evidence of Breeding	Seen Only	Total
Breeding 1968–72	83	54	137
Breeding 1988–94	156	161	317
Breeding 2008–13	98	129	227
Winter 2007/8–2012/13	-	-	307

A small number of birds make short distance movements to coastal areas during the winter and movement prompted by cold weather may also occur (Migration Atlas).

In the London area, the species can be encountered quite widely during winter in both urban and rural areas. As would be expected, many of the well-known sites are in the most well-watched wetland areas but it also uses smaller waterways and ponds.

The Kingfisher was not recorded in Inner London during the breeding seasons of either of the two previous breeding atlases. However, it was recorded in six Inner London tetrads during winter of the current atlas period and was present, though not breeding, in two tetrads during the breeding season. The construction of a Kingfisher bank at one site raises hopes that breeding may occur in Inner London in the future.

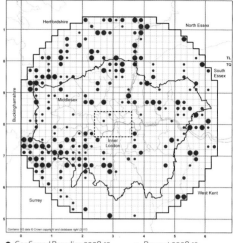

Breeding Distribution

● Confirmed Breeding 2008-13 ・ Present 2008-13
● Probable Breeding 2008-13 ・ Still on Migration 2008-13
● Possible Breeding 2008-13

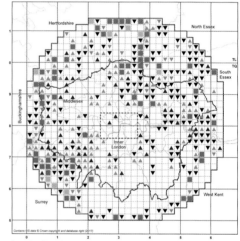

Breeding Change

Breeding Distribution Change
▲ Recent Gain (new in 2008-13) ▲ Old Gain (new in 1988-94)
■ Stable (present in all periods) ■ Variable (absent 1988-94)
▼ Old Loss (last occupied 1968-72) ▼ Recent Loss (last occupied 1988-94)

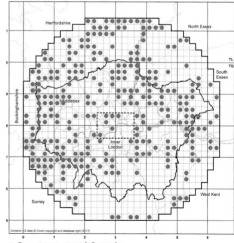

Winter Distribution

● Overwintering 2007/08-2012/13

Wryneck

Jynx torquilla

Scarce passage migrant, former breeder; not listed.

The Wryneck was relatively common in England at the beginning of the twentieth century, when it frequently nested in large suburban gardens (Montier). It was becoming rare in Britain by the 1950s and is now almost extinct here as a breeding bird. Most putative breeding records now come from the Scottish Highlands, including one probable breeding record and several records of singing birds during 2007–11 (National Atlas). The Wryneck remains fairly common and widespread as a breeding species elsewhere in Europe and in Asia. Most of the Wryneck which breed in Western Europe winter in Africa and the very south of Europe (BirdLife).

At the time of the first atlas, the south-east of England and East Anglia were the only regions in England still thought to support breeding Wryneck. It was recorded in just 15 tetrads during the first London Atlas, with breeding confirmed in four of them and evidence of breeding in another seven. Two confirmed breeding records in 1972 were the last records of breeding Wryneck in the London area (Self) and this species is now solely a scarce passage migrant in our area, mostly in autumn. A record of a singing bird in an Essex woodland within our area in May 2009 (Essex Bird Report, 2010) is therefore noteworthy. Although it appeared in the Essex Bird Report and was included as a possible breeding record in the National Atlas, this potential record was not submitted to the London Bird Club ID panel, and is therefore excluded from the table. Interestingly, two other records of passage migrants did occur in the Essex sector in the same month, at Hainault Forest and Purfleet (LBR). Despite this, it seems unlikely that the status of Wryneck in the London area will change soon.

Period	Number of Tetrads		
	Evidence of Breeding	Seen Only	Total
Breeding 1968–72	11	4	15
Breeding 1988–94	0	0	0
Breeding 2008–13	0	0	0

Green Woodpecker
Picus viridis

Common breeding resident; green list.

The Green Woodpecker is found across southern Britain, with the distribution becoming patchier in northern Britain and in western Wales. It is increasing in abundance in the east of its range including the London area but declining in the west (National Atlas).

In the London area, it has continued to expand its distribution further into urban areas since the time of the second London atlas, following gains made between the first two atlases. It has recolonised Inner London, where it last bred in the 1950s (Self), and can now be seen in smaller parks as well as some of the larger parks in the western half of Inner London. In fact, the recolonisation of Inner London occurred in the late 1990s soon after the end of second atlas period (Hewlett *et al.*). The BBS graph for Greater London shows strong population increases at this time and suggests that numbers may have peaked in the early 2000s. Green spaces are limited to the tiniest of squares in the eastern half of Inner London and this heavily built-up area remains unoccupied. The breeding distribution map also shows a small number of unoccupied tetrads in other areas, particularly in south and east London. In terms of abundance, the distribution is fairly even with fewer than four birds recorded in most tetrads during the timed counts. The peak timed count of nine birds in one hour occurred at both TQ68A (Grange Waters/North Stifford area) and TQ16T (Surbiton including Hampton Court Park).

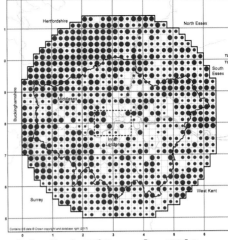

Breeding Distribution

- ● Confirmed Breeding 2008-13
- ● Probable Breeding 2008-13
- ● Possible Breeding 2008-13
- • Present 2008-13
- • Still on Migration 2008-13

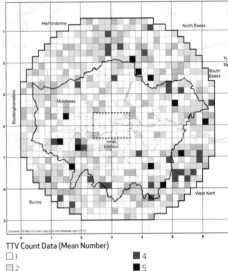

Breeding Abundance

TTV Count Data (Mean Number)
- □ 1
- □ 2
- □ 3
- ■ 4
- ■ 5

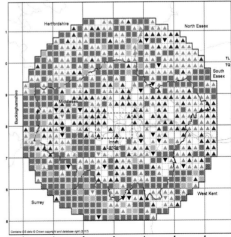

Breeding Change

Breeding Distribution Change
- ▲ Recent Gain (new in 2008-13)
- ■ Stable (present in all periods)
- ▼ Old Loss (last occupied 1968-72)
- ▲ Old Gain (new in 1988-94)
- ■ Variable (absent 1988-94)
- ▼ Recent Loss (last occupied 1988-94)

Period	Number of Tetrads		
	Evidence of Breeding	Seen Only	Total
Breeding 1968–72	259	111	370
Breeding 1988–94	393	189	582
Breeding 2008–13	470	298	768
Winter 2007/8–2012/13	–	–	764

Winter Distribution

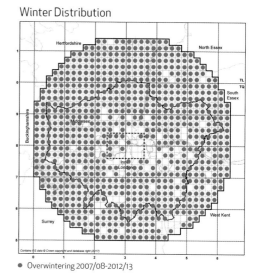

● Overwintering 2007/08-2012/13

The winter distribution of the Green Woodpecker across the London area is similar to the breeding season, with the most significant unoccupied area being the area in and adjacent to the eastern half of Inner London. The species is known to show high site-fidelity throughout the year, usually making only short movements in autumn and winter (Migration Atlas). Minor differences to tetrad occupancy in winter may relate predominantly to the dispersal of juveniles but could also involve local movement by some adults to more open wintering sites that do not contain suitable breeding habitat.

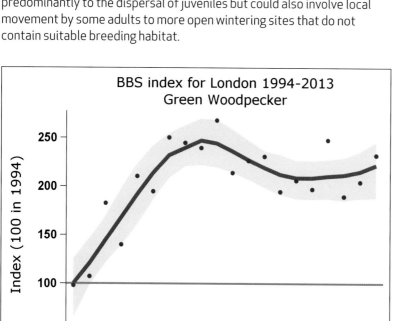

BTO/JNCC/RSPB Breeding Bird Survey (BBS)

Great Spotted Woodpecker

Dendrocopos major

Common breeding resident; green list.

The Great Spotted Woodpecker can be found across Britain and has successfully colonised Ireland during the last ten years (National Atlas). The UK population has increased by between 117% and 154% between 1995 and 2013, with the population in the London region increasing by between 30% and 103% over the same period (BBS).

As in the first two atlases, the Great Spotted Woodpecker remains the most widespread species of woodpecker in the London area. It has further consolidated its status in Greater London, and can now be found even in some of the more heavily urbanised areas of Inner London. Some gaps remain in a few areas, such as along the Thames where there is a lack of suitable habitat in some tetrads. The abundance maps show a clear association with woodland and wooded parkland, with Richmond Park and Wimbledon Common standing out within Greater London.

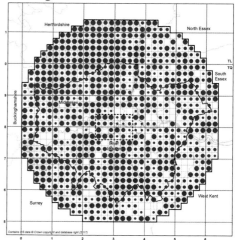

Breeding Distribution

- ● Confirmed Breeding 2008-13
- ● Probable Breeding 2008-13
- ● Possible Breeding 2008-13
- • Present 2008-13
- • Still on Migration 2008-13

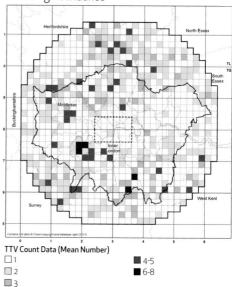

Breeding Abundance

TTV Count Data (Mean Number)
- ☐ 1
- ☐ 2
- ☐ 3
- ■ 4-5
- ■ 6-8

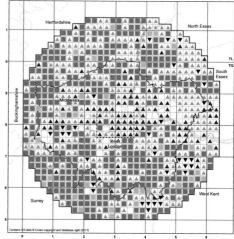

Breeding Change

Breeding Distribution Change
- ▲ Recent Gain (new in 2008-13)
- ■ Stable (present in all periods)
- ▼ Old Loss (last occupied 1968-72)
- ▲ Old Gain (new in 1988-94)
- ■ Variable (absent 1988-94)
- ▼ Recent Loss (last occupied 1988-94)

Period	Number of Tetrads		
	Evidence of Breeding	Seen Only	Total
Breeding 1968–72	286	125	411
Breeding 1988–94	500	177	677
Breeding 2008–13	546	245	791
Winter 2007/8–2012/13	-	-	812

Winter Distribution

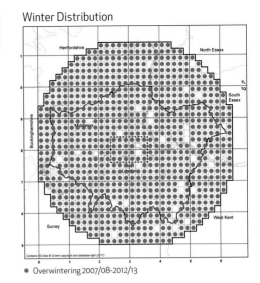

● Overwintering 2007/08-2012/13

As may be expected, the Great Spotted Woodpecker is slightly more widespread during the winter months. During this time, it can exploit feeding opportunities in tetrads containing very little green space and is therefore not restricted by the need to find suitable trees in which to breed. Dead wood can also be a good source of invertebrate food for woodpeckers during the winter months but the provision of food in gardens by people may have helped lessen the reliance of the Great Spotted Woodpecker on its more traditional habitat during winter.

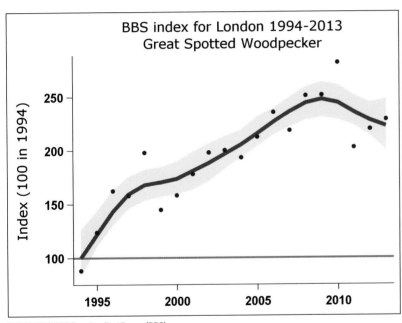

BTO/JNCC/RSPB Breeding Bird Survey (BBS)

Lesser Spotted Woodpecker

Dendrocopos minor

Scarce and declining breeding resident; red list.

In Britain, the Lesser Spotted Woodpecker is restricted to England and Wales. In contrast to the success of the other two woodpecker species, the Lesser Spotted Woodpecker population last peaked in about 1980, during the outbreak of Dutch Elm disease, and has declined since, with numbers halving in the ten years to 1999 (National Atlas). It is believed that this severe decline has continued since then (BirdTrends) but the species is now too rare to be monitored by BBS. It is on the red list of birds of conservation concern and is now considered scarce enough for breeding records to be collated by the Rare Breeding Birds Panel, with the breeding population in Britain estimated to be as low as 1,500 pairs (Musgrove *et al.*, 2013).

The species remains fairly widespread in the London area, as was the case during the two previous breeding atlases, but the distribution is now extremely sparse, with just a scattering of occupied tetrads across previous strongholds in the Essex sector, the Hertfordshire sector and in South London. The only notable cluster of occupied tetrads is in south-west London in Richmond Park, with confirmed breeding also occurring at Tooting Common, Wanstead Flats and several other sites closer to the outer edges of the London area. The change map clearly shows the extent of the decline since the second atlas.

Period	Number of Tetrads		
	Evidence of Breeding	Seen Only	Total
Breeding 1968–72	139	89	228
Breeding 1988–94	195	146	341
Breeding 2008–13	45	76	121
Winter 2007/8–2012/13	-	-	130

The winter map is similar to the breeding map, but with slightly more occupied tetrads in some areas, particularly in west London. This may partly result from birds wandering during winter, and this was certainly the case for the records which came from well-watched sites such as Rainham Marshes and Alexandra Park. The species also often drums in February before becoming silent and more elusive later in the season, so some of the additional winter records may indicate sites where presence during the breeding season later went undetected.

The elusive nature of the Lesser Spotted Woodpecker, when combined with the decline, is likely to have made the species particularly hard to find during this atlas period. It seems likely that the species may have also been present but undetected during the atlas period in some tetrads where coverage was less thorough (for example parts of TQ49, TL40 and TL50 in Essex). Whether or not this was the case, it seems clear that the species is continuing to decline in the London area, as elsewhere, and its future looks bleak unless scientists can identify the causes of the decline and measures to reverse the decline are implemented.

Breeding Distribution

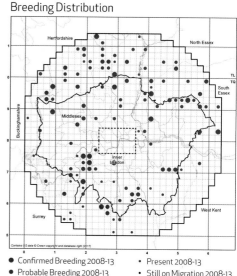

- ● Confirmed Breeding 2008-13
- ● Probable Breeding 2008-13
- ● Possible Breeding 2008-13
- • Present 2008-13
- • Still on Migration 2008-13

225

Breeding Change

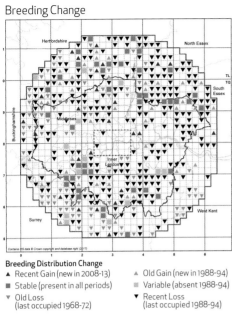

Breeding Distribution Change
- ▲ Recent Gain (new in 2008-13)
- ■ Stable (present in all periods)
- ▼ Old Loss (last occupied 1968-72)
- ▲ Old Gain (new in 1988-94)
- ■ Variable (absent 1988-94)
- ▼ Recent Loss (last occupied 1988-94)

Winter Distribution

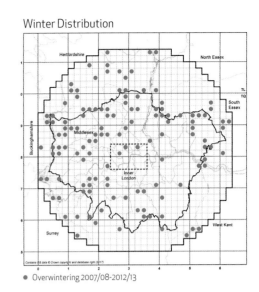

- ● Overwintering 2007/08-2012/13

Red-Backed Shrike

Lanius collurio

Rare passage migrant; red list.

The Red-backed Shrike declined in Britain from the mid-nineteenth century onwards, becoming effectively extinct by the 1990s, with occasional breeding from widely scattered localities occurring since then (National Atlas).

In the London area, the species was still present at the time of the first atlas, when breeding was confirmed in four tetrads and considered probable in a fifth. The last confirmed breeding occurred not long afterwards, in 1975 (Self), and the species appeared in the second London Atlas alongside Wryneck and Cirl Bunting in a section about species lost as breeding birds in our area.

The status remains unchanged and during the current atlas period there were just four breeding season records. Three were short-staying passage birds present for a maximum of two days. The fourth stayed for slightly longer, visiting Lake Farm Country Park intermittently from 11th to 22nd July 2012 (LBR). It seems most likely that this male was an early-returning, failed breeder and, therefore, it is presumed to be a migrant like the others and excluded from the totals in the table below.

However, there have been other recent and widely scattered breeding attempts across Britain (National Atlas). So, it is tempting to speculate that the Lake Farm bird was a wandering bird that had failed to find a mate, and that breeding could possibly occur again in our area if a pair came together in a suitable location early in the season. Sadly, given the status of this species, this seems extremely unlikely and, should it ever occur, it is difficult to believe that it would be anything other than a one-off.

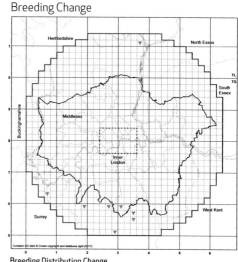

Breeding Change

Breeding Distribution Change
- ▲ Recent Gain (new in 2008-13)
- ■ Stable (present in all periods)
- ▼ Old Loss (last occupied 1968-72)
- ▲ Old Gain (new in 1988-94)
- ■ Variable (absent 1988-94)
- ▼ Recent Loss (last occupied 1988-94)

Period	Number of Tetrads		
	Evidence of Breeding	Seen Only	Total
Breeding 1968–72	5	4	9
Breeding 1988–94	0	0	0
Breeding 2008–13	0	0	0

Magpie
Pica pica

Abundant breeding resident; green list.

The Magpie occurs throughout the British Isles except in the highlands of Scotland and the Northern Isles. Numbers are increasing and it is not of conservation concern.

It is hard to believe that the Magpie was very rare in our area at the beginning of the twentieth century. This was however an artificial situation brought about by the activities of gamekeepers in the surrounding countryside (Montier). The relaxation of persecution resulted in a rapid increase in the Magpie population in the London area from the 1930s onwards (LNHS, 1964). By the time of the first atlas, just over three quarters of the tetrads in our area were occupied by this species, rising to near full occupation by the time of the second atlas. That situation continues today. In fact, the urban areas of Great Britain, including London, have become hotspots for this species, with these areas supporting much greater densities of this species than rural areas. Curiously, the same pattern is not evident in Ireland (National Atlas).

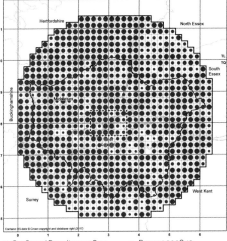

Breeding Distribution

- ● Confirmed Breeding 2008-13
- ● Probable Breeding 2008-13
- ● Possible Breeding 2008-13
- · Present 2008-13
- · Still on Migration 2008-13

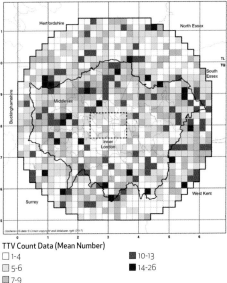

Breeding Abundance

TTV Count Data (Mean Number)
- □ 1-4
- □ 5-6
- □ 7-9
- ■ 10-13
- ■ 14-26

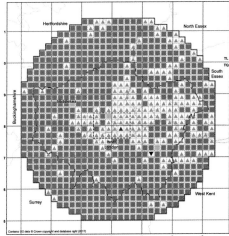

Breeding Change

Breeding Distribution Change
- ▲ Recent Gain (new in 2008-13)
- ■ Stable (present in all periods)
- ▼ Old Loss (last occupied 1968-72)
- ▲ Old Gain (new in 1988-94)
- ■ Variable (absent 1988-94)
- ▼ Recent Loss (last occupied 1988-94)

228

Despite their ability to take eggs, nestlings and even recently fledged young birds of other species, the available research indicates that elevated Magpie numbers do not affect songbird breeding populations (Gooch *et al.*, 1991; Thomson *et al.*, 1998). This appears to be the case even in urban areas (Chiron & Julliard, 2007; Groom, 1993). The authors of these papers suggest that the quality and availability of habitat is the factor which determines song bird populations. Magpie numbers continue to rise in London, a 34% (9% to 65%) increase in the period 1995 to 2013 (BBS), and, despite the research, some observers continue to speculate about the effect this may be having on other bird species.

Period	Number of Tetrads		
	Evidence of Breeding	Seen Only	Total
Breeding 1968–72	490	170	660
Breeding 1988–94	800	52	852
Breeding 2008–13	755	100	855
Winter 2007/8–2012/13	-	-	856

The distribution of the Magpie during the winter, both nationally and in our area, is much the same as during the breeding season. However, large aggregations can occur during this period, with counts of between 30 and 100 not being uncommon (LBR).

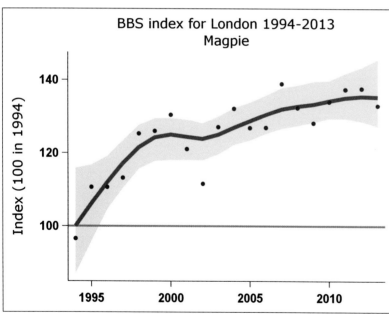

BTO/JNCC/RSPB Breeding Bird Survey (BBS)

Winter Distribution

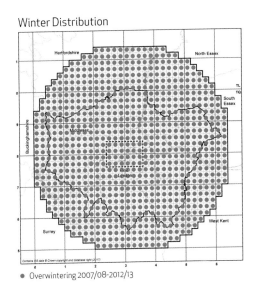

● Overwintering 2007/08-2012/13

Winter Abundance

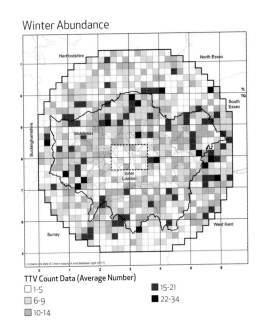

TTV Count Data (Average Number)

☐ 1-5
☐ 6-9
☐ 10-14
■ 15-21
■ 22-34

Jay
Garrulus glandarius

Common breeding bird, the resident population boosted by immigrants in the autumn and winter; green list.

The range of the Jay in the British Isles is expanding northwards and westwards but this species remains at its most abundant in the south-east of England, even though it is declining in this region (National Atlas).

About three quarters of the tetrads in our area were occupied by the Jay at the time of the first atlas, with the only major gap in distribution being along the Thames corridor from central London eastwards, where survey coverage was poor. By the time of the second atlas, this gap was reduced considerably which, coupled with more minor advances elsewhere, resulted in nearly 90% of the tetrads showing some level of occupation by this species. The advancement has continued and the number of tetrads occupied has now risen to 93%. Unsurprisingly, the abundance mapping shows that tetrads with the most extensive areas of woodland support the highest densities of this species. The Jay seems to be as happy in urban woodland and parks as in rural areas.

Period	Number of Tetrads		
	Evidence of Breeding	Seen Only	Total
Breeding 1968–72	417	220	637
Breeding 1988–94	552	209	761
Breeding 2008–13	447	346	793
Winter 2007/8–2012/13	-	-	820

The distribution of the Jay during the winter, both nationally and in our area, is much the same as during the breeding season. However, a higher number of tetrads was found to support this species in the London area during the winter when compared to the breeding season. The Jay is normally highly sedentary. However, occasional, large-scale movements in autumn and winter may occur. Such movements are thought to be related to the availability of acorns and probably involve mostly birds that breed in Britain, as influxes into Britain from birds which breed in Scandinavia are believed to be rare (Migration Atlas).

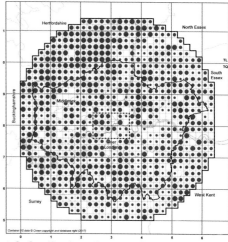

Breeding Distribution

- ● Confirmed Breeding 2008-13
- ● Probable Breeding 2008-13
- ● Possible Breeding 2008-13
- • Present 2008-13
- • Still on Migration 2008-13

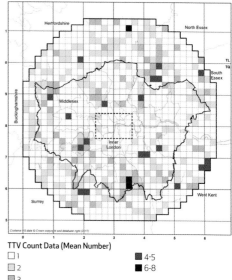

Breeding Abundance

TTV Count Data (Mean Number)
- ☐ 1
- ☐ 2
- ☐ 3
- ▨ 4-5
- ■ 6-8

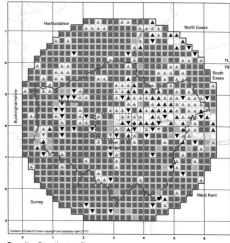

Breeding Change

Breeding Distribution Change
- ▲ Recent Gain (new in 2008-13)
- ■ Stable (present in all periods)
- ▼ Old Loss (last occupied 1968-72)
- ▲ Old Gain (new in 1988-94)
- ▨ Variable (absent 1988-94)
- ▼ Recent Loss (last occupied 1988-94)

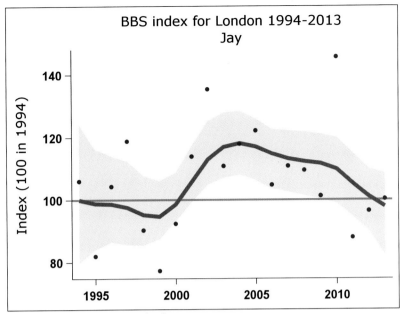

BBS index for London 1994-2013
Jay

Index (100 in 1994)

BTO/JNCC/RSPB Breeding Bird Survey (BBS)

Winter Distribution

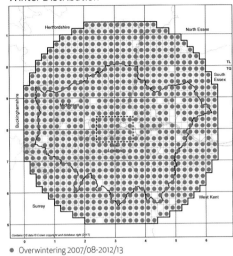

● Overwintering 2007/08-2012/13

Winter Abundance

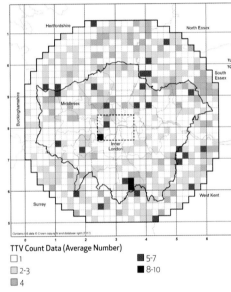

TTV Count Data (Average Number)

☐ 1
☐ 2-3
▨ 4
▨ 5-7
■ 8-10

Jackdaw

Corvus monedula

Common breeding resident and passage migrant, much scarcer in the inner suburbs and city centre; green list.

The Jackdaw is widely distributed throughout the British Isles, only being absent from the north-west of Scotland (National Atlas). The population began to increase in the 1970s and is continuing to do so. For example, in south-east England, the population rose by 72% (45% to 95%) between 1995 and 2013 (BBS, no data for London).

The national atlas clearly shows that the Jackdaw occurs at lower densities in urban areas and this is reflected in the London area, with much more frequent occurrence of this species outside the built-up area than within it.

A comparison of the first and second atlas maps for the London area does not show much change. Both show a population largely confined to the rural margins and larger parks, with some gaps in distribution. Much the same number of tetrads was occupied both times. However, the current atlas shows significant consolidation outside Greater London, with nearly every tetrad occupied, and a significant advance towards the centre of London from all sides.

There was once a small breeding colony in Kensington Gardens but this died out in 1969 (Montier). There were a few records of this species in Inner London during the breeding season in the current atlas period all relating to transient birds. However, it is conceivable that this species will return to breed in Inner London, as suitable nesting habitat is available there.

The abundance map indicates that Richmond Park is a hotspot for this species, presumably due to the high number of old trees containing suitable crevices for nesting. This is also a hotspot for Ring-necked Parakeet and clearly both species are able to find suitable nest sites there. The scientific literature (Newson *et al.*, 2011; Strubbe & Matthysen, 2007) indicates that there is little competition between these two species for nest sites, since Jackdaws prefer larger cavities.

Period	Number of Tetrads		
	Evidence of Breeding	Seen Only	Total
Breeding 1968–72	260	201	461
Breeding 1988–94	240	225	465
Breeding 2008–13	441	215	656
Winter 2007/8–2012/13	-	-	684

The distribution of the Jackdaw during the winter, both nationally and in our area, is much the same as during the breeding season. However, this belies one of our best wildlife spectacles; the flocks of Jackdaw which swirl around the sky at dusk before settling to roost in trees. In our area (and elsewhere), such flocks can comprise more than 1,000 birds (LBR).

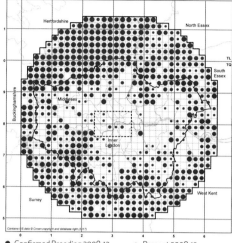

Breeding Distribution

● Confirmed Breeding 2008-13   • Present 2008-13
● Probable Breeding 2008-13   • Still on Migration 2008-13
● Possible Breeding 2008-13

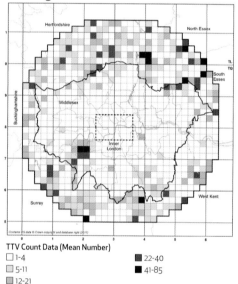

Breeding Abundance

TTV Count Data (Mean Number)
☐ 1-4   ■ 22-40
☐ 5-11   ■ 41-85
▨ 12-21

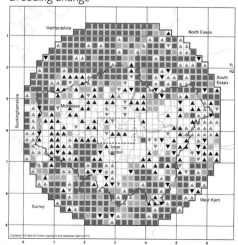

Breeding Change

Breeding Distribution Change
▲ Recent Gain (new in 2008-13)   ▲ Old Gain (new in 1988-94)
■ Stable (present in all periods)   ▨ Variable (absent 1988-94)
▼ Old Loss (last occupied 1968-72)   ▼ Recent Loss (last occupied 1988-94)

Winter Distribution

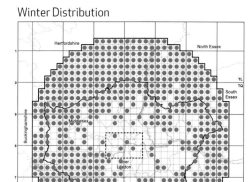

● Overwintering 2007/08-2012/13

Winter Abundance

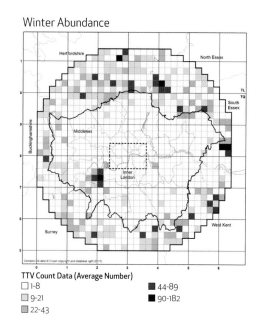

TTV Count Data (Average Number)
- ☐ 1-8
- ☐ 9-21
- ☐ 22-43
- ■ 44-89
- ■ 90-182

Rook

Corvus frugilegus

Common breeding resident in the outer part of the London area, much scarcer in urban localities; green list.

The Rook is widely distributed throughout the British Isles, only being absent from the north-west of Scotland (National Atlas). Whilst the population seems to be declining (BBS), it is not currently of conservation concern.

Despite breeding in Inner London up until 1916, the Rook is very much a rural bird and it disappeared as a breeding bird from this area and most of Greater London as the city grew. The National Atlas shows very clearly that London and the surrounding area now have the lowest density of Rook in lowland England.

The maps from all three London atlases show a similar picture with birds confined largely to the rural areas outside of Greater London. Even in these areas, the breeding population seems to be thinning, with fewer tetrads showing evidence of breeding over time. A few rookeries still persist within Greater London, and in fact the number within the capital has surprisingly increased slightly since the second atlas, although, apart from those in south-east London, they appear to be isolated. Non-breeding birds are occasionally seen in more urban locations, including Inner London, though usually these are flyovers.

Period	Number of Tetrads		
	Evidence of Breeding	Seen Only	Total
Breeding 1968–72	169	124	293
Breeding 1988–94	122	184	306
Breeding 2008–13	107	161	268
Winter 2007/8–2012/13	-	-	331

Nationally, the distribution of the Rook during the winter is much the same as during the breeding season. In the London area, the number of occupied tetrads is higher during winter when compared to the breeding season, with more occupied tetrads on the periphery of Greater London.

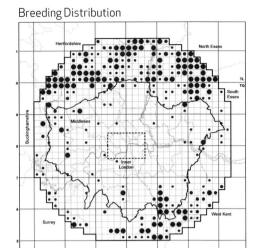

Breeding Distribution

● Confirmed Breeding 2008-13   • Present 2008-13
● Probable Breeding 2008-13   • Still on Migration 2008-13
● Possible Breeding 2008-13

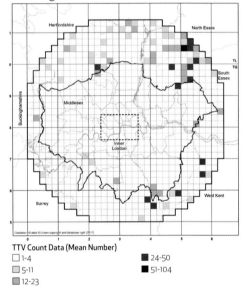

Breeding Abundance

TTV Count Data (Mean Number)
□ 1-4   ■ 24-50
▢ 5-11   ■ 51-104
▨ 12-23

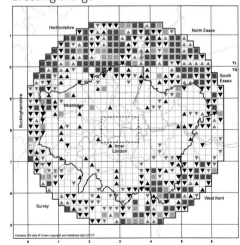

Breeding Change

Breeding Distribution Change
▲ Recent Gain (new in 2008-13)   ▲ Old Gain (new in 1988-94)
■ Stable (present in all periods)   ▨ Variable (absent 1988-94)
▼ Old Loss (last occupied 1968-72)   ▼ Recent Loss (last occupied 1988-94)

Winter Distribution

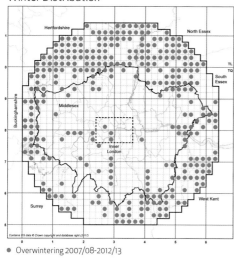

● Overwintering 2007/08-2012/13

Winter Abundance

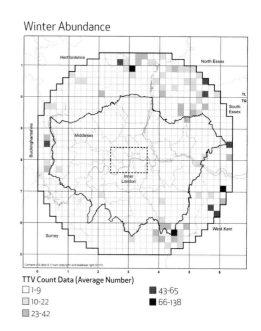

TTV Count Data (Average Number)
☐ 1-9
☐ 10-22
☐ 23-42
■ 43-65
■ 66-138

Carrion Crow

Corvus corone

Abundant breeding resident; green list.

The Carrion Crow is widely distributed throughout the British Isles, only being absent from the north-west of Scotland and Ireland where it is replaced by the Hooded Crow (National Atlas). The population of the Carrion Crow is generally increasing.

Unlike the Rook, the Carrion Crow has adapted well to the urban environment and the National Atlas clearly shows that the London area has some of highest densities of this species in England.

The three London atlases show that this species became ubiquitous sometime between the first and second atlas. In subsequent years (between 1995 and 2013), the Carrion Crow population in the London area increased by 39% (11% to 76%) (BBS) and, during the current atlas period, it was the fourth most commonly recorded breeding species on timed counts within the London area. However, the population growth in our area seems to have levelled off in the last few years (BBS).

Period	Number of Tetrads		
	Evidence of Breeding	Seen Only	Total
Breeding 1968–72	614	153	767
Breeding 1988–94	771	84	855
Breeding 2008–13	743	110	853
Winter 2007/8–2012/13	-	-	856

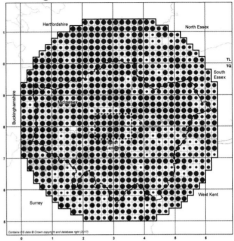

Breeding Distribution

- ● Confirmed Breeding 2008-13
- ● Probable Breeding 2008-13
- ● Possible Breeding 2008-13
- • Present 2008-13
- • Still on Migration 2008-13

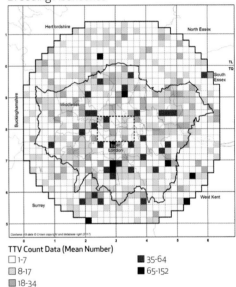

Breeding Abundance

TTV Count Data (Mean Number)
- ☐ 1-7
- ☐ 8-17
- ☐ 18-34
- ☐ 35-64
- ■ 65-152

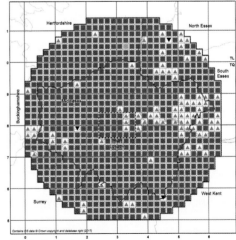

Breeding Change

Breeding Distribution Change
- ▲ Recent Gain (new in 2008-13)
- ■ Stable (present in all periods)
- ▼ Old Loss (last occupied 1968-72)
- ▲ Old Gain (new in 1988-94)
- ■ Variable (absent 1988-94)
- ▼ Recent Loss (last occupied 1988-94)

The distribution of the Carrion Crow during the winter, both nationally and in our area, is much the same as during the breeding season. The winter season provides some large aggregations of this species (which defies the way that many birdwatchers learned to distinguish Carrion Crows and Rooks as a child). Rather than just seeing Carrion Crows in twos or threes, they can be seen fairly often in groups of more than 100, sometimes several hundred, and there is even a record during the current atlas period of more than 3,000 at Beddington Farmlands (LBR). The atlas abundance maps show that the tetrad including Beddington Farmland also recorded the highest timed counts in both seasons, but there are also contemporary records of high numbers from scattered localities throughout the London Area (LBR).

Winter Distribution

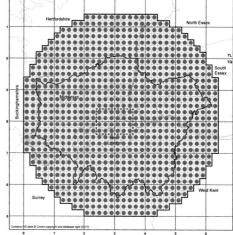

● Overwintering 2007/08-2012/13

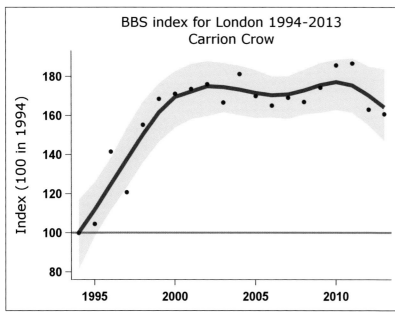

BTO/JNCC/RSPB Breeding Bird Survey (BBS)

Winter Abundance

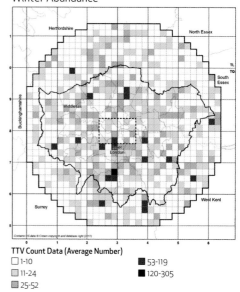

TTV Count Data (Average Number)

☐ 1-10   ■ 53-119

▨ 11-24   ■ 120-305

▨ 25-52

Raven

Corvus corax

Scarce, but increasing visitor; green list.

The Raven is associated with the uplands of western Britain and Ireland, where populations are at their densest. However, this species retreated to these areas in the nineteenth and twentieth centuries as a result of persecution. Happily, the population is currently increasing and expanding eastwards again (National Atlas).

The Raven was once a common species in London and replaced the Red Kite as the main scavenger in the city (Hudson, 1898). However, it disappeared as a breeding species in the London area in the middle of the nineteenth century (Self). During the periods covered by the last two London atlases, the Raven was confined as a breeding species to western and northern parts of the British Isles (National Atlas). Therefore, despite the famous residents of the Tower of London, the Raven did not make an appearance in either publication.

As noted above, the latter part of the last century and the early part of this century saw the breeding distribution of the Raven advance dramatically eastward in a similar fashion to the Common Buzzard. By the time the current atlas period began, the Raven was breeding again in most of the counties around the London area but not within it. There were however many instances of this species passing over our area.

Then, in 2013, the first confirmed record of successful breeding took place in the Kent sector. Two young were successfully raised. Discounting captive birds, this is the first such occurrence since 1845. There is also a record of probable breeding in the Hertfordshire sector of our area, with possibly the same birds observed in several other tetrads in this sector.

The confirmed and probable breeding records have been removed from the breeding map so that the sites cannot be identified.

Period	Number of Tetrads		
	Evidence of Breeding	Seen Only	Total
Breeding 1968–72	0	0	0
Breeding 1988–94	0	0	0
Breeding 2008–13	2	41	43
Winter 2007/8–2012/13	-	-	45

The distribution of the Raven during the winter nationally is much the same as during the breeding season. In our area too, the situation is much the same with mainly wandering birds which can turn up almost anywhere, even Inner London. Most records are still of single birds flying over, including the records from Inner London (LBR). These are likely to account for some dots on the maps, although known flyovers are excluded from the atlas maps. Both maps include a small number of records which were not included in the LBR as they were not submitted to the London Bird Club recorders.

Breeding Distribution

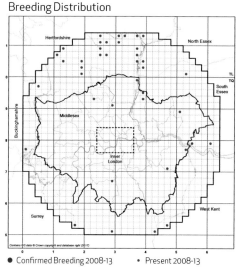

- ● Confirmed Breeding 2008-13
- ● Probable Breeding 2008-13
- ● Possible Breeding 2008-13
- · Present 2008-13
- · Still on Migration 2008-13

Winter Distribution

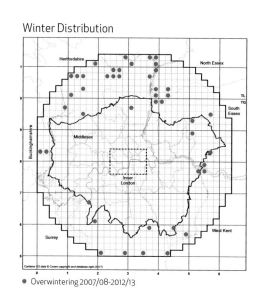

● Overwintering 2007/08-2012/13

Goldcrest

Regulus regulus

Breeding resident, passage migrant and winter visitor; green list.

The Goldcrest has a range which extends across Europe and parts of Asia (BirdLife). The Goldcrest is strongly associated with conifers and has benefited from modern forestry plantations. Perhaps as a result, it is now breeding in most 10km squares in Britain and Ireland (National Atlas).

In the first atlas, this species was shown to be widespread but less often found in the built-up areas of London and also on both sides of the Thames east of London where more open habitats prevail. The second atlas indicates that consolidation had occurred in the intervening period, resulting in more occupied tetrads in Greater London and the open areas to the east. Breeding evidence was recorded in approximately half of the tetrads in our area. The current atlas shows a similar pattern of distribution in the London area, with slightly more occupied tetrads, although there are still a fair number of tetrads where breeding was not recorded. Unsurprisingly, these are most prevalent in the areas where this species was not found in the first atlas.

The population density maps also reflect that pattern with the highest densities typically on the periphery of our area, in more rural locations with plenty of woodland. Northaw Great Wood in Hertfordshire stands out on the abundance map as a population hotspot.

Period	Number of Tetrads		
	Evidence of Breeding	Seen Only	Total
Breeding 1968–72	312	75	387
Breeding 1988–94	418	136	554
Breeding 2008–13	372	255	627
Winter 2007/8–2012/13	-	-	744

The Goldcrest is resident in Britain but the wintering population also comprises migrants, with birds which breed further north arriving in winter, including large falls of migrants from the continent which occasionally occur on British coasts (Migration Atlas). Some birds which breed in northern Britain may also move south, but very few ringing recoveries have been made so this is uncertain (Migration Atlas). The rest of the birds that breed in Britain are thought to be mainly sedentary, especially in the south-east, though this species appears to have a reduced association with conifer woodland in the winter (Snow & Perrins, 1998). Reflecting this situation, and perhaps the larger post-breeding population, the Goldcrest is found more widely in the London area in winter, with presence recorded in 14% more London area tetrads than during the breeding season. The broader picture, however, is that the distribution of this species in winter, both nationally and locally, is much the same as in the breeding season.

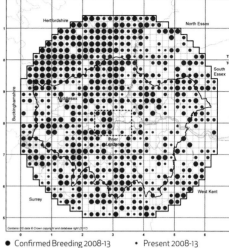

Breeding Distribution

● Confirmed Breeding 2008-13   • Present 2008-13
● Probable Breeding 2008-13   • Still on Migration 2008-13
● Possible Breeding 2008-13

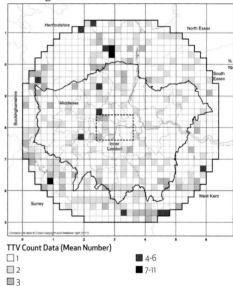

Breeding Abundance

TTV Count Data (Mean Number)
☐ 1   ■ 4-6
☐ 2   ■ 7-11
☐ 3

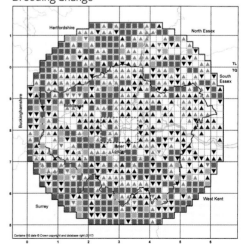

Breeding Change

Breeding Distribution Change
▲ Recent Gain (new in 2008-13)   ▲ Old Gain (new in 1988-94)
■ Stable (present in all periods)   ■ Variable (absent 1988-94)
▼ Old Loss (last occupied 1968-72)   ▼ Recent Loss (last occupied 1988-94)

Winter Distribution

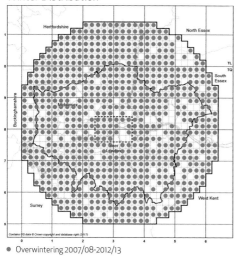

● Overwintering 2007/08-2012/13

Winter Abundance

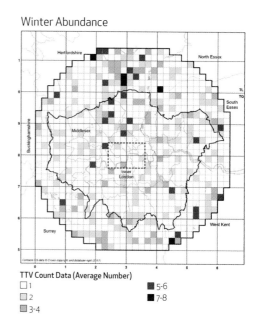

TTV Count Data (Average Number)

□ 1   ■ 5-6
□ 2   ■ 7-8
■ 3-4

Firecrest

Regulus ignicapilla

Scarce passage migrant and winter visitor, rare breeder; amber list.

In Britain, the Firecrest occurs as a breeding bird primarily in south-east England, south of the line between the Wash and the Severn Estuary (National Atlas). This is the northern edge of its range, which extends southwards to North Africa (BirdLife). Like the Goldcrest, the Firecrest is associated with coniferous woodlands and may have benefited from the extensive planting of conifers which occurred in Britain during the twentieth century.

At the time of the first atlas, the Firecrest was a relatively new colonist of the British Isles, and there was no evidence that this species was breeding in the London area despite a handful of records during the breeding season. The first confirmed breeding record in our area was in 1980, followed by another in 1987 (Self). During the six year period of the second atlas, evidence of breeding by this species was recorded in 11 tetrads in total. These were at scattered locations, mainly outside the built-up areas of Greater London but also at Hampstead Heath and Sydenham Hill Wood. The current atlas indicates further colonisation of our area by this species, mostly in the Essex and Hertfordshire sectors outside the built-up areas of Greater London but with scattered records within. Nevertheless, the number of pairs breeding each year is probably fewer than five and most of the records during the atlas period relate to short-staying singing males (LBR) which may have been passage migrants rather than territorial birds.

So that the breeding sites cannot be identified, a sector level summary is shown for the breeding season instead of a tetrad map.

Period	Number of Tetrads		
	Evidence of Breeding	Seen Only	Total
Breeding 1968–72	0	4	4
Breeding 1988–94	11	18	29
Breeding 2008–13	12	34	46
Winter 2007/8–2012/13	-	-	132

The details of migratory movements are poorly known for this species but the resident birds are joined during the winter by birds which probably breed further north and east (Migration Atlas), with passage birds also present in spring and autumn. When coupled with higher post-breeding numbers, the number of tetrads occupied by this species during the winter season is consequently higher than during the breeding season. Interestingly, the number of tetrads where this species was recorded during the winter season is higher in Greater London than outside it, which is the opposite pattern to that shown in the breeding season. It is easy to speculate that this is the result of higher temperatures in the built-up area.

Breeding Distribution

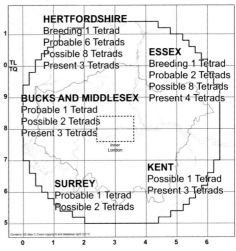

HERTFORDSHIRE
Breeding 1 Tetrad
Probable 6 Tetrads
Possible 8 Tetrads
Present 3 Tetrads

ESSEX
Breeding 1 Tetrad
Probable 2 Tetrads
Possible 8 Tetrads
Present 4 Tetrads

BUCKS AND MIDDLESEX
Probable 1 Tetrad
Possible 2 Tetrads
Present 3 Tetrads

KENT
Possible 1 Tetrad
Present 3 Tetrads

SURREY
Probable 1 Tetrad
Possible 2 Tetrads

Winter Distribution

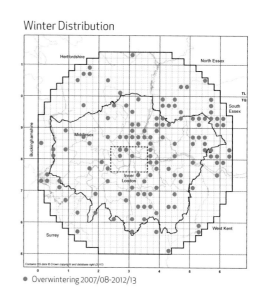

● Overwintering 2007/08-2012/13

Blue Tit

Cyanistes caeruleus

Abundant breeding resident; green list.

The Blue Tit is one of the commonest resident species in Britain and Ireland and, although it is most abundant in lowland England, it is found in nearly every 10km square (National Atlas).

It is also found in every tetrad in the London area. The first atlas shows some gaps in distribution, around the Thames, however, this was a reflection of the completeness of the survey work rather than a real absence at that time. The Blue Tit population in London increased steadily from the end of the second atlas period until around 2005 when it went into decline. It appears that the population has now returned to a similar level to that at the time of the second atlas (BBS). The reasons for the recent decline are not known.

Blue Tit abundance across our area seems to be largely level but with patches of higher density which are mostly associated with greater levels of tree cover and especially extensive woodland.

Period	Number of Tetrads		
	Evidence of Breeding	Seen Only	Total
Breeding 1968–72	743	50	793
Breeding 1988–94	842	14	856
Breeding 2008–13	818	38	856
Winter 2007/8–2012/13	-	-	855

The distribution of the Blue Tit in winter, both nationally and in our area, is the same as the breeding season. Patterns of abundance are also similar.

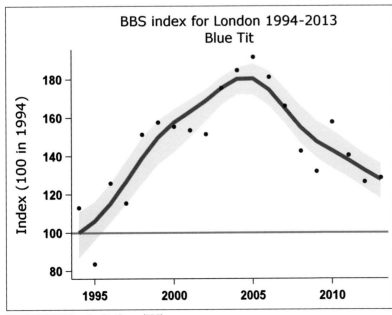

BTO/JNCC/RSPB Breeding Bird Survey (BBS)

Breeding Distribution

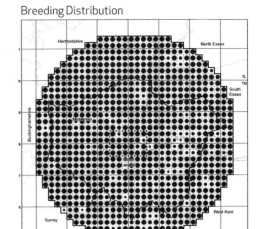

- ● Confirmed Breeding 2008-13
- ● Probable Breeding 2008-13
- ● Possible Breeding 2008-13
- • Present 2008-13
- • Still on Migration 2008-13

Breeding Abundance

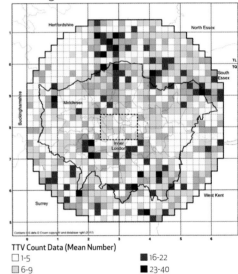

TTV Count Data (Mean Number)
- ☐ 1-5
- ☐ 6-9
- ☐ 10-15
- ■ 16-22
- ■ 23-40

Breeding Change

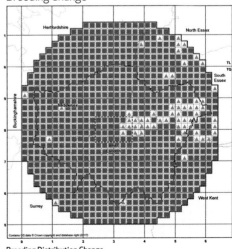

Breeding Distribution Change
- ▲ Recent Gain (new in 2008-13)
- ■ Stable (present in all periods)
- ▼ Old Loss (last occupied 1968-72)
- ▲ Old Gain (new in 1988-94)
- ■ Variable (absent 1988-94)
- ▼ Recent Loss (last occupied 1988-94)

Winter Distribution

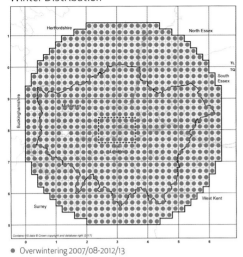

● Overwintering 2007/08-2012/13

Winter Abundance

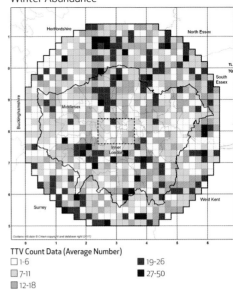

TTV Count Data (Average Number)
☐ 1-6   ■ 19-26
☐ 7-11   ■ 27-50
☐ 12-18

Great Tit

Parus major

Abundant breeding resident; green list.

The timed counts indicate that the Great Tit is not quite as numerous as the Blue Tit, with approximately two Great Tits being counted for every three Blue Tits, both in summer and winter. However, it is just as widespread. The Great Tit population has been steadily increasing since the 1960s and the densest populations are found in south-east England (National Atlas). It can make use of both urban and rural habitats.

Not surprisingly, this species was found in nearly every tetrad during fieldwork for the current atlas and must surely be at least present in the four tetrads where it was not observed during the breeding season. The second atlas shows a similar picture but the first atlas indicates a potential gap in occurrence along the Thames to the east of Inner London. As with the Blue Tit, this gap is due largely to the incompleteness of the survey rather than a real absence.

Like the Blue Tit, Great Tit abundance is fairly level across our area except for higher densities usually associated with areas of woodland. Great Tit abundance has increased markedly in the London area since 1995, perhaps because of the provision of food and nest boxes, but may now be declining (BBS).

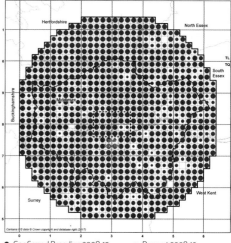

Breeding Distribution

- ● Confirmed Breeding 2008-13
- ● Probable Breeding 2008-13
- ● Possible Breeding 2008-13
- • Present 2008-13
- • Still on Migration 2008-13

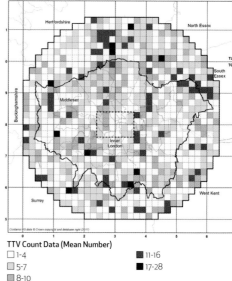

Breeding Abundance

TTV Count Data (Mean Number)

- ☐ 1-4
- 5-7
- 8-10
- ■ 11-16
- ■ 17-28

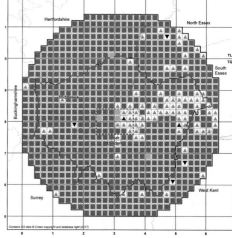

Breeding Change

Breeding Distribution Change
- ▲ Recent Gain (new in 2008-13)
- ■ Stable (present in all periods)
- ▼ Old Loss (last occupied 1968-72)
- ▲ Old Gain (new in 1988-94)
- ■ Variable (absent 1988-94)
- ▼ Recent Loss (last occupied 1988-94)

Period	Number of Tetrads		
	Evidence of Breeding	Seen Only	Total
Breeding 1968–72	706	63	769
Breeding 1988–94	819	30	849
Breeding 2008–13	786	66	852
Winter 2007/8–2012/13	-	-	856

The distribution of the Great Tit in winter, both nationally and in our area, is the same as the breeding season. Patterns of abundance are also similar.

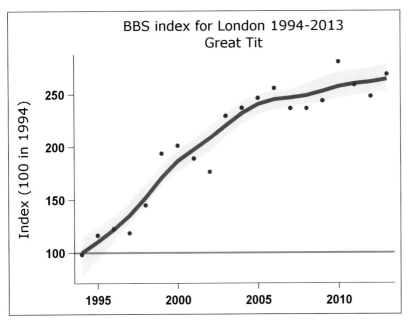

BTO/JNCC/RSPB Breeding Bird Survey (BBS)

Winter Distribution

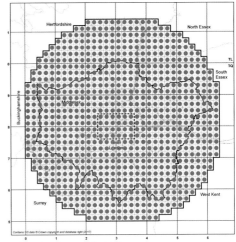

● Overwintering 2007/08-2012/13

Winter Abundance

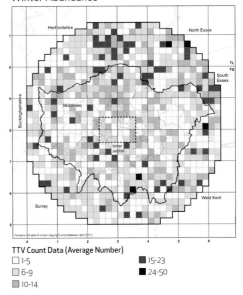

TTV Count Data (Average Number)

□ 1-5
□ 6-9
▨ 10-14
▩ 15-23
■ 24-50

Coal Tit

Periparus ater

Common breeding resident; green list.

The Coal Tit is a resident species across the temperate zone of Eurasia (BirdLife). Except for part of the East Anglia fens, this species is present throughout Britain and Ireland. It is especially abundant in areas with extensive coniferous woodland and in Ireland (National Atlas). The population is stable nationally but may be declining in south-east England (BBS).

In the London area, the distribution of this species has remained much the same across all three atlases, although the number of occupied tetrads has reduced since the second atlas period. Occupied tetrads are mainly in the west and south of our area, with the north-eastern quarter of the London area having the fewest occupied tetrads. The reason for this is unclear but could reflect of the availability of its coniferous woodland habitat.

Period	Number of Tetrads		
	Evidence of Breeding	Seen Only	Total
Breeding 1968–72	423	120	543
Breeding 1988–94	444	133	577
Breeding 2008–13	319	230	549
Winter 2007/8–2012/13	-	-	583

The distribution of this species nationally is pretty much the same during the winter as during the breeding season. In the London area, the Coal Tit is more widely distributed during the winter than during the breeding season, with more occupied tetrads, especially in the east of our area.

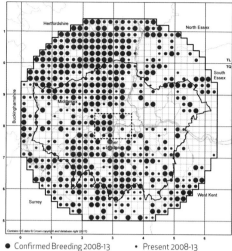

Breeding Distribution

● Confirmed Breeding 2008-13 · Present 2008-13
● Probable Breeding 2008-13 · Still on Migration 2008-13
● Possible Breeding 2008-13

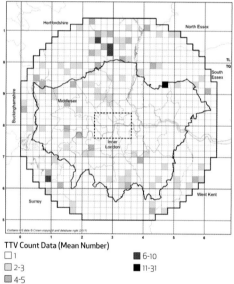

Breeding Abundance

TTV Count Data (Mean Number)
□ 1 ■ 6-10
▨ 2-3 ■ 11-31
▨ 4-5

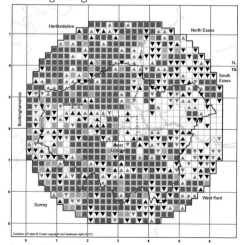

Breeding Distribution Change
▲ Recent Gain (new in 2008-13) ▲ Old Gain (new in 1988-94)
■ Stable (present in all periods) ■ Variable (absent 1988-94)
▼ Old Loss ▼ Recent Loss
(last occupied 1968-72) (last occupied 1988-94)

Winter Distribution

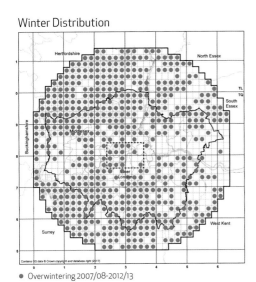

● Overwintering 2007/08-2012/13

Winter Abundance

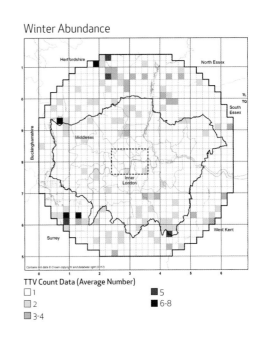

TTV Count Data (Average Number)

☐ 1   ■ 5
☐ 2   ■ 6-8
☐ 3-4

Willow Tit

Poecile montana

Former breeding resident; red list.

The Willow Tit is resident across the temperate zone of Eurasia, including parts of England, Wales and southern Scotland (BirdLife). It is declining and undergoing a range contraction in Britain, with this species becoming scarce south of the line between the Wash and the Severn Estuary and now absent from much of south-east England (National Atlas).

In the first and second atlases, the distribution of this species was much the same as for the Marsh Tit, with records coming mainly from the more wooded areas outside Greater London, to the north, south and west. Again, there was apparently a thinning in the distribution of the Willow Tit between the first and second atlases, particularly in the south of our area, with the overall number of tetrads with breeding evidence just about halving between these two periods. Sadly, there were no records of this species from the London area during the current atlas period, neither as a breeder or vagrant. The last record in the London area was in 2003 (Self). This is part of the wider range contraction in Britain described above. It is thought that habitat degradation, in particular the drying out or loss of young, damp woodlands, may be one of the main reasons for the range contraction and decline (Lewis *et al.*, 2009). The degradation of its habitat could be linked to water abstraction and climate change.

Breeding Change

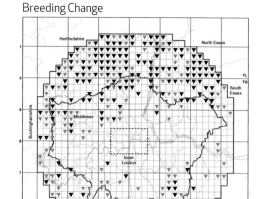

Breeding Distribution Change
- ▲ Recent Gain (new in 2008-13)
- ■ Stable (present in all periods)
- ▼ Old Loss (last occupied 1968-72)
- ▲ Old Gain (new in 1988-94)
- ■ Variable (absent 1988-94)
- ▼ Recent Loss (last occupied 1988-94)

Period	Number of Tetrads		
	Evidence of Breeding	Seen Only	Total
Breeding 1968–72	190	72	262
Breeding 1988–94	101	80	181
Breeding 2008–13	0	0	0
Winter 2007/8–2012/13	-	-	0

Marsh Tit

Poecile palustris

Localised and declining breeding resident and scarce winter visitor; red list

Globally, the Marsh Tit population occurs as in two discrete areas. One of these is centred on Europe and includes parts of Britain, primarily England and Wales (BirdLife). Here, the species is undergoing a long term decline even though its range is broadly unchanged (BirdTrends).

The Marsh Tit is a bird of more rural woodland and so it was recorded mainly outside Greater London in all three atlases. There does, however, seem to have been a general thinning out of the population between the first and second atlas. The current atlas indicates this process has continued, especially in the south of our area. On the other hand, the Essex sector has apparently all but lost its population of breeding Marsh Tit. Survey effort in some parts of this sector was believed to be poorer this time around, so some birds in rural Essex may have been missed, but declines and losses in more well-watched areas such as Epping and Hainault Forest are likely to be genuine, so the same may be true of the losses elsewhere. There were no records from Hainault Forest during the current atlas period at all and no records from Epping Forest in 2012 or 2013. The decline may be continuing in other sectors too and the species may have already gone from some of the other traditional sites where it was recorded early in the current atlas period, for example at Whitewebbs Wood (Middlesex), where the last record was in 2008.

Breeding Distribution

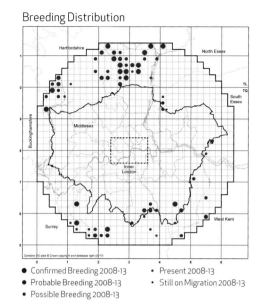

- ● Confirmed Breeding 2008-13
- ● Probable Breeding 2008-13
- ● Possible Breeding 2008-13
- • Present 2008-13
- • Still on Migration 2008-13

Period	Number of Tetrads		
	Evidence of Breeding	Seen Only	Total
Breeding 1968–72	177	100	277
Breeding 1988–94	126	36	162
Breeding 2008–13	32	39	71
Winter 2007/8–2012/13	-	-	105

The Marsh Tit is resident nationally and locally; its distribution in winter is much the same as it is during the breeding season (National Atlas). In the London Area, it is recorded more widely in winter than during the breeding season, including a few records from rural Essex. The Marsh Tit does not normally move very far and the vast majority of ringing recoveries have been within 5km of where they were ringed. Just 4% of these birds moved 10km or more (Migration Atlas), with juvenile dispersal usually occurring in summer soon after they become independent (Broughton *et al.*, 2010). This suggests that most of the winter observations are birds that originated from close by and that this species could breed more widely than is apparent from the breeding season map, but perhaps Marsh Tits may disperse more widely than usual in urban areas in order to find suitable wooded habitat.

Breeding Change

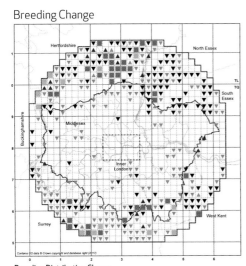

Winter Distribution

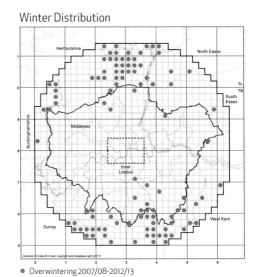

● Overwintering 2007/08-2012/13

Breeding Distribution Change
▲ Recent Gain (new in 2008-13)
■ Stable (present in all periods)
▼ Old Loss
(last occupied 1968-72)

▲ Old Gain (new in 1988-94)
■ Variable (absent 1988-94)
▼ Recent Loss
(last occupied 1988-94)

Bearded Tit

Panurus biarmicus

Uncommon autumn and winter visitor, very rare breeder; amber list.

The Bearded Tit has a patchy distribution across Europe and central Asia driven largely by the distribution of extensive wetland habitats (BirdLife). In Britain, the breeding population is estimated at just 630 pairs (Musgrove *et al.*, 2013) and it is present at isolated localities, mainly in East Anglia and along the south and east coasts of England (National Atlas). Although it is on the amber list, this species is currently expanding its range slightly.

The first reported nesting of this species in the London Area was in 1966 at Stanborough in Hertfordshire (Self). During the period of the first atlas, one successful and two failed breeding attempts occurred here, followed by another subsequent attempt in 1973 (Montier).

By the time of the second atlas, breeding by this species in our area had recommenced with three tetrads having some evidence of breeding and breeding confirmed within one of these. All of these tetrads were in the Thames Marshes and Bearded Tit was observed at another two tetrads in the same area.

Broadly, this picture was unchanged by the time of the current atlas. Rainham Marshes is the main site for this species with birds present sporadically through the summer season and breeding being confirmed in 2011 and 2013. There was also a tantalising breeding season record from the London Wetland Centre, although this related to two overwintering birds in 2013 which were last seen on 19th April.

Period	Number of Tetrads		
	Evidence of Breeding	Seen Only	Total
Breeding 1968–72	1	0	1
Breeding 1988–94	3	2	5
Breeding 2008–13	2	3	5
Winter 2007/8–2012/13	-	-	21

In winter, this species is more widely dispersed, especially inland, but still mainly in southern and eastern England (National Atlas). This is reflected in the results of the fieldwork for the London Atlas, with birds found in more widely dispersed tetrads, but only occasionally away from the lower Thames Marshes. However, winter (November to February) records were made at the London Wetland Centre again, and also at Kempton Nature Reserve, Beddington, Brent Reservoir, Amwell Gravel Pits, Rye Meads, Regent's Park and Hyde Park. Some wandering birds were seen at more than one site in our area: those in Hyde Park in January and February 2013 had been ringed at Rye Meads in November 2012, and almost certainly visited Regent's Park briefly after leaving Hyde Park.

The highest count recorded during the atlas period was 30 at Rainham Marshes in November 2010, but this was unusual and double figure counts are rare in our area (LBR).

With more extensive reed beds now present at several localities in our area as a result of habitat creation (often for Bittern), it is tempting to hope that some overwintering birds, such as those at the Wetland Centre in 2013, will in the near future decide to stay and breed and that by the time of the next atlas breeding will have again been confirmed away from the Thames Marshes.

Breeding Distribution

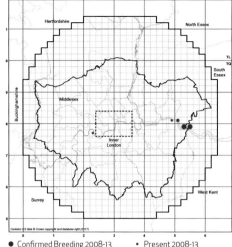

- ● Confirmed Breeding 2008-13   · Present 2008-13
- ● Probable Breeding 2008-13   · Still on Migration 2008-13
- ● Possible Breeding 2008-13

Breeding Change

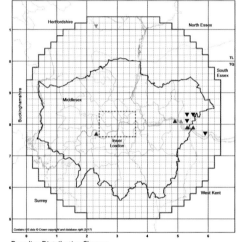

Breeding Distribution Change
- ▲ Recent Gain (new in 2008-13)   ▲ Old Gain (new in 1988-94)
- ■ Stable (present in all periods)   ■ Variable (absent 1988-94)
- ▼ Old Loss (last occupied 1968-72) ▼ Recent Loss (last occupied 1988-94)

Winter Distribution

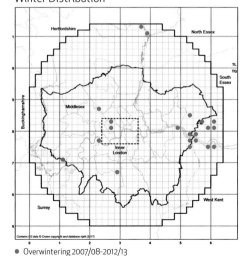

- ● Overwintering 2007/08-2012/13

Woodlark

Lullula arborea

Scarce passage migrant and occasional rare breeder; green list.

The Woodlark has a restricted range in Britain, with the most extensive traditional breeding areas covering the New Forest and, just to the south-west of the London area, the Thames Basin Heaths. Other long-established populations occur in East Anglia and Devon (National Atlas). Recent range expansion and population growth have led to the establishment of new populations in the West Midlands, northern England and South Wales (National Atlas).

Suitable habitat is limited in the London area and therefore Woodlark has always been a scarce bird. Nevertheless, it has bred intermittently at sites near the edge of our area where it overlaps with the north-eastern edge of the Thames Basin Heaths population. The most recent confirmed breeding in the London area occurred in 2007, though a singing male was present at one of the previous breeding sites in 2012 and a single bird was also present there in July 2013. Additionally, a bird was also heard singing at Canons Farm in April 2013.

The breeding map is not shown in order to withhold the location of the previous breeding site.

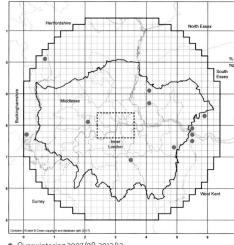

Winter Distribution

● Overwintering 2007/08-2012/13

Period	Number of Tetrads		
	Evidence of Breeding	Seen Only	Total
Breeding 1968–72	6	1	7
Breeding 1988–94	3	1	4
Breeding 2008–13	0	4	6
Winter 2007/8–2012/13	-	-	12

Some of the Woodlark which breed in Britain spend the winter close to the breeding grounds, particularly those breeding in the south, but other birds make longer distance movements (Migration Atlas). In the London area, this species is mostly recorded as a passage migrant, usually at the better watched sites (Self).

Most of the winter atlas records involved birds that stayed for a just a single day or for a few days at most, including single birds at Roding Valley Park and South Norwood Country Park which both arrived during cold weather on 9th February 2012 and both disappeared four days later. The largest flock during the current atlas period also represented the longest staying birds, with up to nine birds feeding in a field in Sidcup, Kent, from 3rd December 2008 to 13th January 2009 (LBR).

The other winter records shown on the map were all present on just one day and occurred at Berrybushes Wood (one bird); Littlebrook Lake (two); Queen Mother Reservoir (one); Wanstead Flats (four); Rainham Marshes (two); South Ockendon (one); and Dartford (two).

Birds seen during the November to February period which are known to have flown straight over are excluded from the map, but some of the single day records shown could also represent flyovers. A winter record from a potential breeding site has also been omitted from the map.

Skylark

Alauda arvensis

Common breeding resident and passage migrant; red list.

The Skylark is a familiar bird in the countryside across the British Isles, particularly during the breeding season when it makes its well-known song-flight. During the winter months, it gathers into flocks in localities where food is available, for example on stubble fields. Along with many other farmland birds, the population has experienced a long-term decline, with an estimated 63% decrease in the breeding population over 1967–2013 (BirdTrends). The decline has continued during the latter part of this forty-year period, with numbers decreasing by 24% (19% to 29%) during 1995 to 2013 (BBS). The UK population may now be 2 million pairs fewer than it was in the early 1970s (BirdTrends).

It is mainly found in the rural areas around the edge of the London area and is also present at some of the larger open spaces within the urban area, particularly those where management supports areas of natural grassland (for example Wanstead Flats, Walthamstow Marsh and Richmond Park). However, birds may find breeding difficult at such sites. For example, a pair attempted to breed at Wormwood Scrubs in 2009 and 2010 but deserted their nest in both years due to disturbance (LBR). Comparison with the second London atlas shows that losses have occurred from tetrads within Greater London along both the Thames and the River Lea and that other gaps have appeared all around the outer parts of the London area. The abundance map suggests that Skylarks are found at fairly low densities across most of our area, with counts of under ten per hour in most tetrads, and that the highest densities are found on the eastern edge of our area, in Essex and Kent.

Period	Number of Tetrads		
	Evidence of Breeding	Seen Only	Total
Breeding 1968–72	596	63	659
Breeding 1988–94	539	71	610
Breeding 2008–13	317	155	472
Winter 2007/8–2012/13	-	-	428

The winter abundance map also suggests that the highest numbers are found in Essex and in Kent. The Skylark was recorded in fewer tetrads during the winter than during the breeding season. This may be explained by the birds flocking together, and retreating into the tetrads with best foraging habitat, or moving frequently from place to place in search of food, making them difficult to detect in any given tetrad. More intensive fieldwork in some of the blank tetrads may well have revealed that birds did use some of these tetrads at some point during the winter. In some cases, birds were absent from tetrads in Essex during visits for most of the winter but reappeared in February when they started taking up territories.

The Skylark can also sometimes be seen flying over central London on passage or during periods of more severe weather and occasionally land in green spaces. Usually, such birds are quickly disturbed by park users and do not stay long.

Breeding Distribution

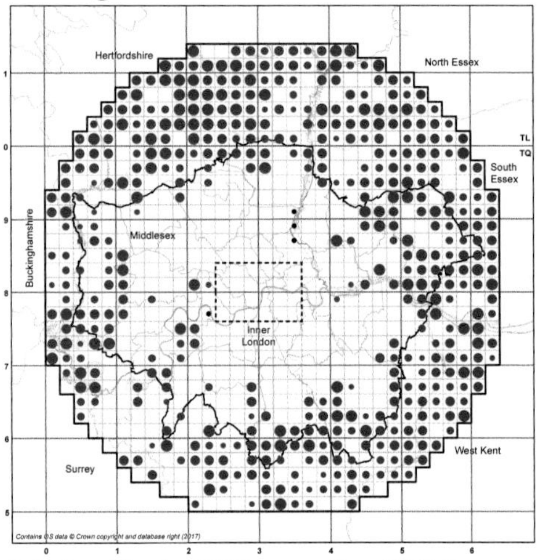

● Confirmed Breeding 2008-13
● Probable Breeding 2008-13
• Possible Breeding 2008-13
• Present 2008-13
• Still on Migration 2008-13

Breeding Abundance

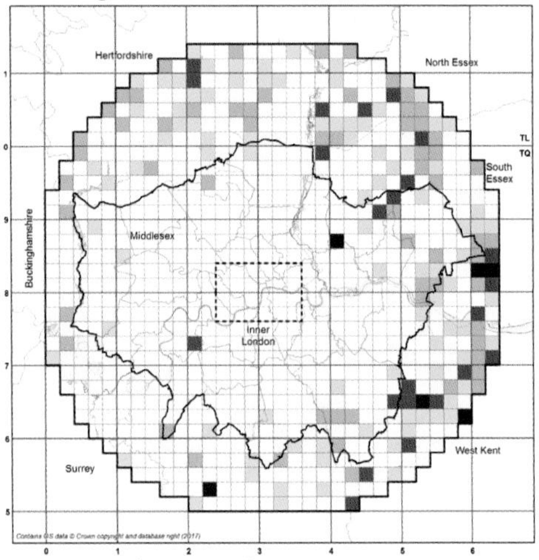

TTV Count Data (Mean Number)
□ 1-2
□ 3
■ 4-6
■ 7-10
■ 11-20

Breeding Change

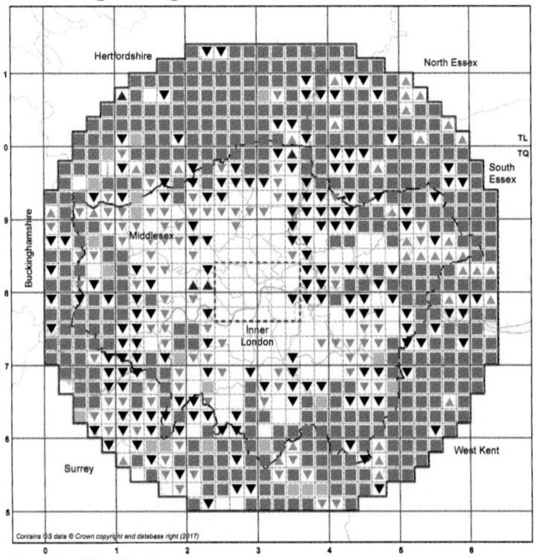

Breeding Distribution Change
▲ Recent Gain (new in 2008-13)
■ Stable (present in all periods)
▼ Old Loss (last occupied 1968-72)
▲ Old Gain (new in 1988-94)
■ Variable (absent 1988-94)
▼ Recent Loss (last occupied 1988-94)

Winter Distribution

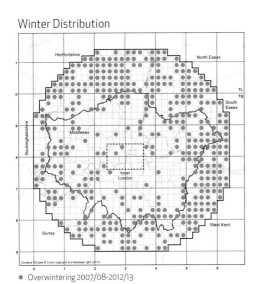

● Overwintering 2007/08-2012/13

Winter Abundance

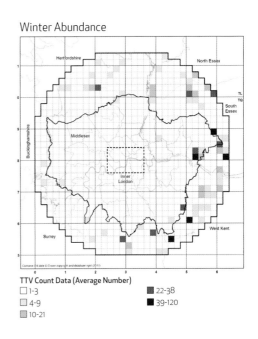

TTV Count Data (Average Number)
- ☐ 1-3
- ☐ 4-9
- ☐ 10-21
- ☐ 22-38
- ■ 39-120

Sand Martin

Riparia riparia

Common summer visitor, localised breeder and passage migrant; green list.

The Sand Martin is found throughout the British Isles. Although the population is increasing in the north of Britain, it is decreasing across much of southern England (National Atlas).

In the London area, the species can mainly be found in areas with river valleys or gravel pits, including the Lee Valley, the lower Thames, the west London waterbodies and parts of the Colne Valley. Although there has been a slight fall in the total number of occupied tetrads, there have been gains in some areas, including in the Docklands area, where breeding was confirmed within Inner London. The spread along the Lee Valley and into Docklands has been made possible by the presence of drainage pipes, which the Sand Martin uses as nest sites, in the banks of the River Lee and elsewhere.

The timed counts indicated quite wide variations in abundance between tetrads, as might be expected for a colonial bird. Also, some of the higher counts may relate to passage flocks. The highest counts made were in the Surbiton area (Surrey Sector) and Eastern Quarry (Kent Sector). During the atlas period, the largest colonies recorded were at Walton Reservoir (172 nest holes in 2008), the London Wetland Centre (72 nest holes visited in 2008) and Holmethorpe Sand Pits (c.45 in 2013) (LBR).

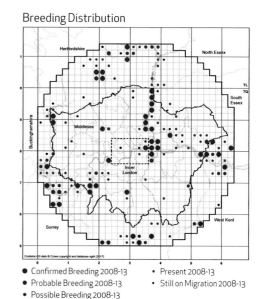

Breeding Distribution

● Confirmed Breeding 2008-13 • Present 2008-13
● Probable Breeding 2008-13 • Still on Migration 2008-13
● Possible Breeding 2008-13

Period	Number of Tetrads		
	Evidence of Breeding	Seen Only	Total
Breeding 1968–72	114	64	178
Breeding 1988–94	80	96	176
Breeding 2008–13	51	92	143
Winter 2007/8–2012/13	-	-	5

The Sand Martin usually returns to Britain in March and leaves in October, so it is perhaps unsurprising that there were a small number of 'winter' records during the current atlas period. Two of these related to early migrants, both seen on 29th February 2008 (at Amwell and Island Barn Reservoir). Three others related to late departures, with the latest one being seen at Richmond Park on 8th November 2008.

Breeding Abundance

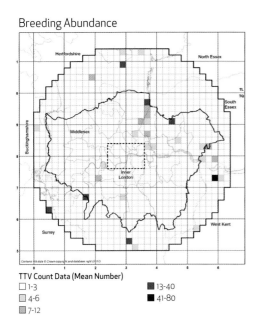

Contains OS data © Crown copyright and database right (2017)

TTV Count Data (Mean Number)
- ☐ 1-3
- ☐ 4-6
- ▨ 7-12
- ▪ 13-40
- ■ 41-80

Breeding Change

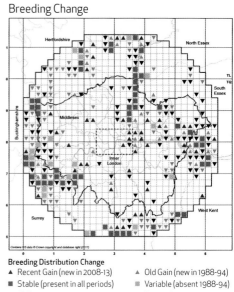

Contains OS data © Crown copyright and database right (2017)

Breeding Distribution Change
- ▲ Recent Gain (new in 2008-13)
- ▪ Stable (present in all periods)
- ▽ Old Loss (last occupied 1968-72)
- ▲ Old Gain (new in 1988-94)
- ▨ Variable (absent 1988-94)
- ▼ Recent Loss (last occupied 1988-94)

Swallow

Hirundo rustica

Common passage migrant and winter visitor, breeding confined to rural areas; green list.

The Swallow can be found across almost the entirety of the British Isles, with the most notable gap in distribution occurring in the built-up part of London (National Atlas). It has increased across the UK between 1995 and 2013 (BBS). However, the comparison of timed counts between 1988–1991 and 2008–11 shows that this species decreased in the London area between these two periods (National Atlas).

The Swallow is now absent from much of Greater London apart from on passage, with most of the confirmed or probable breeding records within the Greater London boundary being restricted to the outskirts. The species has been lost as a breeding species from most formerly occupied tetrads in the lower Lee Valley and along the Thames where it bred during the second atlas period. Perhaps of more concern is the fact that gaps in distribution have also begun to appear in the more rural parts of the London area, particularly in the south and west of our area. The most notable exception to this general picture is at Richmond Park, where the species continues to nest in the Shire horse stables, including in 2013 (LBR).

The Swallow is less colonial than the two martin species and the abundance map shows a relatively even density across the rural parts of our area. Passage birds will be included in some counts, accounting for the records in central London on the abundance maps. Most, if not all, of the dots on the distribution map showing presence in central London will also relate to passage birds which were not marked as such by the observer.

Period	Number of Tetrads		
	Evidence of Breeding	Seen Only	Total
Breeding 1968–72	525	146	671
Breeding 1988–94	484	225	709
Breeding 2008–13	315	276	591
Winter 2007/8–2012/13	-	-	3

The species is known to be one of the later migrants to depart, and was recorded from 3 tetrads during the winter recording period, including one at Valentines Park, Ilford, on the exceptionally late date of 3rd December 2011 (LBR).

Breeding Distribution

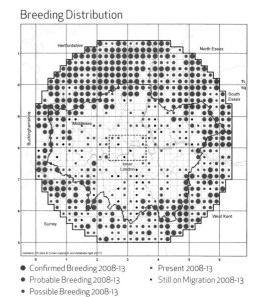

- Confirmed Breeding 2008-13
- Probable Breeding 2008-13
- Possible Breeding 2008-13
- Present 2008-13
- Still on Migration 2008-13

263

Breeding Abundance

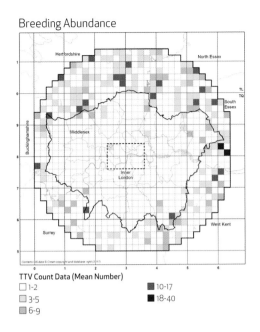

TTV Count Data (Mean Number)

- ☐ 1-2
- ☐ 3-5
- ☐ 6-9
- ■ 10-17
- ■ 18-40

Breeding Change

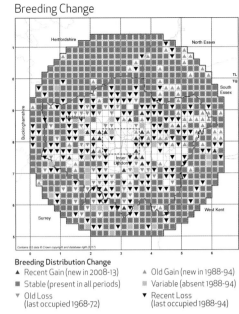

Breeding Distribution Change

- ▲ Recent Gain (new in 2008-13)
- ■ Stable (present in all periods)
- ▼ Old Loss
  (last occupied 1968-72)
- ▲ Old Gain (new in 1988-94)
- ■ Variable (absent 1988-94)
- ▼ Recent Loss
  (last occupied 1988-94)

House Martin

Delichon urbicum

Common but declining breeding summer visitor and passage migrant; amber list.

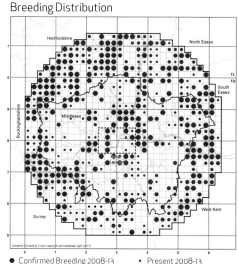

Breeding Distribution

● Confirmed Breeding 2008-13   • Present 2008-13
● Probable Breeding 2008-13   • Still on Migration 2008-13
● Possible Breeding 2008-13

The breeding distribution of the House Martin extends across the British Isles. Like the Sand Martin, it shows differing population trends in the north and the south of Britain, with an increase occurring in Scotland and northern England and a decrease in southern England, which is most marked around the London area (National Atlas).

The decrease is reflected in the large gaps which have appeared in the distribution map across the London area and the substantial fall in the number of occupied tetrads, taking the total well below that of the first atlas. These gaps are most obvious in north and west London and in south-east London, but are noticeable throughout our area, including in the Hertfordshire sector where survey coverage was most thorough. However, the species continues to persist at a few colonies within the urban area, including some within Inner London.

Most timed counts were of fewer than 20 birds per hour, with abundance being highly variable between tetrads, as might be expected for a highly colonial species. Contemporary records indicate that some large colonies do still persist within the London area, with the highest counts during 2008–13 being c.50 pairs on West Hendon Broadway and up to 47 pairs at St. George's Hospital, Hornchurch (LBR).

Period	Number of Tetrads		
	Evidence of Breeding	Seen Only	Total
Breeding 1968–72	626	95	721
Breeding 1988–94	630	182	812
Breeding 2008–13	275	217	492
Winter 2007/8–2012/13	-	-	4

Most birds have left Britain by the end of October and are only occasionally recorded here in November. However, House Martin pairs sometimes raise a second brood, which means that young can be in the nest until September and, exceptionally, into October. During the current atlas period, there were records from three tetrads in early November, and one from Woodford Green, on the incredibly late date of 3rd December 2011 (LBR).

Breeding Abundance

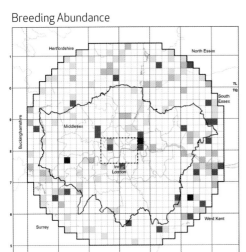

TTV Count Data (Mean Number)
- ☐ 1-3
- ☐ 4-5
- ☐ 6-9
- ■ 10-17
- ■ 18-33

Breeding Change

Breeding Distribution Change
- ▲ Recent Gain (new in 2008-13)
- ■ Stable (present in all periods)
- ▼ Old Loss (last occupied 1968-72)
- ▲ Old Gain (new in 1988-94)
- ■ Variable (absent 1988-94)
- ▼ Recent Loss (last occupied 1988-94)

Contains OS data © Crown copyright and database right (2017)

Cetti's Warbler

Cettia cetti

Increasing resident; green list.

The Cetti's Warbler is a recent colonist of Britain, with breeding confirmed for the first time in Kent in 1973 (Holling & RBBP, 2011). Since then, it has expanded its breeding range substantially; spreading into the English Midlands and Wales with a few breeding pairs occurring even further north (National Atlas).

It was first recorded in the London area in 1975, though the population in London was slow to increase at first, and evidence of breeding was recorded from only four tetrads during the second Atlas, two in the Lee Valley and two in the Ingrebourne Valley (Hewlett *et al.*). Since the second atlas period, the species has spread across the London area, though the areas around the Lee and Ingrebourne Valleys have become clear strongholds. The population of the Ingrebourne valley appears to be the most established, with a maximum count of 42 singing birds in 2012. There were also 21 singing birds at Rainham Marshes in 2013. Breeding numbers are difficult to assess as females sing occasionally and males can pair with more than one female (Snow & Perrins, 1998), but all breeding estimates from other individual sites were of fewer than ten pairs or territories. During the current atlas period, breeding was also either confirmed or thought probable at the London Wetland Centre, Stocker's Lake, the Wraysbury/Staines area, Old Slade Lake, Beddington Farmlands and Sevenoaks Wildlife Reserve, and possible breeding was recorded at several other sites.

Breeding Distribution

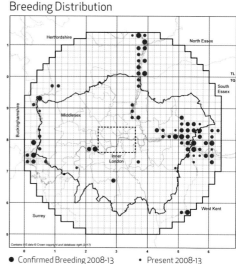

- ● Confirmed Breeding 2008-13
- ● Probable Breeding 2008-13
- ● Possible Breeding 2008-13
- · Present 2008-13
- · Still on Migration 2008-13

Period	Number of Tetrads		
	Evidence of Breeding	Seen Only	Total
Breeding 1968–72	0	0	0
Breeding 1988–94	4	8	12
Breeding 2008–13	39	38	77
Winter 2007/8–2012/13	-	-	60

Although the species is mostly sedentary, dispersal in the autumn and during the winter does occur. Such dispersal may help the species find new sites to colonise and sometimes this leads to birds appearing briefly at small wetland sites where it is not known to breed currently.

Although there were no records of this species in Inner London during the current atlas period in either winter or the breeding season, this species is among the strongest candidates to colonise that area in the coming years.

Breeding Change

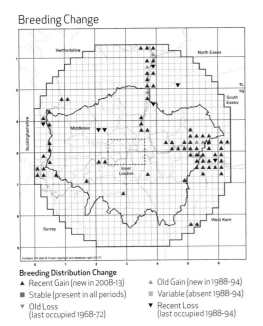

Contains OS data © Crown copyright and database right (2017)

Breeding Distribution Change

▲ Recent Gain (new in 2008-13)   ▲ Old Gain (new in 1988-94)

■ Stable (present in all periods)   ■ Variable (absent 1988-94)

▼ Old Loss   ▼ Recent Loss
   (last occupied 1968-72)   (last occupied 1988-94)

Winter Distribution

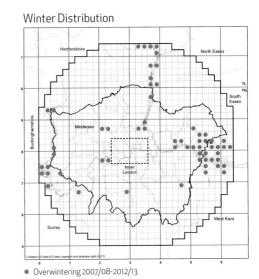

Contains OS data © Crown copyright and database right (2017)

● Overwintering 2007/08-2012/13

Long-tailed Tit
Aegithalos caudatus

Common and widespread breeding resident; green list.

The Long-tailed Tit is a resident species across the temperate zones of Europe and Asia (BirdLife), including Britain and Ireland where it is only really absent from areas without trees, such as the uplands, and some of the Scottish islands (National Atlas). Nationally, the population of this species appears to be increasing (BBS) and its distribution is stable (National Atlas).

At the time of the first atlas, the Long-tailed Tit was largely absent from the built-up areas in Greater London and from the more open habitats to the east in south Essex and north Kent. The second atlas showed a consolidation of its distribution, with 335 additional tetrads being occupied, leaving the inner parts of north-east London as the only real gap in its distribution. The current atlas indicates an increase in the number of occupied tetrads with only a very small number of tetrads having no records of this species during the breeding season. These tetrads are scattered throughout the area and it seems likely that this species is at least occasionally present during the breeding season in some of these tetrads too.

Period	Number of Tetrads		
	Evidence of Breeding	Seen Only	Total
Breeding 1968–72	300	94	394
Breeding 1988–94	618	111	729
Breeding 2008–13	629	174	803
Winter 2007/8–2012/13	-	-	835

In winter, the distribution of this species nationally is much the same as during the breeding season. In the London area, there are more occupied tetrads during the winter than during the breeding season.

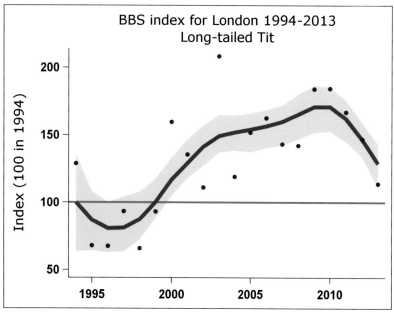

BTO/JNCC/RSPB Breeding Bird Survey (BBS)

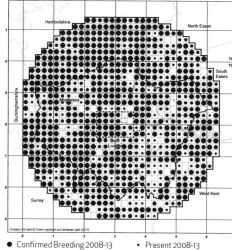

Breeding Distribution

- ● Confirmed Breeding 2008-13
- ● Probable Breeding 2008-13
- ● Possible Breeding 2008-13
- • Present 2008-13
- • Still on Migration 2008-13

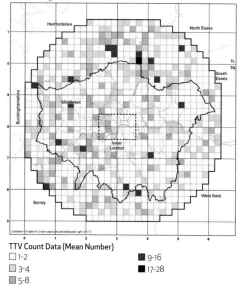

Breeding Abundance

TTV Count Data (Mean Number)
- ☐ 1-2
- ☐ 3-4
- ☐ 5-8
- ■ 9-16
- ■ 17-28

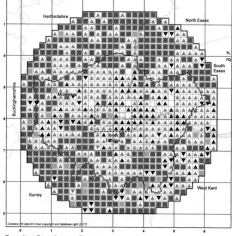

Breeding Change

Breeding Distribution Change
- ▲ Recent Gain (new in 2008-13)
- ■ Stable (present in all periods)
- ▼ Old Loss (last occupied 1968-72)
- ▲ Old Gain (new in 1988-94)
- ■ Variable (absent 1988-94)
- ▼ Recent Loss (last occupied 1988-94)

Winter Distribution

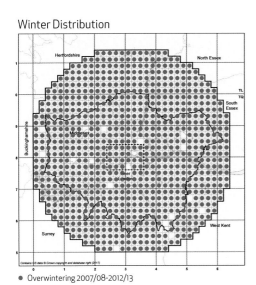

● Overwintering 2007/08-2012/13

Winter Abundance

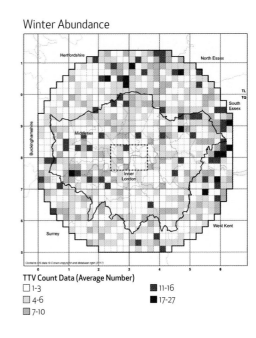

TTV Count Data (Average Number)

☐ 1-3
☐ 4-6
▨ 7-10
▩ 11-16
■ 17-27

Chiffchaff

Phylloscopus collybita

Common and widespread breeding summer visitor and passage migrant, and increasingly widespread in winter; green list.

The Chiffchaff breeds right across Europe and Asia (except the far north) and winters in Africa, mostly from the Sahel northwards, as well as the Middle East and northern India. However, it is also present year round in parts of Western Europe, including southern Britain and Ireland (BirdLife). During the breeding season, this species is common and widespread across lowland Britain and Ireland, especially in the south and south-west (National Atlas). The breeding population in Britain and Ireland is currently increasing (National Atlas; BBS).

The Chiffchaff typically breeds in woodland, or clumps of trees, which do not need to be especially extensive but must include dense vegetation close to the ground, such as brambles (Snow & Perrins, 1998). This preference was shown quite clearly in the first atlas, with breeding evidence coming principally from outside the urban area and the Thames Marshes. Since then, however, this species appears to have consolidated its distribution in our area, with colonisation of woodlands within the Thames Marshes and the urban area of London and only a small number of tetrads apparently lacking at least one breeding pair. The extent of consolidation shown on the atlas map could however be exaggerated by passage birds which stop to sing but ultimately move elsewhere to breed.

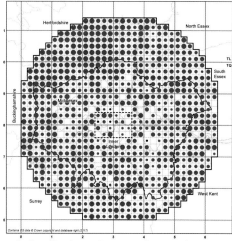

Breeding Distribution

- Confirmed Breeding 2008-13
- Probable Breeding 2008-13
- Possible Breeding 2008-13
- Present 2008-13
- Still on Migration 2008-13

Period	Number of Tetrads		
	Evidence of Breeding	Seen Only	Total
Breeding 1968–72	547	68	615
Breeding 1988–94	605	109	714
Breeding 2008–13	574	225	799
Winter 2007/8–2012/13	-	-	232

The abundance mapping indicates that this species is marginally more abundant in tetrads outside Greater London than within.

Birds that breed in Britain mainly winter further south in Europe and along the Atlantic coast of the Maghreb and West Africa, whereas those that winter in Britain mainly come from continental Europe and from further north (Migration Atlas).

Within Britain and Ireland, the wintering distribution is more southerly than that of the breeding season. Others have reported an association with wetland sites and this association is clearly apparent from the atlas maps, which seem to indicate greater occurrence within the river valleys, such as the Lee, Colne, Thames and Darent. Presumably this is because the invertebrate prey of the Chiffchaff is sufficiently abundant in these areas during the winter.

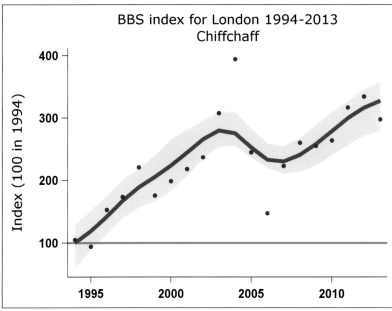

BTO/JNCC/RSPB Breeding Bird Survey (BBS)

Breeding Abundance

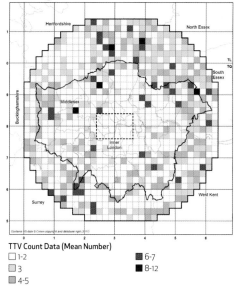

TTV Count Data (Mean Number)
- 1-2
- 3
- 4-5
- 6-7
- 8-12

Breeding Change

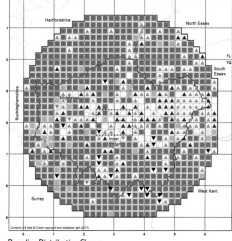

Breeding Distribution Change
- ▲ Recent Gain (new in 2008-13)
- ■ Stable (present in all periods)
- ▼ Old Loss (last occupied 1968-72)
- ▲ Old Gain (new in 1988-94)
- ▨ Variable (absent 1988-94)
- ▼ Recent Loss (last occupied 1988-94)

Winter Distribution

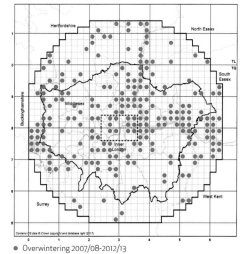

● Overwintering 2007/08-2012/13

Willow Warbler

Phylloscopus trochilus

Common and widespread passage migrant, declining as a breeding species in the London area; amber list.

The breeding global distribution of the Willow Warbler is much the same as the Chiffchaff; however, the Willow Warbler winters only in sub-Saharan Africa (BirdLife). In Britain and Ireland, while the breeding distribution of the Willow Warbler has remained largely unchanged, the population centre is clearly shifting to the north and west. As a consequence, this species has declined markedly in England, especially to the south of a line drawn between the River Ribble and the River Tees, while increasing to the north of this line and in Ireland (National Atlas). The overall picture is one of decline.

The first two London atlases indicate little change in the breeding distribution of the Willow Warbler in our area. Most tetrads outside the built-up area of London held at least one breeding pair and a good number of tetrads within Greater London were similarly occupied, including breeding pairs in Regent's Park and Hyde Park/Kensington Gardens at the time of the first atlas. The distribution of the Willow Warbler very much reflected the availability of its scrub and woodland habitat.

The current atlas indicates an overall thinning of the population, with a significant number of formerly occupied tetrads now without breeding pairs. The situation may be even worse than indicated by the map since some of these records almost certainly involve passage birds which stop to sing but ultimately move on to breed elsewhere. This may include some of the probable breeding records relating to briefly held territories. As an indication of the decline, Wimbledon Common held over 100 pairs in the 1980s, but only 16 to 21 during the second atlas period and between 3 and 14 in the current atlas period (LBR).

Small numbers of breeding pairs (typically fewer than 10) still occur at 20 to 30 sites (some extending over multiple tetrads) within our area which offer suitable habitat. These include Banstead Downs, Wimbledon Common, Richmond Park, Ingrebourne Valley and Rye Meads. There were no confirmed or probable breeding records in Inner London, but single birds held territory just outside Inner London at London Wetland Centre (2013) and Wormwood Scrubs (2011).

Breeding Distribution

- ● Confirmed Breeding 2008-13
- ● Probable Breeding 2008-13
- ● Possible Breeding 2008-13
- · Present 2008-13
- · Still on Migration 2008-13

Period	Number of Tetrads		
	Evidence of Breeding	Seen Only	Total
Breeding 1968–72	595	58	653
Breeding 1988–94	614	139	753
Breeding 2008–13	193	283	476

Breeding Abundance

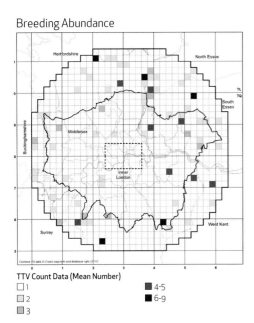

TTV Count Data (Mean Number)
- ☐ 1
- ☐ 2
- ☐ 3
- ■ 4-5
- ■ 6-9

Breeding Change

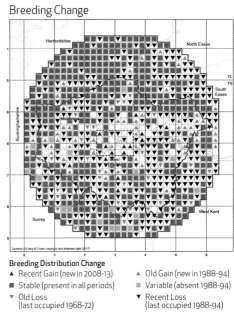

Breeding Distribution Change
- ▲ Recent Gain (new in 2008-13)
- ■ Stable (present in all periods)
- ▼ Old Loss (last occupied 1968-72)
- ▲ Old Gain (new in 1988-94)
- ■ Variable (absent 1988-94)
- ▼ Recent Loss (last occupied 1988-94)

Blackcap

Sylvia atricapilla

Common breeding summer visitor and passage migrant, increasingly common and widespread in winter; green list.

The Blackcap breeds in northern Europe and winters primarily in Africa and the Middle East but also in Western Europe, including parts of Britain and Ireland. During the last four decades of the twentieth century, the breeding population in Britain and Ireland has shown a marked increase (BirdTrends) and range expansion to the north and west (National Atlas). This could potentially be a reflection of climate change (Leech *et al.*, 2004).

In our area, this species has also increased and expanded its distribution through the three atlas periods. The maps show colonisation of the urban area such that this species is now found in almost every tetrad. All that is required is a small patch of woodland or even scrub for this species to be present and it was the most commonly recorded warbler in the London area during the timed counts.

Breeding Distribution

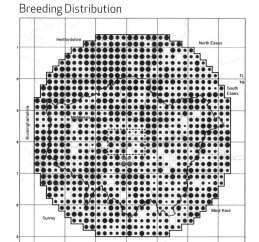

- ● Confirmed Breeding 2008-13
- ● Probable Breeding 2008-13
- ● Possible Breeding 2008-13
- • Present 2008-13
- • Still on Migration 2008-13

Period	Number of Tetrads		
	Evidence of Breeding	Seen Only	Total
Breeding 1968–72	552	60	612
Breeding 1988–94	703	88	791
Breeding 2008–13	659	174	833
Winter 2007/8–2012/13	-	-	343

The Blackcap also winters in our area, although the majority of these birds are thought to breed in central Europe rather than Britain. Increasing wintering numbers in Britain have been attributed to climate change and the increased availability of supplementary food, in particular fats and sunflower hearts, in gardens (Plummer *et al.*, 2015). The atlas map perhaps indicates that, in the London area, the Blackcap has a preference for urban areas and wetland sites during this season, with higher ground less favoured.

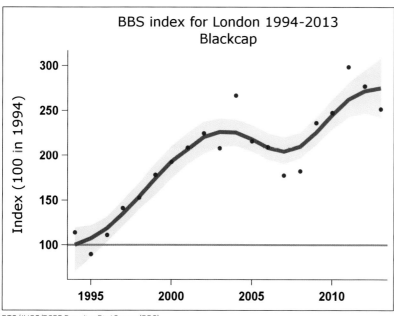

BTO/JNCC/RSPB Breeding Bird Survey (BBS)

Breeding Abundance

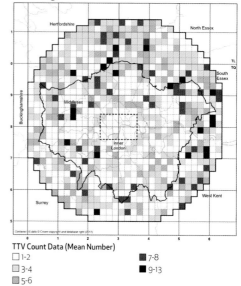

TTV Count Data (Mean Number)
- ☐ 1-2
- ☐ 3-4
- ☐ 5-6
- ■ 7-8
- ■ 9-13

Breeding Change

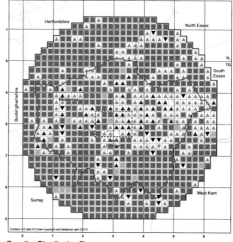

Breeding Distribution Change
- ▲ Recent Gain (new in 2008-13)
- ■ Stable (present in all periods)
- ▼ Old Loss (last occupied 1968-72)
- ▲ Old Gain (new in 1988-94)
- ▣ Variable (absent 1988-94)
- ▼ Recent Loss (last occupied 1988-94)

Winter Distribution

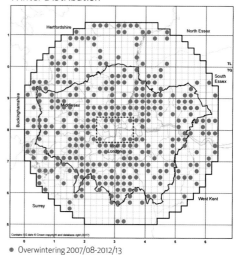

● Overwintering 2007/08-2012/13

Garden Warbler

Sylvia borin

Widespread passage migrant and breeding summer visitor; green list.

The Garden Warbler breeds in northern Europe and winters in sub-Saharan Africa. Its distribution in Britain appears to have changed little during the twentieth century; however this species is declining in the south and east of Britain and increasing in the north and west, where there may also be a slight range expansion (National Atlas). As with the Blackcap, this could reflect climate change (National Atlas; Leech *et al.*, 2004).

In our area, the distribution of this species is clearly influenced primarily by the urban area, with most occupied tetrads occurring in a ring around Greater London. There was little evidence of any real change between the first and second atlases. Much the same pattern can be seen in the current atlas, although there is a suggestion that some thinning out of the distribution in London has occurred, especially in the south and east of our area. That is not to say that this species is absent from the urban area and breeding may occur anywhere there is fairly extensive dense shrubs, and singing birds sometimes occur on passage in the larger Inner London parks. The relative abundance mapping indicates that the Lee Valley is a stronghold for this species.

Period	Number of Tetrads		
	Evidence of Breeding	Seen Only	Total
Breeding 1968–72	318	52	370
Breeding 1988–94	358	135	493
Breeding 2008–13	172	241	413

Breeding Distribution

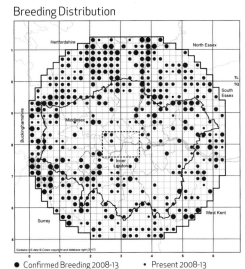

● Confirmed Breeding 2008-13   • Present 2008-13
● Probable Breeding 2008-13   • Still on Migration 2008-13
● Possible Breeding 2008-13

Breeding Abundance

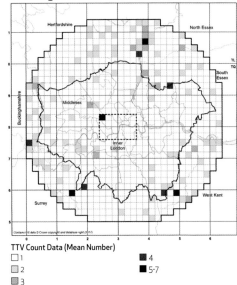

TTV Count Data (Mean Number)

□ 1   ■ 4
□ 2   ■ 5-7
▨ 3

Breeding Change

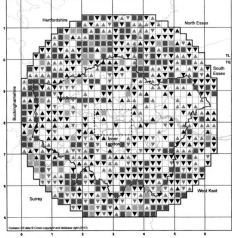

Breeding Distribution Change
▲ Recent Gain (new in 2008-13)   ▲ Old Gain (new in 1988-94)
■ Stable (present in all periods)   ■ Variable (absent 1988-94)
▼ Old Loss   ▼ Recent Loss
  (last occupied 1968-72)   (last occupied 1988-94)

Wood Warbler

Phylloscopus sibilatrix

Scarce passage migrant, former breeding summer visitor; red list.

The Wood Warbler breeds in Europe and winters in sub-Saharan Africa. In Britain and, in particular, England, this species underwent a rapid decline in the last part of the twentieth century (Bird Trends).

The Wood Warbler was described as fairly scarce in the London Area in the first Atlas. Breeding evidence came mainly from scattered locations outside Greater London, particularly in Surrey where suitable woodland habitat is perhaps most abundant. However, this species also showed evidence of breeding at that time from more central locations including Wimbledon Common and Hampstead Heath. The second Atlas indicates a general thinning of the population although singing males were again recorded on Hampstead Heath. In between the second and current atlas periods, the Wood Warbler was lost as a breeding species in our area, with the last confirmed breeding occurring in 1996 (LBR). The records shown in the current atlas are therefore almost certainly passage birds, some of which stop and sing for a while but then move on.

Period	Number of Tetrads		
	Evidence of Breeding	Seen Only	Total
Breeding 1968–72	56	26	82
Breeding 1988–94	34	48	82
Breeding 2008–13	0	28	28

Breeding Distribution

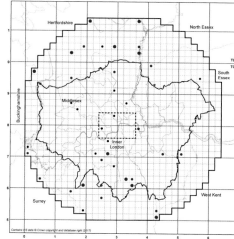

● Confirmed Breeding 2008-13 ・ Present 2008-13
● Probable Breeding 2008-13 ・ Still on Migration 2008-13
● Possible Breeding 2008-13

Breeding Change

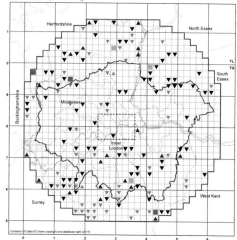

Breeding Distribution Change
▲ Recent Gain (new in 2008-13)   ▲ Old Gain (new in 1988-94)
■ Stable (present in all periods)   ■ Variable (absent 1988-94)
▼ Old Loss (last occupied 1968-72)   ▼ Recent Loss (last occupied 1988-94)

Lesser Whitethroat

Sylvia curruca

Widespread passage migrant and breeding summer visitor; green list.

The Lesser Whitethroat can be found in lowland parts of Britain, having increased its range and colonised areas in Wales and southern Scotland over the last 40 years (National Atlas). The UK population trend is stable overall, but there has been a significant decline of 33% (8% to 54%) in south-east England between 1995 and 2013 (BBS).

The species can still be found across the London area, including in pockets of suitable scrubby habitat within the built-up area. However, the distribution is much patchier than in the second atlas, with gaps particularly noticeable in rural parts of the Essex and Kent sectors and gaps also appearing elsewhere including in the Hertfordshire Sector. As this species is inconspicuous, it may be more widely present than indicated by the atlas maps.

Period	Number of Tetrads		
	Evidence of Breeding	Seen Only	Total
Breeding 1968–72	221	54	275
Breeding 1988–94	391	124	515
Breeding 2008–13	175	239	414

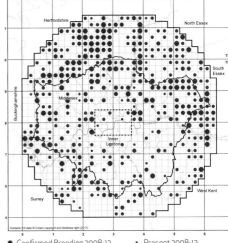

Breeding Distribution

- ● Confirmed Breeding 2008-13
- ● Probable Breeding 2008-13
- ● Possible Breeding 2008-13
- • Present 2008-13
- • Still on Migration 2008-13

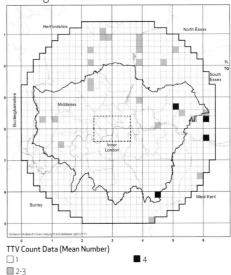

Breeding Abundance

TTV Count Data (Mean Number)
- ☐ 1
- ☐ 2-3
- ■ 4

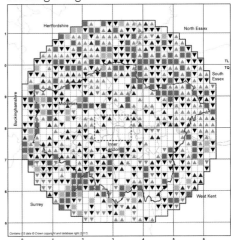

Breeding Change

Breeding Distribution Change
- ▲ Recent Gain (new in 2008-13)
- ■ Stable (present in all periods)
- ▼ Old Loss (last occupied 1968-72)
- ▲ Old Gain (new in 1988-94)
- ■ Variable (absent 1988-94)
- ▼ Recent Loss (last occupied 1988-94)

Whitethroat

Sylvia communis

Common and widespread passage migrant and breeding summer visitor; green list.

During the 1968/69 winter, immediately following the first breeding season of the first atlas survey, the Whitethroat population in the UK crashed by around 70%, from which it has still not recovered (BirdTrends). However, the recent trend is positive and the UK population increased by 38% (29% to 53%) between 1995 and 2013. It is doing even better in south-east England, increasing by 62% (46% to 82%) over the same period (BBS).

The National Atlas shows a distinct reduction in the abundance of this species in the London area relative to the surrounding counties. However, the Whitethroat can be found throughout the outer, rural parts of our area. In the current atlas period, there were slightly more unoccupied tetrads in the Surrey and Kent sectors.

Perhaps reflecting the recent population growth, there have also been gains in occupied tetrads within the built-up area since the second atlas period. These include tetrads in Inner London, where breeding was confirmed in Regent's Park and Burgess Park (LBR). Some of the gains may relate to habitat management, such as at Regent's Park and Richmond Park, where small areas have been fenced to exclude deer and hence allow the establishment of scrub. Elsewhere, the increasing population may be establishing territories in existing suitable habitat, including relatively small areas of scrub, for example, the territory observed along the edge of the railway line at Finsbury Park.

The abundance map shows a relatively even spread across the rural parts of our area, with four or fewer observed per hour in most tetrads during the timed counts, although higher densities were recorded to the east of our area either side of the outer Thames.

Period	Number of Tetrads		
	Evidence of Breeding	Seen Only	Total
Breeding 1968–72	527	69	596
Breeding 1988–94	553	75	628
Breeding 2008–13	531	171	702

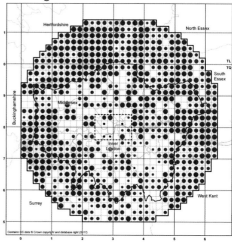

Breeding Distribution

- ● Confirmed Breeding 2008-13
- ● Probable Breeding 2008-13
- ● Possible Breeding 2008-13
- • Present 2008-13
- • Still on Migration 2008-13

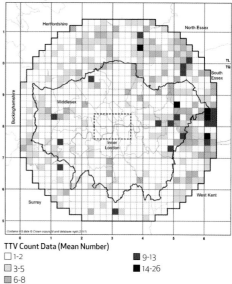

Breeding Abundance

TTV Count Data (Mean Number)
- ☐ 1-2
- ☐ 3-5
- ▨ 6-8
- ■ 9-13
- ■ 14-26

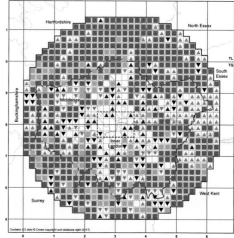

Breeding Change

Breeding Distribution Change
- ▲ Recent Gain (new in 2008-13)
- ■ Stable (present in all periods)
- ▼ Old Loss (last occupied 1968-72)
- ▲ Old Gain (new in 1988-94)
- ▩ Variable (absent 1988-94)
- ▼ Recent Loss (last occupied 1988-94)

Dartford Warbler

Sylvia undata

Rare breeding species, scarce passage migrant and winter visitor; amber list.

The Dartford Warbler is, unusually for a warbler, a mainly resident species in Britain and other parts of Western Europe and North Africa. It was confined to the far south of England at the time of the 1968–72 atlas, but expanded its range during the 1990s and 2000s as far north as the Midlands and East Anglia; though it remains restricted to scattered locations where suitable heathland habitat exists (National Atlas). It is susceptible to severe weather and a substantial population crash occurred as a result of the three successive severe winters at the start of the current atlas period, from 2008/09 to 2010/11. In the Thames Basin and Wealden Heaths Special Protection Areas, just to the south-west of the London area, numbers plummeted from 978 territories in 2008 to just 50 in 2010 (Clark & Eyre, 2012).

In the nineteenth century, the Dartford Warbler was resident on most of the commons in the south of our area and also some in the north (LNHS, 1964). It persisted to breed occasionally at Walton Heath and Wimbledon Common up until 1939 when breeding in our area ceased for a period, resuming again in the 1970s, just after the end of the first atlas period (LNHS, 1964; Self). It was recorded in only a single tetrad during the second atlas period and the most recent confirmed breeding occurred in 2005 (Self), with the last territorial birds in 2007 (LBR). During the current atlas period, in 2008, birds were recorded in two London atlas tetrads and one of these contained a territorial bird, although both records were on the edge of our atlas survey area and outside the official London area boundary and hence not included in the LBR. The species seems to have lost its toehold in the London area entirely during the subsequent severe winter and no further breeding season records occurred during the current atlas period.

Period	Number of Tetrads		
	Evidence of Breeding	Seen Only	Total
Breeding 1968–72	0	0	0
Breeding 1988–94	1	0	1
Breeding 2008–13	1	1	2
Winter 2007/8–2012/13	-	-	24

During winter, the Dartford Warbler disperses more widely and is less strict in its choice of habitat, sometimes lingering for several weeks or longer. During the current atlas period, birds which stayed for relatively long periods were at Staines Moor/Stanwell Moor, Beddington Sewage Farm, Bushy Park, Richmond Park and Rainham Marshes, during one or more winters. Birds which stayed for shorter periods were also observed at a number of other sites, including Wormwood Scrubs, Wanstead Flats, Hounslow Heath and the Ripple Nature Reserve in Barking.

Following the population crash in Britain referred to above, the number of wintering records in the London area has fallen substantially; most of the records shown on the winter distribution map were made before 2010. However, the Dartford Warbler has recovered from previous population crashes, so, unless severe winters continue, it seems likely that numbers will recover again in the future. To protect potentially sensitive sites in the event of a recovery, the breeding season map is not shown.

Winter Distribution

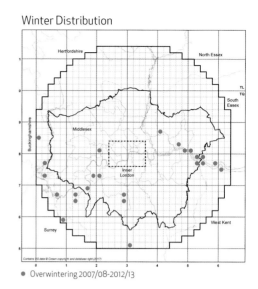

● Overwintering 2007/08-2012/13

Grasshopper Warbler

Locustella naevia

Scarce passage migrant and breeding summer visitor; red list.

The Grasshopper Warbler breeds right across Europe as far east as Mongolia and winters in discrete locations in sub-Saharan Africa (BirdLife). It can still be heard 'reeling' throughout Britain in summer, though the distribution has become patchy (National Atlas). The population underwent a rapid decline during the period between the 1960s and 1980s though the more recent trend, since 1995, is relatively stable (BirdTrends; BBS). However, there are regional differences. In the last 20 years, it has been lost from large areas of southern England but there has been a coincidental expansion and population increase further north and west (National Atlas).

In the London area, the Grasshopper Warbler population has been relatively sparsely distributed since at least the beginning of the twentieth century (LNHS, 1964). For now, the factor governing its distribution is most likely to be the scarcity of its preferred habitat of rough grassland or similar low and dense vegetation, usually with a small amount of taller vegetation such as reeds or bramble (Gilbert, 2012).

The changes in the distribution of this species in the London area are in line with the population trend. Substantial losses occurred in the 1970s and 1980s, especially in Kent, Surrey, the Colne Valley and Hertfordshire (Hewlett *et al.*). This is reflected in the difference in the number of occupied tetrads during the first and second atlas periods. Since the second atlas period, the Grasshopper Warbler has maintained its presence in the London area, at least in terms of the number of tetrads occupied, although there are fewer tetrads with confirmed or probable breeding. The Lee Valley and the outer Thames remain the most important areas, but there has been a mixture of losses and gains elsewhere. The second atlas also showed large numbers of gains and losses, with only a few tetrads showing occupancy both times, and this pattern may therefore reflect the short-term availability of suitable habitat for this species.

Breeding Distribution

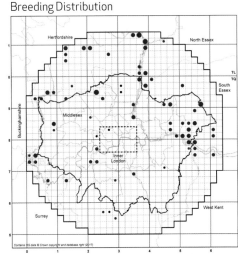

- ● Confirmed Breeding 2008-13
- ● Probable Breeding 2008-13
- ● Possible Breeding 2008-13
- • Present 2008-13
- • Still on Migration 2008-13

Period	Number of Tetrads		
	Evidence of Breeding	Seen Only	Total
Breeding 1968–72	105	26	131
Breeding 1988–94	37	29	66
Breeding 2008–13	23	42	65

Breeding Change

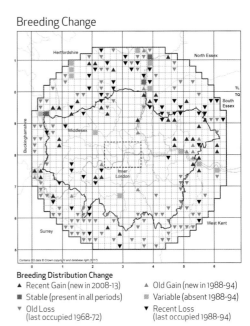

Breeding Distribution Change
- ▲ Recent Gain (new in 2008-13)
- ▲ Old Gain (new in 1988-94)
- ■ Stable (present in all periods)
- ■ Variable (absent 1988-94)
- ▼ Old Loss (last occupied 1968-72)
- ▼ Recent Loss (last occupied 1988-94)

Sedge Warbler
Acrocephalus schoenobaenus

Common and widespread migrant and breeding summer visitor; green list

The Sedge Warbler's breeding range extends right across Europe as far east as Mongolia, while it winters in sub-Saharan Africa (BirdLife). In summer, the Sedge Warbler can be found in lowland areas throughout the British Isles, with its range remaining relatively constant over the long-term. However, the National Atlas abundance counts show that the proportion of occupied tetrads has declined in eastern England since 1988–91.

This decline is reflected in the distribution changes in the London area since the second atlas period. The Sedge Warbler continues to be found in its core areas in the Lee Valley, the outer Thames and the Colne Valley, but has been lost from some tetrads in all these areas, particularly in the Colne Valley. It has also declined substantially in rural Essex, where it formerly bred in drier habitats, including farm fields (Hewlett *et al.*).

Away from its strongholds, it can also still be found within urban areas, where suitable pockets of habitat exist, including the London Wetland Centre, Brent Reservoir, Beddington Sewage Farm and Wanstead Park. Singing birds, almost certainly involving passage birds, were also recorded in Inner London at Bankside, Hyde Park/Kensington Gardens and Regent's Park. The Bankside bird was unusual as it sang for 12 days (1st –12th May 2012), which would merit 'territorial' status, but it has been marked as having possible breeding status as the habitat seems unsuitable. A couple of June records from Regent's Park, including a singing male in June 2013, hint at the possibility that breeding could occur there in future years.

The density mapping suggests that Sedge Warbler is most abundant in the Lee Valley and the lower Thames, with very low numbers being recorded during the timed counts away from these areas, with the exception of Stocker's Lake. Contemporary records support this, with the highest breeding counts during the atlas period coming from Rainham Marshes (92 territories in 2013) and Rye Meads (78 territories in 2009) (LBR).

Breeding Distribution

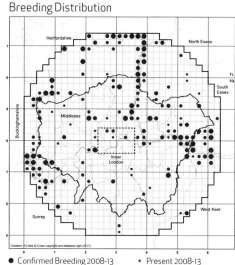

- ● Confirmed Breeding 2008-13
- ● Probable Breeding 2008-13
- ● Possible Breeding 2008-13
- • Present 2008-13
- • Still on Migration 2008-13

Period	Number of Tetrads		
	Evidence of Breeding	Seen Only	Total
Breeding 1968–72	176	30	206
Breeding 1988–94	189	51	240
Breeding 2008–13	82	80	162

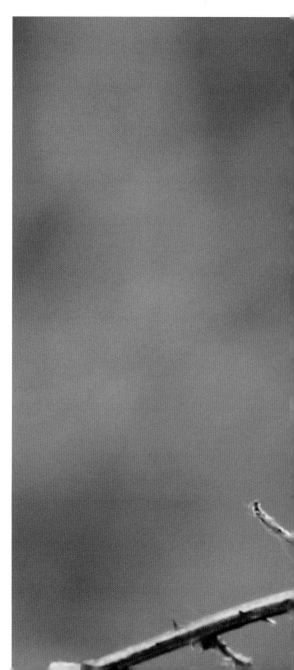

Breeding Abundance

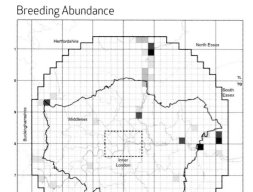

TTV Count Data (Mean Number)

- ☐ 1
- ☐ 2
- ☐ 3
- ■ 4-6
- ■ 7-9

Breeding Change

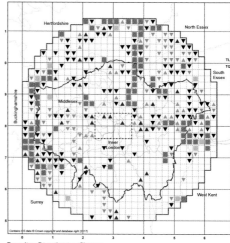

Breeding Distribution Change

- ▲ Recent Gain (new in 2008-13)
- ■ Stable (present in all periods)
- ▼ Old Loss (last occupied 1968-72)
- ▲ Old Gain (new in 1988-94)
- ■ Variable (absent 1988-94)
- ▼ Recent Loss (last occupied 1988-94)

Savi's Warbler

Locustella luscinioides

Vagrant; red list.

Savi's Warbler breeds in wetland areas across much of Europe and as far to the east as Mongolia, though the distribution is patchy away from the centre of its range (BirdLife). It winters in discrete locations in sub-Saharan Africa. It is a scarce breeding bird in the UK, with an estimated breeding population of just two pairs annually (Musgrove *et al.*, 2013). There have only been four records in the London area, all in the Lee Valley (Self). It did not feature in either of the previous London atlases, although one of the previous records was a singing bird present for four days during the second atlas period in May 1989. During the current atlas period, a male was on territory at Seventy Acres Lake throughout the month of May 2009. It therefore qualifies as a 'probable' breeding; record, although it seems unlikely that it would have found a mate.

Marsh Warbler
Acrocephalus palustris

Rare summer visitor and passage migrant; red list.

The Marsh Warbler breeds in continental Europe, wintering in south-eastern Africa, and Britain is at the far western edge of its breeding range (BirdLife). The species still breeds sporadically in eastern Britain but there are no longer any regular breeding populations of this species in the British Isles, following the decline of populations in Worcestershire after the 1950s and in Kent in the 1990s (National Atlas).

In the London area, the species has always been scarce but an increase in the number of records during the 1990s saw the species recorded in seven tetrads during the last atlas period. This included three males on territory for two to four weeks. Although they were not thought to have found a mate (Hewlett *et al.*), the records are shown as having evidence of breeding as they meet the 'probable breeding' definition.

During the current atlas period, three or four singing males were recorded in total in three tetrads; one singing male at Amwell in June 2009, which was within a tetrad included in the London atlas but was actually just outside the official London area, one at Rainham Marshes in 2012 and two at the same site in 2013. The Rainham records came from two different tetrads and at least one pair was confirmed to have bred (Essex Bird Report 2013). This is the first confirmed breeding in the London area since 2001, when three pairs bred (Self).

Period	Number of Tetrads		
	Evidence of Breeding	Seen Only	Total
Breeding 1968–72	0	0	0
Breeding 1988–94	3	4	7
Breeding 2008–13	1	2	3

Breeding Distribution

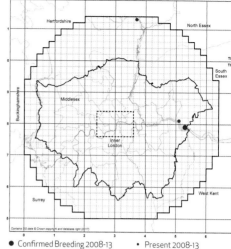

- ● Confirmed Breeding 2008-13
- ● Probable Breeding 2008-13
- ● Possible Breeding 2008-13
- · Present 2008-13
- · Still on Migration 2008-13

Breeding Change

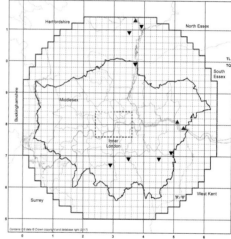

Breeding Distribution Change
- ▲ Recent Gain (new in 2008-13)
- ■ Stable (present in all periods)
- ▼ Old Loss (last occupied 1968-72)
- ▲ Old Gain (new in 1988-94)
- ■ Variable (absent 1988-94)
- ▼ Recent Loss (last occupied 1988-94)

Reed Warbler

Acrocephalus scirpaceus

Common and widespread passage migrant and breeding summer visitor; green list.

The Reed Warbler breeds across Europe and North Africa and winters in sub-Saharan Africa, where it is also resident to the south (BirdLife). In summer, the Reed Warbler is found across much of lowland England and Wales (National Atlas). The UK population is currently stable (BBS) and the long-term trend showing a moderate increase (BirdTrends).

Its strong habitat association means that its breeding distribution is limited mostly to *Phragmites* reedbeds in the London area, as is the case elsewhere. It is therefore not surprising that the main London strongholds for Reed Warbler are the lower Thames, the Lee Valley, the Colne Valley and the west London waterbodies. However, the species can make use of even very small areas of reeds or similar wetland habitat. For example, at Camley Street Natural Park in Inner London during the second atlas period (Hewlett *et al.*).

Since the last atlas, Reed Warbler has continued to benefit from wetland habitat creation and the planting of reedbeds, as predicted by Hewlett *et al.*, and many of the recent gains have occurred at parks and wildlife sites within the urban centre of the London area. In Inner London, it continues to breed in Regent's Park and territories were also recorded at Canada Water/Rotherhithe (in 2008 and 2013), Hyde Park/Kensington Gardens (2013) and St. James' Park (2013).

The density map suggests that Reed Warbler is most abundant in the Thames Marshes, with higher counts also occurring at a number of sites within the Lee Valley and at Stoke Newington Reservoir. Contemporary records show that healthy populations occur at several sites in our area, including: Rainham Marshes (peak count during the current atlas period of 159 territories in 2013), Rye Meads (123 in 2008), London Wetland Centre (65 in 2011), Amwell Nature Reserve (59 in 2009) and Bedfont Lakes (53 in 2011) (LBR).

Breeding Distribution

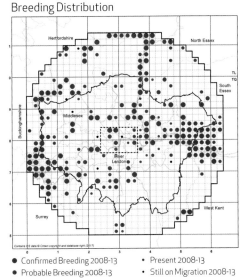

- ● Confirmed Breeding 2008-13
- ● Probable Breeding 2008-13
- ● Possible Breeding 2008-13
- • Present 2008-13
- • Still on Migration 2008-13

Period	Number of Tetrads		
	Evidence of Breeding	Seen Only	Total
Breeding 1968–72	107	11	118
Breeding 1988–94	170	51	221
Breeding 2008–13	156	84	240

Breeding Abundance

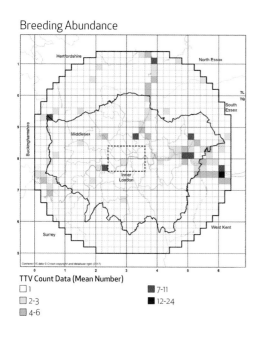

TTV Count Data (Mean Number)
- ☐ 1
- ☐ 2-3
- ☐ 4-6
- ☐ 7-11
- ■ 12-24

Breeding Change

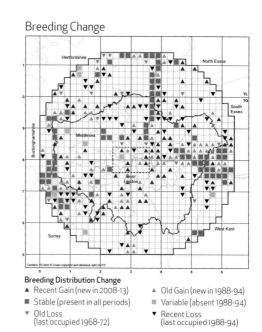

Breeding Distribution Change
- ▲ Recent Gain (new in 2008-13)
- ■ Stable (present in all periods)
- ▼ Old Loss (last occupied 1968-72)
- ▲ Old Gain (new in 1988-94)
- ■ Variable (absent 1988-94)
- ▼ Recent Loss (last occupied 1988-94)

Nuthatch

Sitta europaea

Common breeding resident; green list.

The Nuthatch increased both nationally and in south-east England between the last two atlas periods (BBS), accompanied by a dramatic northwards expansion into southern Scotland (National Atlas).

The distribution of the Nuthatch in the London area is broadly similar during the periods covered by all three atlases but with recent thinning in the Essex sector. As might be expected for a primarily woodland bird, tetrads within the built-up area of Greater London, and areas of open countryside to the east, are occupied with less frequency than those outside the built-up area and in the more wooded counties of Surrey and Hertfordshire. However, this species is also found in areas of woodland encapsulated in urban London.

The abundance mapping for the national atlas shows quite clearly that the areas to the north, west and, especially, south of London support some of the highest densities of this species found in the Britain. The mapping also clearly shows much lower density within Greater London, which fits with the pattern described above. There is some evidence from elsewhere that this species could be suffering from competition for nest sites with Ring-necked Parakeets (Strubbe *et al.*, 2010). However, a study undertaken in England did not detect a significant negative effect on Nuthatch populations so far as a result of competition from the parakeet (Newson *et al*, 2011).

There are historical records of breeding by the Nuthatch in Inner London. It bred in Hyde Park/Kensington Gardens (1997 to 1999), Regent's Park (early to mid-1980s) and perhaps Holland Park (early 1990s). Signs of breeding were also noted in six Inner London tetrads during fieldwork for the current atlas, with breeding confirmed in two tetrads, both relating to nests in Hyde Park/Kensington Gardens.

Period	Number of Tetrads		
	Evidence of Breeding	Seen Only	Total
Breeding 1968–72	325	76	401
Breeding 1988–94	403	111	514
Breeding 2008–13	333	196	529
Winter 2007/8–2012/13	-	-	528

The distribution of the Nuthatch during the winter, both nationally and in our area, is much the same as during the breeding season.

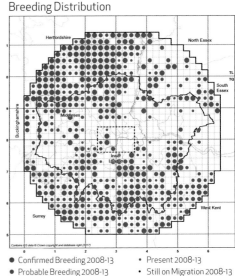

Breeding Distribution

● Confirmed Breeding 2008-13 · Present 2008-13
● Probable Breeding 2008-13 · Still on Migration 2008-13
● Possible Breeding 2008-13

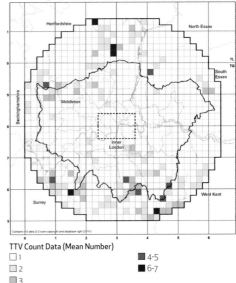

Breeding Abundance

TTV Count Data (Mean Number)
□ 1 ■ 4-5
□ 2 ■ 6-7
▨ 3

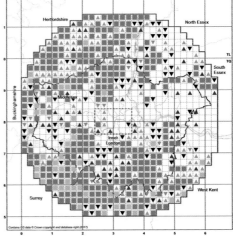

Breeding Change

Breeding Distribution Change
▲ Recent Gain (new in 2008-13) ▲ Old Gain (new in 1988-94)
■ Stable (present in all periods) ▨ Variable (absent 1988-94)
▼ Old Loss ▼ Recent Loss
(last occupied 1968-72) (last occupied 1988-94)

Winter Distribution

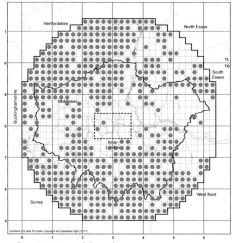

● Overwintering 2007/08-2012/13

Treecreeper
Certhia familiaris

Common breeding resident; green list.

The Treecreeper is found throughout the British Isles, where its population and distribution are stable (BBS, National Atlas).

Like the Nuthatch, the Treecreeper is a woodland species and its distribution in the London area reflects this habitat preference. Although the Treecreeper is the less widely reported, these two species have a high degree of coincidence; with 310 tetrads occupied by both species, 282 tetrads where both species are absent and only 43 tetrads where Treecreeper was recorded but not Nuthatch.

The broad pattern of distribution of the Treecreeper is similar in all three atlases but with a peak in occupied tetrads at the time of the second atlas. In south Essex, this species was apparently absent at the time of the first atlas but had colonised by the time of the second atlas, only to largely retreat from this area during the current atlas period. In north Surrey, there appears to have been a general thinning out of the population which took place between the first and second atlas periods. Finally, this species appears to have retreated a little from Greater London with 104 previously occupied tetrads in this area apparently abandoned since the time of the second atlas. It is feasible that some of these patterns could relate partly to observer effort: for example, the survey coverage in south Essex was most thorough during the second atlas.

The first breeding record for this species in Inner London was in 1945 in Kensington Gardens, with breeding records also coming from Regent's Park and Holland Park in the last half of the twentieth century. During the current atlas period, this species was still breeding in Hyde Park/Kensington Gardens, with one or two pairs annually, but not elsewhere in Inner London.

Period	Number of Tetrads		
	Evidence of Breeding	Seen Only	Total
Breeding 1968–72	288	146	434
Breeding 1988–94	389	121	510
Breeding 2008–13	207	146	353
Winter 2007/8–2012/13	-	-	403

The distribution of the Treecreeper during the winter, both nationally and in our area, is much the same as during the breeding season.

Breeding Distribution

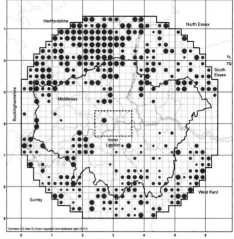

- ● Confirmed Breeding 2008-13
- ● Probable Breeding 2008-13
- ● Possible Breeding 2008-13
- • Present 2008-13
- • Still on Migration 2008-13

Breeding Abundance

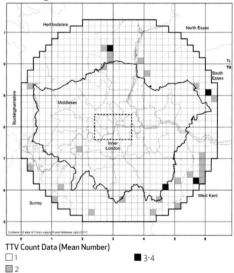

TTV Count Data (Mean Number)
- □ 1
- ▣ 2
- ■ 3-4

Breeding Change

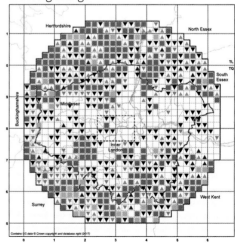

Breeding Distribution Change
- ▲ Recent Gain (new in 2008-13)
- ■ Stable (present in all periods)
- ▼ Old Loss (last occupied 1968-72)
- ▲ Old Gain (new in 1988-94)
- ▣ Variable (absent 1988-94)
- ▼ Recent Loss (last occupied 1988-94)

Winter Distribution

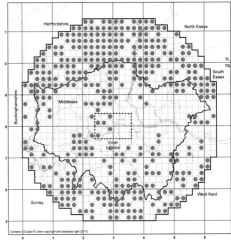

● Overwintering 2007/08-2012/13

Wren

Troglodytes troglodytes

Abundant breeding resident; green list.

The Wren continues to be one of the commonest and most widespread species of bird in the British Isles (National Atlas) and the population has remained stable over the last 20 years (BBS).

It can be found throughout the London area in both the breeding season and in winter. There were some gaps among the occupied tetrads during the first atlas period but it was found in all but one tetrad during the second atlas survey. There was a significant increase in the Wren population in the London area from 1995 to around 2005. This was followed by a slight decline though numbers remain above 1995 levels (BBS). The abundance maps suggest that higher densities are associated with some of the larger green spaces, particularly in suburban areas.

Period	Number of Tetrads		
	Evidence of Breeding	Seen Only	Total
Breeding 1968–72	733	48	781
Breeding 1988–94	838	17	855
Breeding 2008–13	789	61	850
Winter 2007/8–2012/13	-	-	846

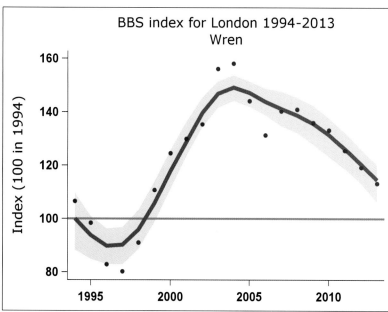

BTO/JNCC/RSPB Breeding Bird Survey (BBS)

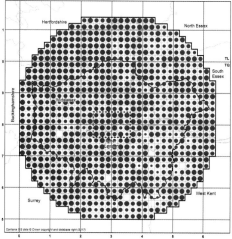

Breeding Distribution

- Confirmed Breeding 2008-13
- Probable Breeding 2008-13
- Possible Breeding 2008-13
- Present 2008-13
- Still on Migration 2008-13

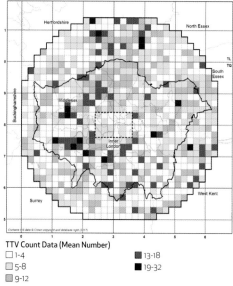

Breeding Abundance

TTV Count Data (Mean Number)
- 1-4
- 5-8
- 9-12
- 13-18
- 19-32

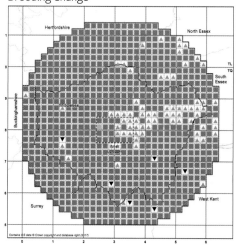

Breeding Change

Breeding Distribution Change
- Recent Gain (new in 2008-13)
- Stable (present in all periods)
- Old Loss (last occupied 1968-72)
- Old Gain (new in 1988-94)
- Variable (absent 1988-94)
- Recent Loss (last occupied 1988-94)

Winter Distribution

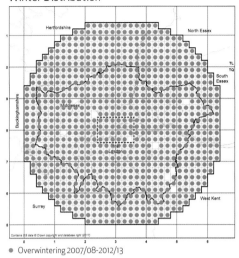

● Overwintering 2007/08-2012/13

Winter Abundance

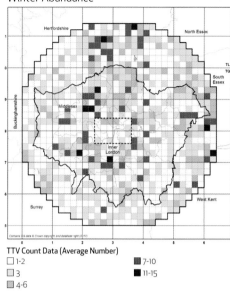

TTV Count Data (Average Number)

☐ 1-2

☐ 3

▨ 4-6

▧ 7-10

■ 11-15

Common Starling

Sturnus vulgaris

Common, but declining, breeding resident, passage migrant and winter visitor; red list.

The Starling is common and widespread throughout the British Isles but its population is declining.

The Starling was recorded in every tetrad in the second atlas and nearly as many in the first, with any gaps potentially attributable to survey effort rather than true absence. It is still a common and widespread species in our area; however, the current atlas indicates a few gaps in distribution which is likely to be an indication of thinning populations. The BBS indicates that the starling in London has undergone a 54% (41% to 63%) decline between 1995 and 2013, which is similar to the figure for the UK as a whole. Fewer than 80 individuals were recorded in most tetrads during the timed counts and the occasional higher count may relate to post-breeding flocks rather than breeding birds.

Despite the decline, the density of the Starling in the London area during the breeding season remains higher than surrounding areas and is much higher than in the west of Britain, making London something of a hotspot for this species in the breeding season (National Atlas). Indeed, the Starling was still the second most commonly counted species in the London area during the atlas breeding season timed counts, behind Woodpigeon.

In winter, the distribution of the Starling in Britain is the same as during the breeding season but the population is at its densest in the west,

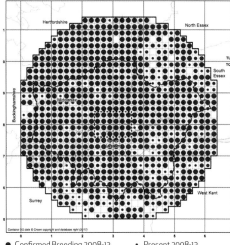

Breeding Distribution

- ● Confirmed Breeding 2008-13
- ● Probable Breeding 2008-13
- ● Possible Breeding 2008-13
- • Present 2008-13
- • Still on Migration 2008-13

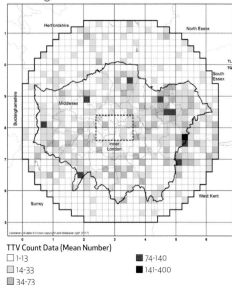

Breeding Abundance

TTV Count Data (Mean Number)
- ☐ 1-13
- ☐ 14-33
- ☐ 34-73
- ■ 74-140
- ■ 141-400

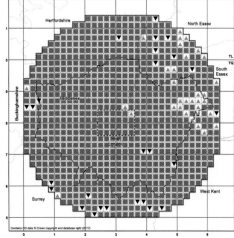

Breeding Change

Breeding Distribution Change
- ▲ Recent Gain (new in 2008-13)
- ■ Stable (present in all periods)
- ▼ Old Loss (last occupied 1968-72)
- ▲ Old Gain (new in 1988-94)
- ■ Variable (absent 1988-94)
- ▼ Recent Loss (last occupied 1988-94)

Period	Number of Tetrads		
	Evidence of Breeding	Seen Only	Total
Breeding 1968–72	796	25	821
Breeding 1988–94	849	7	856
Breeding 2008–13	722	108	830
Winter 2007/8–2012/13	-	-	834

rather than the east. As a consequence, the London area is not the UK hotspot for this species during the winter that it is in the breeding season, with much lower relative densities recorded (National Atlas). The Migration Atlas suggests that birds which breed in Britain are mostly sedentary, and the distribution and numbers of birds in our area are about the same in both seasons. Therefore, a potential explanation for the density pattern is that large numbers of migrant birds arriving from the continent mostly prefer to over-winter in the west of the British Isles.

The Starling is famous for its evening roosts outside the breeding season, comprising many individuals. In the past, there were several such large roosts in the London area, including in Inner London. Historic roost sites included Trafalgar Square, the British Museum (one of the two biggest roosts in 1925) and St Paul's Cathedral (with 7,000 birds in November 1932). The total population of starlings in roosts in London north of the Thames was estimated to be 15,000 to 20,000 in 1932–33, although the author thought this a generous estimate (Fitter, 1943).

Starlings ceased to roost *en masse* on the buildings in Inner London in about 1980 (Bowlt, 2008). However, this species still roosts in some numbers under some of the bridges over the Thames, including Battersea Bridge (Bowlt, 2008) and Wandsworth Bridge, both just outside the Inner London area. In addition, counts of several hundred are not uncommon throughout our area and larger aggregations of this species, comprising several thousand birds, are occasionally made further out from the centre. For example, during the winters of the atlas period, there were counts of around 2,000 at Beddington Farmlands and around 8,000 at Rainham Marshes.

Winter Distribution

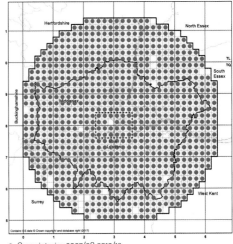

● Overwintering 2007/08-2012/13

Winter Abundance

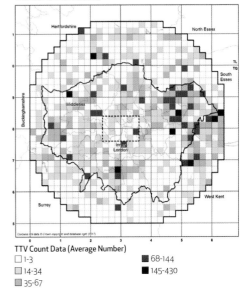

TTV Count Data (Average Number)
□ 1-3   ■ 68-144
□ 14-34   ■ 145-430
□ 35-67

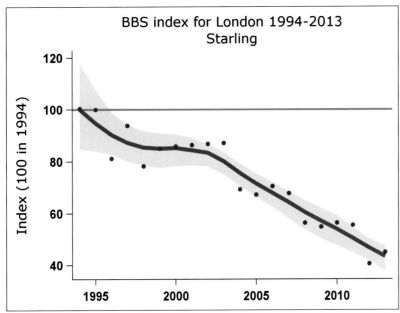

BTO/JNCC/RSPB Breeding Bird Survey (BBS)

Waxwing

Bombycilla garrulus

Uncommon but sometimes numerous irruptive visitor; green list.

The Waxwing breeds in northern Eurasia and is primarily a winter visitor to the British Isles. The birds that winter here are mainly those that breed in Scandinavia. The numbers vary greatly from year to year, with irruptions occurring in some years, when it can be found in almost every 10km square in lowland Britain (National Atlas).

In the London area, this species was recorded in every winter of the atlas fieldwork. However, there were very few reports of this species in the winters of 2007/8, 2008/9 and 2009/10, when all reports were of small flocks. This all changed in the winter of 2010/11, when there was an influx of this species into the London area with numerous reports of flocks exceeding 50 birds. There was a second such influx during the winter of 2012/13 when similar numbers were recorded (LBR). During these periods, the Waxwing can turn up anywhere in the London area. Berries are a common food source during winter irruptions, particularly of rowan and other trees which are often planted in urban streets and gardens. Consequently, many of the records come from urban areas. This effect may be exaggerated by the fact that this species is more easily detected in urban areas than in rural areas, where there are also fewer observers. The highest count made during atlas fieldwork was 367 at Chafford Hundred in January 2011.

During an irruption year, the Waxwing sometimes remains in Britain until late spring. As a result, the species was also recorded during the breeding season atlas surveys. Following the 2012/13 winter, they were particularly late to leave, and the last records were from Walthamstow (2nd May) and Grays (6th May).

Breeding season tetrads: 24

Winter season tetrads: 342

Winter Distribution

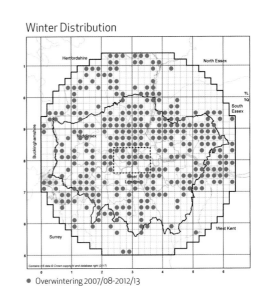

● Overwintering 2007/08-2012/13

Blackbird

Turdus merula

Abundant resident, passage migrant and winter visitor; green list.

The Blackbird remains one of the most widespread species in the London area, both in gardens and the surrounding countryside, and was found in every tetrad in both seasons. It was similarly widespread during both previous breeding atlases, with the few gaps during the first atlas likely to relate to survey coverage rather than true absence.

However, this species seems be suffering in urban areas. Although the UK population increased by 21% (17% to 25%) between 1995 and 2013, the figures for the London region are a statistically significant decline of 27% (14% to 37%) (BBS). Indeed, a decline during the 1990s was also observed in the Royal Parks (Self).

Many of the highest counts of Blackbirds made during the timed visits were in urban and suburban areas, highlighting the importance of gardens and urban green spaces for the species. However, higher counts also occurred elsewhere including in the Hertfordshire and Kent sectors.

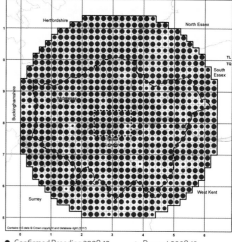

Breeding Distribution

- ● Confirmed Breeding 2008-13
- ● Probable Breeding 2008-13
- ● Possible Breeding 2008-13
- · Present 2008-13
- · Still on Migration 2008-13

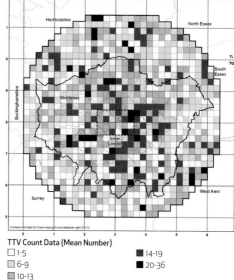

Breeding Abundance

TTV Count Data (Mean Number)
- □ 1-5
- 6-9
- 10-13
- 14-19
- 20-36

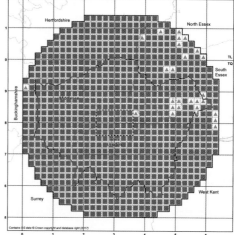

Breeding Change

Breeding Distribution Change
- ▲ Recent Gain (new in 2008-13)
- ■ Stable (present in all periods)
- ▼ Old Loss (last occupied 1968-72)
- ▲ Old Gain (new in 1988-94)
- ▣ Variable (absent 1988-94)
- ▼ Recent Loss (last occupied 1988-94)

Period	Number of Tetrads		
	Evidence of Breeding	Seen Only	Total
Breeding 1968–72	814	15	829
Breeding 1988–94	849	7	856
Breeding 2008–13	842	14	856
Winter 2007/8–2012/13	-	-	856

Winter Distribution

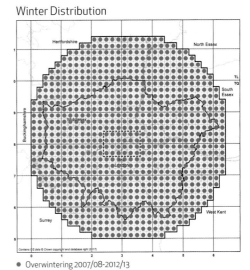

● Overwintering 2007/08-2012/13

In winter, the Blackbird remains widespread in both Britain and the London area. Although many of our breeding birds are likely to be resident, others may head to the south-west, and some of the birds we see here in winter are probably from northern Europe and from Scandinavia (Migration Atlas). However, the timed counts suggest that similar numbers are present in winter (an average of 8.01 birds recorded per hour) to the breeding season (8.46).

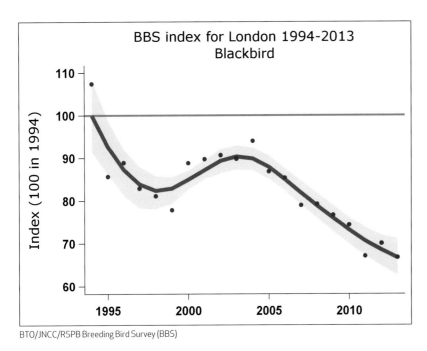

BTO/JNCC/RSPB Breeding Bird Survey (BBS)

Winter Abundance

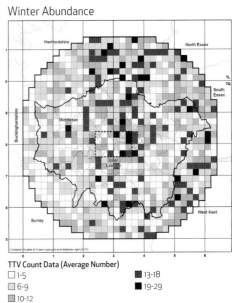

TTV Count Data (Average Number)
- 1-5
- 6-9
- 10-12
- 13-18
- 19-29

Fieldfare

Turdus pilaris

Regular passage migrant and winter visitor; red list.

The majority of the Fieldfare population breeds in Fennoscandia and this species only rarely breeds in the British Isles, mostly in Scotland and northern England (National Atlas).

The breeding record for Fieldfare in the London area at Foots Cray Meadows in May 1991 during the second atlas period (Hewlett *et al.*) is therefore exceptional, with the only other breeding records in our area being from Barking Park in 1980 and 1981 (Self). All the breeding season records made during the current atlas period are likely to be wintering birds, which often do not depart until April. The apparently higher level of tetrad occupancy this time may be due to the differing approaches to recording this species across the three atlases.

The Fieldfare is mostly a winter visitor to the British Isles, when the highest concentrations occur in south-east and central England (National Atlas). During the winter, it is normally easy to find due to its distinctive 'chack-chack-chack' call and its habit of forming large flocks which feed on the ground in the open fields, sometimes alongside the closely related Redwing. However, single birds or small groups feeding in hedgerows can occur occasionally and are less obvious.

Period	Number of Tetrads		
	Evidence of Breeding	Seen Only	Total
Breeding 1968–72	0	0	0
Breeding 1988–94	1	10	11
Breeding 2008–13	0	77	77
Winter 2007/8–2012/13	-	-	742

The Fieldfare is normally present in good numbers each winter in most of the rural areas around the outskirts of London. During milder winter conditions, the Fieldfare is scarce in the urban parts of the area, although a few birds do reach some of the larger green spaces and larger flocks may fly over. In harsher weather, the Fieldfare sometimes invades urban areas in large numbers, being found particularly where fruit and berries are available in gardens or on street trees. Consequently, the majority of urban records of Fieldfare in the current atlas period occurred in the coldest winters; these were 2008/09, 2009/10 and 2010/11. Even in these years, the distribution of the Fieldfare within the urban area is patchier than that of the Redwing.

The density maps produced as a result of the timed counts suggest that the highest numbers in the London area can be found in the Essex, Kent and Hertfordshire sectors. Although timed counts can be less reliable for highly mobile species such as the Fieldfare, the paucity of high counts in the south-west seems to indicate that this part of the London area has a lower wintering population of Fieldfare. This is supported by the higher number of apparently unoccupied tetrads here relative to the other rural parts of our area.

Winter Distribution

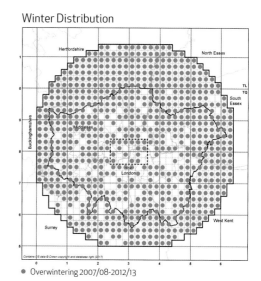

● Overwintering 2007/08-2012/13

Winter Abundance

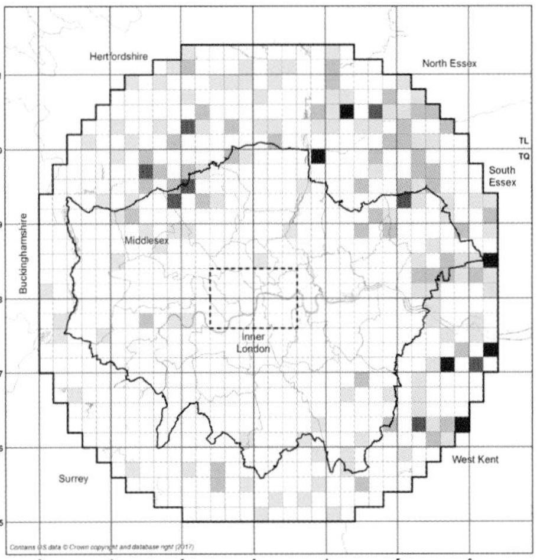

TTV Count Data (Average Number)

- 1-12
- 13-34
- 35-69
- 70-132
- 133-297

Song Thrush

Turdus philomelos

Common, but locally declining, breeding resident, passage migrant and winter visitor; red list.

The Song Thrush remains a common bird in Britain, despite a decline during the 1970s and early 1980s (BirdTrends). There is evidence that the decline may have halted, with numbers being relatively stable since the late 1980s. This has not been seen in London, where the population has decreased by 34% (16% to 49%) between 1995 and 2013 (BBS).

Despite the decline, the Song Thrush can still be found across the London area, where it inhabits gardens, parks and rural areas, as it did in both previous atlas periods. The gaps which have appeared since the second atlas are indicative of the declining London trend and are mainly within Middlesex, the Essex sector and the eastern half of Inner London.

The density map suggests that the Song Thrush is slightly more abundant in the more rural parts of the area, particularly in the Hertfordshire, Essex and Kent sectors, though some parts of Greater London still have good numbers, especially in the west. Lower numbers were recorded in central London and across the eastern half of Greater London, both north and south of the River Thames. The lower abundance in Greater London is also clearly visible on the national abundance maps (National Atlas).

Period	Number of Tetrads		
	Evidence of Breeding	Seen Only	Total
Breeding 1968–72	787	35	822
Breeding 1988–94	814	40	854
Breeding 2008–13	629	183	812
Winter 2007/8–2012/13	-	-	800

Although the majority of the breeding Song Thrush population in Britain is believed to be sedentary, the resident population is supplemented in winter by birds from the Low Countries (Milwright, 2006) and some of

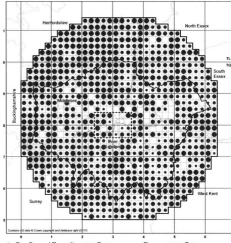

Breeding Distribution

- ● Confirmed Breeding 2008-13
- ● Probable Breeding 2008-13
- ● Possible Breeding 2008-13
- · Present 2008-13
- · Still on Migration 2008-13

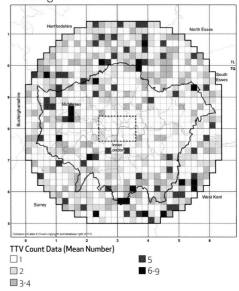

Breeding Abundance

TTV Count Data (Mean Number)
- □ 1
- □ 2
- □ 3-4
- ■ 5
- ■ 6-9

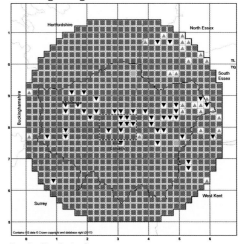

Breeding Change

Breeding Distribution Change
- ▲ Recent Gain (new in 2008-13)
- ■ Stable (present in all periods)
- ▼ Old Loss (last occupied 1968-72)
- ▲ Old Gain (new in 1988-94)
- ▨ Variable (absent 1988-94)
- ▼ Recent Loss (last occupied 1988-94)

those which breed in Britain migrate southwards to the continent and westwards into Ireland (Migration Atlas). Furthermore, birds which breed in Scandinavia are thought to pass through Britain on passage (Migration Atlas). Resident or wintering Song Thrush can be found across most of the London area during winter, although there are a small number of unoccupied tetrads in the heavily urbanised parts of central London. Unlike Redwing, wintering Song Thrush tend to be more unobtrusive and do not tend to occur in flocks, which may have resulted in birds going undetected in some tetrads where they were present. However, males on breeding territories may start singing in late winter and so become easier to detect in January and February. As in the breeding season, the abundance is also lower in Greater London than in the surrounding areas.

Winter Distribution

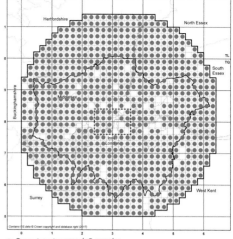

● Overwintering 2007/08-2012/13

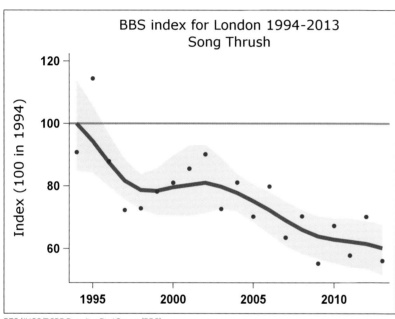

BTO/JNCC/RSPB Breeding Bird Survey (BBS)

Winter Abundance

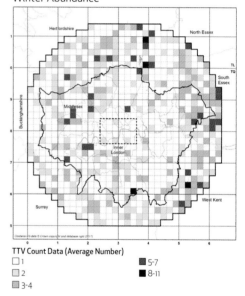

TTV Count Data (Average Number)
☐ 1   ■ 5-7
☐ 2   ■ 8-11
☐ 3-4

Redwing

Turdus iliacus

Common passage migrant and winter visitor; red list.

The Redwing breeds in Iceland, northern and eastern Europe and much of Siberia and winters in western and southern Europe, North Africa and parts of the Middle East (BirdLife). Like the Fieldfare, the Redwing is a rare breeding bird in the north of Britain and a common winter visitor to the British Isles, including the London area (National Atlas). During the winter, it often appears in large flocks and feeding on trees with berries, amongst leaf litter in woodland, and on arable fields or mown recreational grassland. The UK wintering population is estimated to be 690,000 individuals, which is similar to the figure for Fieldfare (Musgrove et al., 2013) and is derived from birds which breed in Iceland and northern Europe (Migration Atlas).

Unlike the Fieldfare, Redwing is not normally restricted to the rural fringes of the London area, and small numbers can be found within the urban area in most winters. In milder winters the Redwing tends to be found in the larger green spaces, for example Hyde Park/Kensington Gardens. Like the Fieldfare, Redwing invades Greater London in much bigger numbers during more severe weather, often in mixed flocks comprising both species. During these 'invasions', birds can be found just about anywhere in the London area, including gardens, the smallest of green spaces, railway verges and feeding on street trees and amenity hedges. For example, a count of 360 in Highbury (Tetrad TQ38C) during a timed count on 8th January 2010 includes a large flock of 350 Redwings, feeding on street trees during a period of harsh weather.

Breeding season tetrads: 77

Winter season tetrads: 825

Winter Distribution

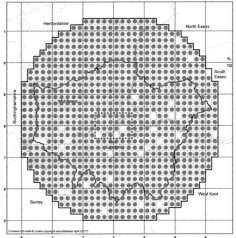

● Overwintering 2007/08-2012/13

Winter Abundance

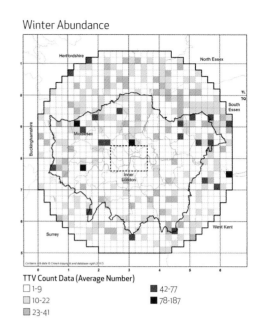

Contains OS data © Crown copyright and database right (2017)

TTV Count Data (Average Number)

☐ 1-9   ■ 42-77
☐ 10-22   ■ 78-187
▨ 23-41

Mistle Thrush

Turdus viscivorus

Common breeding resident; red list.

The Mistle Thrush is our largest resident thrush. Like the other two resident thrush species, it can be found throughout the London area, frequenting parks in urban areas and both woodland and farmland in the countryside. There has been an overall decline in the UK population of around 31% (23% to 37%) since 1995. This is driven principally by declines in the south and east of England (including London), where it has declined by an estimated 57%, and is partially offset by an increasing population in the north and west of Britain (BirdTrends; BBS).

Given the regional declines, it is perhaps no surprise that gaps have appeared on the London distribution map, both within the built-up area and in the rural parts of the Essex and Kent sectors. These losses reverse the gains observed during the second atlas period. Further gaps could appear in future unless the recent declines are reversed.

The Mistle Thrush is generally found at low densities, with most tetrads recording between 0 and 3 birds per hour during the timed counts, with some higher counts relating to family parties.

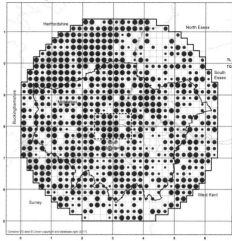

Breeding Distribution

- ● Confirmed Breeding 2008-13
- ● Probable Breeding 2008-13
- ● Possible Breeding 2008-13
- • Present 2008-13
- • Still on Migration 2008-13

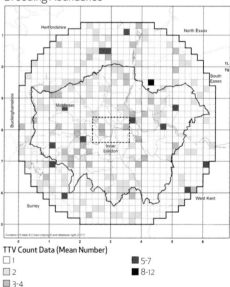

Breeding Abundance

TTV Count Data (Mean Number)
- ☐ 1
- ☐ 2
- ▨ 3-4
- ■ 5-7
- ■ 8-12

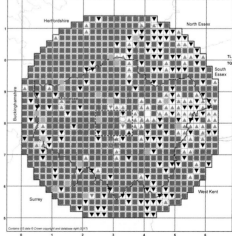

Breeding Change

Breeding Distribution Change
- ▲ Recent Gain (new in 2008-13)
- ■ Stable (present in all periods)
- ▼ Old Loss (last occupied 1968-72)
- ▲ Old Gain (new in 1988-94)
- ▨ Variable (absent 1988-94)
- ▼ Recent Loss (last occupied 1988-94)

Period	Number of Tetrads		
	Evidence of Breeding	Seen Only	Total
Breeding 1968–72	610	124	734
Breeding 1988–94	716	115	831
Breeding 2008–13	483	226	709
Winter 2007/8–2012/13	-	-	764

In winter, the Mistle Thrush is slightly more widespread in our area, although the distribution is similar to that of the breeding season, with gaps in the Essex and Kent sectors, as well as Middlesex and in the western half of Inner London, where there are few green spaces.

Winter Distribution

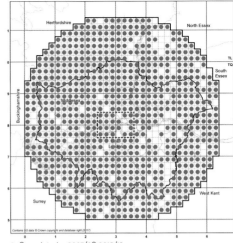

● Overwintering 2007/08-2012/13

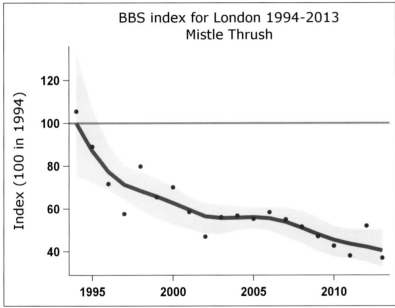

BTO/JNCC/RSPB Breeding Bird Survey (BBS)

Winter Abundance

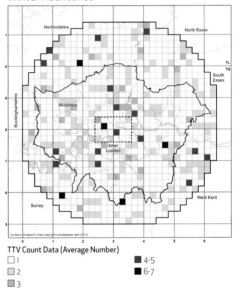

TTV Count Data (Average Number)
- ☐ 1
- ☐ 2
- ☐ 3
- ■ 4-5
- ■ 6-7

Robin

Erithacus rubecula

Abundant breeding resident and passage migrant, with influxes in autumn and winter; green list.

Voted the UK's favourite bird in 2015, the Robin is one of the country's best-known species. It is resident throughout Britain where it is as familiar in gardens as it is in the countryside.

The national atlas abundance maps show that London and the south-east have a higher density of this species than most other parts of Britain. During the first London atlas period, there were some gaps in the breeding range in Inner London and in east London/Essex, though the latter probably related to poor coverage rather than real absence (Hewlett *et al.*). In the second atlas period, the Robin was found in all but two tetrads and it remains ubiquitous in the London area. The population in the UK increased moderately, by approximately 11% (6% to 15%) between 1995 and 2013 but the increase in London has been much greater, around 79% (53% to 130%), over the same period (BBS).

Continental migrants pass through Britain during the autumn but it is believed that these winter further south (Migration Atlas) and hence the majority of birds wintering here are birds which breed in Britain. Given that most resident birds are sedentary, it is unsurprising that the winter distribution is similar to the breeding distribution in both Britain as a whole and in the London area.

Breeding Distribution

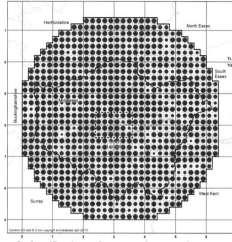

- ● Confirmed Breeding 2008-13
- ● Probable Breeding 2008-13
- ● Possible Breeding 2008-13
- • Present 2008-13
- • Still on Migration 2008-13

Breeding Abundance

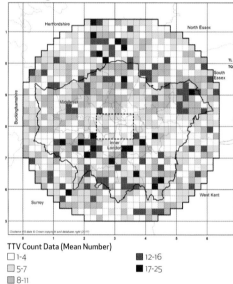

TTV Count Data (Mean Number)
- ☐ 1-4
- ☐ 5-7
- ☐ 8-11
- ☐ 12-16
- ☐ 17-25

Breeding Change

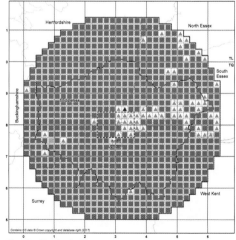

Breeding Distribution Change
- ▲ Recent Gain (new in 2008-13)
- ■ Stable (present in all periods)
- ▼ Old Loss (last occupied 1968-72)
- ▲ Old Gain (new in 1988-94)
- ■ Variable (absent 1988-94)
- ▼ Recent Loss (last occupied 1988-94)

Period	Number of Tetrads		
	Evidence of Breeding	Seen Only	Total
Breeding 1968–72	755	37	792
Breeding 1988–94	841	13	854
Breeding 2008–13	820	36	856
Winter 2007/8–2012/13	-	-	856

Winter Distribution

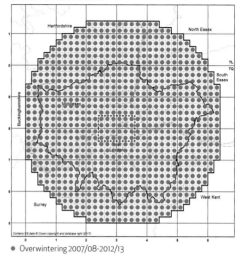

● Overwintering 2007/08-2012/13

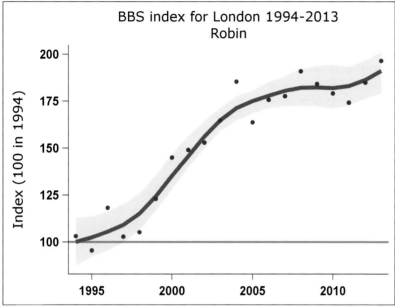

BTO/JNCC/RSPB Breeding Bird Survey (BBS)

Winter Abundance

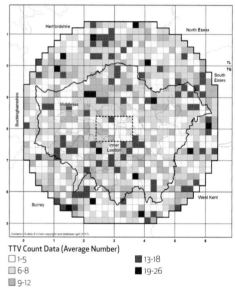

TTV Count Data (Average Number)
☐ 1-5   ■ 13-18
☐ 6-8   ■ 19-26
☐ 9-12

Nightingale
Luscinia megarhynchos

Summer visitor, breeding in small numbers, and scarce passage migrant; red list.

The Nightingale is a renowned songster, which breeds in Eurasia and North Africa and winters in the Sahel (BirdLife).

In Britain, it is restricted to the south where it breeds in areas with clumps of shrubs and, decreasingly, mid-cycle coppiced woodland. It has declined in the last 40 years with a range contraction occurring over this time towards strongholds in Kent, Sussex and Essex. In total, there has been a 43% reduction in the number of occupied 10km squares since 1968–72 (National Atlas).

In the London area, it had already declined substantially by the time of the first atlas (Hewlett *et al*.) and has remained uncommon ever since. Following a reduction in the number of occupied tetrads between the first two atlases, the current distribution map suggests little subsequent change in the London area, with strongholds remaining in the Lee Valley, Epping Forest and the Surrey heaths. There have been losses from tetrads in some areas (for example in Hainault Forest and in the Kent sector) but gains in other tetrads elsewhere (for example in the Lee Valley).

This species may be less widespread than the map suggests, as some of the apparently occupied tetrads are likely to relate to singing passage birds, including a 'probable breeding' record at Wormwood Scrubs, where a bird remained on territory for more than a week in 2011. However, the Nightingale does occasionally breed in unexpected locations, including a confirmed breeding record at Brent Reservoir in 2008. Overall, there may be around 20 to 30 breeding pairs present in the London area each year (LBR).

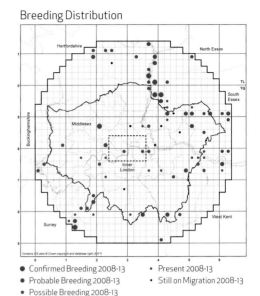

Breeding Distribution

- ● Confirmed Breeding 2008-13
- ● Probable Breeding 2008-13
- ● Possible Breeding 2008-13
- • Present 2008-13
- • Still on Migration 2008-13

Period	Number of Tetrads		
	Evidence of Breeding	Seen Only	Total
Breeding 1968–72	70	19	89
Breeding 1988–94	34	28	62
Breeding 2008–13	24	50	74

Breeding Change

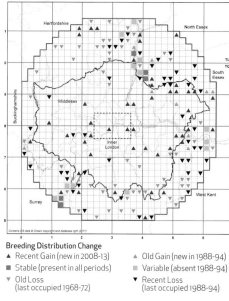

Breeding Distribution Change
- ▲ Recent Gain (new in 2008-13)
- ■ Stable (present in all periods)
- ▽ Old Loss (last occupied 1968-72)
- ▲ Old Gain (new in 1988-94)
- ■ Variable (absent 1988-94)
- ▼ Recent Loss (last occupied 1988-94)

Spotted Flycatcher
Muscicapa striata

Declining breeding summer visitor and passage migrant; red list.

The Spotted Flycatcher is a migratory species which breeds right across Europe and winters in sub-Saharan Africa (BirdLife). It has undergone a rapid and consistent decline in Britain since the 1960s. It is still present as a breeding species in most 10km squares, but the population is concentrated in western and northern parts of the British Isles (National Atlas).

At the time of the first London atlas, the Spotted Flycatcher was widespread if not common, with breeding pairs in the majority of tetrads including seven in Inner London. This included an average of nine occupied territories in Hyde Park/Kensington Gardens during the first atlas period. The distribution of this species at that time appears to have been determined mainly by the availability of suitable habitat, with breeding pairs present in most places where this occurred. At the time of the second atlas, there was some evidence of a decline, particularly in the south-west quadrant of our area, where 55 of formerly occupied tetrads were found to be vacant. For comparison, only one to two territories were reported from Hyde Park/Kensington Gardens. Nevertheless, this species remained widespread in our area, and in spite of the apparent decline in Hyde Park/Kensington Gardens, the number of occupied tetrads in Inner London actually increased.

As might be expected from the national trend, the current atlas shows a dramatic decrease in the numbers of tetrads supporting this species. Greater London and the area to the south had very few tetrads with breeding evidence or even occurrence of this species, with most of the few remaining tetrads where this species breeds being located in the Hertfordshire and Essex sectors. There were fewer than 15 recorded territories in the London area for each year of the current atlas period. The closest of these to central London is Greenwich Park. The national atlas indicates that the London area is a particular low spot in the abundance of this species.

Period	Number of Tetrads		
	Evidence of Breeding	Seen Only	Total
Breeding 1968–72	469	121	590
Breeding 1988–94	412	136	548
Breeding 2008–13	51	59	110

The occurrence of this species in the 10km square TL20 in Hertfordshire, which received a high level of survey effort, suggests that the species may possibly still be more widely present in some of the less well-covered rural areas, such as in Essex, but perhaps be at very low densities and therefore difficult to find. In the 25 tetrads in TL20, breeding was confirmed in ten, and considered probable in one other, during the whole atlas period. These account for 22% of the tetrads with confirmed or probable breeding in the whole of the London area in the same period.

Breeding Distribution

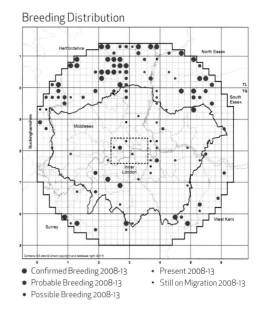

- ● Confirmed Breeding 2008-13
- ● Probable Breeding 2008-13
- ● Possible Breeding 2008-13
- • Present 2008-13
- • Still on Migration 2008-13

Breeding Change

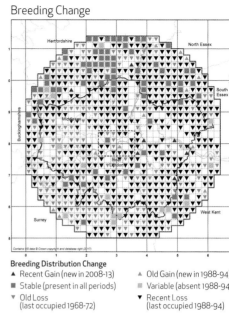

Breeding Distribution Change

▲ Recent Gain (new in 2008-13)   ▲ Old Gain (new in 1988-94)

■ Stable (present in all periods)   ■ Variable (absent 1988-94)

▼ Old Loss
(last occupied 1968-72)   ▼ Recent Loss
(last occupied 1988-94)

Black Redstart
Phoenicurus ochruros

Breeding summer visitor, passage migrant and winter visitor, with small numbers in all seasons; red list.

The Black Redstart is a rare breeding bird in Britain, with a breeding population of just 30 pairs (Musgrove *et al.*, 2013), which occurs principally in urban areas. It is much more numerous elsewhere in its breeding range, which extends across central and southern Europe, Asia and North Africa (BirdLife).

The Black Redstart is one of London's most iconic birds. It colonised London during the inter-war years, with breeding being recorded for the first time in 1926, and prospered during and immediately after the Second World War, making use of bomb sites before they were redeveloped (Hewlett *et al.*). London has since remained one of the strongholds for the species in Britain, with breeding centred on the Lea, the Thames and central London at the time of the last atlas period. During the current atlas period, it was still present in central London and along the Thames but the population in the Brimsdown area appears to have declined.

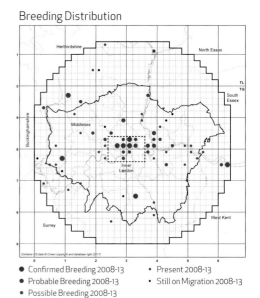

Breeding Distribution

- ● Confirmed Breeding 2008-13
- ● Probable Breeding 2008-13
- ● Possible Breeding 2008-13
- · Present 2008-13
- · Still on Migration 2008-13

Period	Number of Tetrads		
	Evidence of Breeding	Seen Only	Total
Breeding 1968–72	33	8	41
Breeding 1988–94	48	22	70
Breeding 2008–13	13	47	60
Winter 2007/8–2012/13	-	-	39

During the winter, the population of the Black Redstart in the British Isles is perhaps ten times higher than during the breeding season (Musgrove *et al.*, 2013). Passage migrants also occur when moving between their breeding grounds and their wintering grounds in Spain and north-west Africa, especially during the spring (Langslow, 1977). In the winter, the population is much more strongly associated with the coasts of Britain and Ireland than it is the urban areas (National Atlas). Perhaps reflecting this general pattern, the species appears less widespread in central London during the winter and more widespread along the tidal Thames. It is possible that Black Redstart is more widespread in central London in winter than the map suggests, as they will be hard to detect if present on rooftops when they are not singing. However, a more likely explanation for the observed change in distribution is that central London has been largely deserted, due to the scarcity of insect food, and that the birds have moved to take advantage of the greater availability of food along the river, as well as at other wetland sites.

Breeding Change

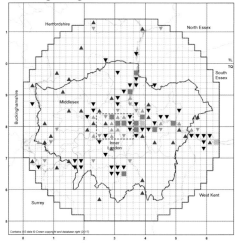

Breeding Distribution Change
- ▲ Recent Gain (new in 2008-13)
- ■ Stable (present in all periods)
- ▽ Old Loss (last occupied 1968-72)
- ▲ Old Gain (new in 1988-94)
- ▥ Variable (absent 1988-94)
- ▼ Recent Loss (last occupied 1988-94)

Winter Distribution

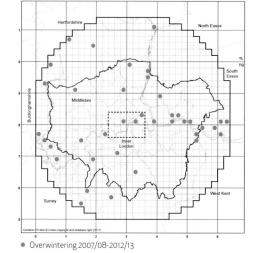

- ● Overwintering 2007/08-2012/13

Redstart

Phoenicurus phoenicurus

Formerly a breeding summer migrant, now an uncommon passage migrant; amber list.

The Redstart is a summer visitor to Britain. Its range has contracted markedly since the first National Atlas, when the species was found across most of mainland Britain. It is now mostly restricted to upland areas, especially in Wales and northern England (National Atlas) and has a very patchy distribution in the lowlands. At the same time, there has been a steep increase in the breeding population in Wales (National Atlas) and as a consequence the UK population has actually grown by approximately 47% (20% to 71%) over the period 1995 to 2013 (BBS).

The pattern in the London area has matched that occurring across much of the south and east of England. Although locally distributed and despite earlier declines, up to 90 territories were present in the early 1960s, concentrated in some of the larger mature woodlands in the Essex and Hertfordshire sectors (Self). During the first atlas period, it was found in 71 tetrads in total. However, numbers continued to fall and it is likely that this species did not breed in the London area between 1977 and 1985 (Self). At the time of the second atlas, it had returned, in a small way, as a breeding species in the London area. At that time, most records were still thought to represent passage birds but three tetrads held territorial birds; one in Epping Forest represented its last stronghold in our area, with six pairs in 1988 and 1989. However, by 1994 just one pair remained at this site (Hewlett *et al.*) and this is the last confirmed record of breeding Redstart in the London area (Self).

Although the current atlas records include an apparently territorial male which was heard singing in the same place in Ongar Park Wood on 5th and 20th May 2008, there was no further evidence of breeding. Most, if not all, of the records undoubtedly relate to passage birds, and a number of records in April from sites with no suitable habitat have been marked retrospectively as migrants. Although occasional, one-off breeding records could potentially occur in future, it is now sadly difficult to envisage the Redstart returning as a regular breeding bird in the London area.

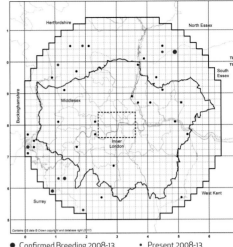

Breeding Distribution

● Confirmed Breeding 2008-13
● Probable Breeding 2008-13
● Possible Breeding 2008-13
· Present 2008-13
· Still on Migration 2008-13

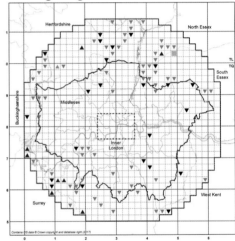

Breeding Change

Breeding Distribution Change
▲ Recent Gain (new in 2008-13)
■ Stable (present in all periods)
▼ Old Loss (last occupied 1968-72)
▲ Old Gain (new in 1988-94)
■ Variable (absent 1988-94)
▼ Recent Loss (last occupied 1988-94)

Period	Number of Tetrads		
	Evidence of Breeding	Seen Only	Total
Breeding 1968–72	42	29	71
Breeding 1988–94	3	21	24
Breeding 2008–13	1	9	10

Stonechat

Saxicola rubicola

Localised breeding resident, regular passage migrant and winter visitor; green list.

Like its relative the Whinchat, the Stonechat is predominantly associated with upland Britain as a breeding species. However, the Stonechat is more widespread in lowland areas, particularly around the coasts and on the downs and heaths of southern England. In contrast to the Whinchat, the Stonechat breeding range and abundance had both increased since the 1988–91 National Atlas. However, the severe winters in 2009/10 and 2010/11 effectively wiped out most of the previous gains in abundance (National Atlas).

In the London area, the Stonechat was found in low numbers on the commons and heaths in Surrey and Kent throughout the twentieth century, before colonising wasteland areas bordering the Thames during the 1980s (Hewlett *et al.*). The Stonechat is still most common in the London area along the Thames, though the number of occupied tetrads has declined here, possibly the result of ongoing development in parts of this area. Elsewhere, a breeding population has persisted in Richmond Park and evidence of probable or confirmed breeding was also recorded at Beech Farm Gravel Pits and at Bushy Park. However, the species appears to have disappeared as a breeding bird on the Surrey heaths, where breeding was already irregular at the time of the second atlas (Hewlett *et al.*). Further development along the Thames Gateway may leave London populations vulnerable and isolated on disparate sites such as Rainham Marshes and Richmond Park.

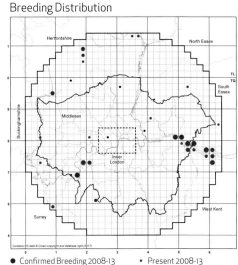

Breeding Distribution

- ● Confirmed Breeding 2008-13
- ● Probable Breeding 2008-13
- ● Possible Breeding 2008-13
- · Present 2008-13
- · Still on Migration 2008-13

Period	Number of Tetrads		
	Evidence of Breeding	Seen Only	Total
Breeding 1968–72	14	4	18
Breeding 1988–94	21	15	36
Breeding 2008–13	14	16	30
Winter 2007/8–2012/13	-	-	155

During winter, the Stonechat is a more widespread visitor across the London area, usually frequenting sites with areas of less-managed scrub and low vegetation and avoiding more tidy parks lacking semi-natural habitat. The distribution in London was noticeably sparser in the latter winters of the current atlas period following the two severe winters, with a corresponding, large fall in the number of records published in the London Bird Reports for 2011 and 2012. Consequently, the winter distribution map almost certainly overstates the winter distribution in our area at the time. It probably also understates the distribution during the early years as some tetrads were not visited until the latter years of the atlas period, by which time Stonechats were scarce.

Breeding Change

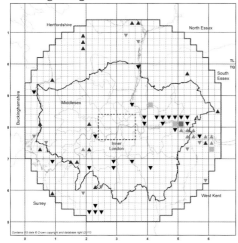

Winter Distribution

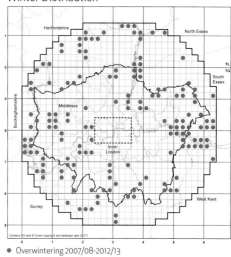

Breeding Distribution Change
- ▲ Recent Gain (new in 2008-13)
- ■ Stable (present in all periods)
- ▼ Old Loss
  (last occupied 1968-72)
- ▲ Old Gain (new in 1988-94)
- ■ Variable (absent 1988-94)
- ▼ Recent Loss
  (last occupied 1988-94)

● Overwintering 2007/08-2012/13

Whinchat

Saxicola rubetra

Formerly a breeding summer migrant, now an uncommon passage migrant; red list.

Like the Redstart, the Whinchat was formerly much more widespread but no longer breeds in most of lowland England. Unlike the Redstart, the Whinchat has declined in abundance across its whole range including in upland areas (National Atlas); the total population decline being approximately 54% (36 to 67%) between 1995 and 2013 (BBS).

In 1955, around 45 pairs bred in the London area, mainly along the river valleys. The population then gradually declined, with evidence of breeding recorded in only 18 tetrads by the time of the first atlas and just six widely scattered tetrads during the second atlas period (Hewlett *et al*.). The last record of breeding in the London area was in 1991 (Self) and the Whinchat can no longer be considered a breeding bird in the London area, although it continues to be a familiar passage migrant in both spring and autumn. The closest breeding population to the London area is now on Salisbury Plain.

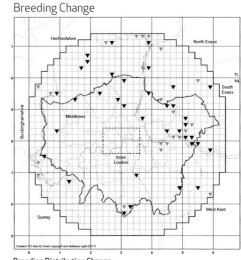

Breeding Change

Breeding Distribution Change
- ▲ Recent Gain (new in 2008-13)
- ■ Stable (present in all periods)
- ▼ Old Loss (last occupied 1968-72)
- ▲ Old Gain (new in 1988-94)
- ■ Variable (absent 1988-94)
- ▼ Recent Loss (last occupied 1988-94)

Period	Number of Tetrads		
	Evidence of Breeding	**Seen Only**	**Total**
Breeding 1968–72	18	7	25
Breeding 1988–94	6	30	36
Breeding 2008–13	0	0	0

Wheatear

Oenanthe oenanthe

Common passage migrant and former breeding visitor; green list.

Formerly occurring more widely, including on downs and heaths in southern Britain, the Wheatear is now mainly restricted as a breeding species to upland and coastal sites in northern and western Britain (National Atlas).

In the early twentieth century, the Wheatear bred on the chalk downlands and heaths of Surrey and Kent and also on Wimbledon Common and in Richmond Park. Since 1930, nesting attempts have only been occasional (Hewlett *et al.*). A handful of probable and possible breeding records were made during the first two atlas periods but the only confirmed breeding records since the beginning of the first atlas period were of one pair in the years from 1978 to 1980 and a pair which attempted to breed in 2000 (Self). Although the second atlas shows a large increase in the total number of occupied tetrads, most of these records were believed to involve passage birds (Hewlett *et al.*).

Records were received from some 140 tetrads during the current atlas period but, with no further evidence to support breeding, these were all assumed to relate to passage birds.

Breeding Change

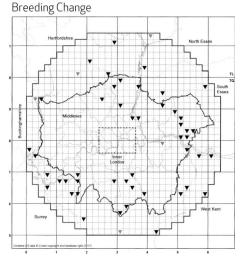

Breeding Distribution Change
▲ Recent Gain (new in 2008-13) ▲ Old Gain (new in 1988-94)
■ Stable (present in all periods) ■ Variable (absent 1988-94)
▼ Old Loss ▼ Recent Loss
(last occupied 1968-72) (last occupied 1988-94)

Period	Number of Tetrads		
	Evidence of Breeding	Seen Only	Total
Breeding 1968–72	3	3	6
Breeding 1988–94	2	45	47
Breeding 2008–13	0	0	0

Dunnock

Prunella modularis

Abundant resident; amber list.

The Dunnock is a widespread resident species. Following a steep decline in Britain from the mid-1970s to the mid-1980s, numbers have increased since but have still not returned to the former level (National Atlas; BirdTrends). It can be found in many different habitats, in both rural and urban areas, and the slight fall in density in central London is barely noticeable on the national atlas relative abundance map.

In the London area, there were gaps in the distribution of the Dunnock during the first atlas period in east London, south Essex and the eastern half of central London. Some of the gains in the second atlas period, when the species was found in all but three tetrads, were attributed to better coverage in these areas (Hewlett *et al.*). The population has been broadly stable in London since the mid-1990s (BBS) and the number of occupied tetrads has hardly changed between the second and current atlas periods.

Period	Number of Tetrads		
	Evidence of Breeding	Seen Only	Total
Breeding 1968–72	747	53	800
Breeding 1988–94	835	18	853
Breeding 2008–13	667	172	839
Winter 2007/8–2012/13	–	–	838

The Dunnock is highly sedentary in Britain, with most birds remaining within a kilometre of where they hatched (Migration Atlas), and the winter distribution, both nationally and locally, is therefore much the same as it is during the breeding season.

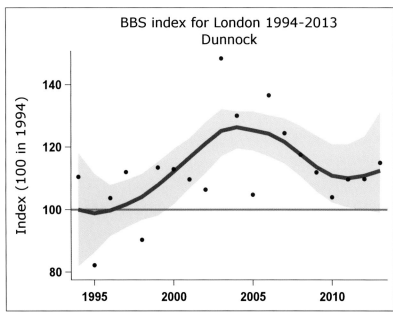

BTO/JNCC/RSPB Breeding Bird Survey (BBS)

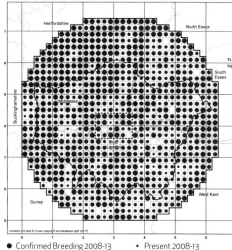

Breeding Distribution

- ● Confirmed Breeding 2008-13
- ● Probable Breeding 2008-13
- ● Possible Breeding 2008-13
- • Present 2008-13
- • Still on Migration 2008-13

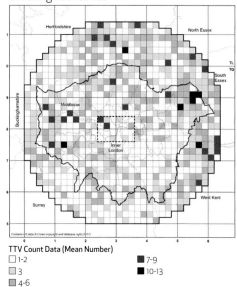

Breeding Abundance

TTV Count Data (Mean Number)
- ☐ 1-2
- ☐ 3
- ☐ 4-6
- ■ 7-9
- ■ 10-13

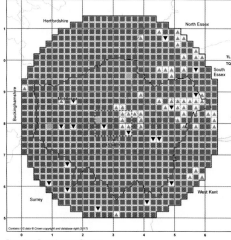

Breeding Change

Breeding Distribution Change
- ▲ Recent Gain (new in 2008-13)
- ■ Stable (present in all periods)
- ▼ Old Loss (last occupied 1968-72)
- ▲ Old Gain (new in 1988-94)
- ■ Variable (absent 1988-94)
- ▼ Recent Loss (last occupied 1988-94)

Winter Distribution

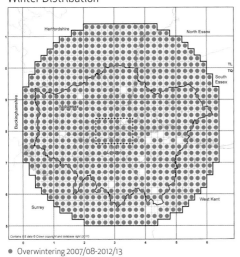

● Overwintering 2007/08-2012/13

Winter Abundance

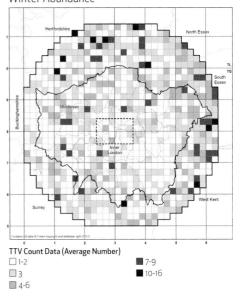

TTV Count Data (Average Number)

☐ 1-2

☐ 3

▨ 4-6

▨ 7-9

■ 10-16

328

House Sparrow
Passer domesticus

Breeding resident, with much lower abundance than previously; red list.

In the UK, the House Sparrow population declined dramatically between the 1970s and the mid-1990s, since when it has been stable overall. This masks regional variations; in some western areas, notably Wales, Northern Ireland and Scotland, the population has been increasing, while in eastern areas, the population has been decreasing. The reason for the decline remains a matter of some speculation (Summers-Smith, 2003; De Laet & Summers-Smith, 2007).

London was once famous for its abundant House Sparrows. The often quoted Kensington Gardens study (Nicholson, 1995; Sanderson, 2013) illustrates why. In 1925, the result of a count of House Sparrows was 2,603 in this locality alone. Hudson (1898), writing about London, "*was frequently amused, and sometimes teased, by the sight and sound of the everywhere-present multitudinous sparrow.*" and the LNHS (1964) reports that "*the house sparrow is at its most dense in central London….*". A decline had, however, already been noticed in the first half of the twentieth century and has continued apace in London; the population declined by 72% (59% to 80%) between 1995 and 2013 (BBS). It also declined, although less dramatically, during the same period in the south-east as a whole (BBS).

The distribution maps in the first and second atlases do not illustrate this decline; while the population certainly reduced in the intervening period, the population remained widespread enough to be recorded in nearly every tetrad, even during the period of the second atlas. The current atlas shows gaps opening up in the distribution of the House Sparrow

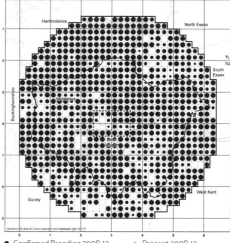

Breeding Distribution

- ● Confirmed Breeding 2008-13
- ● Probable Breeding 2008-13
- ● Possible Breeding 2008-13
- • Present 2008-13
- • Still on Migration 2008-13

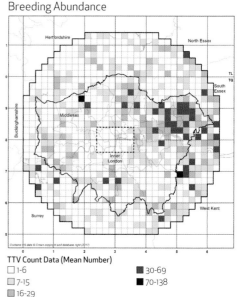

Breeding Abundance

TTV Count Data (Mean Number)
- ☐ 1-6
- ☐ 7-15
- ☐ 16-29
- ■ 30-69
- ■ 70-138

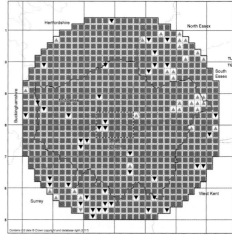

Breeding Change

Breeding Distribution Change
- ▲ Recent Gain (new in 2008-13)
- ■ Stable (present in all periods)
- ▼ Old Loss (last occupied 1968-72)
- ▲ Old Gain (new in 1988-94)
- ■ Variable (absent 1988-94)
- ▼ Recent Loss (last occupied 1988-94)

in London with what seem to be genuine absences from a handful of tetrads, including several in Inner London. In the vast majority of tetrads, fewer than 23 House Sparrows were recorded per hour of survey. Counts of more than 100 birds in a given locality are now unusual and the highest recorded in the atlas fieldwork in any one tetrad during the breeding season was 141. Despite all this, the House Sparrow was still the seventh most common species recorded in London during the breeding season timed counts.

The abundance mapping indicates that the decline and thinning is at its worst in the south and west of the London area and at its least in the north and east, between the River Lea and the Thames. This is something of the opposite of the national picture and may be explained by the observed association of the House Sparrow with less affluent areas (Shaw *et al.*, 2008).

There were no records of House Sparrow in Kensington Gardens in the years 2007 to 2012, though one was recorded in April 2006 (LBR) and one singing male was also recorded there in March 2013; this is not shown on the map as it was outside the atlas survey seasons. Elsewhere in Inner London, there are a handful of small colonies of breeding House Sparrows at, for example, London Zoo and the Tower of London but this is a far cry from the situation one hundred, or even 50, years beforehand.

Period	Number of Tetrads		
	Evidence of Breeding	Seen Only	Total
Breeding 1968–72	795	29	824
Breeding 1988–94	839	16	855
Breeding 2008–13	700	112	812
Winter 2007/8–2012/13	-	-	780

In the winter, the distribution and abundance of the House Sparrow in our area and elsewhere is much the same as during the breeding season.

Winter Distribution

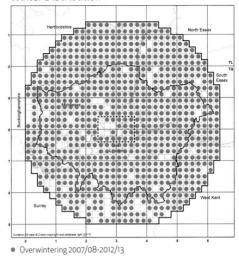

● Overwintering 2007/08-2012/13

Winter Abundance

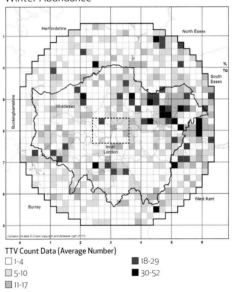

TTV Count Data (Average Number)
- ☐ 1-4
- ☐ 5-10
- ▨ 11-17
- ■ 18-29
- ■ 30-52

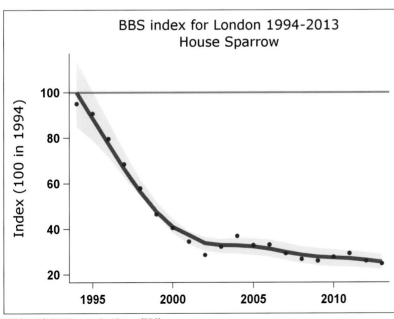

BBS index for London 1994-2013
House Sparrow

BTO/JNCC/RSPB Breeding Bird Survey (BBS)

Tree Sparrow

Passer montanus

Scarce breeding resident, confined to a few sites; red list.

Once a common species throughout most of lowland Britain, Tree Sparrow numbers declined massively between the 1970s and mid-1990s, since when the population has been stable overall, with some regional variations. The decline was accompanied by a range contraction, with this species now absent from much of the south of England (National Atlas).

The first atlas shows the Tree Sparrow to be widespread in the London area, being absent though from densely built-up areas and parts of the North Downs but present in most tetrads outside these areas. It showed quite a strong association with the river valleys and gravel pits (Sage, 1963).

The second atlas showed a huge reduction in distribution, with over 60% of the previously occupied tetrads vacated. The species still held on in Richmond Park, Beddington Sewage Farm and the Lee Valley, as well as some rural areas, especially in Essex (Hewlett *et al.*).

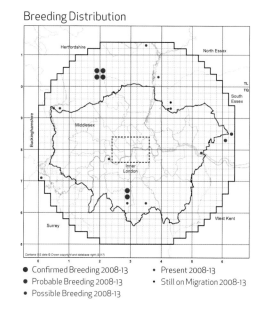

Breeding Distribution

- ● Confirmed Breeding 2008-13
- ● Probable Breeding 2008-13
- ● Possible Breeding 2008-13
- • Present 2008-13
- • Still on Migration 2008-13

The current atlas shows a further range contraction; the Tree Sparrow has vacated 97% of the tetrads which it occupied at the time of the first atlas. There are now just two localities in our area in which this species breeds; one is in Hertfordshire and the other is at Beddington. Records in May from a couple of other rural localities hint at the possibility of the odd pair still breeding elsewhere, but most (if not all) such records may relate to spring passage movement.

The remaining two breeding populations are monitored closely and supported by conservation efforts. The Hertfordshire population averaged just 15.5 pairs during 2007 to 2012 while the Beddington population compromised an average of 80 breeding pairs during the same period. The numbers at Beddington during most of the current atlas period compared favourably to that found at the same location in the mid-1950s, when there were around 65 pairs (LNHS, 1964), and the early 1960s, when there were 70 pairs (Hewlett *et al.*). However, a substantial drop in breeding numbers at Beddington occurred in 2013, to just nine pairs.

Despite the retention of the Hertfordshire and Beddington populations, the position of the Tree Sparrow as regular breeding species in our area is precarious indeed, especially as these two populations have become increasingly isolated.

Period	Number of Tetrads		
	Evidence of Breeding	Seen Only	Total
Breeding 1968–72	411	120	531
Breeding 1988–94	133	72	205
Breeding 2008–13	6	12	18
Winter 2007/8–2012/13	-	-	30

The distribution of the Tree Sparrow during the winter is much the same as during the breeding season. However, a small proportion of the Tree Sparrows that breed in Britain are thought to move south during winter (Migration Atlas) and probably account for some of the records away from the breeding sites. Others may be juveniles which disperse from the breeding sites (D. Coleman *pers. comm.*).

Breeding Change

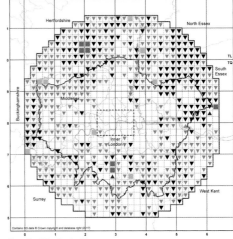

Breeding Distribution Change
▲ Recent Gain (new in 2008-13)   ▲ Old Gain (new in 1988-94)
■ Stable (present in all periods)   ▨ Variable (absent 1988-94)
▼ Old Loss (last occupied 1968-72)   ▼ Recent Loss (last occupied 1988-94)

Winter Distribution

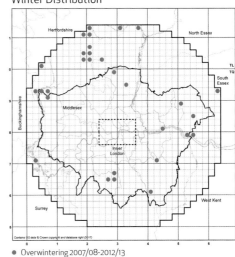

● Overwintering 2007/08-2012/13

Yellow Wagtail

Motacilla flava

Common passage migrant and now scarce and decreasing breeder; red list.

The Yellow Wagtail is a migratory species, with a breeding range which extends all the way across Eurasia (BirdLife). Britain is in the far west of its breeding range and it is largely absent from Ireland (National Atlas). The wintering range lies mostly to the south of the northern 30th parallel; including Africa, South Asia and South-East Asia (BirdLife). Birds which breed in Britain, winter south of the Sahara in western Africa (Migration Atlas).

In Britain, the Yellow Wagtail breeding population has experienced strong recent declines, with numbers falling by 40% (29% to 51%) over the period 1995 to 2013 (BBS). At the same time, its breeding range in Britain has diminished, including within the areas to the south and west of London, and it is now mainly restricted to central and eastern England (National Atlas).

During the first London atlas period, the species was mainly associated with the Thames and the Lee Valleys and the west London waterbodies. Gains were made in other areas by the time of the second atlas, particularly in the Hertfordshire and Essex sectors; some of these may relate to newly available habitats, such as gravel pits and country parks (Hewlett *et al*). The London area is now on the very southern edge of the species' main range in Britain and widespread losses have occurred in our area since the second atlas period.

In the south-western quarter of our area, there was just a single probable breeding record during the current atlas period. This relates to a pair seen in late April only, so these may well have been on migration. The species was also found to have all but disappeared from the river valleys throughout the London area. A scattering of breeding records came from the Essex and Hertfordshire sectors, predominantly associated with arable fields rather than wetland sites. Within Greater London, the only breeding records came from Fairlop Gravel works, the Ingrebourne Valley and the Enfield Chase area. Other records were of passage migrants, and some of the mapped records showing the species as present are likely to involve migrant birds which were not recorded as such. The main arrival in spring is from mid-April and returning birds pass through our area from July to October (Self).

Sadly, with the continued national decline and contraction in range, it seems likely that the Yellow Wagtail will soon be lost as a breeding species within the London area, or will continue to occur only as an occasional opportunistic breeder at temporary sites such as Fairlop Gravel Works.

Breeding Distribution

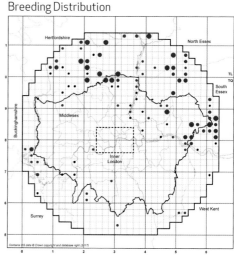

- Confirmed Breeding 2008-13
- Probable Breeding 2008-13
- Possible Breeding 2008-13
- Present 2008-13
- Still on Migration 2008-13

Period	Number of Tetrads		
	Evidence of Breeding	Seen Only	Total
Breeding 1968–72	118	39	157
Breeding 1988–94	147	84	231
Breeding 2008–13	28	48	76

Breeding Change

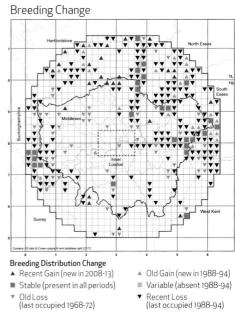

Contains OS data © Crown copyright and database right (2017)

Breeding Distribution Change
▲ Recent Gain (new in 2008-13)   ▲ Old Gain (new in 1988-94)
■ Stable (present in all periods)   ■ Variable (absent 1988-94)
▼ Old Loss   ▼ Recent Loss
   (last occupied 1968-72)   (last occupied 1988-94)

Grey Wagtail
Motacilla cinerea

Breeding resident and passage migrant; red list.

In the north and west of Britain, the Grey Wagtail often shares fast-moving wooded streams with the Dipper *Cinclus cinclus* and densities of the Grey Wagtail are highest in these areas during the breeding season. However, the species vacates some upland areas in winter (National Atlas). The UK breeding population declined by 54% (38% to 64%) over the period 1975 to 2013 (BirdTrends), although breeding numbers in the UK did increase during the late 1990s and the 2000s, before numbers were hit by two severe winters at the start of the current atlas period (National Atlas).

The Grey Wagtail can also be found across many lowland areas of Britain and birdwatchers in the London area will be aware that it is also at home on slow-flowing urban streams, including some with concrete banks. It first bred in the London area in the early twentieth century (Self), and was breeding on several rivers by the time of the first atlas, particularly in the south-west (Montier). Since then, it has continued to spread and can now be found across the London area, including Inner London where it seems to be established as a breeding bird. The majority of sightings occur in the vicinity of water, so it does not yet rank with the Pied Wagtail as a truly urban species, though some breeding records do occur some way away from rivers or other waterbodies for example a nest at Pimp Hall, Chingford in 2010.

The main gaps in the breeding distribution are in the rural areas of the Essex, Kent and Surrey sectors. A lack of suitable watercourses has probably restricted its ability to colonise more widely in these areas.

Breeding Distribution

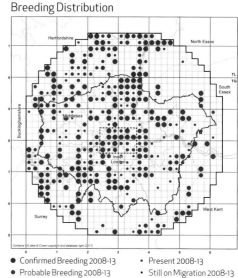

- ● Confirmed Breeding 2008-13
- ● Probable Breeding 2008-13
- ● Possible Breeding 2008-13
- • Present 2008-13
- • Still on Migration 2008-13

Period	Number of Tetrads		
	Evidence of Breeding	Seen Only	Total
Breeding 1968–72	70	37	107
Breeding 1988–94	183	109	292
Breeding 2008–13	217	133	350
Winter 2007/8–2012/13	-	-	463

In winter, populations in the south of Britain are supplemented by birds from the uplands (Migration Atlas). The species becomes more widespread in the London area during this time, with the most obvious gaps occurring in the same areas as during the breeding season.

Breeding Change

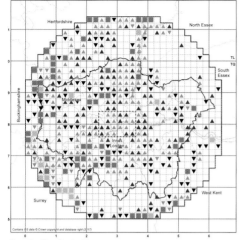

Winter Distribution

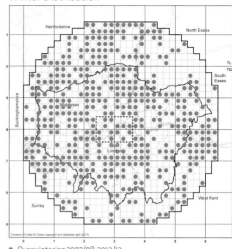

Breeding Distribution Change
- ▲ Recent Gain (new in 2008-13)
- ■ Stable (present in all periods)
- ▼ Old Loss (last occupied 1968-72)
- ▲ Old Gain (new in 1988-94)
- ▨ Variable (absent 1988-94)
- ▼ Recent Loss (last occupied 1988-94)

● Overwintering 2007/08-2012/13

Pied Wagtail

Motacilla alba

Common breeding resident and winter visitor; green list

There are 11 sub-species of *Motacilla alba* of which three have occurred in the British Isles; the common resident subspecies in Britain is *yarrellii* or Pied Wagtail, while the equivalent in continental Europe is subspecies *alba* or White Wagtail, which also occurs in Britain occasionally. The third type is *leucopsis* or Amur Wagtail, which is a rare vagrant in Britain (Addinall, 2010). Records not specified to race have been assumed to be Pied Wagtail and have been aggregated on the atlas maps with records specified as *yarrellii*.

White Wagtail records are not mapped. However, two breeding records involved this race during the current atlas period. A female White Wagtail nested at Wraysbury Reservoir in 2008 but it is unclear whether the male was a White or Pied Wagtail, and a female White Wagtail paired with a male Pied Wagtail at Canons Farm in 2010 and raised two young.

The Pied Wagtail is present as a breeding species throughout the British Isles. The population increased markedly in the early 1970s and has been fluctuating but broadly stable since then (BirdTrends).

The Pied Wagtail was common throughout the London area in first half of the twentieth century (LNHS, 1964) and it remained widespread during both the first and second atlas periods. In both periods, the Pied Wagtail could be found throughout our area but with a patchy distribution (Hewlett *et al*). Despite the recent success of the Grey Wagtail in the London area, the Pied Wagtail remains the most likely to be encountered; it can sometimes be found looking for scraps along busy high streets or for invertebrates on rooftops. The species remains widespread in the London area but it is not as numerous here as elsewhere in Britain (National Atlas).

Breeding Distribution

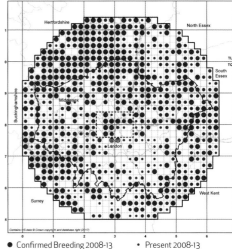

- ● Confirmed Breeding 2008-13
- ● Probable Breeding 2008-13
- ● Possible Breeding 2008-13
- · Present 2008-13
- · Still on Migration 2008-13

Breeding Abundance

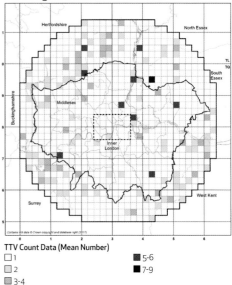

TTV Count Data (Mean Number)
- □ 1
- ☐ 2
- ▨ 3-4
- ■ 5-6
- ■ 7-9

Breeding Change

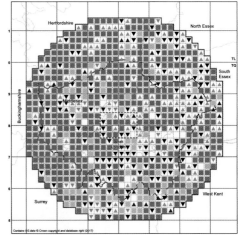

Breeding Distribution Change
- ▲ Recent Gain (new in 2008-13)
- ■ Stable (present in all periods)
- ▼ Old Loss (last occupied 1968-72)
- ▲ Old Gain (new in 1988-94)
- ▨ Variable (absent 1988-94)
- ▼ Recent Loss (last occupied 1988-94)

Period	Number of Tetrads		
	Evidence of Breeding	Seen Only	Total
Breeding 1968–72	451	196	647
Breeding 1988–94	491	216	707
Breeding 2008–13	413	275	688
Winter 2007/8–2012/13	-	-	764

During winter, the Pied Wagtail remains widespread in Britain but vacates upland areas in favour of lowland areas (National Atlas). Its distribution across the London area is similar to that in the breeding season, although more tetrads were occupied. The resident birds may be joined by others which breed further north (Dougall, 1991) and some of those which breed in our area may migrate further south (Chandler, 1979).

In winter, small flocks can sometimes be encountered in rural areas feeding in pasture and arable fields. However, the species is better known at this time of year for forming large urban roosts, perhaps benefiting from the urban 'heat-island' effect. During the current atlas period, the largest roost recorded comprised an incredible 2,000–3,000 birds, at Heathrow Airport in January 2012 (LBR). However, this does not beat the roost of 4,300 birds recorded in Orpington in 1977 (Chandler, 1979); the largest known aggregation of this species in the London area to date (Self). Other roosts recorded during the current atlas period included over 300 at both Welwyn Garden City and Harold Hill.

Winter Distribution

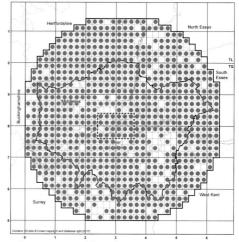

● Overwintering 2007/08-2012/13

Winter Abundance

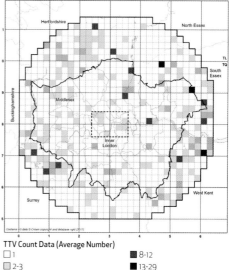

TTV Count Data (Average Number)
☐ 1　　　　　 ■ 8-12
☐ 2-3　　　　 ■ 13-29
■ 4-7

Tree Pipit

Anthus trivialis

Passage migrant and now scarce and decreasing breeder; red list.

The Tree Pipit is a summer visitor to woodland and scrubby areas throughout Britain, but is most numerous in the uplands in the north and west (National Atlas). A sharp population decline occurred between the mid-1980s and the mid-1990s, since when the population has been broadly stable (BirdTrends). The decline was accompanied by a range contraction, with losses of breeding birds in 10km squares occurring principally in central, south-east and northern England and the Scottish central belt (National Atlas).

The decline in south-east England is reflected in the distribution maps for the London area. The Tree Pipit is now restricted to a handful of sites, with confirmed or probable breeding occurring at just three sites. These were Thorndon Country Park (in two tetrads), Epping Forest (two tetrads) and Hatfield Aerodrome, with the probable breeding status at the latter site based on a bird recorded on territory in June, which was only seen on two dates, eight days apart. The majority of the birds recorded elsewhere during the current atlas period are likely to be passage migrants.

The species was found in as many as 192 tetrads (22% of those in the London area) at the time of the first London atlas, when it was widespread in the outer parts of the area. The number of occupied tetrads had already more than halved by the time of the second atlas, when the majority of records were from the Hertfordshire sector. At this time, there were also a few occupied tetrads in the Essex sector and it still persisted within Greater London at Richmond Park and Wimbledon Common.

With the continued severe reduction in occupied tetrads shown by the current atlas project, the outlook for Tree Pipit in the London area looks bleak. Indeed, in 2012 there were no records of territorial birds in the London area for the first time ever and the same was true in 2013 (LBR).

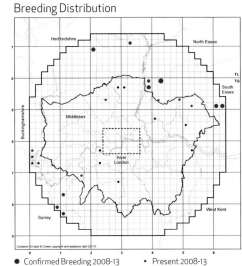

Breeding Distribution

● Confirmed Breeding 2008-13   · Present 2008-13
● Probable Breeding 2008-13   · Still on Migration 2008-13
● Possible Breeding 2008-13

Period	Number of Tetrads		
	Evidence of Breeding	Seen Only	Total
Breeding 1968–72	163	29	192
Breeding 1988–94	54	28	82
Breeding 2008–13	5	14	19

Breeding Change

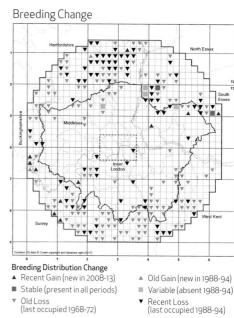

Breeding Distribution Change
- ▲ Recent Gain (new in 2008-13)
- ■ Stable (present in all periods)
- ▼ Old Loss (last occupied 1968-72)
- ▲ Old Gain (new in 1988-94)
- ■ Variable (absent 1988-94)
- ▼ Recent Loss (last occupied 1988-94)

Meadow Pipit

Anthus pratensis

Common passage migrant, winter visitor and localised breeder; amber list.

The Meadow Pipit breeds throughout the British Isles, though it is much more common in upland habitats in the north and west of the country and has a patchy distribution in the south and east (National Atlas). Like its compatriot the Skylark, the Meadow Pipit population in the UK has declined substantially and is now about half what it was in the 1970s (BirdTrends). The decline appears to be continuing, albeit much less steeply than before (BBS).

In the London area, the Meadow Pipit has a restricted distribution during the breeding season. It is absent from most urban areas as well as many rural areas. In the two earlier London atlases, the main breeding areas were concentrated along the Thames corridor and around the west London waterbodies, with breeding occurring at scattered locations elsewhere. The current atlas indicates that the number of occupied tetrads has reduced, including within its former strongholds.

Like the Skylark, the Meadow Pipit continues to breed at suitable open grassland sites within the urban area. For the Meadow Pipit, these sites include Wormwood Scrubs, Wanstead Flats, Lake Farm Country Park and Minet Country Park, but it has been lost from some urban sites, including Brent Reservoir and Wimbledon Common. In the surrounding countryside, the Hertfordshire sector stands out as the only sector where the breeding distribution has been maintained or slightly increased.

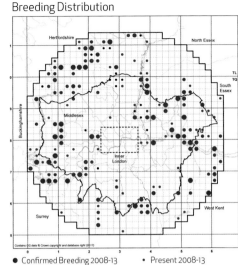

Breeding Distribution

- ● Confirmed Breeding 2008-13
- ● Probable Breeding 2008-13
- ● Possible Breeding 2008-13
- • Present 2008-13
- • Still on Migration 2008-13

Period	Number of Tetrads		
	Evidence of Breeding	Seen Only	Total
Breeding 1968–72	121	73	194
Breeding 1988–94	123	111	234
Breeding 2008–13	68	95	163
Winter 2007/8–2012/13	-	-	432

The Meadow Pipit is much more widespread as a passage migrant and winter visitor, and can be found, usually in small numbers, at farmland sites around the London area, often in the same fields as Skylark and finches. Like the Skylark, the species also makes use of open habitats within the urban area, particularly during periods of harsh weather. However, numbers are generally small and Greater London clearly has a much lower abundance of this species than surrounding areas (National Atlas). In the Lee Valley, small groups can often be found along the grassy banks of some of the larger reservoirs, which do not normally attract Skylark, apart from short-staying birds during harsh weather. Occasional records of Meadow Pipit even occur within Inner London in winter; for example, birds flushed from areas of long grass, which have been deliberately left to grow, in Hyde Park/Kensington Gardens.

Breeding Change

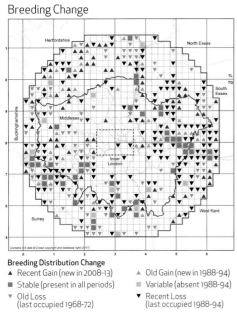

TL
TQ

Winter Distribution

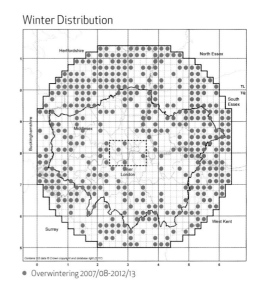

Breeding Distribution Change
- ▲ Recent Gain (new in 2008-13)
- ▲ Old Gain (new in 1988-94)
- ■ Stable (present in all periods)
- ■ Variable (absent 1988-94)
- ▼ Old Loss (last occupied 1968-72)
- ▼ Recent Loss (last occupied 1988-94)

● Overwintering 2007/08-2012/13

Rock Pipit

Anthus petrosus

Passage migrant and winter visitor; green list.

As a breeding bird in Britain, the Rock Pipit is restricted to rocky coasts, including parts of Kent, but is otherwise largely absent from the coastline from Selsey eastwards to Flamborough Head, including the London area (National Atlas).

However, the species winters all around the coastline, with the majority of those in the south-east of England most likely to be continental migrants (National Atlas). This is true of the birds in the London area, with most, if not all, believed to be of the Scandinavian race *littoralis* (Self). Although the Rock Pipit is uncommon in the London area as a whole, it is a regular winter visitor along the Thames east of Barking Creekmouth, where it is usually present from October to March.

The vast majority of records come from Rainham Marshes, where this species is almost certain to be found in winter along the Thames when the tide is not at its highest. Counts of wintering Rock Pipit at Rainham usually reach between 15 and 20 birds, but 32 were recorded on 9th January 2013, the highest count in London since 1971 (LBR). However, the preponderance of records from Rainham probably reflects coverage and ease of access to this site. Regular records also come from other sites including Crayford Marshes, Swanscombe Marshes and West Thurrock and the current atlas distribution map shows that the species can be found along most of the Lower Thames, where they have been wintering since at least the 1950s (Self).

The Rock Pipit is rarely recorded along the Thames further west than Barking, possibly because much of the river is walled in and suitable stony habitat is sparse and often only uncovered at low tide. One observed flying west at Tower Bridge in December 2008 was therefore unusual.

Away from the Thames, birds occasionally turn up at other sites in the London area, particularly at the London Wetland Centre and on the banks of some of the major reservoirs. However, sightings at these sites away from the Thames are more common during spring passage, in March and April, and autumn passage, in October. Around three-quarters of the atlas records away from the Thames occurred during November, and therefore probably related to late migrants rather than overwintering birds.

Breeding season tetrads: 5

Winter season tetrads: 36

Winter Distribution

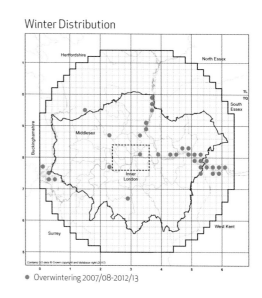

● Overwintering 2007/08-2012/13

Water Pipit

Anthus spinoletta

Regular but localised winter visitor and passage migrant; amber list.

The Water Pipit is a scarce winter visitor to Britain from alpine areas of southern Europe. When in Britain, it is mostly found in the south on the coast but is more likely than the Rock Pipit to be found inland (National Atlas).

Like the Rock Pipit, the Water Pipit is an uncommon winter visitor to the London area. It can also be found wintering at Rainham Marshes and elsewhere along the lower Thames, where it can be picked out by a patient observer amongst its more numerous relative. However, whilst wintering Rock Pipits in the London area are mostly restricted to this part of the Thames, wintering Water Pipits have slightly different habitat requirements and are not constrained by the lack of suitable 'coastal' habitat elsewhere in London. Several other regular wintering sites were used by the Water Pipit during the atlas period, including King George VI Reservoir, Staines Moor, Beddington Sewage Farm and the London Wetland Centre. Rye Meads was also a regular wintering site in the past, being used by one to two birds up until 2009/10 but not subsequently.

Wintering numbers are usually low at all the regular wintering sites, though numbers tend to peak in late winter and early spring, and double figure counts occurred during the winter atlas period at only two sites: Staines Moor (12 in January 2008) and at King George VI Reservoir (ten in February 2008). A count of 12 was also made at Rainham Marshes in March 2009. Elsewhere, the species is mostly recorded as a scarce passage migrant.

Breeding season tetrads: 14

Winter season tetrads: 32

Winter Distribution

● Overwintering 2007/08-2012/13

Brambling
Fringilla montifringilla

Regular autumn migrant and winter visitor; green list.

The Brambling breeds in northern Eurasia and is primarily a winter visitor to the British Isles, when it can be found in almost every 10km square in lowland Britain. The birds that winter here are mainly those that breed in Scandinavia. Numbers occurring in Britain each winter can be variable and are thought to depend on the availability of beechmast and on weather conditions in southern Scandinavia and continental Europe (Migration Atlas).

In the London area, this species has been recorded in every winter in recent years and this situation seems set to continue. The first arrivals usually occur in early October and the last birds are usually seen in early April (Self). It can turn up almost anywhere in the London area, most usually found in flocks of fewer than ten (LBR). However, it can sometimes occur in quite large flocks, which occur principally in the rural parts of our area. For example, there are records of over 1,000 birds in a single flock, such as the one of 1,200 at Canons Farm, Surrey in January 2008.

Breeding season tetrads: 30

Winter season tetrads: 207

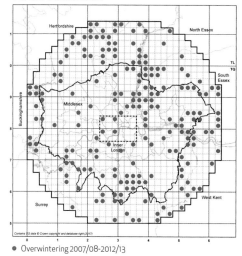

Winter Distribution

● Overwintering 2007/08-2012/13

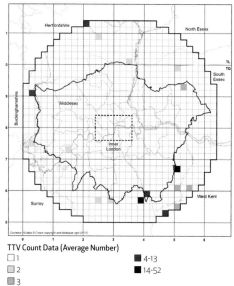

Winter Abundance

TTV Count Data (Average Number)
☐ 1
☐ 2
◻ 3
◼ 4-13
◼ 14-52

Chaffinch

Fringilla coelebs

Common breeding resident and winter visitor; green list.

The Chaffinch is present as a breeding species in nearly every 10km square in the British Isles. Following a period of increase, the population is currently declining (BBS). However, this decline has not been severe enough for the Chaffinch to be added to the list of birds of conservation concern, and the population remains at a higher level than it was in the 1970s and 1980s (BirdTrends).

The Chaffinch is principally associated with woodland and hedgerows and shows a preference for rural areas. Indeed, London is a distinct low spot in Chaffinch abundance (National Atlas). The abundance mapping for the London Atlas also clearly shows that, while this species is present throughout our region, numbers are much lower in Greater London than in the surrounding areas.

The first two atlases indicated that a similar number of tetrads were occupied by this species both times. However, in the second atlas, the gains were thought to be mainly a result of improved coverage and the losses most likely to be genuine. This, coupled with evidence from some sites where the population was monitored, indicates that there was a decline in Chaffinch numbers, and a slight contraction in distribution, between these two atlas periods (Hewlett *et al.*).

From roughly the end of the second atlas period, the Chaffinch population in London underwent a period of growth, peaking at approximately two

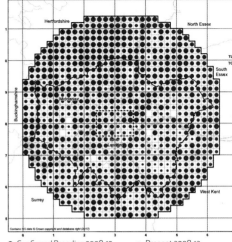

Breeding Distribution

- ● Confirmed Breeding 2008-13
- ● Probable Breeding 2008-13
- ● Possible Breeding 2008-13
- · Present 2008-13
- · Still on Migration 2008-13

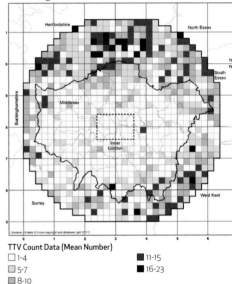

Breeding Abundance

TTV Count Data (Mean Number)
- ☐ 1-4
- ☐ 5-7
- ☐ 8-10
- ■ 11-15
- ■ 16-23

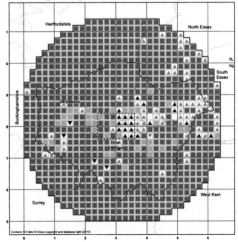

Breeding Change

Breeding Distribution Change
- ▲ Recent Gain (new in 2008-13)
- ■ Stable (present in all periods)
- ▼ Old Loss (last occupied 1968-72)
- ▲ Old Gain (new in 1988-94)
- ■ Variable (absent 1988-94)
- ▼ Recent Loss (last occupied 1988-94)

and a half times larger in 2007 (BBS). The evidence of this is seen in the 2008–13 distribution map with all but seven tetrads occupied by this species in the breeding season. However, perhaps mostly as a result of *Trichomonosis* disease, Chaffinch numbers have now fallen from their peak in 2007 (Robinson *et al.*, 2010). In London, numbers in 2013 were around 20% below what they were in 2007 (BBS) while, in south-east England, the population fell to below the 1995 level. Therefore, it may be that the near 100% occupation of tetrads by the Chaffinch shown on the distribution map is not quite representative of the situation at the end of this atlas period.

Period	Number of Tetrads		
	Evidence of Breeding	Seen Only	Total
Breeding 1968–72	707	63	770
Breeding 1988–94	705	86	791
Breeding 2008–13	676	173	849
Winter 2007/8–2012/13	-	-	846

The distribution of the Chaffinch in winter, both nationally and locally, is much the same as during the breeding season. Although birds which breed in Britain are sedentary, they are joined in winter by birds which bred in continental Europe, mostly from Scandinavia (Migration Atlas). Reports of flocks of more than 100 birds are frequent from the more rural parts of our area, although fewer than 13 birds per hour were recorded in the vast majority of tetrads during the timed counts.

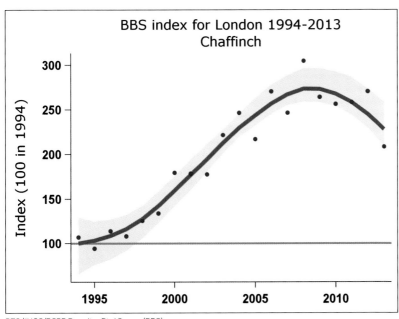

BTO/JNCC/RSPB Breeding Bird Survey (BBS)

Winter Distribution

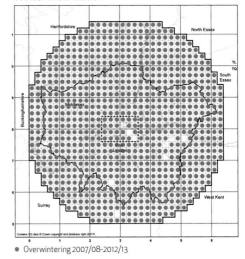

● Overwintering 2007/08-2012/13

Winter Abundance

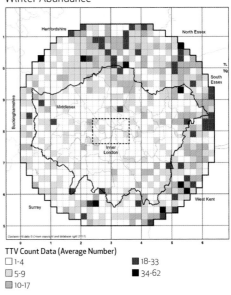

TTV Count Data (Average Number)
☐ 1-4   ■ 18-33
☐ 5-9   ■ 34-62
▨ 10-17

Greenfinch

Chloris chloris

Common breeding resident and passage migrant; green list

The Greenfinch is present as a breeding species in nearly every 10km square in the British Isles; the main exceptions being those in the Scottish Highlands (National Atlas). Like the Chaffinch, the Greenfinch population is currently undergoing a period of population decline following an increase between 1995 and 2005. It is not currently on the list of birds of conservation concern, even though, in 2013, UK population was about 32% below what it was in 1995 and 70% below its 2005 peak (BBS).

At least from the latter part of the twentieth century onwards, the Greenfinch has been less associated with rural areas than the Chaffinch and there is no low spot in Greenfinch abundance in the London area; it is more or less as abundant here as anywhere else in lowland England (National Atlas). The abundance mapping for the London atlas also indicates that this species does not have a particular preference for rural areas.

The Greenfinch population appears to have increased and spread throughout the London area in the first half of the twentieth century. By the time of the first atlas, over 90% of tetrads showed some level of occupation by this species and that situation prevailed in both the second and current atlas periods. There was some evidence of a decline in Inner London at least, between the first and second atlas periods but it remained the commonest finch in central London at that time (Hewlett *et al.*). The population then underwent an increase, more than doubling

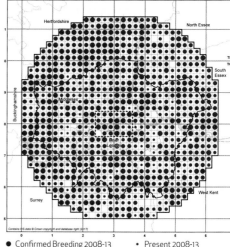

Breeding Distribution

- ● Confirmed Breeding 2008-13
- ● Probable Breeding 2008-13
- ● Possible Breeding 2008-13
- · Present 2008-13
- · Still on Migration 2008-13

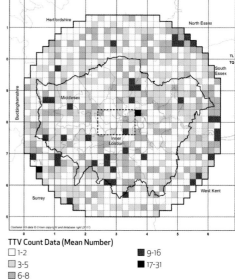

Breeding Abundance

TTV Count Data (Mean Number)
- ☐ 1-2
- 3-5
- 6-8
- 9-16
- 17-31

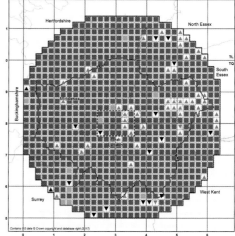

Breeding Change

Breeding Distribution Change
- ▲ Recent Gain (new in 2008-13)
- ■ Stable (present in all periods)
- ▼ Old Loss (last occupied 1968-72)
- ▲ Old Gain (new in 1988-94)
- ■ Variable (absent 1988-94)
- ▼ Recent Loss (last occupied 1988-94)

in the London area between 1995 and 2007, when Greenfinch numbers in London, and elsewhere, reached their peak (BBS). The subsequent fall is attributed to *Trichomonosis* disease (Robinson *et al.*, 2010). In London, Greenfinch numbers have fallen back to their 1995 level and the trajectory is steeply downwards. Despite this, the Greenfinch was still the second most common finch in the breeding season in the London area during the current atlas period, the most common being the Chaffinch (based on atlas timed counts).

Period	Number of Tetrads		
	Evidence of Breeding	Seen Only	Total
Breeding 1968–72	734	69	803
Breeding 1988–94	774	68	842
Breeding 2008–13	619	220	839
Winter 2007/8–2012/13	-	-	827

Small numbers of Greenfinch move away from Britain in winter and are replaced by continental birds, mainly from Norway, but most birds which breed in Britain are sedentary (Migration Atlas). The distribution of the Greenfinch in winter, both nationally and locally, is much the same as during the breeding season. During the winter in the London area, flocks of more than 20 are not unusual but flocks of more than 70 appear to have become a rarity (LBR) over the course the atlas period. The abundance mapping undertaken for the atlas in winter shows a similar pattern, fewer than seven birds encountered per hour of survey in the majority of tetrads and only a handful with more than 19 birds encountered per hour of survey.

Winter Distribution

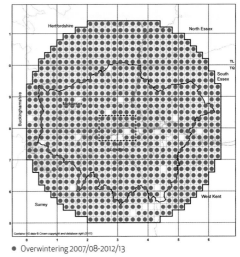

● Overwintering 2007/08-2012/13

Winter Abundance

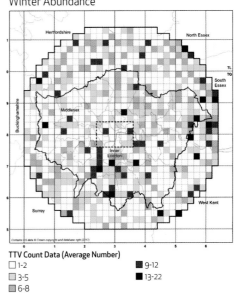

TTV Count Data (Average Number)
☐ 1-2   ■ 9-12
☐ 3-5   ■ 13-22
▨ 6-8

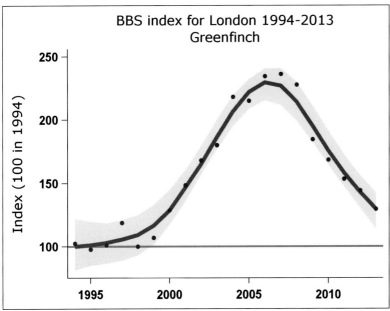

BTO/JNCC/RSPB Breeding Bird Survey (BBS)

Goldfinch

Carduelis carduelis

Common breeding resident and passage migrant; green list.

The Goldfinch is present as a breeding species in nearly every 10km square in the British Isles; the main exceptions being those in the Scottish Highlands (National Atlas). The Goldfinch population in the UK more than doubled between 1995 and 2013 (BBS), however it occurs at a relatively low density in south-east England (National Atlas). There is no evidence that it particularly favours rural areas.

Following a period of population decline, the Goldfinch was considered to be a rare breeding bird in the London area at the beginning of the twentieth century. The population is reported to have then increased again, recovering to the same levels as 100 years previously by the 1950s, at which time it prevailed in suburban London but was also present at sites in Inner London, where bomb sites provided good habitat (Hewlett *et al.*). The first and second atlases show this species to be widespread with more or less 90% of tetrads occupied on both occasions. Between 2003 and 2013, the Goldfinch population in London increased dramatically (BBS), which is in line with the national trend. While it was recorded in nearly every tetrad in the current atlas period, the numbers encountered were not especially high with typically fewer than eleven birds counted per hour of survey.

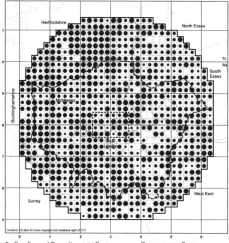

Breeding Distribution

- ● Confirmed Breeding 2008-13
- ● Probable Breeding 2008-13
- ● Possible Breeding 2008-13
- • Present 2008-13
- • Still on Migration 2008-13

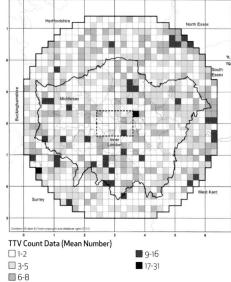

Breeding Abundance

TTV Count Data (Mean Number)
- □ 1-2
- □ 3-5
- ▨ 6-8
- ■ 9-16
- ■ 17-31

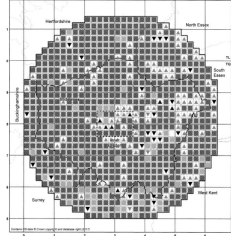

Breeding Change

Breeding Distribution Change
- ▲ Recent Gain (new in 2008-13)
- ■ Stable (present in all periods)
- ▼ Old Loss (last occupied 1968-72)
- ▲ Old Gain (new in 1988-94)
- ▨ Variable (absent 1988-94)
- ▼ Recent Loss (last occupied 1988-94)

Period	Number of Tetrads		
	Evidence of Breeding	Seen Only	Total
Breeding 1968–72	601	133	734
Breeding 1988–94	612	179	791
Breeding 2008–13	574	252	826
Winter 2007/8–2012/13	-	-	826

The distribution of the Goldfinch, both nationally and locally, in the winter is much the same as during the breeding season. The general picture is of slightly higher numbers throughout the London area during the winter period, but there are also records of flocks of more than 100 at a few sites in most winters (LBR). This is despite the Goldfinch being a partial migrant, with a proportion of the British population migrating to France and Spain for the winter (Migration Atlas).

Winter Distribution

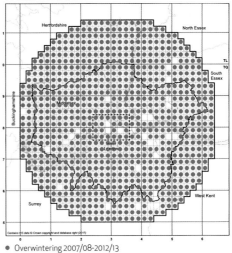

● Overwintering 2007/08-2012/13

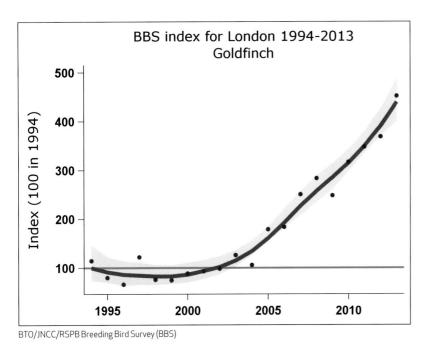

BTO/JNCC/RSPB Breeding Bird Survey (BBS)

Winter Abundance

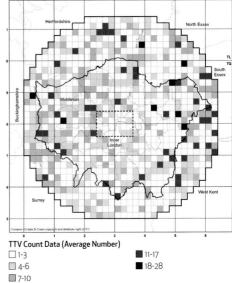

TTV Count Data (Average Number)
☐ 1-3   ■ 11-17
☐ 4-6   ■ 18-28
▨ 7-10

Siskin

Carduelis spinus

Common winter visitor passage migrant and rare breeder; green list.

The three National Atlases reveal a steady consolidation of the breeding range of the Siskin across Britain, although it is still scarce as a breeding species across much of lowland England. Its habitat is primarily coniferous woodland and no doubt the planting of these in the latter part of the twentieth century has helped facilitate this expansion.

The Siskin was recorded as breeding in just one tetrad, in Epping Forest, in the first London Atlas and only recorded as breeding in four in the second atlas. The current atlas shows little change with five tetrads having breeding evidence. However, confirmation of breeding came from just one tetrad and strong evidence come from just one other, in Barnet in 2013 (LBR). The large increase in records showing 'possible breeding' or 'presence' almost certainly relates to late leaving or early returning wintering birds.

Period	Number of Tetrads		
	Evidence of Breeding	Seen Only	Total
Breeding 1968–72	1	5	6
Breeding 1988–94	4	18	22
Breeding 2008–13	5	79	84
Winter 2007/8–2012/13	-	-	487

The Siskin undertakes a partial migration in the British Isles, with some birds also migrating southwards into France and beyond, while other birds migrate to Britain from the north (Migration Atlas). The net effect is that the Siskin occurs at higher abundance and more widely in southern Britain during the winter than during the breeding season. In the London area too, the Siskin is recorded much more widely in winter, typically feeding on the seeds of birches and alder. There are usually several records of more than 100 birds at a handful of sites each year. The largest one hour count recorded during atlas timed counts was 120 in TQ55D (Sevenoaks Wildlife Reserve) and the largest flock during the atlas period was of as many as 600 birds, at Cornmill Meadows in 2010 (LBR).

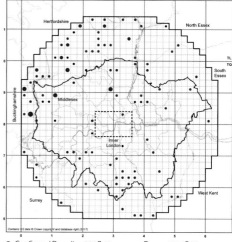

Breeding Distribution

● Confirmed Breeding 2008-13   • Present 2008-13
● Probable Breeding 2008-13   • Still on Migration 2008-13
● Possible Breeding 2008-13

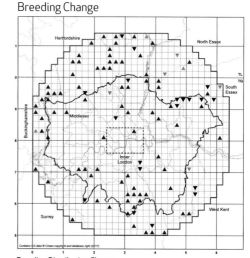

Breeding Change

Breeding Distribution Change
▲ Recent Gain (new in 2008-13)   ▲ Old Gain (new in 1988-94)
■ Stable (present in all periods)   ■ Variable (absent 1988-94)
▼ Old Loss (last occupied 1968-72)   ▼ Recent Loss (last occupied 1988-94)

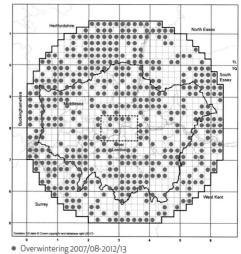

Winter Distribution

● Overwintering 2007/08-2012/13

Winter Abundance

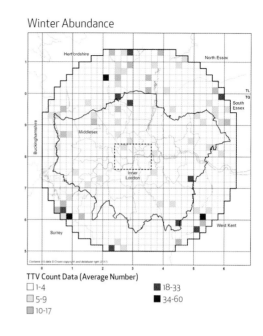

TTV Count Data (Average Number)

- 1-4
- 5-9
- 10-17
- 18-33
- 34-60

Linnet

Carduelis cannabina

Common but declining breeding resident and passage migrant; red list.

The abundance of the Linnet in the UK fell rapidly from the late 1960s to middle of the 1980s, during which period about three quarters of the population was lost. This has been followed by relative stability, with rising populations in the west, particularly in Ireland, being offset by continuing declines in the east of Britain, where this species is still at its most abundant in the British Isles. In south-east England, the Linnet population fell by around 45% (36% to 54%) between 1995 and 2013.

The Linnet is a bird of open countryside and is not well suited to the urban environment. Indeed, there is a distinct low spot of the abundance of Linnet in the London area relative to the surrounding area (National Atlas). The three London Atlases indicate a deteriorating situation for the Linnet. The first two atlases show a relatively consistent picture, with approximately the same number of tetrads occupied both times. However, Hewlett noted that the Linnet had disappeared from some of its former suburban haunts. This process appears to have continued, with the Linnet vacating 28% of formerly occupied tetrads, including many within Greater London. The current distribution shows something of an association with river valleys within Greater London and with rural areas elsewhere.

Period	Number of Tetrads		
	Evidence of Breeding	Seen Only	Total
Breeding 1968–72	532	150	682
Breeding 1988–94	537	181	718
Breeding 2008–13	310	167	477
Winter 2007/8–2012/13	-	-	298

Apart from a retreat from upland areas, the distribution of the Linnet in Britain is largely unchanged in the winter when compared with the breeding season. However, it is a partial migrant; some birds which breed in Britain and Ireland migrate south, with some crossing the channel into France and some of these continuing on to the Iberian Peninsula for the winter (Migration Atlas). One effect of this is that the Linnet is more frequently recorded in larger flocks during the winter in our area, although it was found in fewer tetrads. It is most commonly found in flocks of fewer than ten birds. However, larger flocks of up to 100 birds are recorded fairly frequently, and there are occasional flocks of over 300 birds recorded in most years. Rarely, more than double that number can be found together for example 625 were at Canons Farm on 10th November 2013.

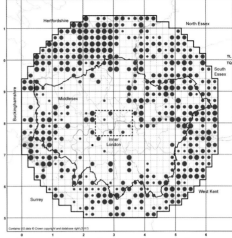

Breeding Distribution

- ● Confirmed Breeding 2008-13
- ● Probable Breeding 2008-13
- ● Possible Breeding 2008-13
- • Present 2008-13
- • Still on Migration 2008-13

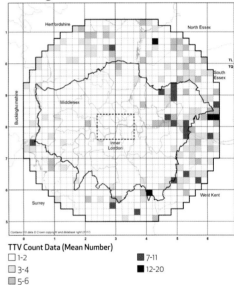

Breeding Abundance

TTV Count Data (Mean Number)
- □ 1-2
- □ 3-4
- □ 5-6
- ▨ 7-11
- ■ 12-20

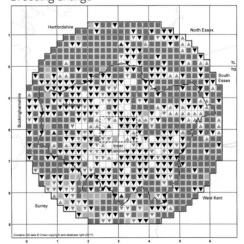

Breeding Change

Breeding Distribution Change
- ▲ Recent Gain (new in 2008-13)
- ■ Stable (present in all periods)
- ▼ Old Loss (last occupied 1968-72)
- ▲ Old Gain (new in 1988-94)
- ▨ Variable (absent 1988-94)
- ▼ Recent Loss (last occupied 1988-94)

355

Winter Distribution

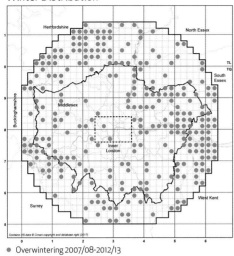

● Overwintering 2007/08-2012/13

Winter Abundance

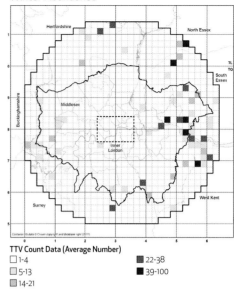

TTV Count Data (Average Number)
□ 1-4   ■ 22-38
□ 5-13   ■ 39-100
▨ 14-21

Lesser Redpoll

Carduelis cabaret

Former breeding resident, winter visitor and passage migrant; red list.

Except for the south-west of England, the Lesser Redpoll was abundant and widespread in the British Isles in the 1970s. Subsequently, the population underwent a substantial decline and has been lost from many parts of lowland England, with the population now concentrated in western and northern Britain, as well as Ireland (BirdTrends; National Atlas).

The first two atlases show a similar frequency of occurrence in the London area; this species was recorded from roughly a third of the tetrads on both occasions. Between the two atlases, there does however seem to have been a shift in distribution from the south and west to the north and the east. This was accompanied by a decline in numbers overall (Hewlett *et al.*) as would be expected given the general decline across the country occurring at that time.

While there are still occasional records of this species in our area during the breeding season, and some evidence of breeding behaviour was noted by the surveyors, this species probably does not breed in the London area currently. The two locations where breeding evidence was recorded were Copped Hall, where a pair were displaying in May 2010, and Broxbourne Woods, where another pair was recorded in April 2009.

Period	Number of Tetrads		
	Evidence of Breeding	Seen Only	Total
Breeding 1968–72	170	78	248
Breeding 1988–94	148	183	331
Breeding 2008–13	2	68	70
Winter 2007/8–2012/13	-	-	326

This species is much more widespread in Britain during winter and is found across much of the lowlands, but prefers more wooded areas is therefore largely absent from more open countryside (National Atlas).

Reflecting this, it was recorded more widely in our area during winter. It is most commonly found in flocks of fewer than ten birds but larger flocks of up to 50 birds are recorded fairly frequently, with occasional flocks of over 100 birds recorded in most years (LBR).

Breeding Distribution

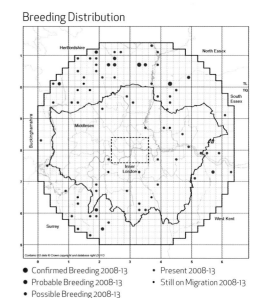

- ● Confirmed Breeding 2008-13
- ● Probable Breeding 2008-13
- ● Possible Breeding 2008-13
- • Present 2008-13
- • Still on Migration 2008-13

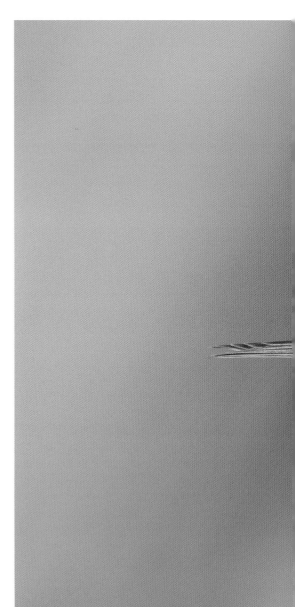

Breeding Change

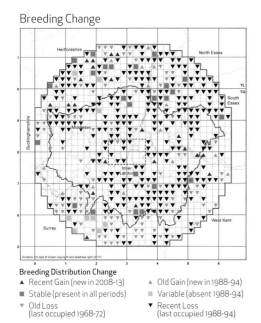

Winter Distribution

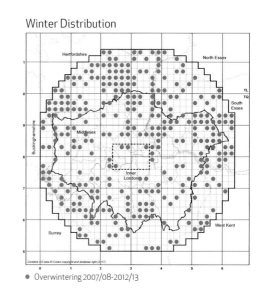

Breeding Distribution Change
- ▲ Recent Gain (new in 2008-13)
- ■ Stable (present in all periods)
- ▼ Old Loss (last occupied 1968-72)
- ▲ Old Gain (new in 1988-94)
- ■ Variable (absent 1988-94)
- ▼ Recent Loss (last occupied 1988-94)

● Overwintering 2007/08-2012/13

Common Crossbill

Loxia curvirostra

Irruptive visitor and rare breeder; green list.

The Common Crossbill has a range which extends across North America and central Eurasia, including Scandinavia and northern Europe (BirdLife) where it feeds mainly on Norway Spruce. In poor years for Norway Spruce seed production, and when Crossbill numbers are high, large numbers of birds undertake mass movements, known as irruptions, typically towards the south-west or west. These irruptions can bring this species into Britain. Newton (2006) reports that there were at least 40 occasions when these have reached Britain in the 120-year period 1881–2000. The birds do not return to their region of origin that year and instead may stay to breed in the region reached during the irruption. The surviving birds and their offspring may then return to their region of origin in a subsequent year (Newton, 2006). This pattern has resulted in fluctuations in the Crossbill population in Britain; it is currently at a high level (BBS), particularly in Scotland and Wales but also other areas with high levels of conifer such as the New Forest and Thetford Forest (National Atlas).

The Common Crossbill was present in the London area during both the first and second atlases but a very small number of tetrads were occupied. In fact, in the first atlas period, these were in just one year (1968) following an irruption the previous year (Montier) and during the second atlas period, these were in just two years (1991 and 1994). The number of breeding pairs in each of these years was probably fewer than ten.

This time it was recorded in a few months in 2007 and then in most months from May 2008 until the end of the atlas period (LBR). Breeding evidence was reported from the same number of tetrads as the second atlas, and the current atlas maps indicate that this species is still a rare breeder in our area, with breeding confirmed in just one tetrad where recently fledged young were seen, and considered probable in six other tetrads. The 14 tetrads with possible breeding status or higher were principally in the Surrey and Hertfordshire sectors. The highest density recorded in any of the timed counts was eight birds per hour of survey during the breeding season.

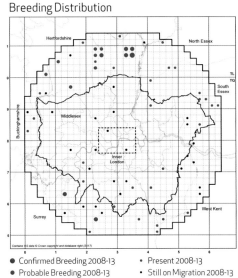

Breeding Distribution

● Confirmed Breeding 2008-13 ・ Present 2008-13
● Probable Breeding 2008-13 ・ Still on Migration 2008-13
● Possible Breeding 2008-13

Period	Number of Tetrads		
	Evidence of Breeding	Seen Only	Total
Breeding 1968–72	2	0	2
Breeding 1988–94	7	18	25
Breeding 2008–13	7	37	44
Winter 2007/8–2012/13	-	-	37

Given the strong association of this species with coniferous woodland, the distribution of the Common Crossbill in the British Isles is much the same in both the breeding season and the winter. In the London area, this also holds true, although small numbers may turn up or fly over almost anywhere in either season. This includes occasional visits to parks in Inner London. Crossbills have a flight call which is distinctive once learnt, and so are often recording flying over. Birds which are known to have flown over without stopping are excluded from the maps, but such records may still account for some of the dots on both maps.

359

Breeding Change

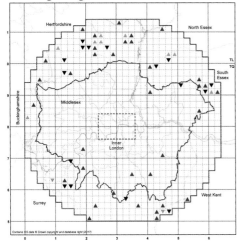

Breeding Distribution Change
- ▲ Recent Gain (new in 2008-13)
- ▲ Old Gain (new in 1988-94)
- ■ Stable (present in all periods)
- ■ Variable (absent 1988-94)
- ▼ Old Loss (last occupied 1968-72)
- ▼ Recent Loss (last occupied 1988-94)

Winter Distribution

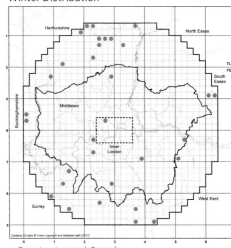

● Overwintering 2007/08-2012/13

Bullfinch

Pyrrhula pyrrhula

Fairly common but probably declining breeding resident; amber list.

The Bullfinch is another small passerine which underwent a large population decline that began in the 1970s (BirdTrends). For the Bullfinch, the decline continued until the year 2000, since when there has been some increase in the UK as a whole, but continued decline in south-east England (BBS). Despite the decline, the overall range of the Bullfinch has not changed; it is still present in most 10km squares in the British Isles, except those dominated by high ground, or the relatively treeless landscape of the parts of the fens.

There is a distinct low spot in Bullfinch abundance in the London area (National Atlas). The first and second London Atlases show a broadly similar picture, with the Bullfinch occurring in roughly 60% of tetrads on both occasions, with those in more densely developed areas less likely to support Bullfinch than more rural localities. Despite the widespread distribution, this species was not common in Inner London and Hewlett reported evidence of a decline at some well-monitored sites. There were, however, still breeding pairs in Regent's Park, for example.

The current atlas map shows a general retreat from the centre of London towards the rural fringe, as well as from the Thames Marshes and parts of Surrey. The Bullfinch distribution in the Essex sector also appears to have thinned out and become patchier over the last 20 years. The observed pattern is commensurate with the decline still occurring in south-east England.

Even where the Bullfinch occurs, numbers are low; in most tetrads where this species was encountered, fewer than three birds were recorded per hour during timed counts and in only one tetrad did counts exceed eight birds. The Bullfinch appears to be faring worse in the London area than elsewhere; the population here suffered a bigger decline since the 1988–91 Atlas than anywhere else in Britain (National Atlas).

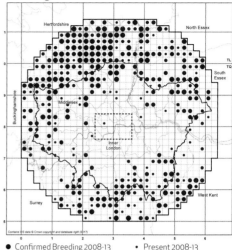

Breeding Distribution

● Confirmed Breeding 2008-13 • Present 2008-13
● Probable Breeding 2008-13 • Still on Migration 2008-13
● Possible Breeding 2008-13

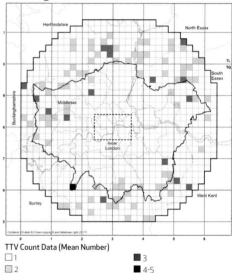

Breeding Abundance

TTV Count Data (Mean Number)
□ 1 ▨ 3
□ 2 ■ 4-5

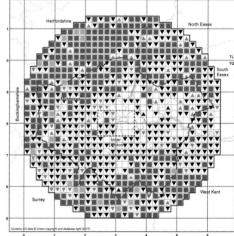

Breeding Change

Breeding Distribution Change
▲ Recent Gain (new in 2008-13) ▲ Old Gain (new in 1988-94)
■ Stable (present in all periods) ■ Variable (absent 1988-94)
▼ Old Loss (last occupied 1968-72) ▼ Recent Loss (last occupied 1988-94)

Period	Evidence of Breeding	Seen Only	Total
Breeding 1968–72	495	166	661
Breeding 1988–94	538	185	723
Breeding 2008–13	229	141	370
Winter 2007/8–2012/13	-	-	462

Number of Tetrads

The distribution of the Bullfinch, both nationally and locally, is much the same during the winter as it is during the breeding season. Ringing recoveries suggest that the species is highly sedentary: although they may make local movements, they are usually found within 20km of where they were ringed (Migration Atlas). It was, however, slightly more widespread in the London area during winter, being recorded in 54% of our tetrads compared to 43% of tetrads during the breeding season.

Winter Distribution

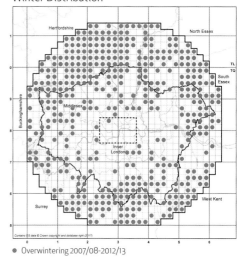

● Overwintering 2007/08-2012/13

Hawfinch

Coccothraustes coccothraustes

Very scarce breeding resident and occasional passage migrant; red list.

The breeding range of the Hawfinch extends right across Eurasia from Japan to Britain. In Europe, the breeding population is estimated to number 2,600,000–5,070,000 breeding pairs and the population is thought to be stable (BirdLife). However, the population in Britain, on the edge of this species' range, has undergone a decline and range contraction, with isolated populations now occurring in just five or six key areas, one of which could be described as a loose aggregation in south-east England (National Atlas). The most recent population estimate for Britain as a whole is 500–1,000 pairs in 2011 (Clements, 2012).

Breeding Distribution

- ● Confirmed Breeding 2008-13
- ● Probable Breeding 2008-13
- ● Possible Breeding 2008-13
- • Present 2008-13
- • Still on Migration 2008-13

The Hawfinch is a bird of extensive woodland and is therefore excluded from less wooded landscapes, rural and urban. In the London area, this species was once more widespread around the periphery and in the suburbs where suitable habitat occurs. In the first half of the twentieth century, it was thought likely to breed at, for example, Wimbledon Common, Tooting Bec Common, Hampstead Heath and Highgate Woods (LNHS, 1964).

The first atlas shows breeding to occur in only about 4% of the tetrads in the London area; the occupied tetrads were scattered around the periphery of Greater London, with the majority in the Hertfordshire and Essex sectors, including Epping Forest (where this species was first confirmed to breed in Britain in 1832 (LNHS, 1964). A notable exception to the general distribution of this species at the time of the first atlas was a breeding population in Kew Gardens.

The second atlas indicates that a slightly greater number of tetrads were occupied by breeding Hawfinch at that time, although it is unclear whether this represents greater recording effort or a genuine expansion. The additional occupied tetrads were mostly in the Essex sector. There do, however, appear to have been genuine losses of breeding Hawfinch from a number of tetrads in the Surrey sector. The nearest record of potential breeding to Inner London at that time was from Hampstead Heath/Highgate where adults and young birds were seen in the summer of 1992 (Hewlett *et al.*).

The current atlas shows a much diminished breeding distribution for the Hawfinch in our area. Breeding evidence came from just two locations (one of these is just outside the official London area), with scattered records from just 11 tetrads elsewhere, including migrants. The number of breeding pairs in the London area is now likely to be fewer than ten. Indeed, Self considers the Hawfinch extinct as a breeding bird in the London area. There are also contemporary records of birds flying over our area, including several flying over Inner London (LBR).

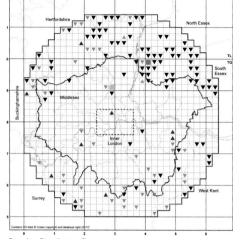

Breeding Change

Breeding Distribution Change
▲ Recent Gain (new in 2008-13)   ▲ Old Gain (new in 1988-94)
■ Stable (present in all periods)   ■ Variable (absent 1988-94)
▼ Old Loss   ▼ Recent Loss
(last occupied 1968-72)   (last occupied 1988-94)

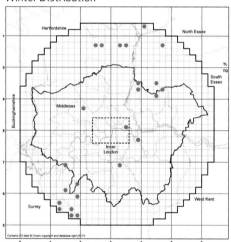

Winter Distribution

● Overwintering 2007/08-2012/13

Period	Number of Tetrads		
	Evidence of Breeding	Seen Only	Total
Breeding 1968–72	35	43	78
Breeding 1988–94	46	47	93
Breeding 2008–13	2	11	13
Winter 2007/8–2012/13	-	-	25

In the winter, the Hawfinch is more than three times as widespread in Britain than during the breeding season (National Atlas). It is also, albeit marginally, more widespread in the London area where this species was recorded from 25 tetrads during the winter. The resident population is joined by birds which breed in northern Europe and the wintering population in Britain is higher than during the breeding season. This results in the occasional presence of large flocks, such as the exceptional one recorded in March 2013 at Juniper Bottom (Box Hill), which comprised up to 130 birds. More usually, just single birds are recorded passing through or over the London area in winter (LBR).

Yellowhammer

Emberiza citrinella

Breeding resident, winter visitor and scarce passage migrant; red list.

The Yellowhammer is another of our farmland passerines which has undergone a decline, although the period of strongest decline took place relatively late on in the twentieth century, beginning in the mid-1980s and continuing to the mid-1990s. The population decline has since continued at a lower rate, particularly in the east and south of Britain where this species is still at its most numerous.

Commensurate with the national pattern of decline in the Yellowhammer population, the number of occupied tetrads in the London area was approximately the same in the first two atlases but fell dramatically between the second and current atlas periods.

The Yellowhammer clearly does not favour urban areas and especially shuns London; there is a clear low spot in Yellowhammer abundance in the London area (National Atlas) and all three London Atlases clearly show this species is pretty much confined to the rural habitats outside Greater London.

The three London Atlases show a picture of retreat. The retreat is on two fronts. Firstly from the suburbs; for example, this species used to breed in Hampstead Heath (ceased in 1960s), Richmond Park, Wimbledon Common (ceased in 1984) and Bushy Park, but no more. Secondly from the river valleys; for example, this species now seems to have been lost as a breeding species from the Thames Valley, and now only occupies a few tetrads in the Lee and Colne Valleys. In this respect, the pattern of occupation is almost the negative of the distribution of the Reed Bunting. Presumably, this is the effect of both species retreating into more favoured areas as their populations decline, but it is possible to speculate that competition between the two species is also a factor.

Breeding Distribution

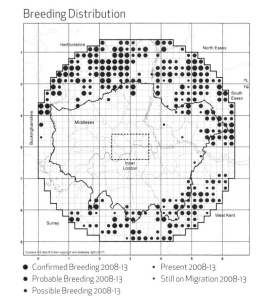

- ● Confirmed Breeding 2008-13
- ● Probable Breeding 2008-13
- ● Possible Breeding 2008-13
- • Present 2008-13
- • Still on Migration 2008-13

Period	Number of Tetrads		
	Evidence of Breeding	Seen Only	Total
Breeding 1968–72	440	67	507
Breeding 1988–94	422	80	502
Breeding 2008–13	186	104	290
Winter 2007/8–2012/13	-	-	245

The distribution of the Yellowhammer, both nationally and locally, is much the same during the winter as it is during the breeding season. Flocks can form at this time of year, typically comprising between 10 and 50 birds but occasionally around 100, such as that at Ridlands in January 2008.

Breeding Change

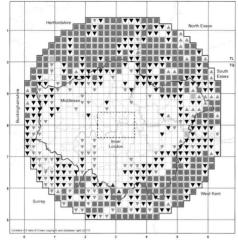

Breeding Distribution Change
- ▲ Recent Gain (new in 2008-13)
- ■ Stable (present in all periods)
- ▼ Old Loss (last occupied 1968-72)
- ▲ Old Gain (new in 1988-94)
- ▦ Variable (absent 1988-94)
- ▼ Recent Loss (last occupied 1988-94)

Winter Distribution

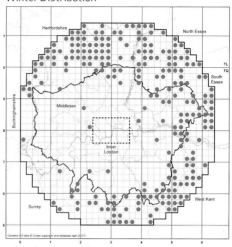

- ● Overwintering 2007/08-2012/13

Reed Bunting
Emberiza schoeniclus

Breeding resident, winter visitor and passage migrant; amber list.

The Reed Bunting is another of our small passerines which declined markedly in the 1970s (BirdTrends). Since then, the total UK population has fluctuated around a new, lower level, with increases in some regions, including south-east England, being offset by decreases in others (BBS). This species occurs throughout the British Isles; however, it is most abundant in areas of land around sea level and least abundant, or absent, in areas of higher ground. As its name and distribution suggest, it is mostly a bird of marsh and wetland; however, it also inhabits drier areas with tall crops.

The first two atlases show a broadly similar distribution and frequency of tetrad occupation. As would be expected, there is a clear association with the main river valleys in our area and a clear avoidance of the higher ground, particularly the North Downs. However, there was some evidence of a decline in numbers at the time of the second atlas (Hewlett *et al.*). The traditional pattern of distribution is still evident in the current atlas but it is clear that the number of tetrads occupied by this species has reduced substantially over the last 25 years. There may now be fewer than 250 pairs breeding in the London area currently (LBR).

Breeding Distribution

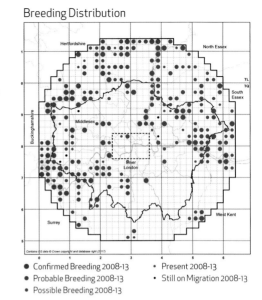

- ● Confirmed Breeding 2008-13
- ● Probable Breeding 2008-13
- ● Possible Breeding 2008-13
- · Present 2008-13
- · Still on Migration 2008-13

Period	Number of Tetrads		
	Evidence of Breeding	Seen Only	Total
Breeding 1968–72	324	63	387
Breeding 1988–94	304	106	410
Breeding 2008–13	164	94	258
Winter 2007/8–2012/13	-	-	235

The distribution of the Reed Bunting, both nationally and locally, is much the same during the winter as it is during the breeding season.

Breeding Change

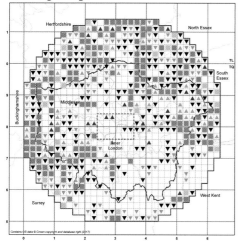

Winter Distribution

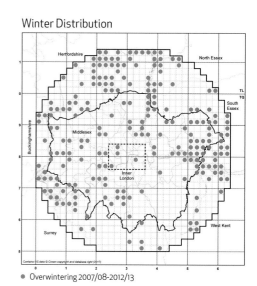

Breeding Distribution Change

▲ Recent Gain (new in 2008-13)   ▲ Old Gain (new in 1988-94)

■ Stable (present in all periods)   ▨ Variable (absent 1988-94)

▽ Old Loss
(last occupied 1968-72)   ▼ Recent Loss
(last occupied 1988-94)

● Overwintering 2007/08-2012/13

Corn Bunting

Emberiza calandra

Localised and declining breeding resident; red list.

Like many farmland bird species, the Corn Bunting population underwent a steep decline between the 1970s and the 1990s. More recently, the population decline has continued but at a much lower rate than previously. Along with the decline, the population has retreated into core areas, principally in lowland England.

The number of tetrads occupied and the distribution of this species were much the same in both the first and second London atlases. However, this species was known to have been more widespread before the first atlas (LNHS, 1964) and there was evidence of a further decline by the end of the second atlas period (Hewlett *et al.*). The stronghold for this species in the latter half of the last century in our area was to the east of London, north and south of the Thames. The current atlas shows a much reduced occurrence of the Corn Bunting. There are a few tetrads within its former stronghold where this species still breeds, plus occasional breeding in the Hertfordshire sector. However, there are now probably fewer than 20 breeding pairs present each year in the whole of the London area. With the ongoing decline, small and fragmented populations are likely to be vulnerable and the future of this species in the London area looks bleak.

Period	Number of Tetrads		
	Evidence of Breeding	Seen Only	Total
Breeding 1968–72	112	32	114
Breeding 1988–94	109	50	139
Breeding 2008–13	12	17	29
Winter 2007/8–2012/13	-	-	28

The Corn Bunting is highly sedentary (National Atlas) and its distribution, both nationally and locally, is much the same during the winter as it is during the breeding season.

Breeding Distribution

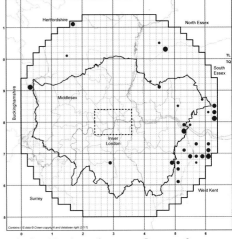

- ● Confirmed Breeding 2008-13
- ● Probable Breeding 2008-13
- ● Possible Breeding 2008-13
- • Present 2008-13
- • Still on Migration 2008-13

Breeding Change

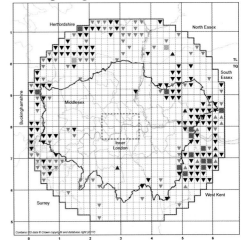

Breeding Distribution Change
- ▲ Recent Gain (new in 2008-13)
- ■ Stable (present in all periods)
- ▼ Old Loss (last occupied 1968-72)
- ▲ Old Gain (new in 1988-94)
- ▨ Variable (absent 1988-94)
- ▼ Recent Loss (last occupied 1988-94)

Winter Distribution

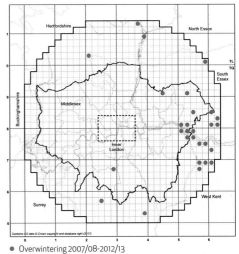

- ● Overwintering 2007/08-2012/13

Birdwatching in London

Written by Gehan de Silva Wijeyeratne, adapted from his article first published in Wall Street International, www.wsimag.com.

Top Three Wildlife Sites

London is surprisingly rich in wildlife and provides a network of fantastic nature reserves with superb visitor infrastructure for birders and wildlife photographers. About 45% of Greater London is green space or open water. In the heart of Central London, participants in nature walks organised by the London Natural History Society (LNHS) look for Tawny Owls and Green Woodpeckers. The LNHS, London Wildlife Trust (LWT) and other London-centric nature organisations have something on almost every week. They welcome non-members at their indoor events (talks, workshops, etc.) and nature walks (a.k.a. field meetings) and coach trips. It is worth checking their programmes on their websites. Visiting photographers may find some of the day trips by coach especially useful. These will take you out of London, usually within a 3-hour drive radius.

In Greater London there are dozens of nature reserves of various sizes. The LWT alone manages over 40 nature reserves. Many of the formal parks are also increasingly managed to have small wild areas to encourage native wildlife. The LNHS, LWT and various local authorities hold nature events in these reserves.

These notes, especially on access, are written with visitors in mind. The problem visitors to London, and the surrounding area, face is not the lack of nature reserves and activities but which ones they should focus on, for the combination of wildlife and visitor facilities. I have therefore focussed on just a few, which are selected on the basis of the following criteria.
• Very good for a mix of wildlife
• Easy to reach with public transport
• Very good visitor facilities
• Oriented to photographers and birdwatchers

The top three sites are based on the criteria listed above. This is a personal selection and others who live in London will have their own favourites. It is advisable to check online for up-to-date details. The details provided below are correct at the time of writing, but can change and should only be used as a guideline.

London Wetland Centre

In a temperate country, the London Wetland Centre is hard to beat for its combination of visitor facilities, matrix of habitats and bird hides. The Tower Hide is heated and has a glass front which is three storeys high. The café is never more than 10 minutes away. Even in cold, wet weather, the excellent visitor facilities make being out here a good experience. In good weather it is just magic. In

London Wetland Centre, Barnes

winter, good numbers of migratory waterfowl are present. In spring, the breeding birds are in full song and flowers are coming out. In summer, butterflies, dragonflies, birds and plants in flower make a visit here very rewarding. Even reptiles put in an appearance and Common Lizards can be seen basking. A number of nature walks run throughout the year. In summer, special bat walks using bat detectors are run in the evenings.

Entry: Admission charge for non WWT members. Summer opening time: from 1 March until October 31; 9.30 a.m. to 5.30 p.m. (last admission 4.30 p.m.). Winter opening time: from 1 November until February 28 (or 29 when relevant); 9.30 a.m. to 4.30 p.m. (last admission 3.30 p.m.).

Visitor Facilities: Car parking and toilets. A big indoor café with a choice of food; hot meals, sandwiches and a

London Wetland Centre, Barnes

RSPB Rainham Marshes

selection of hot and cold drinks. In summer an additional outdoor café is opened. The visitor centre has a big shop with souvenirs and books. There is also a separate retail outlet of 'in focus' who specialise in optics. The visitor centre is best in class as far as nature reserves go.

Getting there: District and Piccadilly lines on the London Underground run frequently to Hammersmith. From the bus station (sign-posted at the tube station) take a 33, 72 or 209 and alight at the Red Lion bus stop, approximately 150 metres walk from the Wetland Centre. These buses are frequent, running approximately every 10 minutes.

The 485 takes you directly to the centre but is infrequent and does not operate on Sundays and public holidays.

Walking from Hammersmith: From the Hammersmith tube station you can walk to the south bank of the River Thames across Hammersmith bridge (about 10 minutes plus) and walk along the Thames Tow Path to the centre. It would help to have a map or a smartphone map. The walk will take about 30 minutes plus. If you have a lot of gear, it may be more comfortable to wait for a bus.

RSPB Rainham Marshes

The reserve boundary is within tens of metres of the River Thames. The Thames is very wide here and telescopes are used by visitors from the balcony at the back of the visitor centre to look for Seals which may be basking on the far shore. Skuas are also at times seen. The reserve comprises a series of waterbodies fringed with

RSPB Rainham Marshes

reedbeds and areas of managed grassland. One of the closest reserves to London where visitors in summer are greeted by singing Skylarks. The reedbeds are alive to the songs of Reed Warblers in spring. There are patches of woodland which are good for warblers and other passerines. The grassland is used by Redshanks and Lapwings for breeding. In winter, good numbers of waterfowl arrive. It is one of the best places in Britain to see and photograph Water Voles.

Entry: Admission charge for non-RSPB members. Car park and reserve trails are open 9.30 a.m. to 4.30 p.m. from 1 November to 31 January and 9.30 a.m. to 5 p.m.

from 1 February to 31 October; closed on Christmas Day and Boxing Day.

Visitor Facilities: Car parking and toilets. A well-equipped café with a choice of food; hot meals and a selection of hot and cold drinks. The café overlooks the reserve from a small height, a terrific location.

Getting there: Trains leave from Fenchurch Street station which is in the eastern part of Central London and very much in the heart of London's old financial district. Take a train to Purfleet (which is the stop after Rainham). Exit the Purfleet Station and turn right onto the main road (going over a railway crossing). Follow the signs to the Thames Towpath and follow the river heading west. You can see city buildings in Canary Wharf in the distance. The visitor centre in an unusual building is about a 15 minutes walk away.

On Saturdays there are two direct trains an hour and it is easy to get to. On Sundays you have to take a train from Fenchurch Street to Barking and change trains.

RSPB Rye Meads

The reserve comprises a number of waterbodies with extensive areas of reedbeds. The hides are well positioned for photographing waterbirds throughout the year. A good site for Water Voles. The walking paths are lined with scrub and trees and a mix of woodland birds is also present. In spring and summer look for warblers and waterfowl in winter.

Access: Generally, the reserve is open daily 9 a.m. to 5 p.m. (or dusk if earlier). Closed Christmas Day and Boxing Day. Free entry. Small car parking charge to non-RSPB members.

Facilities: Car parking and toilets. A tiny café area with some hot and cold drinks and a limited selection of food, mainly snacks. It is advisable to bring your own packed lunch.

Getting there: Trains leave from Liverpool Street station which is in the eastern part of Central London and in the north-eastern border of London's old financial district. Two trains an hour on Saturdays and Sundays to Rye House. Exit the station and turn right. The reserve is about a 5 minutes plus walk. Very easy to get to.

Other Sites

Hampstead Heath

Hampstead Heath is a free entry public space with multiple access points in the north of London. Heavily visited. Easy to access from stations such as Hampstead (on Northern line) and Hampstead Heath (on London

Overground). Some wildlife photographers have commented to me that the animals are habituated to people, allowing good photography. However, I find this to be also the case with sites such as the London Wetland Centre which is preferable for bird photographers with its network of hides. Hampstead Heath does not have bird hides and is managed primarily as a public space and not as a nature reserve for wildlife-centric visitors. Unlike the reserves (where entry is by ticket) managed by the RSPB and WWT, people are free to bring their pets to Hampstead Heath.

Although bird photographers may find the top three sites more productive, all-round nature photographers may find more subject matter in Hampstead Heath because it has old woodland and extensive areas of grassland. It will have a richer flora than the other three sites and also have a wider selection of invertebrate species. it is clearly one of the most important biodiversity sites in London which is also rich in history.

Woodberry Wetlands

Woodberry Wetlands is one of a pair of reservoirs which has been converted to a wetland with reedbeds planted on the edges and islands created in the middle for resting and breeding waterfowl and other birds. The other adjoining reservoir is used for boating. In summer, Reed Warblers are active and sing from just a few feet away from the boardwalk. Cetti's Warbler is also heard. The usual waterbirds as well as species such as Shelduck, which would not normally be seen within such a densely occupied part of London, can be seen here.

Access: Open from 9.00 a.m. to 4.30 p.m. Entrance free.

Facilities: There is a café with toilets but it closes an hour earlier than the reserve. The West Reservoir is used for sailing and also has a café.

Getting There: The wetland is just under a 10 minute walk from Manor House tube station which is on the Piccadilly Line. There is an entrance from the Lordship Road side and also from Bethune Road to the East Reservoir which is now branded as the Woodberry Wetland. The walk from one entrance to the other along the reservoir can be done in 10 minutes. There is a small strip of land between the reservoir and the perimeter through which a woodland trail has been placed. The site has a number of Oak trees which provide a habitat for woodland birds. There is no doubt that this site will result in a number of interesting birding records with around 40 species possible on a good day. Regular visitors have logged more than 100 species over a year.

For wildlife photographers this is unlikely to be as rewarding as the three top sites. But the site is important for bringing people close to nature. It lies in one of the most densely populated parts of London, is free and its courses from introductory birdwatching to wild yoga are a sell-out. The natural reedbeds, the presence of informed volunteer nature guides, the focus in providing a managed nature reserve to city dwellers are all examples of how London is leading as a city that is bringing wildlife to city dwellers.

Richmond Park

Richmond Park is one of two National Nature Reserves (the other is Ruislip Woods) in the south-west of London. Wildlife photographers come here to photograph Red Deer in rut. Keep your distance; every year people are injured by deer. The Park is one of the best places in the country to observe the introduced Ring-necked Parakeet. A free entry public space with multiple access points. It can be reached easily by taking the tube to Richmond (District line) and walking. Heavily visited and has vehicles driving through. No bird hides. Unlike at the reserves managed by the RSPB, LWT and WWT, people are free to bring their pets. As with Hampstead Heath, the presence of old woodland and extensive grassland results in a very rich flora and a diversity of invertebrates.

River Lee Country Park

The train station at Cheshunt acts as the gateway to the River Lee Country Park; a sprawling network of wetlands with 24 hour public access. In spring and summer the location is very good for a variety of woodland and waterside warblers. Entry is within a few minutes walk from the train station. There are toilets at certain entry points. Wardens may be present at the big hide at the Bittern Information point. However there is no café, so bring your own food and water. It has a number of advantages including ease of access by train from London (Liverpool Street and Tottenham Hale) and being open all day with free entry. There are also some good opportunities for wildlife photography.

Other sites

A look at the websites of the LNHS, LWT and RSPB Central London Local Group and other organisations will show that there are a number of good sites for bird watchers, botanists, entomologists and other natural historians. These vary from Hyde Park and Kensington Gardens where patches of woodland will have Nuthatches, Stock Doves, Little and Tawny Owls to Brent Reservoir where wintering ducks such as Scaup may be seen as well as rarities which are passing through. There are literally several dozen sites in London. The above has covered a small handful of the bigger sites. (See also *Where to Watch Birds in the London Area* by Dominic Mitchell.)

Useful Organisations and Apps

Check the social media of the following organisations for useful pointers. Also look at their programmes on their websites for guided walks and coach trips. Coach trips are run at cost and most nature walks are free. Most of the organisations charge a small donation at the door for attending a talk. Non-members are welcome.

The local walks organised by the LNHS, LWT, the Central London Local Group of the RSPB and the Marlyebone Birdwatching Society will introduce you to a wealth of wildlife watching sites for Londoners varying from the Lee Valley Regional Park to Tooting Common. Mature woodlands with Little Owls can be found in seemingly unlikely London boroughs if you go with the right people. It is worth inspecting the programmes of the organisations listed below. The LNHS website also has a large listing of nature organisations with a national or London-centric focus.

London Natural History Society
www.lnhs.org.uk
Twitter @LNHSoc
@LondonBirdClub
Search for #londonbirds to see postings
Facebook http://www.facebook.com/LNHSoc

London Wildlife Trust
www.wildlondon.org.uk
Twitter @WildLondon

Marylebone Birdwatching Society
http://www.birdsmbs.org.uk/
Twitter @BirdsMBS

Central London Local Group RSPB
http://www.rspb.org.uk/groups/centrallondon

Apps

A free App such as City Mapper is very useful as it helps with bus routes and other public transport.

The Trainline app is useful for checking on trains to sites like Rye Meads and Rainham Marshes. The London Underground map is available as a free app and does not need signal to view it once downloaded. MeetUp is a useful app and you can sign up with the LNHS and RSPB Central London group for example. Event notifications are automatically emailed to you. But remember to manage your setting so that you are not overwhelmed with a deluge of emails and you restrict yourself to event notifications from the groups you have joined.

Submitting records

If you would like to contribute your natural history records, smartphone apps such as BirdTrack and iRecord make it very easy. Some of the local ornithological societies continue to have their own recording portals as well.

Gazetteer of Sites

This gazetteer lists the sites mentioned in the book, with the exception of the names of towns and villages and other well-known London landmarks. Each site name is followed by the LNHS recording sector in which it is located (BU = Buckinghamshire; EX = Essex; HE = Hertfordshire; IL = Inner London; KE = Kent; MX = Middlesex & SY = Surrey), and a six-figure Ordnance Survey Grid Reference to enable sites to be located on a map. Note that some of the sites referred to in the text and listed in this gazetteer are strictly private or accessible only with a permit.

Site name	Grid reference	Site name	Grid reference
Aldenham Country Park (HE)	TQ169955	Eastern Quarry (KT)	TQ592735
Alexandra Park (MX)	TQ302900	Enfield Chase (MX)	TQ290988
Amwell Nature Reserve (HE)	TL380125	Epping Forest (EX)	TQ420985
Apps Court Farm (SY)	TQ110673	Fairlop Gravel Works (EX)	TQ462900
Banbury Reservoir (EX)	TQ362915	Fairlop Waters (EX)	TQ459905
Bankside (IL)	TQ320805	Finsbury Park (MX)	TQ317875
Banstead Downs (SY)	TQ252610	Foots Cray Meadows (KT)	TQ480715
Barking Bay (EX)	TQ451816	Gallion's Reach (EX)	TQ445801
Barking Creekmouth (EX)	TQ457814	Gores Brook (EX)	TQ486839
Barn Elms (SY) (now London Wetland Centre)	TQ228770	Grange Waters (EX)	TQ610820
		Greenwich Dock (IL/SY)	TQ361791
Barnes Wetland (SY) (= 'London Wetland Centre')	TQ228770	Greenwich Park (KT)	TQ390775
		Grey Goose Farm, North Stifford (EX)	TQ629807
Battersea Park (IL)	TQ282722	Grovelands Park (MX)	TQ305944
Beddington Farmlands/Sewage Farm (SY)	TQ290662	Hainault Forest (EX)	TQ476932
		Hall Marsh (EX)	TL373017
Bedfont Lakes Country Park (MX)	TQ078726	Hampstead Heath (MX)	TQ273866
Beech Farm Gravel Pits (HE)	TL190086	Hampton Court Park (MX)	TQ470820
Berrybushes Wood (HE)	TL069007	Harmondsworth (MX)	TQ050779
Bowyer's Water (HE)	TL368018	Harrow Lodge Park (EX)	TQ525863
Brent Reservoir (MX)	TQ215870	Hatfield Aerodrome (HE)	TL205085
Brimsdown (MX)	TQ367970	Hayes Farm Trout Lake (KT)	TQ416670
Broadwater Lake (MX)	TQ045892	Hersham Gravel Pits (SY)	TQ128663
Broxbourne Woods (HE)	TL340080	Highgate Woods (MX)	TQ283887
Buckland Sand Pits (SY)	TQ227510	Hilfield Park Reservoir (HE)	TQ158959
Burgess Park (IL)	TQ335778	Hogsmill Sewage Works (SY)	TQ197682
Bushy Park (MX)	TQ273866	Holland Park (IL)	TQ248796
Camley Street Natural Park (IL)	TQ298836	Holmethorpe Sand Pits	TQ295515
Canada Water (IL/SY)	TQ355793	Holyfield Lake (EX)	TL378045
Canons Farm (SY)	TQ248577	Horton Gravel Pits (BU)	TQ005753
Cheshunt Gravel Pits (HE)	TL370030	Hounslow Heath (MX)	TQ123745
Cheverells (SY)	TQ395565	Hyde Park (IL)	TQ270803
Cobham Floods (SY)	TQ106595	Ingrebourne Valley (EX)	TQ538843
Copped Hall (EX)	TL430010	Juniper Bottom (SY)	TQ180525
Cornmill Meadows (EX)	TL380011	Kempton Nature Reserve (MX)	TQ116706
Crayford Marshes (KT)	TQ532775	Kensington Gardens (IL)	TQ270803
Crossness (KT)	TQ478815	Kew Gardens (SY)	TQ182769
Dagenham Riverside (EX)	TQ470820	King George V Reservoir (EX)	TQ374964
Denham Country Park (BU)	TQ048865	King George VI Reservoir (MX)	TQ041732
East India Dock Basin (MX)	TQ391808	Lake Farm Country Park (MX)	TQ090804

Site name	Grid reference	Site name	Grid reference
Littlebrook Lake (KT)	TQ553756	Sydenham Hill Wood (SY)	TQ335722
London Wetland Centre (SY)	TQ228770	Thames Chase (EX)	TQ584863
London Zoo (IL/MX)	TQ282834	The Mores, Brentwood (EX)	TQ561965
Longfordmoor (MX)	TQ042767	Thorndon Country Park (EX)	TQ620916
Malden Rushett (SY)	TQ169615	Thorney Country Park (BU)	TQ048790
Maple Lodge Nature Reserve (HE)	TQ036924	Thorpe Water Park (SY)	TQ030681
Mardyke Valley (EX)	TQ600805	Tokyngton Recreation Ground (MX)	TQ200846
Millwall Dock (MX)	TQ377795	Tooting (Bec) Common (SY)	TQ293720
Minet Country Park (MX)	TQ110800	Tottenham Marsh (MX)	TQ354910
Nazeing Gravel Pits (EX)	TL385072	Troy Mill Lake (HE)	TQ039905
New River, Enfield (MX)	TQ336970	Tyttenhanger Gravel Pits (HE)	TL191865
Northaw Great Wood (HE)	TL285044	Valentine's Park, Ilford (EX)	TQ438878
Old Slade Lake (BU)	TQ040780	Walthamstow Marsh (EX)	TQ350878
Ongar Park Wood (EX)	TL495025	Walthamstow Reservoir (EX)	TQ353890
Orsett Fen (EX)	TQ628833	Walton Heath (SY)	TQ232540
Perry Oaks Sewage Farm (MX) [Site No longer exists]	TQ055755	Walton Reservoir (SY)	TQ122685
Pimp Hall, Chingford (EX)	TQ390937	Wandsworth Park (SY)	TQ248753
Queen Elizabeth II Reservoir (SY)	TQ120670	Wanstead Flats (EX)	TQ410864
Queen Mary Reservoir (MX)	TQ070695	West Hendon Broadway (MX)	TQ221880
Queen Mother Reservoir (BU)	TQ017773	West Thurrock Marshes (EX)	TQ583767
Rainham Marshes (EX)	TQ525800	Whitewebbs Wood (MX)	TQ325997
Redwell Wood Farm (HE)	TL207027	William Girling Reservoir (EX)	TQ367945
Regent's Park (IL)	TQ281828	Wimbledon Common (SY)	TQ247723
Richmond Park (SY)	TQ200730	Wormwood Scrubs (MX)	TQ221818
Ridlands (SY)	TQ422524	Wraysbury Gravel Pits (BU)	TQ015735
Ripple Nature Reserve, Barking (EX)	TQ468827	Wraysbury Reservoir (MX)	TQ025745
Roding Valley Park (EX)	TQ425945	Wyvil Estate, Stockwell (IL)	TQ302775
Rye Meads (HE)	TL383103		
Sevenoaks Wildlife Reserve (KT)	TQ522570		
Seventy Acres Lake (HR/EX)	TL374030		
Shadwell Basin (MX)	TQ352807		
Silvertown (EX)	TQ414798		
South Norwood Country Park (SY)	TQ353684		
St. George's Hospital, Hornchurch (EX)	TQ539855		
St. James's Park (IL)	TQ294798		
Staines Moor (MX)	TQ033734		
Staines Reservoir (MX)	TQ051731		
Stanborough (HE)	TL230108		
Stanwell Moor (MX)	TQ040743		
Stocker's Lake (HE)	TQ046935		
Stoke Newington Reservoir (MX)	TQ326876		
Stone Marshes (KT)	TQ568755		
Surrey Water (IL/SY)	TQ365800		
Swanley Park (KT)	TQ516694		
Swanscombe Marsh (KT)	TQ605760		

List of species recorded during the atlas survey work for which no species account has been prepared

Common Name	Scientific Name	BOU Category
Black Swan	*Cygnus atratus*	E
Swan Goose (Chinese Goose)	*Anser cygnoides*	E
Lesser White-fronted Goose	*Anser erythropus*	AE
Red-breasted Goose	*Branta ruficollis*	AE
Hawaiian Goose	*Branta sandvicensis*	E
Bar-headed Goose	*Anser indicus*	E
Ross's Goose	*Chen rossii*	DE
Emperor Goose	*Chen canagica*	E
Ruddy Shelduck	*Tadorna ferruginea*	BDE
Muscovy Duck	*Cairina moschata*	E
Ringed Teal	*Callonetta leucophrys*	E
Wood Duck	*Aix sponsa*	E
Falcated Duck	*Anas falcata*	DE
American Wigeon	*Anas americana*	E
White-cheeked Pintail	*Anas bahamensis*	E
Yellow-billed Pintail	*Anas undulata*	E
Bernier's Teal	*Anas bernieri*	E
Green-winged Teal	*Anas carolinensis*	A
Blue-winged Teal	*Anas discors*	AE
Marbled Duck	*Marmaronetta angustirostris*	DE
Ferruginous Duck	*Aythya nyroca*	AE
Bufflehead	*Bucephala albeola*	AE
Barrow's Goldeneye	*Bucephala islandica*	AE
Golden Pheasant	*Chrysolophus pictus*	E
Indian Peafowl	*Pavo cristatus*	E
Helmeted Guineafowl	*Numida meleagris*	E
Great White Pelican	*Pelecanus onocrotalus*	DE
Storm Petrel	*Hydrobates pelagicus*	A
Gannet	*Morus bassanus*	A
Little Bittern	*Ixobrychus minutus*	A
Night-heron	*Nycticorax nycticorax*	A
Cattle Egret	*Bubulcus ibis*	A
Great White Egret	*Ardea alba*	A
Purple Heron	*Ardea purpurea*	A
White Stork	*Ciconia ciconia*	A
Spoonbill	*Platalea leucorodia*	A
Honey-buzzard	*Pernis apivorus*	A
Black Kite	*Milvus migrans*	A
Goshawk	*Accipiter gentilis*	A
Osprey	*Pandion haliaetus*	A
Red-footed Falcon	*Falco vespertinus*	A
Lanner Falcon	*Falco biarmicus*	E
Crane	*Grus grus*	A
Spotted Crake	*Porzana porzana*	A
Stone-curlew	*Burhinus oedicnemus*	A
Black-winged Stilt	*Himantopus himantopus*	A
White-tailed Plover	*Vanellus leucurus*	A
Whimbrel	*Numenius phaeopus*	A
Curlew Sandpiper	*Calidris ferruginea*	A
Temminck's Stint	*Calidris temminckii*	A
Sanderling	*Calidris alba*	A

Common Name	Scientific Name	BOU Category
Little Stint	*Calidris minuta*	A
Pectoral Sandpiper	*Calidris melanotos*	A
Wood Sandpiper	*Tringa glareola*	A
Pomarine Skua	*Stercorarius pomarinus*	A
Arctic Skua	*Stercorarius parasiticus*	A
Long-tailed Skua	*Stercorarius longicaudus*	A
Great Skua	*Stercorarius skua*	A
Little Tern	*Sternula albifrons*	A
Whiskered Tern	*Chlidonias hybrida*	A
Black Tern	*Chlidonias niger*	A
White-winged Black Tern	*Chlidonias leucopterus*	A
Sandwich Tern	*Sterna sandvicensis*	A
Roseate Tern	*Sterna dougallii*	A
Arctic Tern	*Sterna paradisaea*	A
Kittiwake	*Rissa tridactyla*	A
Bonaparte's Gull	*Chroicocephalus philadelphia*	A
Little Gull	*Hydrocoloeus minutus*	A
Ring-billed Gull	*Larus delawarensis*	A
Iceland Gull	*Larus glaucoides*	A
Glaucous Gull	*Larus hyperboreus*	A
Cockatiel	*Nymphicus hollandicus*	E
Budgerigar	*Melopsittacus undulatus*	E
Alexandrine Parakeet	*Psittacula eupatria*	E
Green Parakeet	*Psittacara holochlorus*	E
Peach-faced Lovebird	*Agapornis roseicollis*	E
Monk Parakeet	*Myiopsitta monachus*	E
Blue-crowned Parakeet	*Aratinga acuticaudata*	E
Scarlet Macaw	*Ara macao*	E
White-cheeked Turaco	*Tauraco leucotis*	E
Alpine Swift	*Apus melba*	A
Hoopoe	*Upupa epops*	AE
Red-rumped Swallow	*Cecropis daurica*	A
Melodious Warbler	*Hippolais polyglotta*	A
Great Reed Warbler	*Acrocephalus arundinaceus*	A
Pied Flycatcher	*Ficedula hypoleuca*	A
Richard's Pipit	*Anthus richardi*	A
Common Rosefinch	*Erythrina erythrina*	A
Common Redpoll	*Carduelis flammea*	A

BOU Categories (after BOU, 2013)

A   Naturally occurring species since 1950
B   Naturally occurring species 1800 to 1950 but not since
C   Self-sustaining, introduced species
D   Possibly naturally occurring but insufficient evidence
E   Introductions or escapes, not self-sustaining

Notes: Species excluded from the species accounts include escapes, vagrants and passage migrants which are uncommon in the London area

List of Contributors

This section lists the observers and organisations who contributed one or more records within the London Atlas recording area, either directly to the London Atlas database or to BirdTrack. In addition to those listed, we would also like to thank a small number of additional observers who are not listed as they wished to remain anonymous. We would also like to thank all those observers who contributed records to the London Bird Club during the atlas survey period, whose names are listed in the 2007 to 2013 London Bird Reports.

The London Atlas is dedicated to all the observers, without whom this project would not have been possible.

Mr Darren Abbott
Mr David Abrahams
Mr David Ackland
Mr Jason Ackland
Mr Greg Adams
Ms J Adams
Mrs Nikki Adams
Dr Nigel Agar
Mr David Agombar
Mrs Maria Aguado
Mr Sacha Alberici
Mrs Josefina Alcolea J Clover
Mr Peter Alfrey
Mr Simon Allday
Miss Emily Allen
Mr Julian Allen
Mr Mark Allott
Mr Jim Alloway
Miss Jennifer Allsop
Mr Roger Amer
Mr Stuart Ames
Mr Ian Anderson
Mr Jason Anderson
Mr N Anderson
Dr Edwyn Anderton
Mrs Diane Andrews
Mr Rob Andrews
Mr M B Andrews
Mr David Annal
Mr Simon Apps
Mr David Arch
Mr Darren Archer
Mr John K Archer
Miss A Arkinstall
Ms Sheelagh Armour
Mr Grant Armstrong
Mr Richard Arnold
Mr Jd Ash
Miss Kate Ashbrook
Mr Sean Ashton
Dr Kirsten Asmussen
Miss Janet Atkinson
Mrs D I Atkinson
Mr Chris Attewell
Mr John Attiwell
Mr Philip Attwood
Mr Brian Austin
Mr Michael Austin
Mr D Austin
Mr J S Austin
Dr M I Avery

Mr David Avis
Mr G C Avison
Mr James Aylward
Mrs Sharon Aylward
Dr Derek Baggott
Mr David Bagott
Dr Louise Bailey
Mr D Bainbridge
Mr Stephen Baines
Mr Edward Baker
Miss Helen Baker
Mr James Baker
Mr Ray Baker
Mr Ross Baker
Dr M Baker-Schommer
Mr John Ball
Mr Philip Ball
Mr Tim Ball
Ms Dawn Balmer
Mr Brian Banks
Mr Christopher Banks
Ms Helen Bantock
Mrs Elizabeth Barber
Mr Brian Barefield
Mr Andrew Barfoot
Mr Derek Barker
Mr Jeremy Barker
Mr Glen Barnes
Mrs Ruth Barnes
Miss Claire Barrand
Mr J W Barrington
Mr P Barrow
Mr Jerry Bart
Mr Geoff Barter
Mr D W Bastin
Mr A Batchelor
Mr Shaun Bater
Dr Alan Bates
Mr Keith Bates
Mr Rob Bates
Mr Terry Bates
Mr Edward Battersby
Miss Sarah Baulch
Mr Mike Baxter
Mr Chris Beach
Mr Martin Beacon
Mr Matthew Beales
Mr V R Beaney
Mr Michael Beard
Mr Richard Beasley
Mr A J Beasley

Miss Catherine Beazley
Mr Peter Beckenham
Mr K F Beckett
Mr Roy Beddard
Mr K Beddow
Mrs B Bedford
Mr Matthew Beech
Mr A Beeney
Mr Martin Bell
Mrs Sandra Bell
Ms Cynthia Bendickson
Mr Trevor Bending
Mr Bruce Bennett
Mr Gavin Bennett
Mr Simon Benson
Ms Yvonne Benting
Berkshire Ornithological Society
Mrs Christina Bessant
Mr D Bessick
Mr Philip Best
Lieutenant Colonel N W Beswick
Mr K F Betton
Mr E A Bew
Mr Nigel Bewley
Mr Derek Bezuidenhout
Mrs Lisa Bibby
Mrs A Biggs
Dr Stella Bignold
Mr Robert Billingsley
Ms Joan Bingley
Mr Alastair Binham
Dr Keith Birch
Mr Roger Birch
Mr Michael Bird
Birdguides
Mr John Birkett
Mr Graham Bishop
Dr Peter Black
Mr Simon Blackley
Miss Elizabeth Blackwell
Mr Huw Blackwell
Mr Robin Blades
Mr Stephen Blake
Mr Tony Blake
Mr Bjorn Blanchard
Mr Richard Bland
Mr P Blatcher
Mr Innes Blight
Mr Daniel Bluemore

Mr Andrew Bluett
Mr William Blumsom
Mr David Blyth
Mr Trevor Blythe
Mr David Boddy
Mrs Rossana Bojalil
Mr Patrick Bonham
Mr Richard Bonser
Mr Harry Boorman
Mr D J Booth
Ms Reem Bortcosh
Mr Robin Borwick
Mrs S M Bosley
Mr Simon Boswell
Mrs Laura Bower
Mr Alex Bowes
Mr Trevor Bowley
Mr Richard Bowman
Mr Robert Bown
Mr Frank Boxell
Mr David Boyce
Mr Gary Boyes
Mr Brian Boyland
Mr Carl Bradbury
Mrs Mary Braddock
Mr David Bradford
Mr David Bradnum
Mr Hugh Bradshaw
Mr Ian Bradshaw
Mr Andrew Brady
Mr Michael Brady
Mr J A Braggs
Mr Daniel Brand
Mr Keith Brandwood
Mr James Bray
Mr Kane Brides
Ms Genevieve Bridgeman
Mrs Hilary Bridgland
Mr Barnaby Briggs
Mr Alan Bright
Mr Kit Britten
Mr James Brockbank
Mr Adrian Brockless
Mr Robert Brook
Mr Robert Brook
Dr Colin Brooks
Mr David Brooks
Ms Hazel Brooks
Mr Graham Broom
Mr Alastair Brown
Mrs Jean Brown

Mr Lee Brown
Mr Murray Brown
Mrs Nadine Brown
Mr Ray Brown
Mr Mark Brownell
Mr John Brownfield
Mr Ronald Bruty
Mr Daniel Bryan
Ms Lisa Bryan
Miss E M Bryant
BTO Dataset (BBS)
BTO Dataset (GBW)
BTO Dataset (HERON)
BTO Dataset (NRS)
BTO Dataset (WEBS)
BTO Ringers
Mrs Frances Buckel
Buckinghamshire Bird Club
Ms Clare Buckle
Mr Neil Bucknell
Mr R A Budd
Mr R A Budd
Ms Dominique Buesnel
Mr Richard Bufton
Dr R S K Buisson
Mr Phil Bull
Mr Neil Burchett
Ms Hilary Burden
Ms Jennifer Burdett
Mrs Victoria Burger
Mr Colin Burgess
Mr John Burgoine
Mrs N Burgum
Ms Deborah Burkett
Mr G Burman
Mr Craig Burnett
Ms Laraine Burnett
Mr Ian Burrus
Mr P J Burston
Mr Dave Burt
Mr Andrew Burton
Mr Jeff Butcher
Mr Alan Butler
Mr James Butler
Mr Trevor Butler
Mr Philip Butson
Mr Charlie Butt
Dr P A F Byle
Mrs Carolyn Byrne
Dr John Caddick
Mr David Cadman
Mr Tom Cadwallender
Mr Mike Caiden
Mr G D Caine
Miss T S Caine
Mr Bruce Calder
Mr David Callahan
Mr David Callaway

Mr Robert Callf
Cambridgeshire Bird Club
Mr Andrew Camp
Mr James Camp
Mr John Camp
Mr Andrew Campbell
Mr David Campbell
Mr Stephen Campion
Mr Graham Canny
Mrs V Carnell
Mr Ben Carpenter
Miss D G Carr
Mr Paul Carter
Mr Stephen Carter
Mr Tony Carter
Mr S Carter
Ms Jules Cassidy
Mr John Castle
Mr Ian Cater
Ms Shirley Catlin
Mrs Joanna Catterall
Mr Philip Cavalli
M N Chaffe
Mr Scott Chalmers
Mr Jonathan Chamberlain
Mr David Chambers
Miss Dawn Chambers
Mr K Chambers
Mr Bird Champion
Mr Dan Chaney
Mrs Miriam Chaplin
Mr Chris Chapman
Dr Jason W Chapman
Ms Lynda Chapman
Mrs Patricia Chapman
Mr Peter Chapman
Ms Anna Charles
Mr Peter Charles
Mr Erik Charleson
Mr Philip Chasteauneuf
Mr Steve Chastell
Mrs Joanne Chattaway
Mr Graham Checkley
Mr Adam Cheeseman
Professor Robert Cheke
Dr Peter Cherry
Mrs S A Chesson
Mr Steve Chilton
Mr Andrew Chipchase
Mr Philip Chown
Dr Peter Christian
Dr Stephen Christmas
Dr Roger Christopher
Mr Phil Church
Mr Marcell Claassen
Mr David Clark
Mr David Clark
Mr Frank Clark

Mr John Clark
Mr John Clark
Mrs Deborah Clarke
Miss Felicity Clarke
Ms Jean Clarke
Mrs J M Clarke
Mr Graham Clarkson
Dr Andy Clements
Mr John Clements
Mr R J Clements
Mr Aaron Clements-Partridge
Mr K J Clench
Mr B D Clews
Mrs G E K Clode
Mr Dominic Coath
Mr Martin Coath
Mr Nicholas Coats
Mr Tony Coatsworth
Mr Anthony Cobb
Mrs Sharon Cocker
Mr Shaun Cohen
Mr Simon Cohen
Ms Yvonne Cohen
Dr David Coldrey
Mrs Felicity Cole
Mr Melvyn Cole
Mr Robin Cole
Mr Derek Coleman
Mr John Coleman
Dr Peter Coleman
Mr Michael Collard
Mr Hugh Collings
Mr Hugh Collings
Ms Alex Collins
Mrs Jeanette Collins
Mr Michael Collins
Mr Philip Collins
Ms Catherine Collop
Mr Sam Collyer
Mr Steve Coney
Mr James Connor
Mr Nick Connor
Mrs Moira Convery
Mr Christopher N Cook
Mrs Frances Cook
Mr Henry Cook
Mr Paul Cook
Mrs G M Cook
Ms Chantal Cooke
Mr Gervase Cooke
Dr Alison Cooper
Mr Andrew Cooper
Mr Simon Cooper
Mr Richard Cope
Mr Paul Corbet
Mrs T Corcoran
Mr Gert Corfield
Dr Nigel Corp

Ms Lydia Costello
Mr David Cotton
Mr Mark Coventry
Mrs Dawn Cowan
Dr Richard Cowie
Mr Andrew Cox
Mr Brian Cox
Mr Gordon Cox
Miss Judith Cox
Dr Simon Cox
Dr Helen Crabtree
Mr Michael Craig
Mr Alan Crawford
Mr Richard Crawford
Mrs M Crecraft
Mr Robert Cripps
Mr Andrew Cristinacce
Mrs Rosa Crockett
Mr Simon Crockford
Mr Harry Crook
Mr Paul Cropper
Ms Lois Crouch
Mrs Jenny Croxson
Mr David Crump
Mr Michael Cuff
Mrs Colette Cullen
Dr Patrick Cullen
Dr Andrew Culshaw
Mrs Kathleen Curran-White
Mr Mark Cutts
Dr J R Dagley
Mr Chris Dale
Mr Richard Dale
Mr Adam Dalton
Ms Elise Daniels
Mr Mike Daniels
Mr Roger Darsley
Ms Anne Davage
Mrs Amanda Davies
Mr Gerry Davies
Mr Matthew Davies
Mr David Davis
Mr James Davis
Mrs Sue Davis
Dr J B Davis
Miss Michelle Dawkins
Dr D G Dawson
Miss Emma Dawson
Mr B Dawton
Mrs Aideen Day
Dr Richard De Souza
Mr Rod Dean
Tim and Janet Dean
Mr John Dedman
Mr Chris Dee
Ms M Dee
Mr P Delaloye
Mr Brian Demby

Mr Nick Denman
Mr M D Dent
Mr R A Denyer
Miss Deb Depledge
Dr K J Derrett
Mr R A Dewey
Mr Oscar Dewhurst
Mr T D Dick
Mr Keith Dickens
Mr Ian Dillon
Mr Lee Dingain
Mr John Dingemans
Mrs Helen Dixon
Mr James Dixon
Mr Mark Dixon
Mr Martin Dixon
Mr G Dixon
Miss Holly D'mello
Mr Frank Dobson
Mr Nigel Dodd
Mr Nicholas Donnithorne
Miss Brigitte Donovan
Mr Martin Dorling
Mr Anthony Dorman
Ms Angela Dougall
Mr Shaun Dowman
Dr Iain Downie
Mr Andrew Downing
Reverend Frances Downing
Mr Stephen Drake
Miss Emily Dresner
Mr Ed Drewitt
Mr Peter Driver
Mr Robin Dryden
Ms Nicola Duckworth
Mr Francis Dummigan
Mr Kevin Duncan
Mr Rob Duncan
Mr Brian Dyke
Ms Lynne Dymond
Mr Roger Eagles
Mr Tim Earley
Mr Michael East
East London Birders Forum
Mr J R Easton
Dr Mark Eaton
Mr Eirwen Edwards
Mrs Nicola Edwards
Mr Les Edwins
Ms Ruth Elder
Ms Karen Eldridge
Mr Trevor Eldridge
Mrs Jan Elliott
Miss Sarah Elliott
Mr Greg Elliott-Moustache
Mr Ian Ellis
Mr John Ellis
Mr Nick Ellis
Mrs Pamela Ellis

Mr D Ellisdon
Mr Nicholas Elsey
Ms Marion Emberson
Mr Roger Emmens
Mr John Emms
Miss V Enright
Ms Claire Etches
Dr Anna Evans
Mr Gareth Evans
Mr Glyn Evans
Mr Glyn Evans
Mr Hugh Evans
Mr Michael Evans
Mr Simon Evans
Mr Colin Everett
Mr Luke Everitt
Mrs Claudien Everson
Mr Michael Faint
Mr Malcolm Fairley
Miss Rachel Falkingham
Mr Charles Farrell
Mrs Ann Farrer
Mr Matthew Farrier
Mr Jack Fearnside
Dr Mark Fellowes
Mr Jonathan Fenton
Mr D M Ferguson
Mr David Fernleigh
Miss Dianna Ferry
Mrs Anna Field
Mr Paul Field
Mr Stuart Finch
Mr S Findell
Mr Jimmy Finn
Mr Ian Fisher
Mr Ian Fisher
Mrs Janice Fisher
Mr Stuart Fisher
Mr M Fitch
Mr Terence Flanagan
Mrs Joy Fleck
Mr K Fleming
Mr Ricky Flesher
Mrs M Fletcher
Mr M R Fletcher
Mrs Gillian Flinn
Mr Paul Floyd
Ms Aideen Flynn
Mr Phil Flynn
Mrs Jacqueline Fogden
Mr Joe Foley
Mr Peter Follett
Mr Sean Foote
Mr Neil Forbes
Mr Stuart Forbes
Mr Eric Ford
Mrs Tina Ford
Mr William Fordham
Miss Eleanor Forrest

Mrs Jill Forshaw
Professor Malcolm Forster
Mr Chris Forsyth
Mr E M Forsyth
Mrs Audrey Fossey
Mr Christopher Foster
Mr Neill Foster
Mr David Fouracre
Ms Teresa Fowler
Mr Timothy Fox
Mr Richard Francis
Mr P Franklin
Mr Roger Frankum
Mr Ben Fraser
Mrs S D Frearson
Mr Daniel Free
Mrs Danielle Free
Mr Nick French
Mr Peter Frost
A P Fullen
Dr Richard Fuller
Professor R J Fuller
Mrs Valerie Fullforth
Dr Sandy Fung
Ms Alison Fure
Mr Christopher Furley
Mrs Vanessa Gabbay
Mr John Gale
Mr Terence Gale
Mr B Galpin
Sir ANTHONY Galsworthy
Mr Jeremy Galton
Game & Wildlife Conservation
    Trust
Mrs L Gammage
Dr Ernest Garcia
Mr Alan Gardiner
Mr John Gardner
Mr Graeme Garner
Mr Richard Garrett
Ms Aimee Gasston
Mr Jeremy Gates
Mr S J Gates
Mr Nick Gatward
Mr Stephen Gent
Ms Alison Giacomelli
Mr Alasdair Gibb
Mr Anthony Gibbs
Dr Geoff Gibbs
Mr John Gibson
Mr Robin Gibson
Mr Trevor Gibson-Poole
Mrs Susan Giddens
Mr D L Gifford
Mr Derek Gilby
Mrs Jean Gilby
Dr Thomas Giles
Mrs Elizabeth Gill
G W Gill

Mr Simon Ginnaw
Mr Derek Girvan
Mrs Emma Gladwell
Reverend T W Gladwin
Mrs Catherine Glenister
Mr David Glue
Mr Allan Goddard
Dr David Gompertz
Mr John Gooch
Mr G Goodall
Mr Chris Goodey
Mr Jeff Gooding
Mr P Goodman
Mr Ralph Gordon
Miss Janice Gosden
Miss S J Gough
Mrs E Gower
John Gowers
Mr Stuart Graham
Mr Martin Grant
Mr Mark Grantham
Mr R Graves
Mrs Charlotte Gray
Mr Peter Gray
Mrs Sue Grayston
Mr Philip Green
Ms R Green
Dr A E Green
Mr T T Green
Mr Malcolm Greenaway
Miss Louise Greenwood
Mr Stuart Greer
Mr R Greer
Mrs Gillian Gregory
Mr Mark Gregory
Mr Paul Gregory
Mr Gi Grieco
Mr Mark Griffin
Mr David Griffiths
Miss Dilys Griffiths
Mrs Marian Griffiths
Mr Robin Griffiths
Mr R Grimmond
Mr Andrew Grimsey
Mrs R D Gross
Mr Martin Grounds
Mr Derek Gruar
Mrs R Grummett
Mr John Guard
Mr Andrew Guest
Mr John Guiver
Ms Sunnuva Gulklett
Miss Tracy Gunn
Mrs Suzan Gunnee
Mr Michael Gunstone
Mr Graham Guthrie
Mr Anthony Gutteridge
Mr Philip Hacker
Mr Paul Hadland

Mr William Haines
Mr Allan Hall
Mr Rob Hall
Ms Samantha Hall
Mr Stephen Hall
Mrs C P Hall
Mr Richard Hallam
Mrs Kay Halley
Ms Rosemary Hamilton
Mr William Hamilton
Mr Maurice Hammond
Mr Michael Hamzij
Mr Tom Hankinson
Mr Anthony Harbott
Mr Alan Hardie
Mr Clive Harding
Mr Richard Hards
Mr Roger Hardy
Mr Stewart Hares
Mr Robin Harley
Miss Frauke Harms
Mr Peter Harrigan
Mr Alan Harris
Mr David R Harris
Mr Jason Harris
Mr Joe Harris
Mr Kevin Harris
Mr Nigel Harris
Mr Ray Harris
Mr Robin Harris
Mr Simon Harris
Mr D G Harris
Mr Andrew Harrison
Mrs Barbara Harrison
Mr John Harrison
Mr D W Harrison
Mr Ben Harrower
Dr Alistair Hart
Mr Patrick Hart
Mr Robin Hart
Miss Susan Hart
Miss E M Hart
Mr Michael Harvey
Ms Linda Haslam
Mr Muhammed Hassan
Mr Martin Hatfield
Mr Chris Hatherill
Miss Caroline Hattersley
Mrs Wendy Hatton
Mr Gavin Hawgood
Mr Kenneth Hawkins
Mr Paul Hawkins
Mr John Haworth
Mr John Hawtree
Mrs Suzanne Hay
Mr Alan Haycock
Mr Richard Haydon
Mr D E Hayes
Dr Bill Haynes

K S Hayward
Dr Grant Hazlehurst
Mrs Sue Healey
Ms Carolyn Heathcote
Mr Peter Heathcote
Mr Brian Hedley
Mr Andrew Henderson
Mr Martin Henderson
Mr Daniel Hercock
Mr James Herd
Herts Bird Club
Richard and Marion Hetherington
Mr Roger Hewitt
Mrs E R Hewitt
Mr P J Hewitt
Mrs Jan Hewlett
Mr James Heyes
Mr Richard Hibbert
Ms Johanna Hickey
Mr David Hicks
Mr R Hicks
Mrs M Higham
Mr Jonathan Hiley
Mr Kelvin Hill
Miss Marion Hill
Mr Richard Hill
Mr Ronald Hill
Mr Eddie Hillion
Ms Julie Hillman
Mr Matt Hines
Mr J J Hoare
Mr Nick Hobbs
Mr Alan Hobson
Mr John Hobson
Mr Peter Hodge
Mr Tim Hodge
Ms Debbie Hodges
Miss Sarah Hodgetts
Ms Julie Hogg
Mr John Holder
Dr P K Holland
Dr Rob Hollingworth
Mr Mark Hollinsworth
Mr Ryan Holm
Mr Andy Holmes
Mr Robert Holmes
Mrs Jenny Holter
Mr Ray Hooper
Mr M S Hooper
Ms Rachel Hopkins
Mr Rob Hopkins
Dr R Horrocks
Mrs Christine Horsley
Mr Richard Horton
Mrs Diana Housley
Mr A M Howard
Mr G N Howard
Miss Heather Howes

Mrs A V Howett
Mr Graham Howie
Mr Anthony Hozier
Mr Alan Hubbard
Mr Graham Huckstepp
Mr Alan Hudson
Mr James Hudson
Miss Joanna Hudson
Mr S Huggins
Mr Neil Hughes
Mr C Hull
Mrs Jacqui Humphreys
Mr Richard Humphreys
Mr Robert Humphreys
Mr Alan Hunt
Mr David Hunt
Mr Geoff Hunt
Mr Marcus Hunt
Mr Mark Hunt
Mrs Nicola Hunt
Mr Stephen Hunt
Mrs Belinda Hunter
Ms Frances Hurst
Mr R A Husband
Mr Kevin Huscroft
Mr Edward Hutchings
Mr J V P Hutchins
Mr David Hutley
Mr Colin Hyde
Mrs S Hyde
Mr Philip Hynes
Mr Michael Ilett
Mr Marshall Iliff
Mr J B Ingham
Mrs Susan Ingle
Mr Roy Ingleston
Mrs Ruth Iredale
Mrs Elizabeth Irwin
Mr Andrew Jackson
Mr Ian Jackson
Mr John Jackson
Mr John Jackson
Mr Robert Jackson
Miss Sally Jacobs
Mr David James
Mr Garry James
Mr Gary James
Sir Jeffrey James
Mr Paul James
Miss A C James
Ms Sue Jarrett
Mr Kevin Mark Jarvis
Miss Vanessa Jeffs
Mr Joshua Jenkins Shaw
Mrs Janet Jennings
Miss Rachel Jennings
Mrs Sally Jennings
Mr Colin Jervis
JNCC Seabird Data

Mr David Jobbins
Mr Graham John
Mr Kevin Johns
Mr Lee Johnson
Ms Liz Johnson
Mr Michael Johnson
Mr Philip Johnson
Mr Stuart Johnson
Miss Phillipa Johnston
Mr Barry Jones
Mr Barry Jones
Mr Ceri Jones
Mr Chris Jones
Dr Edward Jones
Miss Eleanor Jones
Mr Ethan Jones
Mr Glenn Jones
Mr Ian Jones
Mr Meurig Jones
Mr Peter Jones
Mr Philip Jones
Mr Richard Jones
Mr Roger Jones
Miss Rosy Jones
Mr Sam Jones
Miss Trudy Jones
Miss Valerie Jones
Mr P D Jones
Mr Daniel Jordan
Mr Jaroslav Jordan
Mr Martin Jordan
Ms Tania Joyce
Mr Charles Joynson
Mr Derek Julian
Dr Sonia Jupp
Mr C R Jupp
Mr K W S Kane
Ms Jacqui Katze
Mr Thomas Kearney
Dr Michael Keates
Mrs Julia Keddie
Ms Sheelagh Keddie
Mr Peter Keeble
Mr G H Keeble
Mrs C Hristine Keen
Mr Andrew Kellett
Mr Neil Kemp
Miss Tracie Kemp
Mr A D Kennelly
Mr David Kennett
Kent Ornithological Society
Mr George Kernahan
Mr Bruce Kerr
Mrs Virginia Kerridge
Miss Claire Kerry
Miss Rebecca Kessock-Philip
Mr M M Kettell
Mr Ron Kettle
Miss Nicole Khan

Mr Ian Kightley
Mr Robert Kilby
Dr David King
Mr David King
Mrs Jane King
Mr J King
Mr M King
Mr Melvyn Kirby
Mr G R Kirk
Mr John Kirkman
Mr Stephen Kitchen
Mr Roger Kitchener
Dr P Kitchener
Mr Thomas Kittle
Mrs Christine Knight
Mr David Knight
Mr Graham Knight
Mr A R Knight
Mr Simon Knott
Mr Peter Knox
Ms E M Kondla
Mr John Kornjaca
Mr Derek Kortlandt
Mr Kenneth Kyllo
Mrs Marina Kyriacou
Ms Tajinder Lachhar
Mr Chris Lamsdell
Mr Richard Langley
Dr R H W Langston
Ms Patricia Lathey
Mr L W Lawes
Miss Alison Lawrance
Mrs Eleanor Lawrence
Mr John Lawrence
Mr Andrew Lawson
Mr Marcus Lawson
Mr Peter Lawton
Sir J H Lawton
Mrs Sheila Lay
Mr A R Layfield
Mrs Helen Layton
Mr Jordan Layton
Mr John Le Gassick
Mr Derek Lea
Miss Helen Leach
Mr Nicholas Leahy
Mr E J Leahy
Mr Alan Lean
Mrs Karen Ledgerton
Mr David Lee
Dr Philip Lee
Mr Richard Lee
Mr Emerson Leerjet
Mr Niall Leighton
Dr Brian Lennox
Mrs Avril Leonard
Mr Stuart Leslie
Mr Jonathan Lethbridge
Mr Gareth Lewis

Mr Paul Lewis
Dr G H Lewis
Mr S J Lewis
Mrs Ann Lidington
Ms Christine Lindsay
Reverend Frederick Linn
Mrs Angela Linnell
Mr Roger Little
Mrs Jane Lobstein
Miss Diana Lockton
Mr Carey Lodge
Mr Martin Longhurst
Mrs Janet Longley
Mrs Anthea Lovatt
Mr Anthony Lovegrove
Mrs Jane Lowe
Dr D P J Lowman
Ms Alison Lowton
Mr William Luckhurst
Mrs Kathryn Ludlow
Mr Neil Lukes
Mr Jeremy Lunn
Miss Zoe Lyons
Mr Andy Mabbett
Mr Ben Macdonald
Mr Matthew Macfadyen
Mr Mel Mackinnon
Mrs Frankie Macrow
Miss Kathleen Maddams
Mrs Jean Maginn
Dr Nathalie Mahieu
Ms Sam Main
Ms Sue Malcom
Miss Helen Mandley
Mr David Manger
Mr T Manning
Mrs Frances Manthos
Mr Andrew Manwaring
Mr Alun March
Mr John Marchant
Mrs Anna Marett
Mrs Emma Margrave
Mr Nick Marriner
Mr Richard Marsh
Mr Stephen Marsh
Mr Robert Marshall
Mr Stephen Marshall
Dr Adrian Martin
Mrs Ellen Martin
Mr Jeff Martin
Mr John Martin
Mr Jonathan Martin
Dr Keith Martin
Mr Lindsay Martin
Mr Peter Martin
Mr Bob Martinelli
Mr John Maskell
Mrs Carole Mason
Professor Chris Mason

Mr Nick Mason
Mrs Pamela Mason
Ms Sheila Mason
Mr Alex Massey
Miss Anna Mathias
Mr Cliff Matthews
Mr Daniel Matthews
Mrs J Matthews
Mr Clive Maxwell
Mr Philip May
Mr R May
Mr E B Mayer
Mr Dave Mayfield
Mr Robert Mcallister
Mr Jack McArdle
Mr Billy Mcaree
Mr Stephen Mcavoy
Dr David Mcbeth
Mrs Laura McBrien
Mr Bernard Mccabe
Mr Martin McCleary
Mr Ian McCulloch
Mr Angus McCullough
Mr Conor Mcelhinney
Mr Brian McGhie
Miss Katy McGilvray
Mr Marco McGinty
Mr Paraig Mcgovern
Dr Alistair McGowan
Mr James Mcinerney
Mr Neal Mckenna
Mr Mark Mckenzie
Mrs Pauline Lloyd
Ms Pat Mckeown
Ms Catherine Mclaughlin
Ms Pam McLeod
Mrs E K McMahon
Mr Mark Mcmanus
Mr David Mcnee
Mr John McSweeney
Mr Derek McWalter
Mr Gary Mead
Mr David Melville
Mr Stephen Menzie
Miss Florence Mercer
Mr Andrew Merritt
Mr Craig Messenger
Mr Scully Michael
Mr A Middleton
Mr Richard Middleton
Mr Stephen Middleton
Mrs Pauline Midwinter
Mr C Miers
Miss Kate Miles
Lord Stephen Miles
Mr Andrew Millar
Mr John Millar
Ms Lorraine Miller
Mrs Myra Miller

Mr Nicholas Miller
Mr H J Miller
Miss Jenny Mills
Mrs Sarah Mills
Mrs Helen Milne
Mr Chris Miskimmin
Ms Elaine Mitchell
Mr John Mitchell
Mr Melvyn Mitchell
Mr Lorn Money
Mr David Montier
Mrs Jane Moody
Mr Andrew Moon
Mr Christopher Moore
Ms Hilary Moore
Miss Pamela Moore
Dr P D Moore
Mr P W Moore
Dr R C Moore
Mr Richard Moores
Mr Nick Moran
Mrs Sally Morgan
Mr Glenn Morris
Mr Paul Morris
Mr David Morrison
Mr Roger Morton
Mr Robert Moss
Mr Keir Mottram
Mr Tom Moulton
Mr Tony Moverley
Mr Paul Mulcahy
Mr Vic Mummery
Mr Clive Murgatroyd
Mrs Margaret Murphy
Miss Michele Murphy
Mr Neil Murphy
Mr Alan Murray
Mr John Murray
Mr A J Murray
Mrs Nicki Murtagh
Dr Andy Musgrove
Mr David Mutters
Mr R Myatt
Mrs Di Napier
Mr Richard Nash
Mr John Neal
Mr W D Neate
Miss Kaitlin Neeson
Mr Edward Neller
Mr M J Netherwood
Mr Peter Newbound
Mr Ken Newman
Mr Peter Newmark
Mr Des Newton
Mr Bruce Nicholls
Dr Peter Nicholls
Mr Andrew Nichols
Mr Steven Nichols
Mrs Alison Nicholson

Mrs Helen Nicholson
Mr Jim Nicholson
Mr W A Nicoll
Mr Joshua Nightingale
Miss Lucy Nixon
Mrs Jane Noakes
Mr Brian Nobbs
Mr Kenneth Noble
Mr S D Noble
Mrs Jo Norman
Mr Derek Norris
Mr Martin Norris
Mr Stephen North
Mr Peter Northcote
Mr Alan Nottage
Mr John Nundy
Mr Gavin Ó Sé
Mr Mike Oakland
Mr John Oakley
Mr Darren Oakley-Martin
Mr Darren Oakley-Martin
Mr Steve Oates
Dr Paula O'Donnell
Mr Ian Offer
Mr Colm O'Flynn
Mr Peter Ogden
Mr J O'Hanlon
Mr Peter Oliver
Mr Craig Omus
Mr M J Orchard
Mr Patrick Orme
Mr Stephen Ormondroyd
Mr Duncan Orr-Ewing
Mr Geoffrey Orton
Mr Terry Osborn
Mr P Osborn
Miss Beryl Osborne
Mr Graham Osborne
Mr Graham Osborne
Mr John Osmond
Mr G H C Ottley
Mr Doug Owen
Mr E Owen
Miss Susan Oxlade
Mr Roy Page
Ms Dawn Painter
Mr Kieron Palmer
Mr Matthew Palmer
Mr Rchard Palmer
Ms Samira Pandor
Mr Simon Papps
Miss Claire Parfrey
Dr Nicole Parish
Mr J C Parish
Ms Teresa Parker
Mr S J Parker
Mr David Parkinson
Mr Paul Parmenter
Mr Martin Parr

Dr Charles Parry
Mr Keith Parry
Dr M Parry
Mr Shailesh Patel
Rev Nigel Paterson
Mr Sandy Paterson
Mr Stephen Patmore
Mr Allan Payne
Mrs Anita Payne
Mr David Payne
Ms Kirsty Payne
Mr Adrian Pearce
Mr Gary Pearce
Mr Kelvin Pearce
Mr Steven Pearce
Mr Mark Pearson
Mr Roger Peart
Miss Hannah Peck
Mr Ronald Peck
Mr Robert Pedder
Mr Alan Pedliham
Mr Chris Peers
Mr Robert Pell
Dr Theresa Pell
Dr Chris Pendlebury
Mrs Angela Pennock
Mr Andy Pepper
Mr P Peretti
Mr Samuel Perfect
Miss Lorraine Perry
Miss Helen Perryman
Ms Scheherazade Pesante-
    Mullis
Mrs Liz Ann Petch
Mr Jeremy Peters
Ms Jacky Pett
Mrs Christine Phelps
Mr Roy Phillips
Mr Vernon Phillpot
Mr R H Pickering
Mr Gordon Pickett
Mr Robert Pickett
Mr S Piotrowski
Mr Adrian Platt
Ms Debbie Pledge
Ms Alison Plumridge
Ms Helena Poldervaart
Mr Clive Poole
Mrs Elizabeth Popham
Dr Robert Pople
Mr Stephen Posen
Mr Stephen Posen
Mrs Mary Poulton
Mr John Powell
Mr Duncan Poyser
Ms Cathy Preece
Mr Jonathan Preston
Ms Gillian Price
Mr Neil Price

Mrs Pat Pridham
Mrs Joanna Priestnall
Mr Simon Priestnall
Miss Holly Pringle
Ms Anne Pringle Davies
Mr Malcolm Prior
Mr William Prior
Mr David Pritchard
Mrs J S Pritchard
Dr A D Prowse
Mr Robert Putnam
Mr M Puxley
Mr Rupert Pyrah
Mrs Lynne Queisser
Mr A Quinn
Mr Rob Rackliffe
Mrs Sue Radford
Rainham Rspb
Mr Ian Ramsay
Miss Nicky Ranger
Dr Graham Rankin
Dr Neil Rawlings
Mrs Esther Rawlinson
Mr Howard Ray
Ms Catherine Reay
Redbridge Birdwatching
Mr Simon Redwood
Mr Barry Reed
Dr Gareth Rees
Mr Scott Reeves
Mr Andrew Reid
Mrs Jose Relton
Mr Erwyn Rentzenbrink
Mr Graham Richardson
Mrs Gillian Riches
Mr Ollie Richings
Mr Malcolm Riddler
Mr Jonathan Ridge
Mr M J Ridley
Dr Renton Righelato
Dr Christine Riley
Ms Miriam Rinsler
Ms Kate Risely
Mr Michael Rist
Mr John Rivoire
Mr Ivor Roberts
Ms Maria Roberts
Mr Patrick Roberts
Mr William Roberts
Ms Glynis Robertson
Mr Malcolm Robertson
Mr Robert Robertson
Mr Darren Robinson
Mr David Robinson
Mr David Robinson
Miss Louise Robinson
Mr Steven Robinson
Mr Simon Roddis
Ms Joanne Rodwell

Ms Lesley Rogers
Mr Tony Rogers
Mrs Carolyn Roissetter
Miss Julia Rolf
Mr Alan Roman
Mr Ken Rome
Mr Andrew Rooke
Miss Sinead Rooney
Mr Ian Rose
Mr J E Rose
Miss Nathalie Rosin
Mr Chris Ross
Mr Leonard Ross
Mr Nick Rossiter
Mr Derek Rothery
Mr J C Roughton
Mr Martin Routledge
Mr Ian Rowbotham
Dr George Rowing
Mr John Roy
Mr Kevin Roy
RSPB Croydon Local Group
RSPB Dataset (GENERAL)
Mr Barry Ruck
Mr David Rugg
Miss Linda Runham
Miss Fiona Rusbridge
Mr Mark Ruscoe
Mr Steve Rush
Mrs Claire Rushton
Mr John Ruskin
Ms Louise Russell
Mr Mark Russell
Mr Mike Russell
Mr P J Rutt
Dr Colin Ryall
Mr Kevin Ryan
Miss Clare Ryland
Mr Kevin Rylands
Mr Christopher Rymer
Mr D G Salmon
Mrs Delwen Samuel
Mr J R Samuel
Mr Roy Sanderson
Mrs Linda Sank
Mr Neil Santy
Ms Linda Sargent
Mr Stephen Saunders
Mr D Saunders
Mr Gavin Saville
Mr Vince Scannella
Mr Gunter Scheller
Mr M J Schickner
Ms Nathalie Schorbon
Mr Stuart Scott
Mr M Scott-Ham
Mr Terry Seabrook
Mrs Joan Seale
Mr Richard Seargent

Mr John Seaton
Mrs Bronya Seifert
Mr Andrew Self
Mr Michael Sell
Mr Barrie Senior
Dr Margaret Shackell
Mrs T E Shailer
Mr Thomas Shannon
Miss Kathy Sharman
Mr Mark Sharpe
Mr Marc Shaw
Mr C I Shaw
Mr Kevin Shea
Mr Alan Shearman
Mr Andrew Sheerin
Ms Diana Shelley
Mrs Lorraine Shelley
Dr Jane Shemilt
Mr Martin Shepherd
Mr C N Shepherdson
Mr Mel Shepherd-Wells
Mrs Amanda Sherwood
Mr Thomas Shields
Mr Ewan M Shilland
Mr Robin Shrubsole
Mr Stephen Shutt
Mrs J M Sibson
Mr Steven Simmonds
Mr Cyril Simmons
Mr Oliver Simms
Dr Michael Simons
Mr Brian Simpson
Ms Charlotte Simpson
Mr Christopher Sims
Ms Mary Sims
Miss Chantil Sinclair
Mr David Sinclair
Mr Peter Sketch
Mr Leigh Skilton
Mr Andrew Skotnicki
Dr Jeremy Smallwood
Ms Corinna Smart
Mr Peter Smart
Mrs Sally Smart
Mr Mark Smedley
Mr David Smith
Mr Graham Smith
Dr Graham Smith
Miss Gwendolen Smith
Mr Ivor Smith
Mr Jim Smith
Mr Keith Smith
Ms Laura Smith
Mr Martin Smith
Mr Max Smith
Mr Mike Smith
Mrs Sue Smith
Mr Tom Smith
Mr Wilfred L Smith

Mrs Yvonne Smith
Dr K W Smith
Mr P A Smith
Mr R E Smith
Mr Steve Smithee
Mr P A C Smout
Miss Jodie Southgate
Ms Janet Southwood
Mr T S Spall
Mr Derek Sparkes
Miss Jade Spence
Mr Paul Spencer
Mr Robert Spencer
Mrs Judith Spicer
Mr Michael Spittles
Mr S J Spooner
Dr David Spratt
Dr Chris Spray
Prof Christopher Spry
Ms Barbara Squire
Mr Martin Sreeves
Mrs I A Stachnicki
Mr Tim Stainton
Mr Bill Stallard
Mr Andrew Stanger
Ms Jennifer Stanley
Mr M P Stanyer
Ms Sharonina Star
Dr Jennifer Steel
Mr Martin Stevens
Mr Paul Stevens
Mr Thomas Stevenson
Miss Ann Steventon
Mr Les Steward
Mr Gavin Stewart
Mr Graeme Stewart
Mr Ken Stewart
Ms Annemarie Stiegler
Mr Colin Stanley Stinton
Mr Brian Stone
Mr Peter Stoppard
Mr James Storrar
Mr Ashley Stow
Mr Alf Strange
Mr Peter Strangeman
Mr Paul Stretch
Mrs Anna Stribley
Mr R F Stuckey
Mr Ian Sturgess
Mr Martin Sullivan
Dr Malcolm Summers
Mr Neil Sumner
Surbiton and District Bird
    Watching Soc
Mr Paul Sutton
Mr J L Swallow
Mrs Jane Swann White
Mr Owen Sweeney
Mr Owen Sweeney

Mr Anthony Sweetland
Mr Robert Swift
Mr W Swinglehurst
Mr Szymon Szary
Ms Chooi-Leng Tan
Mr Karl Tarratt
Miss Sarah Tash
Mr Mark Tasker
Mrs Beth Taylor
Miss Carole Taylor
Mr Ian Taylor
Mr Ian Taylor
Ms Jean Taylor
Miss Kerry Taylor
Ms Marci Taylor
Mr Roger Taylor
Mrs Tessa Taylor
Ms Penny Taylor-Pearce
Mr Jim Terry
Miss Susan Thairs
Mr Brian Theakston
Mr Roger Theobald
Mrs Andrea Thomas
Mr Andrew Thomas
Mr Brian Thomas
Mr Julian Thomas
Miss Kelly Thomas
Mr Malcolm Thomas
Mr Ernest Thomason
Mr Clive Thompson
Mr Ian Thompson
Mrs Joan Thompson
Mrs Emma Thomsen
Miss Maxine Timmis
Mr Neil Timms
Mr Trevor Tinlin
Mr Ralph Todd
Mr A B Tomczynski
Mr Richard Tomlin
Mr Alan Tomlinson
Mr Mike Toms
Mr Andy Tongue
Mrs Kate Towler
Mr Andrew Townsend
Mr Ben Tragett
Mr Ken Travers
Mr Ian Traynor
Mr Paul Treen
Mr Paul Tregenza
Mr Simon Trenerry
Mr Peter Trew
Mr Charles Trollope
Mr Neil Trout
Mr Freddy Try
Mr Mike Tubb
Mr Raymond Tuck
Mr Ray Tucker
Mr Simon Tucker
Mr K Tucker

Mr David Turner
Mr Derek Turner
Mr Turner
Mr Raymond Turner
Mr Mike Turton
Mr Sash Tusa
Mr Derek Tutt
Mr Glenn Tutton
Mr Gary Twells
Mr Gordon Twinberrow
Mr David Tyler
Mr Peter Tyler
Mr Adrian Tysoe
Mr Brian Unwin
Mr Nick Unwin
Mr Jeff Upex
Mr Michael Upstone
Mr Brian Utton
Mr John Vallas
Mr Nicolaas Van Der Veen
Mr Tim Vaughan
Mr Hugh Venables
Dr David Venters
Mr Graham Vine
Mrs Kim Visocchi
Miss Kathy Vivian
Ms Anne Waite
Mr Robert Wakelam
Mr Marek Walford
Mr Stuart Walker
Mr Trevor Walker
Mrs Vaila Walker
Ms Michelle Wallington
Mr Richard Wallis
Mr Chris Walsh
Mrs Laura Walsh
Mr Lee Walther
Dr Oliver Walton
Mr Dave Warburton
Mr Clive Ward
Mr Keith R A Ward
Dr Stephen Ward
Mr John Warren
Mr Roger Warren
Mrs Maggie & Derek
    Washington
Mr David Waters
Mrs Janet Waters
Mrs Linda Waterworth
Dr Daphne Watson
Mr John Watson
Mr Michael Watson
Mr Nigel Watson
Mr Peter Watson
Mr Robert Watson
Mr Geoffrey Watt
Mr Iain Watt
Mr Patrick Watters
Dr D Wawman

Mr Richard Webb
Mr Stephen Webb
Mr Steve Webb
Mr William Webb
Mr Christopher Webster
Ms Jackie Wedd
Mr D J Wedd
Mrs H J Wellard
Mr John Wells
Mr Tom Wells
Miss Ann West
Mr Carl West
Mr Clive West
Mrs Jan West
Mr Robin West
Mr Samuel West
Miss Sarah West
Mr Andrew Westwood
Ms Jamian Wetlaufer
Mr Jeffery Wheatley
Mrs Jo Wheeler
Mr Gary Whelan
Mr Mark Whitaker
Mrs Helen Whitall
Mr Bernard White
Mr Chris White
Mr Ken White
Mr Michael White
Mr Richard White
Mr Samuel White
Mrs Sarah White
Mr J R White
Mr Stephen Whitehead
Mr Adam Whitehouse
Dr David Whitehouse
Mr Andrew Whitfield
Mrs Janet Whitfield
Mr Andrew Whitney
Mr Matt Whittle
Mr Christopher Whyte
Mr Rory Whytock
Mr Christopher Wicks
Mr J P Widgery
Mr Simon Wightman
Mr Jan Wilczur
Mr P J Wild
Ms Val Wilders
Mr Tony Wileman
Mr Philip Wilkins
Mr David Wilkinson
Mr David Wilkinson
Mr Tony Wilkinson
Mr James Willett
Mr Shaun Willett
Mr Alan Williams
Mr Andy Williams
Dr Anne Williams
Mr Boyd Williams
Mr Charles Williams

Prof Ingrid Williams
Mrs Penny Williams
Dr Richard Williams
Mr Robert Williams
Ms Rosie Williams
Mr G Williams
Mr John Williamson
Mr C S Williamson
Mr Nigel Willits
Mr David Wills
Mr Adam Wilson
Mr Brian Wilson
Mr Colin Wilson
Mrs Gill Wilson
Mr Ian Wilson
Mrs Deborah Wiltshire
Mr Ian Wiltshire
Mr Alan Wingrove
Mr Mark Wingrove
Mr Alan Winn
Mr Richard Winston
Mrs L K Wiseman
Mrs Tina Wishart
Mr Antony Witts
Ms Estelle Wolfers
Mr Andrew Wood
Mr Steve Wood
Mr Terence Wood
Mr S D Wood
Mr Christopher Woodham
Mr Roger Woods
Mr A E L Woods
Mr Ian Woodward
Mr Roy Woodward
Dr J K A Woodward
Mr David Wooldridge
Mrs Jenni Workman
Miss Lynsey Wrigglesworth
Mr Barry Wright
Ms Karen Wright
Mr Tim Wright
Mr G Wright
Mr M R Wright
Mr Max Wurr
Ms Clare Wyatt
Ms Freda Wyn
Mr Stephen Yates
Mr Geoffrey Young
Mr Ian Young
Mr John Young
Mr John Young
Mr John Young
Mr D Younger
Mr Elisha Zadok
Mrs Fiona Zobole

References

Common references

Shortened referencing conventions are used for frequently used references, as listed below, including the previous London Atlases, the Birds of London and various BTO publications and reference sources. Note also that any references to the 'first atlas' in the species accounts refer to Montier, and any references to the 'second atlas' refer to Hewlett *et al.*:

'BBS': Harris, S.J., Massimino, D., Newson, S.E., Eaton, M.A., Balmer, D.E., Noble, D.G., Musgrove, A.J., Gillings, S., Proctor, D. & Pearce-Higgins, J.W. (2015) *The Breeding Bird Survey 2014. BTO Research Report 673*. British Trust for Ornithology, Thetford.

'BirdLife': BirdLife International (2016/2017) IUCN Red List for birds. (Viewed on http://www.birdlife.org between October 2016 and February 2017).

'BirdTrends': Robinson, R.A., Marchant, J.H., Leech, D.I., Massimino, D., Sullivan, M.J.P., Eglington, S.M., Barimore, C., Dadam, D., Downie, I.S., Hammond, M.J., Harris, S.J., Noble, D.G., Walker, R.H. & Baillie, S.R. (2015) *BirdTrends 2015: trends in numbers, breeding success and survival for UK breeding birds. Research Report 678*. British Trust for Ornithology, Thetford.

'Hewlett *et al.*': Hewlett, J. (Ed) (2002) *The Breeding Birds of the London Area*. London Natural History Society. London.

'LBR': London Bird Report.

'Montier': Montier, D (Ed) for the London Natural History Society (1977) *Atlas of Breeding Birds of the London Area*. B.T. Batsford Ltd. London.

'National Atlas': Balmer, D.E., Gillings, S., Caffrey, B.J., Swann, R.L., Downie, I.S., & Fuller, R.J. (2013) *Bird Atlas 2007–11: the breeding and wintering birds of Britain & Ireland*. BTO Books, Thetford.

'Migration Atlas': Wernham, C., Toms, M., Marchant, J., Clark, J., Siriwardena, G & Baillie, S. (2002) *The Migration Atlas: movements of the birds of Britain & Ireland. T & A.D.* Poyser. London.

'Self': Self (2014) *The Birds of London*. Bloomsbury Publishing. London.

'WeBS': Frost, T.M., Austin, G.E., Calbrade, N.A., Holt, C.A., Mellan, H.J., Hearn, R.D., Stroud, D.A., Wotton, S.R. & Balmer, D.E. (2016) Waterbirds in the UK 2014/15: The Wetland Bird Survey. BTO/RSPB/JNCC. Thetford. www.bto.org/volunteer-surveys/webs/publications/webs-annual-report.

Full Reference List

Addinall, S. G. (2010) 'Amur Wagtail' in County Durham: New to Britain and the Western Palearctic. *British Birds*, **103**, 260.

Aebischer, NJ (2013) The National Gamebag Census: released game species. *Game Conservancy Annual Review*, **44**, 34–37.

Alisauskas, R.T., Klass, E.E., Hobson, K.A. & Ankney, C.D. (1998) Stable-Carbon isotopes support use of adventitious color to discern winter origins of Lesser Snow Geese. Journal of Field Ornithology, **69**, 262–268.

Baker, D. J., Freeman, S. N., Grice, P. V. & Siriwardena, G. M. (2012) Landscape-scale responses of birds to agri-environment management: a test of the English Environmental Stewardship scheme. *Journal of Applied Ecology*, **49**, 871–882.

Balmer, D.E., Gillings, S., Caffrey, B.J., Swann, R.L., Downie, I.S., & Fuller, R.J. (2013) *Bird Atlas 2007–11: the breeding and wintering birds of Britain & Ireland*. BTO Books, Thetford.

Banks, A. N., Burton, N. H. K., Calladine, J. R., & Austin, G. E. (2007) *Winter Gulls in the UK: Population Estimates from the 2003/04-2005/06 Winter Gulls Roost Survey*. British Trust for Ornithology.

BBS [Breeding Bird Survey]: Harris, S.J., Massimino, D., Newson, S.E., Eaton, M.A., Balmer, D.E., Noble, D.G., Musgrove, A.J., Gillings, S., Proctor, D. & Pearce-Higgins, J.W. (2015) *The Breeding Bird Survey 2014. BTO Research Report 673*. British Trust for Ornithology, Thetford (See Common References).

BirdLife: BirdLife International (2016/2017) IUCN Red List for birds. (Viewed on http://www.birdlife.org October 2016 to February 2017) (see Common References).

BirdLife International (2004) *Birds in Europe: population estimates, trends and conservation status*. BirdLife International, Cambridge, U.K.

BirdTrends: Robinson, R.A., Marchant, J.H., Leech, D.I., Massimino, D., Sullivan, M.J.P., Eglington, S.M., Barimore, C., Dadam, D., Downie, I.S., Hammond, M.J., Harris, S.J., Noble, D.G., Walker, R.H. & Baillie, S.R. (2015) *BirdTrends 2015: trends in numbers, breeding success and survival for UK breeding birds. Research Report 678*. BTO, Thetford (see Common References).

Black, J.M., Prop, J. & Larsson, K. (2014) *The Barnacle Goose*. T & A D Poyser. London.

Bond, G., Burnside, N. G., Metcalfe, D. J., Scott, D. M., & Blamire, J. (2005) The effects of land-use and landscape structure on barn owl (*Tyto alba*) breeding success in southern England, UK. *Landscape ecology*, **20**, 555–566.

BOU [British Ornithologist's Union] (2013) The British List: A checklist of Birds of Britain (8th Edition). *Ibis*, **155**, 635-676.

Bowlt, C. (2008) London's Missing Starlings. *London's Changing Natural History*, 27–28, London Natural History Society, London.

Bright, J.A., Morris, A.J., Field, R.H., Cooke, A.I., Grice, P.V., Walker, L.K., Fern, J. & Peach, W.J. (2015) Higher-tier agri-environment scheme enhances breeding densities of some priority farmland birds in England. *Agriculture, Ecosystems & Environment*, 203, 69–79.

Broughton, R.K., Hill, R.A., Bellamy, P.E. & Hinsley, S.A. (2010) Dispersal, ranging and settling behaviour of Marsh Tits *Poecile palustris* in a fragmented landscape in lowland England. *Bird Study*, **57**, 458–472.

Brown, A. & Grice, P. (2005) *Birds in England*. T. & A.D. Poyser, London.

Cadbury, C.J. & Olney, P.J.S. (1978) Avocet population dynamics in England. *British Birds*, **71**, 102–121.

Chamberlain, D., Gough, S., Vaughan, H., Appleton, G., Freeman, S, Toms, M., Vickery, J. & Noble, D. (2005) *The London Bird Project. BTO Research Report 384. A report to the Bridge House Estates Trust*. BTO, Thetford.

Chandler, R. J. (1979) Two urban pied wagtail roosts. *British Birds*, **72**, 299–313.

Chiron, F. & Julliard, R. (2007) Responses of Songbirds to Magpie Reduction in an Urban Habitat. *Journal of Wildlife Management*, **71**, 2624–2631.

Clark, J.M. & Eyre, J. (2012) Dartford Warblers on the Thames Basin and Wealden Heaths. *British Birds*, **105**, 308–317.

Clements, R. (2012) A UK population estimate for the Hawfinch. *British Birds*, **106**, 43–44.

Cramp, S. & Teagle, W.G. (1952a) A Bird Census of St. James's Park and the Green Park, 1949–50. *London Bird Report No. 15 for the year 1950*, 48–52.

Cramp, S. & Teagle, W.G. (1952b) The Birds of Inner London 1900–1950. *British Birds*, **45**, 433–456.

Crick, H.Q.P., Robinson, R.A., Appleton, G.F., Clark, N.A. & Rickard, A.D. (eds). (2002) *Investigations into the causes of the decline of Starlings and House Sparrows in Great Britain. BTO Research Report 290*. Defra. Bristol.

Dawson, D. & Gittings, T. (1990) *The effect of suburban residential density on birds*. London Ecology Unit, London.

De Laet, J., & Summers-Smith, J. D. (2007) The status of the urban house sparrow *Passer domesticus* in north-western Europe: a review. *Journal of Ornithology*, **148**, 275–278.

Defra (2015) Wild Bird Populations in the UK, 1970 to 2014. Annual Statistical Release. 25 October 2015. www.gov.uk/government/statistics/wild-bird-populations-in-the-uk; viewed on 01/10/2016.

Dougall, T. W. (1991) Winter distribution and associated movements of northern Pied Wagtails *Motacilla alba yarrellii*, as shown by ringing. *Ringing & Migration*, **12**, 1–15.

Drewitt, E. (2014) *Urban Peregrines*. Pelagic Publishing, Exeter.

Drewitt, E. J. A. and Dixon, N. (2008) Diet and prey selection of urban-dwelling Peregrine Falcons in southwest England. *British Birds*, **101**, 58–67.

Eaton, M., Aebischer, N., Brown, A., Hearn, R., Lock, L., Musgrove, A., Noble, D., Stroud, D. & Gregory, R. (2015) Birds of Conservation Concern 4: the population status of birds in the UK, Channel Islands and Isle of Man. *British Birds*, **108**, 708–746.

Eglington, S. M., Davis, S. E., Joys, A. C., Chamberlain, D. E., & Noble, D. G. (2010) The effect of observer experience on English Breeding Bird Survey population trends. *Bird Study*, **57**, 129–141.

Evans, I.M., Summers, R.W., O'Toole, L., Orr-Ewing, D.C., Evans, R., Snell N. & Smith, J. (1999) Evaluating the success of translocating Red Kites *Milvus milvus* to the UK. *Bird Study*, **46**, 129–144.

Fitter, R.S.R. (1943) The Starling roosts of the London Area. *London Naturalist*, **22**, 3–23.

Fitter, R.S.R. (1949) *London's Birds*. Collins. London.

Frost, T.M., Austin, G.E., Calbrade, N.A., Holt, C.A., Mellan, H.J., Hearn, R.D., Stroud, D.A., Wotton, S.R. and Balmer, D.E. (2016) *Waterbirds in the UK 2014/15: The Wetland Bird Survey*. BTO/RSPB/JNCC. Thetford. http://www.bto.org/volunteer-surveys/webs/publications/webs-annual-report

Fuller, R.J., Noble, D.G., Smith, K.W. & Vanhinsbergh, D. (2005) Recent declines in populations of woodland birds in Britain: a review of possible causes. *British Birds*, **98**, 116–143.

Gibbons, D.W, Reid, J.B. & Chapman, R.A. (1993) *The New Atlas of Breeding Birds in Britain and Ireland: 1988–1991*. T. & A.D. Poyser, London.

Gilbert, G. (2012) Grasshopper Warbler *Locustella naevia* breeding habitat in Britain. *Bird Study*, **59**, 303–314.

Gillings, S. & Newson, S.E. (2005) Winter availability of cereal stubbles attracts declining farmland birds and positively influences breeding population trends. *Proceedings of the Royal Society B.*, **272**, 1564.

GLA (2004) *The London Plan: Spatial Development Strategy for Greater London*. Greater London Authority. February 2004.

GLA (2005a) *Crazy paving: The environmental importance of London's front gardens*. Greater London Authority Environment Committee. September 2005.

GLA (2005b) *Dereliction of duty? A report on brownfield development in London*. Greater London Authority Environment Committee. November 2005.

GLA (2008) *Living Roofs and Walls. Technical Report: Supporting London Plan Policy*. Greater London Authority. February 2008.

GLA (2016) *The London Plan. The Spatial Development Strategy for London consolidated with alterations since 2011. Greater London Authority. March 2016.* [An overview of the plan in 2016]. The full plan is now published online at http://www.london.gov.uk/what-we-do/planning/london-plan/current-london-plan (viewed on 11/10/2016).

Gooch, S., Baillie, S.R. and Birkhead, T.R. (1991) Magpie *Pica pica* and Songbird Populations. Retrospective Investigation of Trends in Population Density and Breeding Success. *Journal of Applied Ecology*, **28**, 1068–1086.

Groom, D.W. (1993) Magpie *Pica pica* predation on Blackbird *Turdus merula* nests in urban areas. *Bird Study*, **40**, 55–62.

Hamilton, J.C. (1997) *Kingfishers*. Colin Baxter Photography, Scotland.

Harris, A. (2006) Roosting behaviour of wintering Eurasian Bitterns in the Lee Valley. *British Birds*, **99**, 174–182.

Harrison, C. & Davies, G. (2002) Conserving biodiversity that matters: practitioners' perspectives on brownfield development and urban nature conservation in London. *Journal of Environmental Management*, **65**, 95–108.

Harting, J.E. (1866) *The Birds of Middlesex*. John van Voorst, London

Helbig, A., Berthold, P, Mohr, G. & Querner, U. (1994) Inheritance of a novel migratory direction in central European blackcaps. *Naturwissenschaften*, **81**, 184–186.

Henderson, I (2009) Progress of the UK Ruddy Duck eradication programme. *British Birds*, **102**, 680–690.

Henderson, I (2013) UK Ruddy Duck Eradication Programme. http://www.rinse-europe.eu/assets/_files/bestpracticepresentation_ruddyduck.pdf. (Viewed 27/06/2016).

Heward, C.J., Hoodless, A.N., Conway, C.J., Aebischer, N.J., Gillings, S. & Fuller, R.J. (2015) Current status and recent trend of the Eurasian Woodcock Scolopax rusticola as a breeding bird in Britain. *Bird Study*, **62**, 535–551.

Hewlett *et al.*: Hewlett, J. (Ed) (2002) *The Breeding Birds of the London Area*. London Natural History Society. London. (See Common References).

Hewson, C.M., Amar, A., Lindsell, J.A., Thewlis, R.M., Butler, S., Smith, K. & Fuller, R.J. (2007) Recent changes in bird populations in British broadleaved woodland. *Ibis*, **149**, 14–28.

Hewson, C.M., Thorup, K., Pearce-Higgins, J.W. & Atkinson, P.W. (2016) Population decline is linked to migration route in the Common Cuckoo. *Nature Communications*, **7**, 12296.

Holling, M. & RBBP [Rare Breeding Birds Panel] (2011) Rare breeding birds in the United Kingdom in 2009. *British Birds*, **104**, 476–537.

Holling & RBBP [Rare Breeding Birds Panel] (2013) Rare breeding birds in the United Kingdom in 2011. *British Birds*, **106**, 496-554.

Holt, C., Austin, G., Calbrade, N., Mellan, H., Mitchell, C., Stroud, D., Wotton, S. & Musgrove, A. (2012) *Waterbirds in the UK 2010/11: The Wetland Bird Survey*. BTO/RSPB/JNCC, Thetford.

Hudson, R. (1965) The spread of the Collared Dove in Britain and Ireland. *British Birds*, **58**, 105–139.

Hudson, W.H. (1898) *Birds in London*. Longmans Green & Co, London. Reprinted in 1969 by David & Charles Reprints, London.

JNCC [Joint Nature Conservation Committee] (2016) Natura 2000 Standard Data Form. Thames Marshes. http://jncc.defra.gov.uk/pdf/SPA/UK9012021; generated by JNCC 25/01/2016 (viewed 01/10/2016).

LBR [London Bird Report]: See Common References.

Lack, P.C. (1986) *The Atlas of Wintering Birds in Britain and Ireland*. T. & A.D. Poyser, Calton.

Langslow, D. R. (1977) Movements of Black Redstarts between Britain and Europe as related to occurrences at observatories. *Bird Study*, **24**, 169–178.

Langston, R. H. W., Wotton, S. R., Conway, G. J., Wright, L. J., Mallord, J. W., Currie, F. A., Drewitt, A.L., Grice, P.V., Hoccom, D.G. & Symes, N. (2007) Nightjar *Caprimulgus europaeus* and Woodlark *Lullula arborea* - recovering species in Britain?. *Ibis*, **149 (s2)**, 250–260.

Leech, D.I., Crick H.Q.P. & Rehfisch, M.M. (2004) *The effect of climate change on bird species in the UK BTO Research Report 369*. British Trust for Ornithology, Thetford.

Lehikoinen, A, Jaatinen, K., Vähätalo, A.V., Clausen, P., Crowe, O., Deceuninck, B., Hearn, R., Holt, C.A., Hornman, M., Keller, V., Nilsson, L., Langendoen, T., Tománková, I., Wahl, J. & Fox, A.D. (2013) Rapid Climate driven shifts in the centres of gravity of the entire wintering range of three common waterbirds species. *Global Change Biology*, **19**, 2071–2081.

Lewis A.J.G., Amar. A, Charman, E.C. & Stewart, F.R.P. (2009) The decline of the Willow Tit in Britain. *British Birds*, **102**, 386–393.

LNHS [London Natural History Society] (1964) *The Birds of the London Area (Revised Edition)*. Rupert Hart-Davis, London.

Loss, S. R., Will, T., Loss, S. S., & Marra, P. P. (2014) Bird–building collisions in the United States: Estimates of annual mortality and species vulnerability. *The Condor*, **116**, 8–23.

Maclean, I.M.D., Austin, G.E., Rehfisch, M.M., Blew, J., Crowe, O., Delany, S., Devos, K., Deceuninck, B., Gunther, K., Laursen, K., van Roomen, M. & Wahl, J. (2008) Climate change causes rapid changes in the distribution and site abundance of birds in winter. *Global Change Biology*, **14**, 2489–2500.

388

Mayer, E (2014) Swifts – why we must help them survive and thrive. *London Naturalist*, **93**, 23–43. London Natural History Society, London.

Meek, W. R., Burman, P. J., Nowakowski, M., Sparks, T. H., & Burman, N. J. (2003) Barn owl release in lowland southern England—a twenty-one year study. *Biological Conservation*, **109**, 271–282.

Met Office (2016) www.metoffice.gov.uk/climate/uk/interesting/dec2010 (viewed on 19/02/2016).

Migration Atlas: Wernham, C., Toms, M., Marchant, J., Clark, J., Siriwardena, G & Baillie, S. (2002) *The Migration Atlas: movements of the birds of Britain & Ireland*. T & A.D. Poyser. London (see Common References).

Milwright, R. D. P. (2006) Post breeding dispersal, breeding site fidelity and migration/wintering areas of migratory populations of Song Thrush *Turdus philomelos* in the Western Palearctic. *Ringing & Migration*, **23**, 21–32.

Mitchell, P. I., Newton, S. F., Ratcliffe, N., & Dunn, T. E. (2004) *Seabird populations of Britain and Ireland*. T & AD Poyser, London.

Montier: Montier, D (Ed) for the London Natural History Society (1977) Atlas of Breeding Birds of the London Area. B.T. Batsford Ltd. London. (see Common References).

Musgrove, A.J., Austin, G.E., Hearn, R.D., Holt, C.A., Stroud, D.A. & Wotton, S.R. (2011) Overwinter population estimates of British waterbirds. *British Birds*, **104**, 364–397.

Musgrove, A., Aebischer, N., Eaton, M., Hearn, R., Newson, S., Noble, D., Parsons, M., Risely, K. & Stroud, D. (2013) Population estimates of birds in Great Britain and the United Kingdom *British Birds*, **106**, 64–100.

National Atlas: Balmer, D.E., Gillings, S., Caffrey, B.J., Swann, R.L., Downie, I.S., & Fuller, R.J. (2013) *Bird Atlas 2007 –11: the breeding and wintering birds of Britain & Ireland*. BTO Books, Thetford (See Common References).

Newson, S.E., Marchant, J.H., Ekins, G.R. & Sellers, R.M. (2007) The status of inland-breeding Great Cormorants in England. *British Birds*, **100**, 289–299.

Newson, S.E., Johnston, A., Parrott, D. & Leech, D.I. (2011) Evaluating the population-level impact of an invasive species, Ring-necked Parakeet *Psittacula krameri*, on native avifauna. *Ibis*, **153**, 509–516.

Newson, S., Marchant, J., Sellers, R., Ekins, G., Hearn, R. & Burton, N. (2013) Colonisation and range expansion of inland-breeding Cormorants in England. *British Birds*, **106**, 737–743.

Newton, I. (2006) Movement patterns of Common Crossbills *Loxia curvirostra* in Europe. *Ibis*, **148**, 782–788.

Newton, I & Wyllie, I. (1992) Recovery of a sparrowhawk population in relation to declining pesticide contamination, *Journal of Applied Ecology*, **29**, 476–484.

Newton, I., Wyllie, I. & Asher, A. (1991) Mortality causes in British Barn Owls *Tyto alba*, with a discussion of aldrin-dieldrin poisoning. *Ibis*, **133**, 162–169.

Nicholson, E.M. (1995) *Bird-watching in London: a Historical Perspective*. London Natural History Society, London.

O'Connor, R.J. & Mead, C.J. (1984) The Stock Dove in Britain, 1930-1980. *British Birds*, **77**, 181–201.

Oliver, P.J. (1985) Breeding Tufted Ducks in the London Area. *London Bird Report No. 49 for the year 1984*, 104–110.

Oliver, P (2011) The establishment of the Common Buzzard as a breeding species in the London Area. *London Bird Report 72 for the year 2007*, 199–205.

Olsen, K.M. & Larsson, H. (2003) *Gulls of Europe, Asia and North America*. Christopher Helm, London.

Pithon, J.A. & Dytham, C. (2002) Distribution and population development of introduced Ring-necked Parakeets *Psittacula krameri* in Britain between 1983 and 1998. *Bird Study*, **49**, 110–117

Plummer, K.E., Siriwardena, G.M., Conway, G.J., Risely, K. & Toms, M.P. (2015) Is supplementary feeding in gardens a driver of evolutionary change in a migratory bird species? *Global Change Biology*, **21**, 4353–4363.

Raco, M & Henderson, S. (2006) Sustainable urban planning and the brownfield development process in the United Kingdom: lessons from the Thames Gateway. *Local Environment*, **11**, 499–513. http://dx.doi.org/10.1080/13549830600853098

Robinson RA, Lawson, B., Toms MP, Peck KM, Kirkwood JK, Chantrey J, et al. (2010) Emerging Infectious Disease Leads to Rapid Population Declines of Common British Birds. *Plos One* , **5**, e12215.

Ross-Smith, V.H., Robinson, R.A., Banks, A.N., Frayling, T.D., Gibson, C.C. & Clark, J.A. (2014) The Lesser Black-backed Gull *Larus fuscus* in England: how to resolve a conservation conundrum. *Seabird*, **27**, 41–61.

RSPB [Royal Society for the Protection of Birds]/London Biodiversity Partnership (2003) *Where have all the sparrows gone?* Survey Report 2002, updated 2003. RSPB, Sandy, Beds.

Sage. B.L. (1963) The Breeding Distribution of the Tree Sparrow. *London Bird Report No. 27 for the year 1962*, 56–65.

Sanderson, R. (2013) Autumn Bird Counts in Kensington Gardens, 1995–2010. *London Bird Report No. 75 for the year 2010*, 209–215.

Sangster, G., Collinson, J.M., Helbig, A.J., Knox, A.G. & Parkin, D.T. (2005) Taxonomic recommendations for British birds: third report. *Ibis*, **147**, 821–826.

Sauter, A., Korner-Nievergelt, F. & Jenni, L. (2010) Evidence of climate change effects on within-winter movements of European Mallards *Anas platyrhynchos*. *Ibis*, **152**, 600–609.

Self: Self (2014) *The Birds of London*. Bloomsbury Publishing. London (See Common References).

Shaw, L. M., Chamberlain, D., & Evans, M.J. (2008) The House Sparrow *Passer domesticus* in urban areas: reviewing a possible link between post-decline distribution and human socioeconomic status. *Journal of Ornithology*, **149**, 293–299.

Smith, C., Dawson, D., Archer, J., Davies, M., Frith, M., Hughes, E & Massini, P. (2011) *From green to grey; observed changes in garden vegetation structure in London, 1998–2008*. London Wildlife Trust, Greenspace Information for Greater London & Greater London Authority, London.

Smith, K.W., Dee, C.W., Fearnside, J.D. & Ilett, M. (2015) *Birds of Hertfordshire*. Hertfordshire Natural History Society, Welwyn Garden City.

Snow, D.W. & Perrins, C.M. (Eds) (1998) *The Birds of the Western Palearctic. Concise Edition. Volume 2: Passerines*. Oxford University Press, Oxford/New York.

Strubbe, D. and Matthysen, E. (2007) Invasive ring-necked parakeets *Psittacula krameri* in Belgium: habitat selection and impact on native birds. *Ecography*, **30**, 578–588.

Strubbe, D., Matthysen, E. and Graham, C. H. (2010) Assessing the potential impact of invasive ring-necked parakeets *Psittacula krameri* on native nuthatches *Sitta europeae* in Belgium. *Journal of Applied Ecology*, **47**, 549–557.

Summers-Smith, J. D. (2003) The decline of the House Sparrow: a review. *British Birds*, **96**, 439–446.

Thomson, D.L., Green, R.E., Gregory, R.D. & Baillie, S.R. (1998) The widespread declines of songbirds in rural Britain do not correlate with the spread of their avian predators. Proceedings of the Royal Society B, 265, 1410.

Townshend, D.J. (1985) Decisions for a lifetime: establishment of spatial defence and movement patterns by juvenile Grey Plovers Pluvialis squatarola. *Journal of Animal Ecology*, **54**, 267–274.

UKBAP [UK Biodiversity Steering Group] (1995) Biodiversity: The UK Steering Group Report – Volume II: Action Plans: Coastal and Floodplain Grazing Marsh (December 1995, Tranche 1, Vol. 2). Joint Nature Conservation Committee, Peterborough.

Underhill-Day, J. (1998) Breeding Marsh Harriers in the United Kingdom, 1983-95. *British Birds*, **91**, 210–218.

Vincent, K.E. (2005) Investigating the causes of the decline of the urban House Sparrow Passer domesticus population in Britain. PhD Thesis. De Montfort University, Leicester. URI: http://hdl.handle.net/2086/10742.

WeBS: Frost, T.M., Austin, G.E., Calbrade, N.A., Holt, C.A., Mellan, H.J., Hearn, R.D., Stroud, D.A., Wotton, S.R. & Balmer, D.E. (2016) *Waterbirds in the UK 2014/15: The Wetland Bird Survey*. BTO/RSPB/JNCC. Thetford. www.bto.org/volunteer-surveys/webs/publications/webs-annual-report. (See Common References).

Wilby, R.L. (2003) Past and projected trends in London's urban heat island. *Weather*, **58**, 251–260.

Wood, S. (2007) *The Birds of Essex*. Christopher Helm, London.

Woodward, I.D. (2016) The Breeding Bird Survey in London. *London Bird Report No. 79 for the year 2014*, 186–188.

Woodward, I. & Arnold, R. (2012) The changing status of the breeding birds of the Inner London area. *British Birds*, **105**, 433–457.

Index

Authors' Acknowledgements

The London Atlas project would not have been possible without the time and effort committed by members and volunteers of the British Trust for Ornithology (BTO), the London Bird Club, and many other organisations and bird clubs covering parts of the London area. We dedicate this publication to these volunteers.

The London Atlas project was initiated as a result of the National Atlas project 2007–11, organised by the BTO, the Scottish Ornithologists' Club and BirdWatch Ireland. The National Atlas team was led (in England) by Dawn Balmer and Simon Gillings, and the online development work for the atlas was led by Iain Downie. Without the National Atlas, and the development of the excellent online atlas system, undertaking the London Atlas project would have been at best daunting, and we would like to thank Dawn, Simon, Iain and the many other BTO staff members who were involved in the National Atlas and who also supported us in our endeavour.

Some parts of the London area overlap with other recording areas, and hence atlas survey work was co-ordinated by voluntary BTO regional representatives in these areas, in Buckinghamshire (David Lee & John Gearing), Essex (Simon Cox), Hertfordshire (Chris Dee), Kent (Sally Hunter) and Surrey (Hugh Evans). In Hertfordshire, the Herts Bird Club undertook their own local atlas project (Smith et al., 2015), achieving particularly comprehensive survey coverage in this part of the London area and we would like to thank the whole Hertfordshire atlas team for their contribution.

We would also like to thank all the members of the London Bird Club committee and the LNHS Council for their help and support over the course of the London Atlas project. As well as general encouragement, the committee has contributed towards decisions on the treatment of sensitive species and the bird club recorders helped with decisions regarding records of scarcer species. The work of the recorders has also enabled us to add extra records to the atlas. The membership of both the committee and the council has changed over the course of atlas fieldwork and subsequent writing up of the results. We are grateful to all those who contributed especially Pete Lambert, David Darrell-Lambert, David Lindo, Bob Watts and the recorders (John Archer, Richard Bonser, Sean Huggins, Des McKenzie, Andrew Moon, Mark Pearson, Andrew Self, Steve Spooner, Nick Tanner, Joan Thompson and Roy Woodward).

Several sub-editors of the London Bird Report commented on our draft species accounts, and provided useful suggestions for the species that they cover for the bird report (with some also commenting on additional species). These include several people already mentioned plus Derek Coleman, Ian Ellis, Alan Lewis, Angela Linnell and Paul Whiteman.

Some of the larger sites within the London area fall across more than one tetrad and we would like to thank the following observers whose local knowledge helped us allocate records from these sites to atlas tetrads either during the atlas fieldwork or retrospectively, including Bob Watts (Alexandra Park), Tony Duckett (Regent's Park), Howard Vaughan (Rainham Marshes), David Morrison (Ingrebourne Valley), David Darrell-Lambert (Grays/Chafford Hundred area), Roy Woodward (KGV/William Girling Reservoirs) and Martin Shepherd (Sewardstone area). Many other observers did the same by inputting tetrad level records themselves over the course of atlas fieldwork.

Special thanks go to Gehan de Silva Wijeyeratne and Jan Hewlett. Gehan co-ordinated the selection of photographic images, made arrangements with our publisher and pushed us onwards to complete the work. Jan Hewlett provided detailed comments on the introductory sections and Jan and the LNHS also kindly allowed us to closely copy two paragraphs describing the London area from the second atlas publication.

Thanks also to Tara Wikramanayake who proofread the first page proofs and made a number of useful suggestions and corrections.

We have shown Breeding Bird Survey (BBS) trend maps for London for species for which they are available, and so would also like to thank all BBS surveyors in London. The BBS is run by the BTO, and jointly funded by the BTO, the Joint Nature Conservation Committee (JNCC, the statutory adviser to Government on UK and international nature conservation, on behalf of Natural Resources Wales, the Department of Agriculture, Environment and Rural Affairs, Northern Ireland, Natural England and Scottish Natural Heritage) and the Royal Society for the Protection of Birds (RSPB).

Richard also expresses his thanks to his family, Judy, Katie, Sophie and Tim, for putting up with his long hours at the computer, and the team at Thomson Ecology, especially the graduate ecologists including Robert Allen and Charlotte Hewitt, who spent many hours inputting data.

We are also grateful to the photographers, who have contributed images to be used in this publication, as credited on p. 4 and all at John Beaufoy Publishing, for the hard work in making the publication a reality.

Chair's Acknowledgements

As Chairman of the LBC, on behalf of the committee I have to say a huge thank you to Ian Woodward, Richard Arnold and Neil Smith for undertaking a Herculean task. A number of people assisted them and I will not repeat their names here as they are covered in the authors' acknowledgements.

I would also like to acknowledge the enormous time and effort put in by the various current and past holders of committee positions and other roles in the different sections of the LNHS. Their efforts make the London Natural History Society one of the most active local natural history societies of its kind in the world.

In October 2015 I was invited to be the Chairman of the London Bird Club, not because I was a London birder of any note. On the contrary the expectation was that I would bring in ordinary work skills, experience and enthusiasm to support the work of the committee. My arrival coincided with London Bird Atlas (LBA) being a key item in the agenda. It has been my privilege to be involved in some of the behind-the-scenes work to support the publication of it and thanks are due to a large number of people.

The London Bird Atlas was the subject of many LBC committee meetings and my thanks to all of those who contributed to those discussions. It is not possible for me to mention all of the committee members who have contributed in some way, directly or indirectly over the last few years. But I would like to mention Angela Linnell, Kat Duke, Pete Lambert, Helen Baker and Shalmali Paterson as key contributors at London Bird Club Committee discussions. Pete Lambert commented on the need to publish within a reasonable time from the completion of the survey period, so as to not have an adverse impact on sales. This was useful and gave me a sense of urgency at a time when I had just joined the committee. I would also like to thank Angela who through her 20 years of service as Committee Secretary has provided a stable core to the LBC Committee and in no small way helped me to find the time for the enormous amount of back stage work I had to engage in. Many members of LHS council participated in discussions. I would like to thank Jan Hewlett for flagging the need to raise external funding and for sharing her experience of issues relating to funding and print runs learnt from her experience with the publication of the Breeding Bird Atlas of London published in 2002. Michael Wilsdon, Mike West and David Howden and others in the LNHS Administration and Finance Committee and the authors assisted with tailoring a standard publishing contract which suited the society and the publisher.

A number of options from electronic to print needed to be evaluated together with the various distribution models for a book. Over the years, a number of publishers and editors of magazines and newspapers have shared their publishing experience with me, for which I was grateful. With specific regard to the LBA,

I am grateful for a number of helpful discussions with various people including. Ken and Linda Smith of the Hertfordshire Natural History Society and Keith Betton of the Hampshire Ornithological Society. They provided a number of useful insights with their experience of the recent atlas publications for Hertfordshire and Hampshire respectively. To evaluate whether the LNHS should seek to independently publish or not, Ken and Linda Smith made a number of useful introductions. Nigel Partridge (Nigel Partridge Design Ltd), Mike Dawson (Swallowtail Print), Jack Fearnside (LTD Design Consultants), Richard Chalmers (Dolman Scott) very kindly provided quotes and talked me through options for self-publication. Jim Martin of Bloomsbury provided a useful perspective from an established and large ornithological publisher. Jim also offered suggestions on smaller, specialist publishers. John Beaufoy and Rosemary Wilkinson of John Beaufoy Publishing (JBP) invested much time in exploring options for how the LNHS could leverage their publishing and distribution platform for a joint publication. We ultimately decided to go with them because in addition to the quality and design that comes from an established natural history publisher, it removed from the LNHS the burden of storage, distribution, marketing, sales and collection of revenues. I was pleased with this outcome as being one of the authors of JBP publications, I was intimately aware of the advantages. Funding a joint publication with a publisher only became possible because the LNHS brand could be monetised through advertising support.

The LNHS traces its origins back to 1858 and has survived for over 150 years. One reason for its longevity is its strong system of governance through an expansive array of committees involving a large number of people. I am grateful to those who served on the LBC Committee, the LNHS Council, the LNHS Administration and Finance Committee and the London Bird Report Editorial Board in 2016 and 2017, for their comments on various documents including a terms of reference, the publishing contract as well as various other guidelines and FAQs that were drafted to support the publication of the LBA. My thanks to Tara Wikramanayake for copy editing various documents including the 'Key Points for Advertisers' and 'Guidelines for Contributors'. My thanks to Kat Duke, Mike Trier, Mike West and others for their comments on early drafts of these various documents. My thanks also to present and past committee members and contributors who have been involved in the publication of the London Naturalist, the London Bird Report and the quarterly Newsletter.

The annual London Naturalist (LN) has had over 90 issues published and the London Bird Report (LBR) published since 1937 sets a benchmark for publications of this genre. All of these publications were useful when I needed to prove the track record of LNHS as a publisher and past copies of the LN and LBR were very useful in the many face-to-face meetings I held with prospective advertisers.

I am grateful to following photographers who contributed images. Andrew Moon, Dominic Mitchell (www.birdingetc.com), Edmund Fellowes, Garth Peacock, Graham Brownlow, Joe Beale, John Hawkins, Jonathan Lethbridge, Julian Bhalerao, Lee Dingain, Martin Bennett, Michael Darling, Nirosh Perera, Peter Alfrey, Peter Warne, Richard Bonser, Roger Riddington and Roy Woodward. Their contributions are listed in the photo credits. Many of them were patient with my request to output images afresh from their RAW files to obtain the quality necessary for publishing in the larger than usual size used in this atlas. Their images have played a key part in the design ethos of this atlas which is designed to appeal to a wider audience. Andrew Self and Richard Bonser reviewed the final selection of images and made helpful comments on revising the selection.

Keith Betton, Viki Harley and Ken Smith, who are not photographers, very kindly made introductions to photographers. Martin Bennett and Peter Warne in turn introduced me to other photographers. Peter Warne was introduced through the excellent programme of talks organised by Kat Duke as the Indoor Meetings Secretary of the London Bird Club. At the start of the process Kate Suttle helped with contacting photographers for images. Pete Lambert and Jonathan Lethbridge, the Chair and Photographic Editor respectively of the London Bird Report Editorial Board assisted with introductions to regular contributors of the LBR.

This book has been entirely funded through advertising support. Besides the obvious financial benefit, I was pleased to engage with corporates as it demonstrates that the LNHS brand and its membership have a commercial value. Furthermore, the LNHS will become stronger by engaging more with corporate sponsors in line with other successful conservation organisations. A huge thank you to the corporates who have supported the publication through advertising. If you are a keen birder or wildlife traveller, please visit their websites and consider travelling with them.

A bird atlas is a specialist publication not familiar to many people and I appreciated the corporates putting in time for face-to-face meetings with me and Shalmali Paterson to better understand how supporting it can be mutually beneficial. James Jayasundera and Shalmali Paterson of Ampersand Travel deserve a big thank you for being the first corporate to come on board and for introductions to Swarovski Optics and the companies from India who signed up. Ampersand Travel also signed up as a Principal Supporter, which got our fundraising off to a very strong start. Shalmali who initially met me on other business subsequently joined the London Bird Club Committee as the Field Meetings Secretary which pleases me immensely as she brings very useful work skills and strengthens the corporate engagement which the LNHS is now pursuing on the lines of leading conservation charities.

I would also like to thank Mike West and Robin Blades the LNHS Treasurer and Deputy Treasurer and others on the LNHS A&F Committee for guidance on issues of VAT and other matters related to invoicing. Mike also spent much time in liaising with me over collection of advance payments. A key factor in winning advertising support was the look and feel of the LNHS website, which was overhauled in 2016. My thanks to the LNHS website sub-committee, the LNHS Webmaster Malcolm Kendall, LNHS Secretary David Howdon and Mick Massie Chairman of the Ecology and Entomology Section who with me were key supporters of the overhaul. Malcolm spent a large part of the summer of 2016 working on the website overhaul with Chris Dee who was awarded the contract. Malcolm was also very proactive in creating new webpages to support the publication process and fundraising efforts. He was also very prompt in placing the logos of advertisers once they made a commitment, to demonstrate the speed and efficiency of the LNHS. All of this helped with the fundraising.

It is not possible to list every individual from the corporates who have enthusiastically supported the publication and assisted with the underlying administration. But I have listed some of them with whom I have engaged in correspondence and apologies to anyone I have missed.

Ampersand Travel (James Jayasundera, Shalmali Paterson, Chloe Goolden and Moiz Taherboy), Cinnamon Nature Trails (Chitral Jayatilake and Johan Antonypillai), Gateway Resort, Corbett (Ruth Goodwin, Anoop Kharabandara and Rakesh Singh), Heritance Kandalama (Susith Jayawickrama, Renusha Gomis, Trinisha Suzette Collas and Stasshani Jayawardana), Jetwing Tented Villas (Angie Samuel, Prasanna Wellangoda, Upashama Talgaswatte and Hiran Cooray), Kulu Safaris (Javana Fernando and Natasha Muttettuwegama), Leica (Jason Heward, Nanette Roland and Selena Barr), Leopard Trails (Arshad Nihaz and Radheesh Sellamuttu), Palmyrah House (Ajith Ratnayaka and Raja Gnanam), Pugdundee Safaris (Kanushree Matanhelia and Manav Khanduja), Resplendent Ceylon (Malik Fernando, and Nalintha Rodrigo), Swarovski Optik (Peter Antoniou, Christine Peter and Dale Forbes) and Taj Safaris (Pallavi Gopal, Ritesh Bhatt and Pankaj Khanna).

My thanks also to Ram Pratap and Anu Singh for the invitation to attend the Uttar Pradesh Bird Fair (UPBF) and for hosting me for an extended stay at the Chambal Safari Lodge. Nikhil Devasar had invited some excellent speakers. The UPBF resulted in a number of useful contacts. This included meeting Martin Kelsey who in turn introduced me to John Hawkins who contributed a number of images including species that were difficult to source.

It was also at UPBF that I met Nanette Roland from Leica who introduced me to Jason Heward, MD of Leica Cameras in London.

Ian Lycett of Birdwatch magazine assisted by being a sounding board on various topics ranging from VAT to benchmarking the pricing of the advertising. Madushan Perera of Jetwing Eco Holidays (JEH) refreshed contact details of a number of British and international tour operators whom I had lost touch with. Paramie Perera of JEH provided a summary of advertising rates in British wildlife magazines to assist with calibrating the pricing of the advertising support.

John Beaufoy and Rosemary Wilkinson were enthusiastic about the joint publication of a book which is quite time consuming and complicated. They were also quite patient as the details of the agreement were navigated through the many internal committees of the LNHS. One of the challenges of the atlas was to marry the strong factual and indeed scientific content of an atlas with a visually strong design that would help to recruit others into birdwatching. Their designers supported our efforts by putting up with multiple iterations of the sample pages to introduce a book with visual impact to complement the scientific content. Tara Wikramanayake helped with copy editing during the page proofing stage.

My article on top birding sites has been adapted from a series of articles originally published in the online magazine Wall Street International (www.wsimag.com) during 2017. My thanks to Nathalie Dodd, the Editor of WSI for permission to reproduce the articles with modifications.

Finally, a big thank you to my wife Nirma and my two daughters Maya and Amali who put up with me burying myself in administrative work on the London Bird Atlas rather than spending time with them.

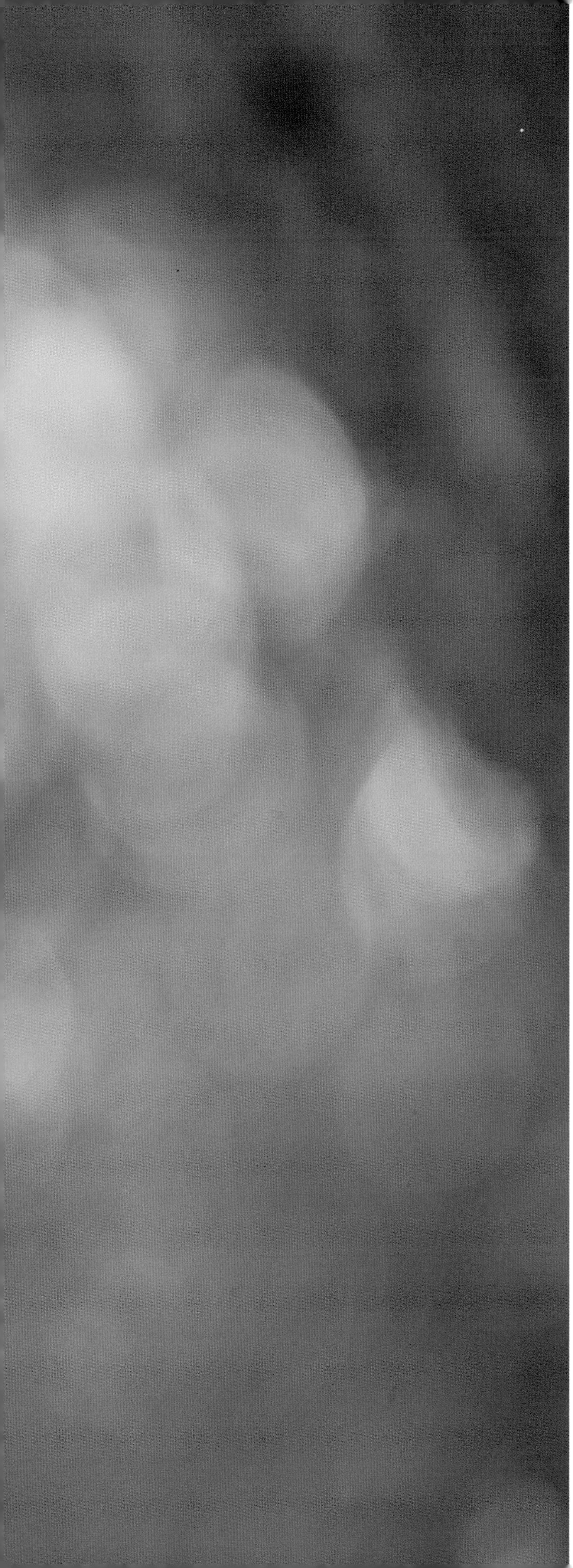

Principal
Sponsor

Ampersand Travel

Long-eared Owl

www.ampersandtravel.com

info@ampersandtravel.com

Beauty is in the detail

A fresh perspective can lead to the most wonderful discoveries. This holds true for both our cultural and wildlife tailor-made holidays.

Our carefully chosen guides have the ability to make the ordinary extraordinary, and to reveal the world in a whole new light.

Advertising Supporters

Cinnamon Nature Trails
Gateway Resort, Corbett
Heritance Kandalama
Jetwing Tented Villas
Kulu Safaris
Leica
Leopard Trails
Palmyrah House
Pugdundee Safaris
Resplendent Ceylon
Swarovski Optik
Taj Safaris

Note: The full page advertisements from the Advertising Supporters will follow in this section in alphabetical order.

Short-eared Owl

BIRDING ISN'T JUST A HOBBY, IT'S A LIFESTYLE!

Enjoy Sri Lanka's amazing bird life while at Cinnamon Lodge Habarana, Habarana Village by Cinnamon or Cinnamon Wild Yala together with expert naturalist guides from Cinnamon Nature Trails our award winning eco-tourism arm.

Over 450 species of birds in this island rich in diversity can make unforgettable memories. Let us inspire you to experience the most of our 34 endemic species and plenty of other non-endemic Asian species that will make you want to return back for more.

NATURE TRAILS
A Cinnamon Holiday Experience

W : www.cinnamonhotels.com | www.cinnamonnaturetrails.com E : Chitral@Cinnamonhotels.com | Johan@Cinnamonhotels.com
Facebook: www.fb.co/cinnamonhotels | www.fb.co/NatureTrailsLanka

explore corbett
like never before.

Home to many rare species of wild flora and fauna, The Corbett National Park is the latest destination for the Taj. Set alongside the picturesque Kosi River, the hotel is a perfect getaway for adventure hunters and holiday seekers. Sprawled across acres of dense greens, the property comes with the finest of Indian and international dining options that include Treetop – the all-day diner that also serves Active Foods for the health conscious, Tusker – the watering hole for the wild-spirited and Jim's Grill – a perfect spot for sundowners. Indulge in some holistic wellness at our award-winning Jiva Spa. Unwind at the pool or simply rejuvenate with Yoga. However, for those who wish to explore or just lose themselves, a word of caution – we have 521 kms of National Park as our backyard.

For bookings, call Taj Reservations Worldwide on 1800 111 825 / +91 5947 266 600 or email: gateway.corbett@tajhotels.com

THE**GATEWAY**RESORT
CORBETT NATIONAL PARK

f thegatewayhotel 🐦 thegatewayhotel

www.gateway.tajhotels.com

Rediffusion-Y&R/Mum/Gateway/0170

HERITANCE KANDALAMA…
AN ESCAPE INTO
TRUE WILDERNESS

- Flanked by two UNESCO world heritage sites, the Dambulla Rock Temple & the Sigiriya Rock Fortress
- Recognized the world over for its sustainable practices
- Most awarded hotel in Sri Lanka
- First hotel in the world to be LEED certified and first hotel in Asia to be Green Globe 21 certified
- 152 well-appointed rooms and suites overlooking a beautiful tropical landscape

WILDLIFE

- Situated within a dry zone scrub forest with the feel of a private nature reserve
- Over 150 species of birds can be seen in and around the hotel during the migrant season on a 2-3 night stay
- Our team consists of professional nature guides for wildlife watching and birding around the hotel and also for excursions to experience the Elephant Gathering in Minneriya
- We also arrange Loris watching at the Popham Arboretum located close to the hotel

Committed to the UNWTO
**Global Code of Ethics
for Tourism** Supported by the United Nations

(+94) 66 5555 000
www.heritancehotels.com/kandalama

FIND LUXURY IN THE
MOST UNEXPECTED SPACES

Committed to the UNWTO
Global Code of Ethics
for Tourism Supported by the United Nations

Welcome to a world away from it all, cocooned in the comfort of nature. A camp of ten extravagant tented villas with endless acres of wilderness to one side and stretches of golden sands to the other. Discover how we put the glamour in glamping with fluffy white sheets on snug lush beds, a personal butler awaiting to serve you, BBQ day outs and bonfire nights, all amidst the wild. Welcome to Jetwing Tented Villas for the ultimate glamping experience.

For more information contact us on +94 11 4709400
resv.tentedvillas@jetwinghotels.com #jetwingtentedvillas

Jetwing
TENTED VILLAS
YALA · SRI LANKA

www.jetwinghotels.com

An idyllic island for the quintessential birding experience

Kulu Safaris is the most experienced, environmentally responsible, and high-end wildlife operator in Sri Lanka. Our local knowledge is unsurpassed, conservation is in our DNA, and we take pride in impressing the most discerning of clients.

Our portfolio of low-footprint luxury camps, private beach villas, and exclusive bungalows is spread out across our island with access to rainforests, wetlands, dry scrub jungle, highlands, and a wild coastline – all of which are hosts to a rich tapestry of birdlife and wildlife.

For an unforgettable birding tour,

Quote **#LBA** and write to us at **safari@kulusafaris.com**

Or for more information visit **www.kulusafaris.com/birding**

NEW!

LEICA NOCTIVID.
UNPARALLELED
VIEWING EXPERIENCE.

Distilled from 110 years of experience. Named after the Athene noctua, the symbol of wisdom, knowledge and insight, the Leica Noctivid are the best binoculars we've ever made. Stylish and compact, they offer the perfect balance of attributes for crystal clear seeing experiences. Easy one-handed use, large eyepieces, incredible depth of field, clean contrasts and the perfect combination of light transmission and colour fidelity. Unparalleled viewing.

Leica Camera Ltd | 34 Bruton Place | London | W1J 6NR | www.leica-sportoptics.com

Guided safaris into Yala and Wilpattu
National Park in Sri Lanka

LEOPARD TRAILS
www.leopardtrails.com

PALMYRAH HOUSE
SERENDIP.ITY RETREATS | MANNAR

Mannar Island is on an international migratory flyway and has internationally significant numbers of waterfowl, waders and gulls wintering on the island and on coastal wetlands immediately across the mainland. It is also home to a number of birds and other animals confined to the northwest and northern peninsula of Sri Lanka. The Adam's Bridge chain of islands is a protected breeding ground for a number of pelagic seabirds, some of which are rarely seen in this part of the Indian Ocean. The Palmyrah House has for many years been the first choice of accommodation for visiting birders, photographers and naturalists.

THE PALMYRAH HOUSE,
Thalaimannar Rd, Mannar Island,
SRI LANKA.
Telephone   +94 112 594467,
Mobile   +94 722 227154
Website: www.palmyrahhouse.com
E mail: info@palmyrahhouse.com

Bespoke Ornithological Tours of Central India

Central India is the heart of India's wildlife. The Tiger country in its diverse habitat of wetland, fields, marsh lands and broad leafed forests nestles majority of India's Tiger populace and more than 400 avian species. Experience bird watching and photography in endless landscape of scrubs and extensive forests for a truly Indian safari experience.

Write to us for bespoke safari tours in any of the six Central India national parks. Tours are complete with exceptional English speaking naturalists and a memorable stay at our unique eco-lodges accredited for hospitality.

For a Bespoke Birding Experience
Call: +44 (0) 7772017988 | +91- 9540537711, +91-124-2970497
Email : salesdesk@pugdundeesafaris.com | info@pugdundeesafaris.com
Website : www.pugdundeesafaris.com

Denwa Backwater Escape – Satpura • Ken River Lodge – Panna • Pench Tree Lodge – Pench
Kings Lodge & Tree House Hideaway – Bandhavgarh • Kanha Earth Lodge • Barahi Jungle Lodge – Chitwan

YOU CAN FIND OUR PRODUCTS
AT EXCLUSIVE SPECIALIST RETAILERS
AND ONLINE AT **WWW.SWAROVSKIOPTIK.COM**

BY APPOINTMENT TO
HER MAJESTY QUEEN ELIZABETH II
SWAROVSKI OPTIK
SUPPLIER OF BINOCULARS

EL FAMILY
LIMITLESS
PERFECTION

The EL Family from SWAROVSKI OPTIK is the best ever.
Its FieldPro package takes comfort and functionality
to a new level. Its perfect optical performance and precision,
outstanding ergonomics, and revamped design add
the finishing touches to this long-range optical masterpiece.
Enjoy moments even more – with SWAROVSKI OPTIK.

SEE THE UNSEEN
WWW.SWAROVSKIOPTIK.COM

SWAROVSKI
OPTIK

BRING ALIVE KIPLING'S JUNGLE BOOK EXPERIENCE IN MOWGLI'S VERY OWN FOREST.

Experience the unparalleled beauty of the jungles in the Indian subcontinent. With its towering, ancient trees, enchanting chorus of forest birds, and herds of gentle chital, this is a travel experience unlike any other. Enjoy jungle drives twice a day, conducted in the comfort of an open 4x4 safari vehicle, direct from our unique and luxurious Safari Lodges.

Call Taj Reservations Worldwide on 00 800 4588 1825
or write to us at reservations@tajhotels.com, tajsafaris@tajhotels.com

BAGHVAN
PENCH NATIONAL PARK
A TAJSAFARIS LODGE

pashan garh
PANNA NATIONAL PARK
A TAJSAFARIS LODGE

MAHUA KOTHI
BANDHAVGARH NATIONAL PARK
A TAJSAFARIS LODGE

BANJAAR TOLA
KANHA NATIONAL PARK
A TAJSAFARIS LODGE

Rediffusion-Y&R/Mum/Taj/2545

Merrill J. Fernando, Founder of Dilmah

RELAIS &
CHATEAUX.

www.resplendentceylon.com

Conceived by the Fernando family, prominent Sri Lankan tea producers and founders of Dilmah Ceylon Tea, **Resplendent Ceylon** is creating a collection of small, luxury resorts that offer the discriminating traveller a unique circuit across Sri Lanka, with a range of authentic cultural experiences, while contributing towards local communities and the environment through the MJF Foundation & Dilmah Conservation.

Ceylon Tea Trails is the world's first tea bungalow resort, perched at an altitude of 1250 metres in Sri Lanka's panoramic Ceylon tea region, bordering the World Heritage Central Highlands. 5 historic tea planters bungalows offer 27 exquisite rooms & suites, including the owner's cottage.

Cape Weligama is the most sumptuous resort along this fabled island's palm fringed shores. Thirty minutes east of Galle, 39 villas and suites, the largest in Sri Lanka, inhabit 12 tropical acres atop a singular promontory rising 40 metres above the Indian Ocean.

Wild Coast Tented Lodge sits where jungle meets beach on the edge of Yala National Park, the leopard hotspot. 28 vaulted Cocoon tents offer the comfort of a luxury hotel with the excitement of a safari-style wilderness experience.

Our exceptional circuit of eventually six resorts, all connected by seaplane, is the finest way to experience Sri Lanka; the Resplendent Isle.

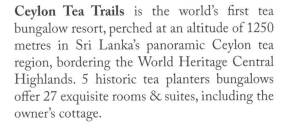

Total number of species in each tetrad in the breeding season and in winter.

Breeding

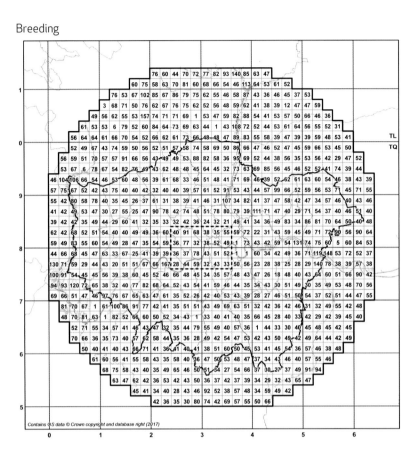

Winter

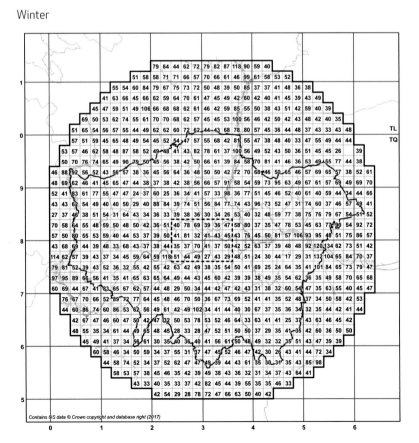

About the Authors

Ian Woodward

Ian is from Chingford in north-east London and has lived in this area for most of his life. He began birdwatching at the age of ten, and, since then, has regularly visited sites in Epping Forest, the Lee Valley and elsewhere in London. From 2005 until 2017, he was the Regional Representative for the British Trust for Ornithology (BTO) in North London, a voluntary position organising BTO surveys in the area and working closely with the London Natural History Society (LNHS). Ian has worked for the BTO as a Research Officer since 2014 and became an LNHS Council Representative in 2015.

Richard Arnold

Richard originates from north London but is now firmly settled in the south. He is the Regional Representative for the British Trust for Ornithology (BTO) in South London and a professional ecological consultant at Thomson Ecology. Previous publications include Thomson Ecology's Handbook, as well as co-authoring a paper published in the Journal of Applied Ecology (Hill & Arnold, 2012). He served on the council of the Chartered Institute of Ecology and Environmental Management (CIEEM) and helped develop CIEEM's guidelines on ecological impact assessment.

Ian and Richard have previously published a paper on London's birds in the journal British Birds (Woodward & Arnold, 2012). Between them, they co-ordinated the survey work and wrote the species accounts for the London Bird Atlas.

Neil Smith

Though originally from the Chilterns, much of Neil's early ecological and ornithological experience stems from living and working in Edinburgh and the west coast of Scotland. He trained as an ecologist, with an emphasis on botany and habitat surveying, and in doing so, developed an interest in the use of geographical information systems (GIS) in conservation and ecology. Neil currently works alongside Richard, as a professional GIS consultant at Thomson Ecology. Neil managed the dataset and produced all the maps for the London Bird Atlas.

Woodward, I. & Arnold, R. (2012). The changing status of the breeding birds of the inner London area. British Birds 105: 433-457

Hill, D., & Arnold, R. (2012). Building the evidence base for ecological impact assessment and mitigation. Journal of Applied Ecology, 49(1), 6-9.

About the London Natural History Society

The London Natural History Society traces its history back to 1858. The Society is made up of a number of active sections that provide a wide range of talks, organised nature walks, coach trips and other activities. This range of events makes the LNHS one of the most active natural history societies in the world. Whether it is purely for recreation, or to develop field skills for a career in conservation, the LNHS offers a wide range of indoor and outdoor activities. Beginners are welcome at every event and gain access to the knowledge of some very skilled naturalists. On top of its varied public engagement, the LNHS also provides a raft of publications free to members. The London Naturalist (with over 90 issues so far) is its annual journal with scientific papers as well as lighter material such as book reviews. The annual London Bird Report published since 1937 sets a benchmark for publications of this genre. Furthermore, there is a quarterly Newsletter that carries many trip reports and useful announcements.

The LNHS Programme is sent to members in print form twice a year and is packed with events. The programme on the website can be synced with your calendars and event notifications can also be obtained through the LNHS group on the MeetUp app. The LNHS maintains its annual membership subscription at a modest level, representing fantastic value for money. Membership can be obtained and paid for online at www.lnhs.org.uk. The LNHS and its sections are also on a variety of social media including Facebook and Twitter.